Puyo Runa

Puyo Runa

Imagery and Power in Modern Amazonia

NORMAN E. WHITTEN JR. AND
DOROTHEA SCOTT WHITTEN

UNIVERSITY OF ILLINOIS PRESS

Urbana and Chicago

Library of Congress Cataloging-in-Publication Data
Whitten, Norman E.
Puyo runa : imagery and power in modern Amazonia /
Norman E. Whitten Jr. and Dorothea Scott Whitten.
p.   cm.
Includes bibliographical references and index.
ISBN-13: 978-0-252-03239-4 (cloth : alk. paper)
ISBN-10: 0-252-03239-X (cloth : alk. paper)
ISBN-13: 978-0-252-07479-0 (pbk. : alk. paper)
ISBN-10: 0-252-07479-3 (pbk. : alk. paper)
1. Canelos Indians—History.
2. Canelos Indians—Politics and government.
3. Canelos Indians—Social life and customs.
4. Puyo (Pastaza, Ecuador)—History.
5. Puyo (Pastaza, Ecuador)—Social life and customs.
6. Napo River Valley (Ecuador and Peru)—History.
7. Napo River Valley (Ecuador and Peru)—Social life and customs.
I. Whitten, Dorothea S. II. Title.
F3722.1.C23W463   2008
305.898'4—dc22   2007019534

Contents

Preface and Acknowledgments   ix

Notes on Orthography and Pronunciation   xxi

Notes on Pronouns, People, and Pseudonyms   xxv

1. Puyo Runa and Nayapi Llacta   1

2. Cultural Reflexivities, Images, and Locality   30

3. Empowerment, Knowledge, and Vision   59

4. Connections: Creative Expressions of Canelos Quichua Women
   Dorothea Scott Whitten   90

5. Imagery and the Control of Power   119

6. Cultural Performance   140

7. Aesthetic Contours: History, Conjuncture, and Transformation
   Dorothea Scott Whitten and Norman Whitten   167

8. Return of the Yumbo: The Caminata from Amazonia to
   Andean Quito
   *Norman Whitten, Dorothea Scott Whitten, and
   Alfonso Chango*   200

9. *Causáunchimi!*: Processes of Empowerment   231

Glossary   259

References   271

Index   293

The Puyo Runa people of Amazonian Ecuador tell us that to learn something of significance one must be prepared to "see." Through their ancient and contemporary ceramic art, women potters show us how to "see" into their lives, their cosmos, their pasts, and their futures in the time of cunalla, *"right now." Shamans, who are men, create seances in which blurred visions arrive as spirit images, called* muscui, *and it is the women, again, who clarify the images so that people may "see," "right now," just what is emerging that unites pasts, presents, and futures with different places. Images are controlled by "one who knows,"* yachaj, *shaman; and by "one who 'sees'—owner or possessor of images—"* mus-cuyuj, *ceramist. The imagery of the cosmos includes the place of humans and all other beings in it, as well as that of other people, who think and speak through other cultures,* shuj shimita yachai. *To be fully human is to know other cultures, because through this knowledge one comes to know one's own. Power emanates from imagery.*

Imagery and power do not exist in a vacuum. They are grounded in many realities. Among them are the physical founts of daily existence—the cultural traditions and their dynamic creativities that allow people to wrest a livelihood from their environment. Other people, living and dead, constitute that environment, as do their souls, souls of others, spirits, and the imagined and real mysteries that such forces entail. Life itself, causai, *as it is experienced and remembered, and the actions that it engenders, constitute the power, the imagery, and the central feature of all knowledge.*

The phrase causáunchimi!, *which means "We are living!" in Amazonian Quichua, sums this up: We are living! (as fully human beings). Listen to us!*

Preface and Acknowledgments

In this book we seek to understand the modern and millennial dimensions of increasingly self-essentialized cultural systems in a setting of wrenching national transformation and competing macro-ideologies. Ecuador is an Andean nation that, together with Venezuela, Colombia, Peru, and Bolivia, seems to be moving in directions that often bewilder and befuddle powerful planners and ideologues. Myriad cultural systems, often unknown or misunderstood, are likely to be classified as "primitive" or "peasant," as opposed to "modern" or "progressive." Some academics and planners circumvent these unfortunate labels and dichotomies by setting boundaries to specific peoples in nation-states, thereby overlooking the montage of diversity that characterizes many regional systems.

In Amazonian Ecuador such specificities are attached to the Achuar and Shuar Jivaroans, the Waorani, the Zaparoans, the Siona and Secoya Tucanoans, and the Cofán. Excluded are the Canelos Quichua and the Napo Runa, people who fall, *according to some academic or scholarly imposed criteria*, between Andean and Amazonian sectors of professional endeavor. A purpose of this work is to present the reader with essays aimed at understanding and appreciating the scope of lifeways and the depth of humanity of the Puyo Runa people of Canelos Quichua culture, themselves deeply embedded in the forces of history and modernity, and sometimes generative of processes of millenniarity. We seek to offer an ethnography of empowerment.

Cushi Tampo, Amazonian Ecuador, 1987

We were designing a temporary exhibition for the Art Gallery of the Central Bank of Ecuador, a setting that carried the prestige of a gallery exhibition in the Smithsonian in the United States. We had moved from Puma Llacta to Cushi Tambo, a new hamlet on a dirt, stone, and mud road that led from the main road from Puyo through the Comuna San Jacinto del Pindo, a large indigenous communal territory inhabited by about two thousand people in eighteen similar hamlets. Although the hamlet was new, it was in the area where its founder, our *compadre,* Marcelo Santi Simbaña, formerly lived with his first wife, Corina Vargas, prior to her death during childbirth. Now, Marcelo, his wife, Faviola Vargas Aranda, from Canelos, and their young children had returned to found a new territory with both localized and dispersed residences.

Early in the week, in Puyo, where we were working in a studio setting with Marcelo's sister, Clara Santi Simbaña, and her son, Alfonso Chango, among others, we had come up with a tentative title, *causanchimi* (we are living), for the upcoming exhibit and accompanying booklet. Our interest, and that of the people with whom we were working, was to stress the contemporaneity of living people creating imagery through their arts in the canopied rain forest at the base of the Andes.

Later, at a work party in Cushi Tambo, we publicly mentioned the concept of *causanchimi* and asked, "What should we name the exhibition?" People had already agreed that "*Arte*" (art) should be in the title, as well as a reference to Amazonia. After thinking about the title, the first to speak was Luis Vargas Canelos (Lucho), who had come from near Canelos, after the death of his first wife, to marry Marcelo Santi Simbaña's last daughter by Corina Vargas. He was then the vice president of the Organization of Indigenous People of Pastaza Province (OPIP), which he had been instrumental in founding in 1981.

He suggested *causáunchimi* with an emphasis, which we present in English with an exclamation mark. We paused, as did others. Sibby (Dorothea Scott Whitten) had learned in her Quichua course with Frank Salomon and Carmen Chuquín that this use of a diphthong marks a "continuitive" in Quichua. But Lucho's first language, like that of the late Corina, was Achuar, not Quichua. Others pondered and quickly a consensus emerged that this term was perfect. Lucho explicated what we already knew: *causana* means "to live" and *causai* is a life force. *Nchi* means "we," and *mi* signifies stress or emphasis. We knew that *causanchimi* means "we are living," implying "we are here." It is a rather pedestrian term; it carries no special emotional tone or evocative force, and it was a forceful trope that we sought to name the exhibition of art made by and for living people.

Delicia Dagua, daughter-in-law of Marcelo and Faviola, who is also a master potter and image maker, next spoke up: "When you say *causáunchimi!* it means that we, the real people (*runapura*), are here, that we are speaking. People should listen to us. They should 'see' that we are here." Delicia is from the Río Bufeo area east of Montalvo; we knew that she was familiar with other languages, but only learned in 2005 that she spoke phrases of Andoa (a Zaparoan language also known as Shimigae). We learned then that her late brother was bilingual in Andoa and Quichua. She had traveled when she was young to Llanchama Cocha, where Záparo was spoken, and she later learned Spanish in Quito, where she worked as a maid for two years. She is familiar with Achuar people and culture, too.

Then Marcelo's sister, Clara Santi Simbaña said, "We are ready, *compadre. Shayarinchi"* (we are ready). "We are living and we are ready! *Causáunchimi!* is a good name for our exhibit (*ñucanchi exposición*)." *Causáunchimi!*, as we have come to understand it, is empowering.

Puyo and Urbana, 2006

This book is about an Amazonian people who live on the fringe of Western Amazonas, in an Andean nation. Following the 1941 war with Peru, President José María Velasco Ibarra proclaimed that Ecuador "has been, is, and will be, an Amazonian nation." People of both Amazonian and Andean Ecuador share dialects of Quichua, variants of the Andean political language of the imperial Inca, Quechua. The Inca Empire reached its apex by about 1470, ranging from southern Colombia to central Chile, less than a quarter century before Columbus set off to discover the western sea route to India and Asia in 1492. The Spanish conquest of the Central and Northern Andes took place in 1532, some forty years later, at a time when civil war was raging from Quito to Cuzco. How the Canelos Quichua people acquired their language is murky, but the process clearly entailed socioeconomic relationships between Andean and Amazonian (and coastal) people prior to and outside of the processes of Incaic and Spanish conquest.

Canelos Quichua are tropical-forest-dwelling people who live in a modern Andean republic. In 1992 they marched collectively to the capital city, Quito, and returned triumphantly with legally sanctioned usufruct over more than a million hectares of land, river, and forest. They confound national stereotypes of just who are and who are not "authentic indigenous people."

The Canelos Quichua of the Upper Amazon-Andean Piedmont are one of the many indigenous peoples of Ecuador whose cultural orientations resonate with one another, different though they may be in specifics. From time to time the indigenous people, along with others in various socioeconomic classes, have moved as a chiliastic political force united by intersecting cultural systems to change the face of the nation. In this work we seek to understand reflexively the undergirding processes that create a sense of a transformation in a people of considerable flexible endurance.

The territory of the Canelos Quichua abuts those of Jivaroans to the south and east, and the Waorani and Napo Runa to the north. Within their territory Shiwiar Jivaroans and Andoa-Zaparoan and Zápara-Zaparoan ethnicity are emergent. The Canelos Quichua "appear" in history in the sixteenth century as a sustained cultural moment of ethnogenetic emergence out of a merger of Achuar Jivaroan and Andoa-Zaparoan peoples whose system of trade and cultural transmission is communicated through the Quichua language. They reemerge in indigenous memory as a cultural force of Amazonia at a time when the Liberal Republic of Ecuador appears on the world capitalist stage in the 1890s. This is appropriately remembered as "times of destruction."

Paradoxically, in spite of numerous publications on their dynamic lifeways and rich cosmological system, the Canelos Quichua remain relatively unknown to Ecuadorians in particular and to the world at large. Their cultural system, however, receives considerable attention by Lawrence Sullivan, a specialist in comparative religion, in his groundbreaking book on South American religion, *Icanchu's Drum*.

In the nine essays in this book we present salient facets of our understanding of the social and cosmological underpinnings of cultural endurance, flexibility, and transformation that served and serve as forces to motivate people to take extraordinary risks to change the very fabric of the national system. At the same time, these forces propel the inner workings of local-level organizations to transform over the past quarter century into a focal system of indigenous resistance in the Western Hemisphere. We seek to explicate indigenous culture and knowledge—*ñucanchi yachai*—as a dynamic template for cultural transformation, and to present our understanding of their senses of other cultural systems—*shuj shimita yachai*—as an axis for interculturality. Taken together the template and the axis provide a dynamic basis for empowerment. We present historical and contemporary lifeways of the people as recorded in the literature and as we have known them since 1968.

We zoom down especially on Puyo Runa—those living, real people who become part of national and global forces through urban Puyo, the capital of Pastaza Province, Amazonian Ecuador. The people about whom we write, and with whom we have shared experiences for nearly forty years, come from many locations where different languages, especially Achuar and Quichua but also Shiwiar, Shuar, and Záparo (Andoa-Shimigae, Zápara), have been, or are, spoken. Whether or not one speaks one or more of these languages, they all figure in the imagery of being human by those about whom we write.

Causáunchimi!, we are living!, is our theme.

Acknowledgments

To understand Canelos Quichua lifeways through time and across space, one must move back and forth through ethnographies and histories of Jivaroan-, Zaparoan-, and Quichua-speaking peoples, past and present. Rafael Karsten's book *Headhunters of Western Amazonas* has helped us for years. Karsten's ethnography is one of motion among peoples, and it is our challenge to transform observations made in the early twentieth century to mesh with our own observations and interpretations. Michael J. Harner sent us a copy of his new book, *The Jívaro,* in 1972 while we were getting deeply into our ethnography with the Puyo Runa and other Canelos Quichua peoples. Our attempt to understand the great differences between Harner's data and those presented (and omitted) by Karsten influenced our interpretations and publications, our queries and our quests. In the early 1970s the late Udo Oberem provided us with notes about the similarities and differences between the Canelos Quichua and the Napo Runa-Quijos Quichua. More importantly, he sent us annotated photos that he took in 1955. They were taken in the very areas where we later worked, and they included a very young Apacha Vargas, her parents, siblings, and other relatives. Forty-one years later—in 1996 and again in 2001—Apacha's exegetical discourse on the photos and her identification of every person in them became a new stimulus for more ethnohistoric querying. During the 1970s Carolyn Orr also provided valuable technical assistance with language and concepts, and encouraged us in the very directions our research was taking. We are indebted to these fine scholars for considerable insight and for their great willingness to share.

In 1968 we met Joe Brenner, who had recently arrived in Puyo, and began a friendship that lasted for many years, up until we lost touch with him about a year before his death in 1995. Among our first Canelos Quichua acquaintances in the greater Puyo area were the late Gonzalo Vargas, Olimpia Santi, the late Camilo Santi, the late Delfina Maianchi, the late Narcisa Vargas, the late Soledad Vargas, Camilo Santi Simbaña, Alonso Guatatuca, and Victoria

Santi. In 1970 these people plus the late Venancio Vargas, the late Pastora Guatatuca, Teófilo Santi, Saraita Vargas, Severo Vargas, the late Fernando Vargas, and Apacha Vargas of the Comuna San Jacinto del Pindo helped greatly to establish a base of understanding that ranged from Puyo south to Chiguasa, east to the Copataza River region, north to Sarayacu-Sarayaquillu and back west to Pacayacu and Canelos.

In 1970 Norman attended a kinship festival in Pacayacu and also saw the *lanceros* perform during the Dominario. There he met Absalóm Guevara, the local school teacher. As fate would have it, Absalóm was transferred to the indigenous hamlet Puma Llacta (a pseudonym) when we were living there from 1972 to 1975. It is one of the communities subsumed under the pseudonym Nayapi Llacta in this book. Absalóm has remained a friend and constant supporter of our research, for which we are most grateful.

Marcelo Santi Simbaña and Faviola Vargas Aranda have been enduring friends since 1971 and, with others, continued to help us expand our horizons of inquiry into a cultural system heretofore marginalized by vicissitudes of scholarly, popular, and official stereotyping. The debt we owe them is enormous and has been acknowledged in some detail in other publications. In Sarayacu-Sarayaquillu the late Eucevia Vargas, the late Alicia Canelos Aranda, and Amadora Aranda Canelos jump-started our understanding of a template of enduring symbolism through their ceramic arrays and by their outstanding and unanticipated expositions of evocative imagery.

From 1972 through 1975 we worked especially closely with Virgilio Santi, Bolívar Santi Simbaña, Clemencia Vargas, Juana Catalina Chango, Leonardo Santi, Gladys Salazar, Abraham Chango, Clara Santi Simbaña, Theresa Santi, Alberto Chango, Luis Vargas Canelos, Celia Santi, René Santi, Rubén Santi, Delicia Dagua, Elsa Vargas, Venancio Vargas, Balvina Santi, Segundo Vargas, Rosaura Gualinga, and Pancracio Santi, plus those mentioned above and many others. In the next generation we became particularly close to Alfonso Chango and Luzmila Salazar as we became friends, *compadres,* and valued research collaborators and coauthors.

In the Sierra of Ecuador work with Rudecindo (Rudi) Masaquiza, Francisca (Pancha) Jérez, and later Julio Chicaiza was sustained and became enhanced by two visits to the United States by Rudi and Julio (and one by Pancha). In addition to their own travels, Rudi and Julio gave exhibitions at the University of Illinois at Urbana-Champaign and accompanied us to the American Ethnological Society Meetings in Lexington, Kentucky. Back in 1972–73, and subsequently, Rudi visited us in Puyo and the Comuna San Jacinto and attended one *ayllu jista* that we also attended in Unión Base and San Jacinto.

On her return from years outside the area, Estela Dagua became a very close associate in our various research endeavors. Her constant tutelage, and later that of her daughter, Marta Jobita Vargas Dagua, was also carried to the United States when she and another daughter, Mirian Vargas Dagua, accompanied us to Urbana, and then through southern Illinois and back, until their return to Ecuador to resume a life that we share annually.

While teaching Quichua with Frank Salomon at the University of Illinois at Urbana-Champaign, Carmen Chuquín greatly helped and encouraged Sibby in translating Quichua song texts into English, and assisted both of us in editing *Yachaj Sami Yachachina* by Alfonso Chango. Her collegiality through the years has been outstanding.

One does not just come and go to Ecuador to undertake project after project without substantial support and encouragement from host scholars and administrators. Those who have facilitated our work in more ways than we can describe include especially María del Carmen Molestina Zaldumbide through the Instituto Nacional de Patrimonio Cultural and the Museos del Banco Central; Diego Quiroga, Carlos Montúfar, Santiago Gangotena, and Nancy Orellana of the Universidad San Francisco de Quito, and Amparo Ferri de Quiroga, of Quito. Other formal sponsors of research at different times include the Casa de la Cultura Ecuatoriana and the Instituto Nacional de Antropología y Historia.

In anthropology N. Whitten has been particularly influenced by the scholarship of Clifford Geertz, the late Victor Turner, the late Peter Worsley (who met Julio and Rudi in Lexington at the AES meeting), Jonathan Hill, the late Irving Goldman, Steve Gudeman, Frank Salomon, Jean Rahier, David Guss, and Mick Taussig. Over the years a number of scholars who have worked with us as well as independently have influenced our scholarship. They include, especially, the late Ronald Stutzman, Mary-Elizabeth Reeve, Kathleen Fine-Dare, Mary Weismantel, Diego Quiroga, Rachel Corr, and Michelle Wibbelsman. Recently Julie Williams has offered assistance on many occasions. Steven Holland worked with us to complete all maps and line figures.

Three outstanding ethnographers and ethnohistorians have, through their publications and interactions, enhanced our abilities to continue to contribute to the understanding of people in this complex region, and we are grateful to Anne-Christine Taylor, Philippe Descola, and Michael Uzendoski.

The foundations that have facilitated our work in this region begin in 1968 with a grant from the National Institute of Mental Health and the Latin American Studies Program of Washington University, St. Louis, and continued in 1970 through 1972 and then again in 1973 through 1975 by the National

Science Foundation (Grant G5-2999). Other grants include those from the Social Science Research Council, a John Simon Guggenheim Fellowship, three Wenner-Gren Awards (3287, 4405, and 5232), a Fulbright Summer Research Fellowship, the Illinois Humanities Council, various awards and grants from the Center for Advanced Studies, Program for Study in a Second Discipline (tropical ecology), Center for Latin American and Caribbean Studies through its Title VI National Resource Center funds, the Research Board of the Graduate College, the College of Liberal Arts and Sciences, and the Graduate College of the University of Illinois at Urbana-Champaign.

For many years now Douglas Brewer, Director of the Spurlock Museum, and Dee Robbins, Assistant to the Director, have provided us with a productive and collegial academic milieu for which we are indebted. Dee has maintained communications with us while we undertook (and undertake) research in Ecuador over many years.

Finally, we thank Joan Catapano, editor-in-chief of the University of Illinois Press, for inviting us to submit this manuscript for publication, and for handling all matters from development to publication with generosity and good sense. Rebecca Crist and Cope Cumpston coordinated final editing and the placement of illustrations.

In places, some of these essays draw from other works of ours, especially *Sacha Runa: Ethnicity and Adaptation of Ecuadorian Jungle Quichua* (1976), *Sicuanga Runa: The Other Side of Development in Amazonian Ecuador* (1985), *From Myth to Creation: Art from Amazonian Ecuador* (1988), and elsewhere, as indicated in the acknowledgments of chapters 4 and 8. The three books cited are out of print and difficult to obtain. Earlier observations and insights not included in previous publications are presented here, together with recent information, materials, interpretations, and analyses.

Ecuador, with insert showing South and Central America.

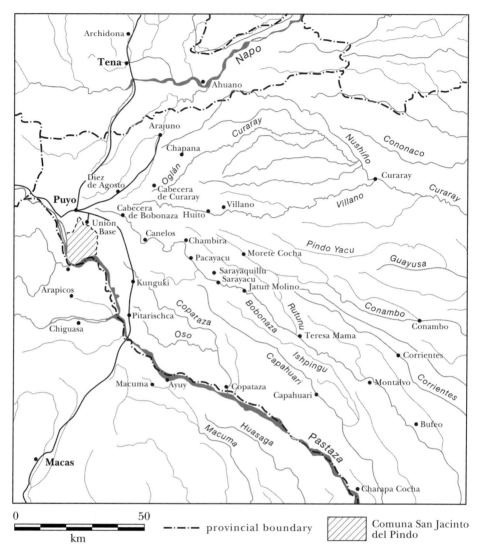

Pastaza Province and immediate environs.

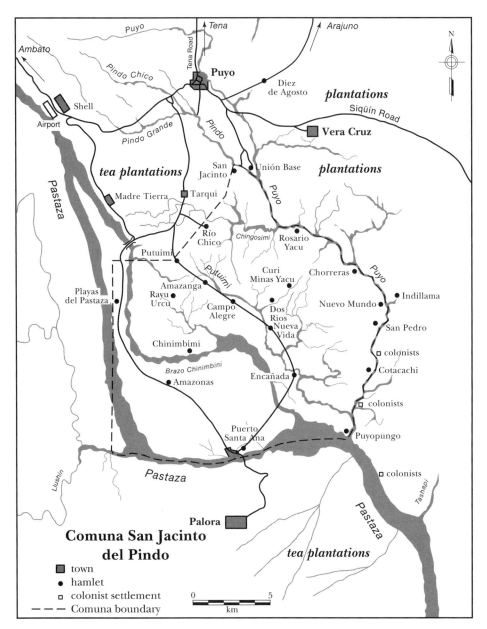

Comuna San Jacinto del Pindo, 1986. In 2006 each hamlet has divided to create more named settlements, but the overall population is more dispersed now than twenty years ago.

Notes on Orthography and Pronunciation

Spanish orthography is standard for the Americas. Unless diacritics are added, emphasis is placed on the penultimate syllable, including proper names and place names. Quichua orthography follows Orr and Wrisley (1965) and is close to Spanish, with some exceptions: [w] is used instead of [gu] or [hu] as in *wasi* (house) except when the word is widely recognized by its Spanish spelling, as in *ayahuasca* (soul vine). In both Spanish and Quichua the /j/ morpheme is pronounced as the English [h], as in Jurijuri spirit or *jista* (festival), pronounced "Hurihuri," or "hista."

An alternative orthography for Quichua that we do not employ here is based on English. Particularly prominent is the use of [w], more expansively than is used in this work, and [k] instead of [c], [j], [g], and [qu]. Examples include Kichwa instead of Quichua, and *yachak* instead of *yachaj* or *yachac* (one who knows, shaman). In this work [j], [c], [g], and [qu] are retained instead of [k] because they correspond to most (but not all) Quichua-Spanish dictionaries. This use also allows us to represent dialect differences and variants more accurately. Also, we continue to use the /u/ grapheme rather than [w] in such words as *asua* (manioc brew), *shua* (lie, liar), and Shuar (people in Jivaroan languages), rather than *aswa, shwa, and Shwar*.

All place names and proper names are rendered in their most common spelling, as in Tungurahua and Zumbagua (both endings are pronounced "wa"), and Guatatuca (pronounced "Watatuca"). All names for political parties or social movements are presented with their common spelling, so Pachakutik is the social movement with political purposes, but *pachacutij* is used otherwise as an episteme of transformation from one space-time system to another.

Words in other languages are rendered in the most accessible manner for English speakers by use of variants of the International Phonetic Alphabet. Grammatically, for convenience of English readers, we use the English [s] instead of the Quichua plural; we use the plural of house as *wasis* and the plural of indigenous territories as *llactas*. However, we keep the proper noun "Runa" for both individual Quichua speakers and for aggregates of Quichua speakers (e.g., *pi runa pasa*, what person is going by; Canelos Runa, people of Canelos). For other people we also use a singular proper noun (Siona, Secoya, Waorani, Shuar, Achuar, Shiwiar) rather than adding the English plural [*s*].

There is variation in morphology. For example, some ceramists say *mucaja* instead of *mucawa* (ceramic drinking bowl), *shilquillu* instead of *shinquillu* (tree resin for coating ceramics), Nunguli instead of Nungüi (and one woman insists on Unguli) for the master spirit of pottery and garden soil. Use of the words as rendered in this book, however, will confuse no one in this cultural area.

Specific Canelos Quichua Orthography

Vowels

a   Spanish *a*

i   Ranges from Spanish *i* to Spanish *e*

u   Ranges from Spanish *u* to Spanish *o* (vowel is rounded when preceded by a nasal, so *nuspa* (crazy) is pronounced more like *nospa*, and *mucawa* (drinking bowl), sounds like *moncawa*.

Consonants

b   English *b*

c   Unaspirated *k*

ch   Unaspirated *ch*, voiced after nasals to give French *je* sound, so *puncha* (day) sounds like *punzha*, or English *punja*. Because of this sound feature we do not list a consonant *zh*. This applies to Canelos Quichua phonemics and varies in other Quichua dialects.

d   English *d*

g   English *g*

j   English *h*, a fricativized *k* (voiceless velar fricative) sound when terminal, so *jauya* (in-law) sounds a lot like *how ya*, and *yachaj* approaches *yachak*, except final sound is almost silent.

l   Spanish *l*

ll   Spanish *ll* that varies from *ll* in Amazonia to *zh* in the Andes. This is why some Andean people write *punlla* instead of *puncha* or *punzha.*

m   English *m*

n   English *n*

ñ   Spanish *ñ*

p   Spanish *p*

qu   Unaspirated *k* before *i,* so that Quichua is pronounced like Kichua and *quilla* (moon) like *killa.*

r   Spanish *r*

s   English *s*

sh   English *sh*

t   Spanish *t*

ts   Similar to Spanish *ch* or German *z* but often aspirated and sometimes voiced.

w   English *w.* Again, this substitutes for Spanish *gu* and *hu* preceding /a/ and /i/ but does not substitute for /u/ (*asua,* not *aswa,* manioc brew).

y   English *y*

z   English *z* (sometimes pronounced almost like *ts*)

Notes on Pronouns, People, and Pseudonyms

Because the essays in this book are written from different perspectives, from N. Whitten's, from D. S. Whitten's, and from both Whittens', our pronouns shift from first person singular to first person plural. Sometimes only one of us experienced a particular event about which she or he decided to write; sometimes we experienced an event together, but one of us undertook the interpretation; and sometimes an oeuvre is truly joint. For that reason the pronouns shift, and we have taken pains not to confuse the reader. As to the overall work, though, each of us has revised and worked on each chapter, and what is published is a joint decision.

Some people with whom we have lived and worked since the early 1970s—the dark years when Ecuador was under seven years of military dictatorship, with its ethnocidal educational and indoctrination policies—emerge in these essays with their proper names and backgrounds. There are many others, however, all thanked in various publications such as *Sacha Runa* and *Sicuanga Runa,* who wish to be disguised personally but who want the events properly recorded. The people mentioned are quite conscious of our endeavors to present facets of their lifeways through publication, and choose to have this information made public, which we are pleased to be able to do.

Pseudonyms were developed in *Sicuanga Runa* by N. Whitten, in consultation with D. S. Whitten and others familiar with the area, to allow a flow of text about similar events in which at least three people in at least three settings participated at one time or another, together with one or both of us. The disguised real people, through their merged pseudonyms, and the events in which they participated and participate are very real; nothing is a figment of our imagination; nothing is "made up." These events and the discourses that entail the use of consistent pseudonyms were deemed by many as essential to protect the specific people involved but critically important in terms of content expressed. The stories and narratives with pseudonyms seek to explicate reality while obscuring the actual actors in the particular places. Real people, mostly still living, designated or represented here as Lluwi, Sicuanga, Rosario, Challua, Marta, María, Taruga, Elena, Blanca, and Carlos are aware of the content and renditions herein portrayed and have approved of the ways in which we have handled the materials.

Puyo Runa

1

Puyo Runa and Nayapi Llacta

At 5:00 A.M., May 12, 2005, a shrill blast of a trumpet awakened the residents of Central Puyo. The military band from Shell then played the national anthem. Simultaneous musical announcements throughout the growing city proclaimed the official founding day of Puyo to be May 12, 1899. The history of the date comes from Dominican documents that erroneously claim that all of greater Puyo's indigenous people came here as an ecclesiastical delegation from the Dominican administrative center at Canelos in 1899. There, according to this official regional and national mythology, Friar Álvaro Valladares became the true civilizer and founder of Puyo, for, it is publicly and redundantly recited, he brought "half-civilized Indians" from Canelos with him to create a new order at the previously savage site in the rainy forested valley at the base of the Andes. Thus, it is claimed, began the inexorable march toward "acculturation" into a nation governed by "whites" who proclaimed the motherland to be "mestizo, Christian, and civilized" (Anonymous 1935; see also Monteros 1937; Yépes 1927).

The polarity of civilization and savagery is publicly celebrated every year on this day as the founding day of Puyo (N. Whitten 1976a; D. Whitten 1981). This year though, and in subsequent years, there was a new twist: the eleventh of May was declared "the day of the nationalities" (indigenous people) and given over to indigenous marches, thereby separating the urban citizenry into "Indian" and "non-Indian" in a modern replication of the colonial construction of the Republic of Indians and the Republic of Spaniards. Once again, indigenous historicity was silenced. While the polarity of savagery and civilization and the triumph of the latter over the former continues to be celebrated every twelfth of May in Puyo, and while this has become part of national myth, other versions of the founding and cultural makeup of the Puyo Runa exist.

Indigenous Mythohistories

Nayapi's Christian name was Javier Vargas. According to many indigenous people who "remember" their origins, this legendary leader came to Puyo from Shuar territory, south of the Pastaza River, and he was cradle bilingual in Quichua and Shuar. He may have spoken other languages and dialects too. A story seldom told, though, is that Nayapi was closely related to two Achuar men who came from Peru to settle the territory between the mouth of the Puyo River and the Llushín River, a region where Shuar and Achuar mingled, where tensions were constant, and where people spoke Quichua.

Nayapi belongs to the Times of the Grandparents. His parentage is buried in the Times of Destruction. Pierre (1983) and Valladares (1912:24–25), the early history writers, state with their own authority that the population of Puyo had been decimated around 1870 by a "Chirapa" attack led by the warrior Sharupe, and that at the time of the arrival of the group from Canelos in the late nineteenth century there were already fourteen native families, two families from Baños, and one from Macas. Nayapi was there at the arrival, and he was and continued to be a great leader.[1]

In the 2000s older people remember the early families, especially those headed by shaman-warriors—*yachaj runa* and *sicuanga runa* as they were called over the last century, *shamanes* and *guerreros* as they are often called in the 1990s and the new millennium—who became the founders of the separated indigenous territories that go back past grandparental times, beyond the times of destruction, to *callarirucuguna,* the beginning times-places.

A Founding Indigenous Myth

In today's nature, which emerged at beginning times-places, Nayapi is a swallow-tailed kite (*Elanoides fortificatus*). Mythically, Nayapi was a great fisherman, predator of riparian life. In the long and complicated myth of Nayapi there are many events as the great man travels from house to house. Others are traveling too, men and women, and the way these stories are told involve narrative spirals and songs intersecting with other narratives and sung spirals. Two women, Manduru Warmi (red woman) and Widuj Warmi (black woman), also trek from house to house in the Nayapi myth, sometimes with him, sometimes not. In some tellings of the myth Nayapi is accompanied by a hideous brother, Tsuna (puss person), who leads the women astray in multiple sexual adventures.

As the story we tell here proceeds it is punctuated by many events, interpretations, interruptions by listeners and pauses by tellers. Manduru and Widuj come to the house of a foreign person, Machin Runa. While the women are asleep in the center of Machin's great oval house, he—the Capuchin monkey in today's world—ties them up with *chambira* palm fiber. When they awaken at dawn they find that the fiber has turned into spiny bamboo. They are trapped in a cage of painful thorns that could impale them if they were to struggle. They cry out—"Who can help us?" Hearing their cries, the game birds of the forest arrive, one by one. First comes Paushi (helmeted currassow, *Pauxi pauxi*); he tries so hard to help; he cuts and he cuts and he dulls his beak trying. He just cannot cut the bonds; he is powerful, but he lacks the capacity to liberate. Then comes Pawa (Spix's guan, *Penelope jaquacu*) and the same thing happens. Yami (pale wing trumpeter, *Psophia leucoptera*) and many others try—still failure, still inability to accomplish the task of freeing the women. All of these birds were warriors, according to the knowledge of the Puyo Runa and of the other real people in their cultural territory.

Sicuanga Runa arrives with his great machete and he cuts and slashes and takes the spines out of the bamboo and he frees the two women. Then they blow their magical breath on Sicuanga, "*suuuuuuuu* Sicuanga Runa," they say, "*saquiringui!*" ("Stay this way!"). Widuj paints him black with *Genipa americana*; then Manduru paints his beak, collar, and the area between his tail and his body red and yellow. She paints with her coloration, the *Bixa orellana* (annatto) paint. Together they give him white, fluffy cotton for his chest. He becomes, and he stays, Sicuanga. He flies with his beak pointing forward like a lance; he is the toucan bird, *sicuanga*; his spiritual force is humanoid, Sicuanga Runa. The two women then change other birds into their present, diverse avian forms, and they make game animals for humans to hunt and then to cook and eat. They blow on Machin and make him a monkey person, almost human, and he, too, stays that way. Then the two women ask, "What will we be?" One says, "I'll be *manduru*," and the other says, "I'll be *widuj*," and they transform themselves into the two trees whose seeds provide red and black dyes to the Runa.

When one listens to stories of Nayapi, whether told by Quichua, Shuar, or Achuar speakers, events such as the one just sketched are brought into memory. Sicuanga Runa appears in many of the spiraling and intersecting tales that punctuate the telling of pasts and understandings of presents.

There is an enduring message to be conveyed. Anthropologists and others now call the message "indigenous historicity." By this we mean that one is listening to someone tell about an event or person that is salient in people's past times. The salience of liberation emerges very clearly in this tale. The modern representation of Sicuanga is crucial if we are to understand one of the root metaphors from which the branching stories radiate: Outsiders—foreigners—correspond to the mythical Machin Runa. Machin Runa is human, but the nature of his humanity is not known, nor is it clear whether he has a Runa-like soul, or whether spirit substances exist in his inner "will" (*shungu*), which defines much of the good and evil of the self. Foreign monkey-person is, however, part of the human universe and he will remain so.

In the beginnings Machin Runa, this foreign male person, tied up two women; Sicuanga Runa freed the women. They continued and continue their adventures from house to house, turning beings into their present forms by blowing upon them with their magical breath. Manduru and Widuj made animals for humans to eat. In the processes of such creation everything is clearly related: all animals, plants, inanimate objects, spirits, humans. They created the colors red and yellow on black and white to provide beauty to the world. Images, *muscui,* must be beautiful and rooted in knowledge. From knowledge comes the ability to understand the pasts and places of real people, and to "see" events of the present times and places. Sicuanga freed the two women so that they could continue their adventures, and so that the world would be as we can know it today. All this begins in the mythic tales of Nayapi, and modern history begins with Nayapi, the real person and ancestor of many contemporary Puyo Runa.

Puyo Runa Historicity

Nayapi was a real person in the Puyo area. He was *sinchi curaga,* a strong leader. As *sinchi curaga* Nayapi derived his authority from close relationships with the Dominican priests of Puyo and Canelos. From these *curas* Javier Vargas obtained and redistributed valued trade goods such as machetes, pots and pans, ax heads, powder, caps, and shot. He was also known as *curaga* because he could, when necessary, rally the dispersed, dissenting native people in the greater Puyo area against the threat of unacceptable encroachment. But just as he rallied people against the Church, from time to time, he also drew them together for the Church and for the state, which the Church represented.

Nayapi was a legendary power broker between Church-state centralized authority and dispersed indigenous dissidence. Today real people remember the resistance side of Nayapi's *curagazgo.* In Spanish-Quichua mix he was known as *gobiernoshina,* like a government. They see the swallowtail kites wheeling around and attacking the palm trees in search of small birds, eggs, and reptiles. They tell of Nayapi's legendary resistance, which is Sicuanga Runa's side of ongoing native life. Most don't usually remember, however, who the brothers of Javier Vargas were, what language they spoke, or where Nayapi lived and where he died. Memory of him now attaches to different ancestors, and while the force of indigenous historicity is transmitted generation to generation, its specifics lie with fewer and fewer people.

One such set of remembrances, which may be learned in different places with different variations, comes out of the region of Nayapi Llacta. They unfold in this way. Nayapi and his wife, Dila, and their children maintained a swidden garden near Puyo. They also maintained distant *chagras* six- to seven-hours' hard trek south of town in a rugged forest territory known by national and international explorers as a no-man's land. Nayapi acquired access to about two thousand hectares of land when, it is said, he confronted a Jurijuri spirit in a great but hidden opening in a formidable rain-forest hill near a rocky feeder stream of the Pazyacu River. There, at midday, alone, near the Jurijuri's secret cave, Nayapi prepared and drank the powerful hallucinogen *Brugmansia suaveolens,* called *wanduj* by the Runa and until recently called Datura in English. He then traveled in the spirit world with the forest spirit Amasanga, also known as Sacha Runa, forest person. Together, spirit and *curaga* drove the Jurijuri—overseer of rain-forest animals, especially monkeys, and other people—from his lair, and as the worlds of spirit and animals and humans again separated from one another three days later, Nayapi controlled the land while Amasanga controlled the forest and environing weather, upon which the fecundity of the land depends. In conquering this territory and making it his *llacta,* Nayapi created a bond between nature and supernature that developed and consolidated into his binding social space. A *llacta* is domesticated by male and female activity; its ecological dynamics are known and respected. People live there, hunt and fish there, and garden there. This space contrasted with Machin Runa *allpa*—foreigner's turf; it became Nayapi Llacta, his territory, and that of his consanguineal and affinal heirs.

Mamach, one of Nayapi's daughters, first expanded her *chagra* in Nayapi Llacta. Her husband, Lluwi, cleared the trees for her, and she brought hundreds of stems of manioc to plant. But before she planted she put one manioc stem in front and one on each flank of the pile; the main stick was the *curaga* and the two other sticks assistants. Then she painted the manioc *curaga* sticks and the two assistants with *manduru* and she painted her face with the same *Bixa orellana* paint. In stories of beginning times-places, the spirit master Nungüi emerges. This is a strictly feminine spirit who is very aggressive. Manioc sticks are her daughters and any perceived aggression or disrespect toward them incurs retaliation against one's human children.

Mamach, together with her older sister, wife of a powerful shaman from the Napo River region, and two unmarried daughters sang and danced to the garden spirit Nungüi. Manduru protected them and tamed the manioc stems so that they would not suck blood from humans—especially babies—or destroy the forest. When women paint manioc stems and themselves red they respect their spirit mother Nungüi and her root-crop children. By the mediation of Manduru, Nungüi refrains from sucking the blood from Runa children. Nungüi left stones, one red, one black, for Mamach to find. Once found they were quickly hidden in the garden region; only Mamach and Nungüi knew their locations. The stones were water polished, smooth, and pretty—*sumaj*. Each contained the soul (*aya*) of a spirit woman who could communicate between the spirit master and the master gardener.

The next day Mamach and her daughters began to plant in the cleared forest-garden domain while Nungüi worked in the undersoil–leaf litter forest-garden domain. Mamach and her female partners worked by day, and while they slept Nungüi worked by night, pushing the manioc sprouts up and helping other planted crops, including the poisonous *barbasco,* which is for fishing—and which is botanically closely related to manioc—to grow into something of a lattice of food-giving life. Just before dawn the planes of growth, one nourished by Nungüi and one nourished by the women gardeners, come close together. It is during this time that waking people can "see" the world of humans and spirits as overlapping, as existing on the same plane of vision and knowledge.

Mamach's husband, Lluwi, was a strong shaman (*sinchi yachaj*), "strong one who knows." Many people came to him when they were ill, some trekking there from the high Andes or deeper Amazonia. Together, patient and shaman would drink another hallucinogenic brew, called *ayahuasca* (soul vine). While the visionary world of darkness flickeringly interacted with the Runa world of the barely discernible night fire, shaman and client would discuss the illness and its possible sources. Then, while sitting on a *bancu,* a carved wooden stool in the shape of a water turtle, Lluwi would fly to distant lands, where he would ward off incoming darts, lances, and other missiles sent by hostile or jealous shamans. Then he would return, with greater shamanic

A clearing for a swidden garden (*chagra*) in the forest south of Puyo.

A new house in the center of a new manioc swidden garden south of Puyo.

capacity than before. He whistled, chanted, and sometimes played a Runa-style three-string violin (where the third string is a spirit-bringing drone), or readjusted it to a two-string Achuar-style violin, which has no drone.

Lluwi's passages into and out of the spirit world were facilitated by his growing and developing relationship with forest spirit-master Amasanga, through whom he communicated with the first shaman and spirit master of the water domain, Sungui, who is also known as Yacu Supai (water spirit). Through time he had acquired water-polished spirit stones from many regions, river banks, hills, rivulets, forests, and the stomachs of animals and fish. These served as the tangible media to his multiple communicative spirit networks.

After his displays of power, and after gaining the strength of universal forces, Lluwi would suck out magical darts sent by evildoers to the vulnerable people in the kinship network and household of another powerful person. If the evil were intentional Lluwi would retaliate by sending killing missiles of his own back at the odious, living shamanic source. Lluwi's power to heal and to inflict illness was drawn from the spirit domain of the encompassing water system, from Sungui, an ever-present spirit force that is kept under control by forest master spirit Amasanga. Amasanga in turn is controlled by feminine Nungüi forces. Lluwi, many people said, would one day become a dangerous and powerful *bancu,* a seat of power for the spirits, and then he would "see" beyond time. He might even acquire the transformational power of *tsumi,* which would allow him to return to this world after his death, as a great black jaguar.

* * *

Whatever was to transpire in the future with Lluwi and Mamach, their children and grandchildren would not be in a global vacuum nor would they be in a national backwater region. Royal Dutch Shell Exploration Company, a British tea company named Cotts, and other international concerns had moved into the Puyo area in the 1930s, and World War II brought an armed Peruvian invasion up the various rivers, just east and north of Puyo, in 1941. In 1945 Acevedo Vargas, Llandro Vargas, and Atanacio Vargas—sons of relatives of Javier Vargas—together with allies Camilo Santi, Estanislaw Santi, Virgilio Santi, among others, each the founder of a *llacta* or close relative of a founder, asked the president of the Republic of Ecuador, Dr. José María Velasco Ibarra, for the land they now collectively controlled. This request was granted and the Comuna San Jacinto del Pindo was created in 1947.

Virgilio Santi, who hails from the Copataza River region and was married to a woman, Antonia Simbaña, from the Upper Curaray River region of Chapana, on the Río Oglán, had earlier sold his land in Puyo to a German refugee and moved permanently to Nayapi Llacta. Known to most as a "Shuar" from Méndez, south of Sucúa in Shuar territory, he and his growing family took care to fan out to the fringes of their territory, Puma Llacta, where they encountered other former indigenous residents of Puyo, and other people, too, similarly engaged in territorial occupation and boundary marking. At first Nayapi Llacta and Puma Llacta became tied by kinship to the settlement of San Jacinto located on the Puyo River. This area nucleated just south of Puyo in the 1930s. But in the 1950s, after the formation of the *comuna,* some of the children and grandchildren, and their spouses and children, firmly broke bonds of ensnarement in hamlet San Jacinto proper and moved as two interrelated groups to the region radiating out of the site where Mamach first made her *chagra,* and where her now-aged husband, Lluwi, continued to demonstrate his shamanic curing powers.

A decade later, in the 1960s, both expanding groups declared themselves to be a separate, proper (*quiquin*) *llacta* with ancient roots that connect only tentatively to close relatives of other people consolidating and nucleating in other territories. In the twenty-first century, tales of Javier Vargas, Acevedo Vargas, Eliseo Vargas, Isaac Vargas, Camilo Santi, Virgilio Santi, Atanacio

Vargas, Llandro Vargas, and so many others have taken on varied legendary qualities and merged into streams of social knowledge that convey fundamental messages of liberation and establishment, while they obscure specific genealogical, affinal, and cultural ties to the past.

Let us return to just one founder, Virgilio Santi. According to church archives and memories of older generations, Virgilio's father, Yu, had come to Canelos and then to Puyo long ago. Some say he was "stolen" from the Shuar or the Achuar by Palati. In Canelos he married Eucevia Vargas, the mother of Virgilio and his siblings. Nayapi's epoch in the Puyo region was coterminous with that of Yu, who the priests of Canelos sometimes inscribed as "Carlos Yu" and "Yumáa." He was always referred to as a "Jívaro" in official records from Canelos.

"Jívaro" in Ecuador is opposed to *cristiano*, which means at least semi-civilized human being. Virgilio was baptized in Canelos, but where he obtained his Santi name is unclear. What emerges from indigenous historicity are the actions of the Vargases and Santis (and others) while in Canelos territory. They waged constant war with the "Chirapas" (who the priests also called "Jívaro") just south of the Pastaza River, in the areas known as Chiguasa, Arapicos, and Macuma. Although classed in perpetuity as heathen, wild savages, these people were also baptized from time to time. Indeed, the renowned Chirapa warrior Sharupe was baptized with great ecclesiastical pomp and circumstance as José María Sharupe in Riobamba in the 1890s (time of Alfaro; Ruiz n.d.:15, from Valladares 1912).

It is said that such raids by the people of Canelos—often in alliance with the Sarayacu Runa and sometimes with the Achuar of the Upper Copataza—against the Chirapa Jivaroans to the south of the Pastaza would take place after the annual or semiannual kinship festival in Canelos. They would be organized by dancers called "lancers" who, with *sicuanga runa* warriors, sallied forth to raid and to kill, if possible. Such warriors, in 1917 (see Karsten 1935:53, 62–68), took a *muqui* (reduced human head; the word is used in Quichua but derives from the Shuar *muca,* and Achuar *muuk,* head) and held a hidden festival with the head as the festive base somewhere in the Sigüín mountains, ancient territory of the Caninche (called "primitive Canelos" by Pierre 1983:234), not far from the mouth of the Puyo River, where it empties into the Pastaza (in earlier sources this is often called the Pindo, or Pindu, River). Yu gained tremendous prestige from this ceremony, and Virgilio and others inherited some of the yet-to-be-reciprocated killing debts that could one day follow. The aura and those debts continued to descend through children, through his *ayllu,* and to become attached to territory.

As the years passed the people of Nayapi Llacta married not only others from adjacent *llactas* but from the Capahuari area as well. Achuar from that area were related to people from other areas, and individuals in the ramifying networks of Achuar came to be regarded as potential spouses to members of the expanding groups of Puyo Runa. The Achuar rule of marriage residence is that the man should move to his father-in-law's site, and many do so. Nayapi Llacta saw the in-movement of some Achuar men, one of them nicknamed Challua, and it witnessed the out-movement of some Puyo Runa men. Some men and women married northward too, into the territory of Virgilio's first wife (he remarried after her death), who had come from the mountainous Upper Curaray River region, an area where Záparo and Waorani once resided in conflict with one another (Pierre 1889; Reeve 1985, 1993–94; Cabodevilla 1994).

In 1967 the nucleated portion of Nayapi Llacta was named Nueva Esperanza, "New Hope." The hamlet of some two hundred people flourished, as did about seventeen similar nucleations of *llacta* formations within the San Jacinto indigenous territory. There were many fights there; shamanic activity continued until the death of Lluwi in the late 1970s; and many people, including Sicuanga and his large family, left the plaza area to live on the *llacta's* territorial fringes, near other growing hamlets.

Nueva Esperanza, 1968

On June 13, 1968, Sicuanga's brother Jaime (whose nickname is Shiny Shoes) looked out the door of the house he was building on the south side of the recently cleared and very muddy plaza of the hamlet called Nueva Esperanza (New Hope). Dawn was just beginning to break, but his sharp eyes, attuned to every nuance of the cleared space beyond his home, instantly saw what he then took to be a horrible anomaly. He saw four big frogs, a foot long and a foot wide, sitting on a split-bamboo mat. They were sort of like *juing* (*Dendrobatis* species), similar to the South African giant bullfrog, but much larger. Although they had no teeth he was afraid they were there to devour him. He wasn't asleep, he wasn't dreaming, but he "saw" something that he knew didn't exist. He turned away and went inside, then turned back and looked out, and they were still there. Now there seemed to be lots of them, all unknown, and they went *waugh, waugh*. He killed two with his machete and again went into the house; then he came back and they were all still there. Again he went inside the house, returning to look when the sun was up, and there were no frogs.

Really shaken now, Jaime crossed the plaza to visit Lluwi, the aging sha-man and founder of the new community. Lluwi listened carefully to Jaime's tale, focusing attention on the fear of being eaten. "Prepare a soul-vine brew," he told Jaime, "and we will 'see' tomorrow night what these things are that so terrify you and that you believe could devour you." Jaime did as he was told, and the next night he and Lluwi drank *ayahuasca* together an hour after sunset. As the spirit world unveiled its other realities, and after conversing with *yacu mama* as black anaconda, Lluwi "saw" just what the frogs were. They were *maquinaria*: big, heavy-duty machinery. Such machinery had not yet arrived in urban Puyo, and there was no road to Nueva Esperanza in the Upper Amazonian rain forest. Nonetheless, Lluwi could "see" the future transformation of the frogs into a large Komatsu bulldozer, a road scraper, and seven dump trucks working one behind the other, first coming up a hill, then turning and backing to the area in front of Jaime's house before dumping their loads of heavy stones taken from the Pastaza and Puyo riv-ers. There was also a heavy roller there making everything flat, squeezing the water out of the plaza and making a giant Andean-type *cancha,* cleared space, that would become sun-parched hardpan eventually, with lagoons in the low spots, unless modern trenches were dug and maintained.

This is what Lluwi "saw" in his *Banisteriopsis*-induced trip to the spirit world, and this is what would exist in the Runa's everyday waking world be-fore many more years passed. Jaime, explained Lluwi, had glimpsed a reality lying between the other world of the spirits and the world of people; both exist, but the plane of existence is different. Sometimes, though, just before dawn, these planes come together in strange but interpretable ways.

Lluwi told Jaime of the machinery going *roooom, vrrroooom aaarrrgggh.* "This is why we have made our plaza," Lluwi explained patiently; "what you saw yesterday morning is what is coming soon." Now Jaime was not fright-ened. The next day he resumed work on his house, completed it, and lived without fear, wondering when the great *maquinaria* that no one in urban Puyo had ever seen would arrive in front of his house. As Sicuanga listened to Jaime tell of Lluwi's insight a few days later, he thought deeply about the past, present, and future of linear time, and shook his head. Looking at his wife, María, he said, "Many, many outsiders will come soon and Shiny Shoes will want whatever their machinery will make. Then he'll need lots of money, and get himself all wrapped up; and change our lives along with his."

* * *

I first visited Nueva Esperanza in 1970, walking there on a partially cordu-roy rain-forest trail to attend a general assembly of the entire Comuna San

Jacinto. I returned near there with Sibby (Dorothea Scott Whitten), in 1971, to begin a set of associations described elsewhere (N. Whitten 1976a). In 1972 we moved into Puma Llacta, near Nueva Esperanza, and lived there for one year, alternating that residence in the Comuna San Jacinto with another residence in Puyo. During that period the trail remained and the system of forests, river, and *chagra* exploitation could be described as a variant of indigenous Upper Amazonian cultural ecology. In 1979 a road was constructed to Nueva Esperanza and we moved to the edge of the *caserío* there; by 1981 the road was all-weather, with a foundation of about six feet or more of five- to forty-pound stones. They were dredged from the Pastaza and Puyo rivers, hauled in large trucks, dumped, and then rolled, overlaid with a couple of feet of smaller stones and gravel, and rolled again. Sugar cane and cattle—both significant commercial commodities—were being purchased roadside by 1980, and some of the Runa were tied up in economic nets of debilitating bank loans, debts, and obligations to competing religious orders (Dominican Catholic and evangelical Protestant).

On May 23, 1982, I attended the inauguration of a new bridge over the Chingosimi River, as well as the encompassing celebration accompanying the completion of the road right up to the school on the south side of the plaza in Río Chico, a hamlet analogous to Nueva Esperanza. On the afternoon before the inaugural celebration I was told the story of Jaime, the frightening frogs, and Lluwi's prognostication about change. The teller didn't know me well; why he told this tale I do not know. The intensity by which others watched the telling, and watched me think and reflect, will never be forgotten, by me, or by others present. I was taken, others later said, to the conjuncture of the times-spaces of then and now. I was offered a brief glimpse of Lluwi's imagined future which is now our present reality. I was offered an insight of a past when the future was "seen" by Lluwi, son of founder Nayapi, father of Sicuanga.

On that day Clara Santi Simbaña arrived at our house at dawn. She wanted to sing, so a stereo recorder was put on a turtle stool and a microphone on another stool. She sang and she sang as the sun came up; by 8:00 A.M. the trucks and bulldozer and road scrapers came up the hill, making the very sound that Lluwi told Shiny Shoes about back in 1968. As the heavy machines droned beside our residence, and right outside her home, Clara sang this song:

> I'm toucan woman, I'm toucan,
> yao sicuanga woman,
> just standing on the big hilltop,
> eating only nuts, I walk, just walk.
> Toucan woman, eating another nut for her belly,

I walk, looking at the sunbeams.
Distant and alone,
this toucan woman doesn't kill in eating this way.
She's just walking, just singing this way.
Toucan woman,
"Don't eat her flesh,"
it seems she sings, it seems she sings.

In 1985 we moved to Cushi Tampo, along another new road cutting through the Comuna San Jacinto, and in 1990 we decided to continue to conduct our extended, multi-sited ethnography primarily in Puyo and other regions of the Bobonaza and Pastaza region. Factionalism within the Comuna was combining with a unity aimed at creating a new indigenous space of social justice and political enfranchisement for all the people of Ecuador. Our extended presence in small hamlets was catalytic, we think, to exacerbated factionalism, so we "pulled back." Since the early 1990s we have undertaken our systematic work with those who come to us from their territories to the Puyo area and with those now living in the Puyo area. N. Whitten has also continued some work in Canelos and the Achuar settlement of Charapa Cocha (D. Whitten and N. Whitten 1993c). During the time of our "pull back" many Puyo Runa families surged forward into Puyo and its expanding region. Consequently, our interaction frequency with many people actually increased. As more and more Puyo Runa entered Puyo and created new *barrios* some also intensified their efforts to firmly establish their *purina* territories, areas to which a trek is made once or twice a year. We were able to understand radical change and remarkable continuities, both from the standpoint of ongoing cultural transformations and social dynamics, with very little difficulty.

In 1990 Ecuador underwent its first Levantamiento Indígena (indigenous uprising), which began to radically reform the nation by drawing dramatic attention to the extraordinary injustice done to native people. In the Puyo area roads were blockaded and heavy equipment confiscated. In Sarayacu the airstrip was blockaded and two planes were confiscated. In 1992 people about whom we are writing embarked on a March (Caminata) for Land and Life from Puyo to Quito, during which period they gained official control of all noncolonized areas of Ecuadorian Amazonia, 1,115,574 hectares, about ¾ of this rain-forest–riparian region.

The year 2000 found Ecuador transformed by the actions of indigenous people, including those about whom we have written, with whom we have lived and worked in their settings, and with whom we continue to work in the growing city of Puyo. Carlos Antonio Vargas Guatatuca, from *caserío* Unión Base, where Acevedo Vargas was once a renowned *tambero,* and where Eliseo Vargas cured his clients while chanting in Záparo, became the president of the national indigenous organization of Ecuador, CONAIE (Confederación de las Nacionalidades Indígenas del Ecuador). His father's father was Eliseo Vargas. We do not know the name by which Eliseo Vargas was known in the late 1800s when he arrived in this area of Puyo. His father was a Zaparoan-speaking person from the hinterland of Sarayaquillu, the cultural heartland of Sarayacu, a site on the Bobonaza River. It is said by relatives and others that Eliseo cured Dr. José María Velasco Ibarra of malignant forces. On January 21, 2000, during the action in Quito known as the *"golpe del 21 de enero,"* Antonio Vargas was part of a junta that ousted the national president, Jamil Mahuad Witt; Vargas served, thereon, for three hours, as vice president of the Republic of Ecuador (see N. Whitten 2003b and chapters 4 and 9 in this volume).

Liberation is occurring for indigenous people of Ecuador, though the cages of spiny thorns constructed by the mythical *machin runa* still have the ability to impale. Whenever collective indigenous action occurs in Ecuador people become confused. "Who are these Indians?" is an often-asked question, "Where do they come from?" When Quichua- and Spanish-speaking people come from Amazonia to the Andean capital of the republic, Quito, to restructure an old modern nation-state, confusion reigns in the minds of most. Try though they will, journalists and other scholars just can't seem to pinpoint the "tribes" in action. Anthropologists often seem to have the same problem. Indeed, prominent social science scholars even today label indigenous movements for human rights as "the Indian question" (Postero and Zamosc 2004:1–31).

The people from Amazonia know who they are. But they use many cultural representations and identity referents to communicate their sporadic oneness in diversity (e.g., Reeve 1993–94). When they use such words as Shuar, Achuar, Shiwiar, Záparo, Andoa, Waorani and seem to shift their markers from one to another they are not signaling or suggesting any "crisis of identity." Quite the opposite; these designations and representations are tied to spaces and places that constitute the living network of past events and times that swirl and spiral into a dynamic present. They help to construct a multicultural, and at times intercultural, modernity radically different but perhaps inextricably tied to the modernities of global forces anchored and dislocated by the contemporary nation-state and transnational corporations. More on this later, as the messages of this ethnography unfold.

Real People, Real Places

In 1971, a year before Sibby and I took up residence in Puma Llacta, Marcelo Santi Simbaña and I set out to understand, from his reference points, the way by which humans in the greater Puyo Region live and the backgrounds of their lived realities.[2] I was interested in indigenous reflexivity: the way by which people take the role of others to understand more of the self. Marcelo's ability to understand what I was trying to understand led to a relationship that culminated in an extended period of residence in his hamlets, out of which we continued our sojourns. In late August 1972, we took up residence in Puma Llacta. Marcelo, with the help of others, had constructed a small oval house of peach-palm posts and split peach-palm floor, split bamboo sides, and a roof thatched with a low ground palm called *ucsha*.

While we were still something of a novelty in the hamlet, people gathered every evening to tell us of mythical events, some of which are narrated again in English in this book. It was only by moving through, across, into, and out of indigenous spaces and places, though, that we could come to an understanding of the multiple historicities that constitute the frameworks of times-places to which people alluded. Women involved Sibby in many of their activities, particularly in seeking health care for their families. She frequently accompanied them for treatment at Hospital VozAndes in Shell, which they came to trust and to choose over other options. At their request, we developed a medical-care delivery program that continues today through this hospital-clinic. In this way she, too, built up a store of native knowledge.

Puyo Runa is how the people referred to themselves. *Runa,* in Quichua, means human being, fully human being; a Runa has a fully developed soul, a life force, and abilities to know in a traditional manner, to perceive and understand what is going on around oneself on a day-to-day basis, to reflect and think critically, and to "see." We shall return to these properties of humanity through the entire volume.

Quichua itself refers to the northern dialects of Quechua. Quechua was the official language spoken by the fifteenth-century Imperial Inca at the time of their Andean conquest north to southern Colombia and south to the Atacama desert in central Chile. This conquest was completed a scant forty years prior to the beginning of the Spanish conquest in the Caribbean and northern South America, Central America, and Middle America.

As Norman, Marcelo, and others walked and talked, stopped, visited for from an hour to a day, moved from place to place, ever outward from any one residential complex and then back again by a different route, the differ-

ent Runa locations emerged. The Puyo Runa are made up of three groupings: those of the Comuna San Jacinto; those children of Peruvian *regatones*
(the Portuguese word for "trader" in Western Amazonas) and women from
Sarayacu who settled in urban Puyo itself; and those of the complex of San
Ramón, Jatun Paccha, San Antonio and Klm cuatro y media (also called
Américas) of the Vía Napo, many of whom had ancestors who hailed from
the Napo or from the Arajuno River region. Canelos Runa consisted and
consist of a wide-flung aggregate of people ranging from Canelos proper
north to the Upper and Central Villano River region, south to the Copataza
River, and west to the Tingüiza River.

The axes of Puyo-Canelos are the Cabecera de Bobonaza, northeast of
Puyo, and Indillama, southeast of Puyo. Both of these sites are important
historically as well-known hinges between the Ecuadorian Andes and its
eastern land from whence comes a type of cinnamon (Uzendoski 2004b),
known historically as *ishpingo* (*ishpingu* in Quichua), and *canela* (from which
derives Canelos) in Spanish. (It is not really cinnamon but *Ocotea quixos*
[Latorre 1995:39].) Historically, Canelos itself ranges through the expanding
and contracting spatial diamond of Puyo–Cabecera de Bobonaza–Indillama–
contemporary Canelos. Indillama (the place of the sloth) is on the Puyo River,
which flows into the Pastaza River. According to Pierre (1983:118), it is at this
riverine juncture that the Dominicans "converted" the Caninche heathens
and began to try to nucleate the site of Canelos in 1581 (see also Karsten 1935;
Naranjo 1977), thirty-seven years after Francisco de Orellana's voyage down
the Napo and Amazon, and a mere three years after the first major rebellion
of the Quijos in the north in 1578 (Oberem 1971:72–75) and two years after a
similar revolt by the Shuar to the south in 1579 (Santos-Granero 1993:217).

According to Requena y Herrera (1784) as reported by Cabodevilla
(1994:476), this sector of the Andean foothills–Upper Amazon was the jump-
ing-off point for the Jesuits for travel into the Marañon territory of the Mission of Maynas. By the eighteenth century, and probably before that, Canelos
was the cultural switchboard not only between the Andes and Amazonia, but
also for the Zaparoans of the Napo, Curaray, and Bobonaza river systems,
the Achuar of the Capahuari and Copataza river systems, and some of the
Shuar to the south (Cabodevilla 1994:108–9). Marcelo Naranjo (1977) argues
that Canelos emerged and endured as a *refuge region* for people from all of
these areas, and as such was the site of preference for traveling curates and
explorers seeking labor and knowledge.

At the beginning of sporadic nineteenth-century Dominican dominion
(N. Whitten 1976a) over the territory of the Canelos people ranged from

the focal zone north to the Upper Curaray and Villano rivers, east to Saray-acu and perhaps Montalvo, and southeast to the Copataza, Capahuari, and Pastaza river systems, including in this system Quichua-speaking, Zaparoan-speaking, and Jivaroan- (mostly Achuar) speaking peoples. The pipeline to Quichua language was from the Puyo-Canelos sector northward to the Napo and southward to the Upano. North was considered a sector of relative safety, and the south always represented danger.

* * *

Because Canelos was the linkage between Upper Amazonia and Sierra in this region of Ecuador, and since Canelos proper and Puyo contained, from time to time, aggregates of people speaking Jivaroan, Quichua, and Zapa-roan languages, I chose "Canelos Quichua" as a working designation of the Quichua speakers for whom Canelos itself was and is a focal representation. What I learned was that "places" and indigenous spaces are inextricably as-sociated with indigenous genealogy and events that punctuate space-time and human continuities. Such punctuations, in turn, create the intercultural continuities themselves (N. Whitten 2002).

By walking from one point to another, I could learn of the ways by which indigenous people mark their spaces to create and activate the neural net-works that allow them to retrieve the culturally stored information. Some-times we would come to what to me was an unremarkable spot in the forest, one where an underground stream could be found after one pawed the under-growth. There I might learn of a special stone, to keep in my mind for future reference to the shamanic power it connoted. Or I learned how to find crab or shrimp or eel to capture and cook and eat. At a larger terminus, a house or a hamlet, Marcelo would sit next to me as we drank *asua* and I would learn from whoever sought to teach. Redundancy in information is not a cultural pattern of the Runa ways of knowledge transmission, so if people thought I knew something, that knowledge was implicit in our conversations. *Ricsina* was mine to acquire and to process. If I were to walk in this land, then I had to grow in experiential knowledge. I would also have to learn to integrate such knowledge with imagery and deep knowledge if I were ever to build the depth of perception that constitutes the fully human being.

To continue this learning process of significant places, I traveled by air, sometimes alone, sometimes with Marcelo and others. After landing I made my way by foot or canoe. Far to the north of Canelos, near where the Vil-lano River flows into the Curaray River, is Curaray, a hamlet reestablished by Canelos Runa around the turn of the twentieth century (Reeve 1985, 1988a,

1988b, 1993–94). Identity as Curaray Runa involves life in a low Amazonian ecotone, as well as sustained interaction with the military, who established a base there after the invasion of Peru in the "War of '41." It also involves memories of the Amazon Rubber Boom, Zaparoan ancestry, conflicts with the Waorani, and conflicts in Canelos that led people to leave there (Reeve 1985, 1988b, 1993–94; Stanfield 1998).[3]

Eastward on the Bobonaza River is Pacayacu; its inhabitants identify as Pacayacu Runa. Over 60 percent of the Pacayacu Runa have the surname of Gaye. Gaye was originally the upriver Andoa dialect of Záparo (Shimigae). Pacayacu Runa extend their territory northward to Villano on the Villano River, and to the sectors where they overlap with Canelos Runa. Farther eastward on the Bobonaza is Sarayacu, with its Sarayacu Runa. In many ways, though it is said to be "essentializing" to say such things in the twenty-first century, Sarayacu represents the epitome of Canelos Quichua culture. A focal sector of Sarayacu is Sarayaquillu, where powerful shamanic activity by some men, beautiful and meaningful ceramics by women, and wide-flung trade networks involving Canelos Quichua speakers, Achuar Jivaroan speakers, Zaparoan speakers, and Peruvian Mestizo (Spanish and Quichua) speakers conflate. To me, Sarayaquillu represents a condensation and intensive miniaturization of the entire Canelos Quichua cultural region. Many indigenous people share my perhaps nostalgic representation.

Farther to the east is Teresa Mama, named from the Jivaroan word for manioc, and then Montalvo, previously known as Juanjiri, which became the nexus of the Upper Amazonian Rubber Boom in this area. Radiating out of Montalvo one finds bi- and trilingualism to include Canelos Quichua, Peruvian Amazon Quechua, Záparo and Andoa Zaparoan, Shuar, Achuar, and Shiwiar Jivaroan. Obviously, the Runa territories cannot be talked about as "the Quichuas" on the one side, and "the Jívaros" on the other side, though this silencing polarization of the dynamic lifeways of people is the way they are usually treated, even by professional ethnographers (e.g., Descola 1994, 1996; Taylor 1999).

* * *

In his youth Marcelo Santi sometimes delivered mail from Puyo to Canelos, Pacayacu, and on to the Copataza River region. I didn't learn about this activity of his until the early 1980s. He also served, once or twice, as a *sillero* on parts of the trail from Puyo through Chontoa and on to Canelos. To be a *sillero* is to have a chair strapped to his back. The visiting priest sits in the chair and travels backwards in a rocky-tipsy seat as the Runa burden carrier for Church and state bears him ever forward over the very difficult terrain to his destination in Canelos, from whence the savage "Jívaro" was to be converted, or at least "tamed" or "hybridized."

Marcelo would tell such stories, chuckling at his remembrances of times when he would let the curate out of his chair, orient him to a tippy canoe, and then get a couple of friends to prop up the priest by the legs so that the representative of God could arrive at the landing site with arms spread outward to form a human cross. At the time of these tellings I could not always contextualize what he was talking about or why he would tell such a tale just as we were arriving at a new destination. What seemed out of place for me at the time was actually an introduction of an important reference point of indigenous reflexivity and historicity. Without the indigenous people to transport them and to prop them up, the Church would not have taken hold here or elsewhere.

In 1972 Marcelo and I together with Luis Vargas Canelos made a special sojourn to Sarayacu. I had been there three times before and knew some people, especially in Sarayaquillu. It was also clear to me that there were Achuar living there, as in Canelos. Lucho (Luis Vargas Canelos) was described by Marcelo as a "Shuar" who came from the Copataza area. I accepted the superficial "Shuar" representation, but I knew better. I had previously traveled to Capahuari and knew of the Achuar territory north of the Pastaza, and I knew that Lucho was of this region. I had come to understand that it was not up to Marcelo or others to mark or label people. He was not a maker of representations; but Lucho began about this time to characterize the social world as he knew it and as he envisioned it becoming.

As Lucho began to see what I had learned without his help, he quickly moved to the role of teacher. His brother Venancio, known as Japa (Deer) in Achuar, had walked over from Copataza to meet us in Sarayacu, and they spoke Achuar to one another. Lucho simply explicated the situation that those north of the Pastaza formed an interconnected aggregate of Achuar who called themselves "Shuar" in and around Puyo, and never used the word Achuar in any of the Runa territories for fear of retaliations for past hostilities. He knew that I had already figured this out, and wanted to be sure that I "knew" and "saw" rather than "thought about" these matters of intercultural connection and intercultural decorum. He wanted me to "see" various levels of social life in this complex cultural system. He helped to fashion intracultural and intercultural images that could adhere to my observations.

During this period of our sojourns out of Puma Llacta and through Nueva Esperanza and other hamlets such as Unión Base, and into other Runa territories, Ecuador was under military dictatorship. The governor of the province, Colonel Alejandro Duque, was suspicious of everything Sibby and I and Marcelo Naranjo did. Among other things we were making a collection of contemporary material culture for the Museum of the Central Bank of Ecuador, in Quito, and this seemed to agitate the colonel no end. We were working with graduate students from Ecuador and the United States who were also in and out of Puyo. There were also Peace Corps volunteers in Puyo, so the foreign gringo presence was quite strong. Sibby and I established a system where indigenous people could stay in our house in Puyo when they came in from the various territories on weekends. We would be visited by not only people from the Comuna San Jacinto, but also by Canelos Runa, Curaray Runa, Pacayacu Runa, Sarayacu Runa, and occasionally by others, as well. Visiting with native people in Puyo was the reciprocation of our own visits to their hamlets and territories. But it was not the constant interaction between us and native peoples that apparently agitated the governor, Alejandro Duque, to the point that he contemplated publicly our expulsion.

In Sarayacu, as Lucho took on the role of teacher, he made a connection that we never would have guessed: Duque's brother-in-law, Luis Mena, ran a tawdry "museum" of "primitive culture" at the tourist site Mitad del Mundo fifteen miles north of Quito. He also ran occasional "tourist trips" for visiting scientists, adventurers, and explorers to the Copataza River region, Lucho's homeland. There, Lucho explained, Mena would send word in advance that the adventurers were coming, and the "Jívaros" would prepare for an all-night party in the "Jivaría." Lucho vividly remembered how, when he was a child, one group of filmmakers arrived to film a final head-taking feast, and how they brought their own *tsantsa*, shrunken head, with them, even though the Achuar do not practice head reduction. Things became clearer thanks to indigenous knowledge of nonindigenous networks: we were competing with the brother-in-law of the military governor of the province of Pastaza. We were interfering with the profitable commercial flow of goods and knowledge between Quito and the Copataza River system.

Marcelo joined in telling of the routes the adventurers would take: from Baños to Río Topo, on through Puyo to Canelos via one of the two connecting routes, down the Bobonaza to Sarayacu where they would walk across into "Jívaro" territory. Alternatively, they would trek south from Canelos and move down the Copataza. The "Jívaros" were regarded as quintessential savages, comparable to the "Auca" (Waorani) to the north of Canelos Quichua territory. The Canelos Quichua and the Runa territories exist between peoples of great interest to the outside world; such outsiders, however, see these people as lackluster, misplaced, or "acculturated" people who speak an "Andean language" rather than a "proper" or "traditional" Amazonian one. More about this later.

The Puyo Runa in the twenty-first century are acutely aware of and finely attuned to their ties to outsider-others with whom their histories are interconnected. They are also acutely aware of their multiple connections to ancestral peoples. Some leaders cultivate ties to representatives of global organizations such as Cultural Survival, the Interamerican Foundation, and the Rainforest Action Group, which, in turn, foster the development of tribalization and localization. The more people from the Runa territories expand the indigenous space of political and economic transformation of the Republic of Ecuador, and the more they move into a life of alternative modernity and globalization, the more they are forced by others to fit a globalized version of restricted identity and confined ethnicity.

Runa Shimi Spoken Here

Runa shimi means "human speech" in Quichua. *Auca shimi* means "speech of others of Amazonia." The "others" have been transformed by many writers to mean "savages," or "wild Indians" (*indios bravos*), so that, if one insists on locating Quichua as a strictly "Andean language" spoken by pacified and "semi-civilized hybrids" as many scholars still do, then by syntagmatic and contrastive association, those Amazonian people who speak *runa shimi* are called people out of place—recent migrants, parts of a lost Andean diaspora, people of little note, and certainly not bona fide Amazonian people whose praxis may change an established hegemony. By such negative ascriptions indigenous people are deprived of an ethnography of empowerment.

No wonder sophisticated journalists and scholars in Quito and elsewhere cry "who are these Indians?" and "where did they come from?" when they arrive in the capital city to change and remake the nation-state. Some Quiteños say of such arrivals that the people are *fuera de su lugar* (away from their [proper] place). They call them "Yumbos." The hegemonic polarity creates a historical silence that denies the very existence they observe. Listening to Quiteños talk about *indios,* unless they can class them as "Jívaro" or "Auca," is like listening to Jaime talk about magical frogs that could devour him, even though he knows they don't exist.

In Amazonian Ecuador *runa shimi* is spoken in three dialects, one of which is Canelos. Another is located east of Papallacta, in the region radiating out of Baeza to the Colombian border and east to Archidona. This region has long been known as the Quijos area. The Quijos may have been descendants of Cofán people (Kohn 2002a) who took up the Quichua language before, during, or after the Inca and Spanish conquests. East of the Quijos Quichua region is the riverine system of the Napo River, whose inhabitants identify in Ecuador as Napo Runa (Napo people; see Uzendoski 2005b; Macdonald 1979; Muratorio 1991) and in Peru as Quechuaruna and Napo Runa. The so-called "Peruvian Amazonian Mestizos," people who live in urban areas such as Iquitos and Pucallpa, share a shamanic lore that is chanted in *runa shimi* (e.g., Dobkin de Rios 1972, Luna and Amaringo 1991). In the Putumayo area of Colombia, both in highland and lowland sectors, *runa shimi* speakers are known as Inga. They, too, control powerful shamanic paradigms in great favor with some Colombian intelligentsia, as well as with poor and well-to-do Colombian peasants and landholders who fall on bad times (Taussig 1987).

The word "Auca" in Ecuador and Peru has long been used for yet another people, the Waorani (Huaorani) who live north of the Curaray River (Reeve 1985, 1988a, 1988b; Cabodevilla 1994; Rival 2002). Waorani is another "isolate" language, not connected, as far as linguists now know, to any other language. In the recent past, and today, there have been many Zaparoan people (probably Záparo and Arabela and maybe Andoa) in what is now Waorani territory, and the language is still known to some speakers there. The Canelos people sometimes call the Waorani the Awa Shiri, or Tawa Shiri, which means to them "high ground people."

Who We Are and Where We Live

The Bobonaza River region is and has long been the locus of Canelos Quichua culture. It extends north to the Curaray River region (Reeve 1985, 1988a), which includes the territories between the Bobonaza and Curaray. *Runa shimi* is spoken here as a common language, and the dominant representation of communality is that of Runa, fully human being. The word Quichua itself is not usually used in intraindigenous quotidian or ritual discourse. But in political discourse it ascends as the "*nacionalidad* Quichua"—the nationality of Quichua-speaking peoples spanning Andes and Amazonia. In this region there are three residential patterns: a localized one in a hamlet and its hunting-gardening-fishing areas, the broader *llacta* represented by the hamlet, and a trekking (*purina*) region, which may be from a day to several days' walk. "Where did your father trek?" is a common question, in *runa shimi*, when one is getting to know new people. Without the "trekking" with Marcelo, and with others as well, and on my own, I could have learned little if anything of this area. Laura Rival's (2002) phrase "trekking through history" is as apt for the Canelos Quichua people as it is for the Waorani (see N. Whitten 2004).

When we trekked we looked, talked, listened. Hearing rain coming across the canopy we would quickly seek refuge in a briefly erected lean-to structure, and in waiting out a storm people would talk of other storms, in other places, the power of the rain, the forces of the forest. A trip with the spirit master of the Datura might be recalled, which itself involves the forces of death and rebirth. Encountering a stream we would look at (not "for") special rocks, the memories of which help us to "see" what our dreams mean, and aid us in dreaming well. The huge flying buttress tree (Ila) that we pass has been a site of shamanic gnosis in the past. Today there is a powerful Uchuputu (kapok tree) spirit living there. During rain storms he pounds a club on the trunk, *thunk boom, thunk boom.* This is fearsome. It is no place for humans to dwell. But humans must "know" of this, so that they are aware of what they may "see." Wherever we go we dwell at times in the places of other dwellings. We are not nomads, but settled people. The trek is from settlement to settlement, from process to process, from place to place, from knowledge to more knowledge. We cannot be rooted if we do not travel to learn; and we cannot travel and learn without knowing our roots.

Staying still in a hamlet, or in the adjacent areas to a hamlet, times-spaces enter the identity-placement process and locate all rooted people in the far-flung nexuses of their recent beginnings. A person's "proper territory," *quiquin llacta,* is where one's grandparents came from. The article "from" or "of" in Quichua is a suffix, *-manda.* If one is "from Sarayacu," she is Sarayacumanda, or Sarayacumanda Runa or Sarayacumanda *warmi.* More often than not, we find a pattern where a woman's mother's mother's husband is "from" Sarayacu, and her father's father's wife is "from" Copataza. She may be married to a man whose father's father's wife comes "from" the Napo River region, and his mother's mother's husband comes "from" the area just north of Montalvo. This gives us a couple in a household with four distinct "proper places" of origin in "times of the grandparents."

The use of concepts of grandparental time, the application of *purina* activities on a regular or irregular basis, and the system of individual memory transmitted through narrative, shamanic activity, ceramic motifs, and song establishes a regional cultural system that is manifest in every locality, from Achuar territory through Canelos Quichua regions, through the Shiwiar and Zaparoan systems and the Napo River region. All of the imagery of all of these connections comes together in a montage of stylized activity during an annual or semiannual kinship festival (N. Whitten 1976a; Reeve 1985, 1993–94). This is the subject of chapters 5 and 6.

Unión Base, 1968

In 1968, the year when Jaime "saw" the frightening frogs in Nueva Esperanza, we first visited Unión Base where we were greeted by an elderly woman, Narcisa Vargas, who volunteered to "watch over" our Volkswagen rental car while we walked on to Rosario Yacu to visit for the first time with people who would be important in our lives over the next three decades or so and who were to constitute part of the make-up of the type-site called Nueva Esperanza/Nayapi Llacta (N. Whitten 1985). We sat and talked in Spanish to her on our return from Rosario Yacu, and soon she told us something of her genealogy, stressing that her father was a *"Záparo del monte,"* a Záparo speaker (Andoa dialect) from the rain forest north of Sarayacu, probably from the Rutunu River region where many from Sarayaquillu today have distant gardens. She, her brothers—Eliseo Vargas and Isaac Vargas—and mother had come from Sarayaquillu to join the famous *tambero,* Acevedo Vargas, in leading adventurers and traders eastward.

Acevedo, or Severo as he is now known, received a small pension from the government to take people from Unión Base down the Puyo River to Indillama, where they either picked up other guides or continued with him through Chontoa, over the Sigüín mountain range (territory of the Caninche people, who probably spoke an Achuar dialect, but where Andoa Zaparoan may also have been spoken), on to Canelos. Severo would also find guides for adventurers seeking experiences with the *untsuri* (numerous) Shuar. Such trips would begin at the mouth of the Puyo River, and continue to Palora, Chiguasa, and Arapicos, where different routes could be taken.

In 1970 the wife of Eliseo Vargas was shot to death, allegedly by Shuar raiders, while she and Eliseo slept in their house on the other side of the Co-muna San Jacinto. Eliseo moved again into Unión Base, where he served as resident shaman into the late 1970s, when he died of natural causes at a very old age.

Unity and Divisions

Language and ethnic hatreds seem to go hand in hand in the region. We first learned this linkage in Unión Base, where people who were descendants of Zaparoans told of vendettas against them. Later, in Puma Llacta, where an

Left, powerful shaman Eliseo Vargas plays flute at Unión Base festival, 1972.

aged shaman—Virgilio Santi—was focal to social life we were told other tales of vengeance across language borders. According to people in Runa territories, especially the Comuna San Jacinto, Canelos and Pacayacu, Shuar and Achuar people have been and are at "war" with all Zaparoans, and would like to silence them forever, down to the last man, woman, and child.

A grandson of Eliseo Vargas, son of the late Venancio Vargas, is Carlos Antonio Vargas Guatatuca, usually just known as Antonio Vargas. Antonio grew up in a world of contradictions imposed by Western hegemony. Runa territories for him became a world of unity. Although he was clearly Puyo Runa, his "proper territory" is Sarayaquillu (stretching north to the *purina* region of the Rutunu River, where Zaparoan was once spoken), where his father's father's relatives came from. When indigenous federations began to form in 1979 Antonio spent extended periods of time in Sarayaquillu, alternating his days between that site and the meeting house in the school on the plaza of Sarayacu (now known as Centro Sarayacu). He learned from the elders of his proper territory, just as he learned of the new strategies for altering the space of indigenous people in the Republic of Ecuador in the schoolhouse on the plaza.

Unión Base in the new millennium is smaller than it was in 1968, but abutting it is the office complex of the Confederation of Indigenous Peoples of Amazonian Ecuador (CONFENIAE). The confederation itself is often, but not always, dominated by Shuar from *untsuri* Shuar territory (which is also called *muraya* Shuar, high-ground people). Nonetheless, all the hostilities and remembrances notwithstanding, a tenuous indigenous unity in the face of nationalist adversity reigns and can be activated in times of perceived crisis. Puyo, like Quito, is a center for indigenous unity, a region where people insist on letting the world know that they are part of an Ecuadorian nation *and* that they are also real *living* people. Indigenous people. *Runapura.*

Knowledge and Learning

A lot of terminology has been given to the reader here. There is a reason for this. As the history of this region of South America is written from multiple perspectives, silences emerge that interfere with indigenous imagery, historicity, and imagined destinies by those now forging a national and international future. To write of "the Quichuas" on the one hand and "the Jívaros" on the other hand, as an enduring contrast set suggests half-civilized and hybrid (Quichua) versus the pristine savage (Jívaro). Whether so written by bureaucrats, curates, or anthropologists, this binary deception violates the fundamental indigenous postulate that to be fully human is to know other cultures as well as one's own. It produces a profound silence in the gap between what prominent scholars such as Descola (1994, 1996) and Taylor (1999) persistently put forth as the Quichua–hybrid–semi-civilized–semi-Incanized–Andeanized–generic "Indian" and the Jívaro-tribal-traditional-Amazonian "Indian."

Regardless of which side of the polarity the writer is on, the subject of the discourse is "Indian," not "human." Indigenous historicity is silenced, and Western hegemonic history presses on. In the ensuing eight chapters we continue to pursue the themes of imagery, power, and the dynamic and changing dimensions of culture as we have come to understand them through multiple intersubjectivities in different locations over many years.

Notes

1. Earlier people recorded by Dominican curates in the Puyo-Canelos area included "Santis, Caninches, Gayes, Imundas, Gualingas," among others, dating from the late 1700s (Pierre 1983:119). All of these names are common today among the Puyo Runa and in all Runa territories of the Canelos Quichua system, and among the Napo Runa.

2. We began with a joint reconnaissance trip in 1968 to visit Canelos Quichua, Napo Runa, Shuar, Cofán, Secoya and Siona, with a visit to the SIL/WBT base in Limoncocha during a time when indigenous people from throughout the Oriente and northwest coast were present. N. Whitten began subsequent research in 1970 when he resided in Puyo and spent extensive periods of time in Unión Base and Rosario Yacu, with daily treks throughout the immediate region. He made another reconnaissance trip on the Napo River and tributaries, and visited Villano, Curaray, Sarayacu, and Montalvo. In 1971 we resided in Puyo and began a relatively systematic reconnaissance of thirteen hamlets and dispersed residences of the Comuna San Jacinto del Pindo, with N. Whitten visiting Cabecera de Bobonaza, Canelos, Pacayacu, Sarayacu, Curaray, Villano, Chapana, and other sites in Canelos Quichua territory. Together we visited various groups of Napo Runa–Quijos Quichua of the Upper Napo–Jatun Yacu and Misahuallí region and of the Andean foothills of Archidona-Cotundo. N. Whitten traveled to Capahuari in Achuar territory, and Ayuy and Macuma in Shuar territory. In 1972 we moved into Puma Llacta, and later into Nayapi Llacta/Nueva Esperanza. The fullest expositions of our ethnography are to be found in *Sacha Runa: Ethnicity and Adaptation of Ecuadorian Jungle Quichua* (1976) and *Sicuanga Runa: The Other Side of Development in Amazonian Ecuador* (1985). Our most succinct summary of archaeology, history, and ethnohistory is in *From Myth to Creation: Art from Amazonian Ecuador* (1988). While serving as head of the Department of Anthropology at the University of Illinois from 1983 to 1986, N. Whitten continued the research in brief but intensive spurts alone for two years, before we both returned in 1986 for a full year to take up residence in Cushi Tampo.

As we conducted our research two other scholars, Theodore Macdonald (1979) and Mary-Elizabeth Reeve (1985), initiated and completed studies in Arajuno and Curaray, respectively, as part of the study of the "Lowland Quichua" initiated by the Whittens in 1968–69. Marcelo Naranjo (1977) joined us in Quito and Puyo in 1971–73 and worked on ethnohistory augmented by ethnography through 1976, when he began to concentrate on his doctoral research in Manta, Manabí.

Thanks to the work of Dominique Irvine (1987), Blanca Muratorio (1991), and Michael Uzendoski (e.g., 2004b, 2005b), the ethnography and ethnohistory of the Napo Runa are well documented by serious, sustained, and ongoing anthropological research. The excellent ethnohistorical and ethnographic research by Eduardo Kohn (2002a, 2002b) contributes greatly to our understanding of the Quijos Quichua people of the eastern Montaña.

Key references to Shuar culture at the time we began our field research are Harner (1961, 1968, and 1979). For the historical derivation of the Spanish "Jívaro" from indigenous "Shuar" see Gnerre (1973). For Andoas-Shimigae and Zápara Zaparoan see Peeke (1954), Ortiz (1940), Osculati (2000), Rospide (1911), Sweet (1969 and 1975), and Wise and Shell (1971). Significant early and contemporary works to consider interethnic regional culture include Ferdon (1950), Ferguson and Whitehead (1999), Flornoy (1953), Gow (1994), Handelsman (2005), Izquierdo Ríos (1960), Karsten (1923 and 1998), Luna (1994), Niles (1923), Oberem (1974), Porras Garcés (1999), Simson (1886), Sorensen (1967), and Stewart and Métraux (1948). For excellent overviews of colonial Ecuador with an eye to Coast and Amazonian regional culture, as well as those of the well-known Sierra, see Lane (2002) and Phelan (1967); for a productive comparison with Peru see Silverblatt (2004).

3. For an extended collection of redundant historical snippets loosely connected by unsupported linguistic, ethnohistorical, and ethnographic speculations, see Trujillo (2001). Cabodevilla (1994, 1997), by very strong contrast to Trujillo, presents an excellent analytical narrative based on the same sources.

2

Cultural Reflexivities, Images, and Locality

"Reflexivity requires bending experience to image."
—Lawrence Sullivan, *Icanchu's Drum*

Stylized Interaction: Reflecting on Our Mutual Humanity

Well before dawn we start walking up the rivulet trail that Marcelo Santi Simbaña altered in 1986 after he and his family split from Nueva Esperanza to form the *caserío* Cushi Tambo on the new road cutting through the Comuna San Jacinto. He chose his house site for many reasons: Faviola liked the forest growth of old garden areas for the beginning of new manioc and other crops; his small field of Cuban grass for his cow or young bull or horse, established a decade earlier on the fringe of Nayapi Llacta, was nearby; and there were the caves, streams, rivulets, and odd deep pools that were familiar sources of power. This power goes back to his youth when Virgilio Santi, founder of Río Chico out of San Jacinto, began to train him in the ways of being fully human.

In his lifetime Marcelo has been involved in the movements back and forth between a *llacta* with a hamlet nucleus and two different areas to which treks (*purina*) are made. The *purina* territories are significant for his and his family's livelihood. About a half century ago, maybe earlier, Marcelo married Corina Vargas, whose Achuar parents had migrated westward from Peru and joined the Puyo Runa on the *comuna* and adjacent territory in their defense of land against Andean colonization and against a branch of the *untsuri* (numerous) Shuar, known as Chirapa, to the south. They lived in a very rugged forest area between the Putuimi and the Pastaza rivers. Corina's father was Ramón Vargas, brother of Javier Vargas (Nayapi), who enters our story at the beginning of the previous chapter. At least he seemed to be Nayapi's brother, though sometimes Marcelo recollected that Nayapi was Ramón's father. He is sure, though, that the two of them, and another brother, Wanchij, "he who kills," were all *quiquin ayllu;* they shared the same "proper" or "real" kin structure.[1]

Kinship is like that; it descends through time with its binding relationships connected by reference points in human actions and bonds established and set in specific places. But as time passes differences between a "brother" and a "father" may fade from memory. People who are clearly remembered as ancestors may merge and their exact consanguinity or affinity may shift (see, e.g., Price 1983; Price and Price 1999). Corina had a sister, Isabel Vargas, who married a powerful shaman, Samuel Grefa, from the San Ramón Runa territory, which is closely connected to the Arajuno Runa, part of the Napo Runa people. This shaman became so powerful that people in the area banded together in the mid-1960s to accuse him formally of *brujería,* sorcery, which is illegal in Ecuador. The shaman was arrested from his hamlet in San Jacinto, near Unión Base, and sent to the Ambato jail in the Andes. When he returned he established a new *llacta* with his sons and sons-in-law and until his death in 2000 maintained barriers not normally seen in the Runa territories.

The road from Shell-Mera to Puyo was completed in 1947, the year the *comuna* was nationally recognized by presidential decree (e.g., Ledesma Zamora [n.d.]a, [n.d.]b). With the road came Andean colonists, and many of them moved to the edge of *comuna* territory, or into the *comuna* itself. Alliances were made by local Runa and the people of the Sierra, but conflict was rife. Marcelo sometimes remembers lying in wait for *machin runa* intruders near the mouth of the Pazyacu River with descendants of Nayapi and firing .410–gauge muzzle-loading shotguns (*chimineas*) to frighten them off. This was long ago, though, when times of the grandparents and times of destruction ran together. And sometimes he remembers that this even occurred in Nayapi Llacta where he was accompanied by two Peruvian Cocama brothers, turned Runa, who Virgilio brought from Curaray during the war of '41. The thoughts of *ayllu* and *llacta* frame memories of peoples and events. The people were there and the events occurred, but the flexible structure of memory anchored in *ayllu* and *llacta* propels their historicity as agents of social change and continuity.

Corina died in childbirth with their fourth child, Celia. After her death Marcelo's life changed radically. To earn hard cash to support his family he allowed himself to be lured into a position of debt peonage, called *enganche,* by a labor recruiter in Puyo. In 1958 he left his children in the care of his sister and brother-in-law, Clara Santi Simbaña (Quillara) and Abraham Chango (Paushi), and went off to work in the western lowland region radiating out of Quevedo. He remembers best the trip from Latacunga over the high Páramo, through the land of the Cotopaxi Runa, then down to the hot and hilly plantation zone inland from the coast.

He left plantation labor before becoming dependent on it and traveled back to the eastern rain forests, where he resided in Canelos between 1960 and 1967. There he married Faviola Vargas Aranda, with whom he has six children and many grandchildren. Faviola was born and reared in Canelos, where most of her relatives still live. Marcelo and Faviola made their own home near the Villano River, at the northwestern edge of Canelos territory. Virgilio, with other native people from Canelos, had once cleared a wide swath through the forest all the way from Puyo to Curaray, including Marcelo's and Faviola's Villano site near Huiduj (Widuj), for what was to have been an Ambato-Amazonian railroad. While there they heard many stories about such clearing and about the days of the Amazon Rubber Boom and its ravaging effects (e.g., Reeve 1988b:24; Stanfield 1998). They remember their home deep in the forest with great nostalgia, and are currently reconstructing a *purina* region near there, in a place now known as Yana Puma, black jaguar.

Going back in time again, the 1890s exemplify Times of Destruction interspersed with times of the grandparents. In the Andes and the Coast the great *caudillo* Eloy Alfaro emerged to create an international image of Ecuador as a Liberal society, one open to capitalist enterprise. He also moved to curtail and suppress the power of the medieval, colonial Church authority. Sometimes known as *el indio alfaro,* he also championed indigenous and black rights, and built something of a power base on the foundation of coastal capital and indigenous knowledge.

As Ecuador emerged as a national self-identifying system to enter the world of economic dependence on a capitalist basis, Canelos itself emerged in national political consciousness as a source of indigenous labor and a force to be controlled, if possible. Many tell us that in the times of Alfaro Rucuguna chaos reigned from Canelos northward into the river regions of the Villano and the Curaray, where the Amazon Rubber Boom brought terrifying brutality to many and prosperity to a few (Cabodevilla 1994; Casement 1912; Stanfield 1998; Reeve 1993–94). When Marcelo and Faviola took up their residence between Canelos and the Villano-Curaray systems in the 1950s, the stories about the Rubber Boom were very much alive.

In the late 1800s in Canelos, a powerful *curaga* whose name was Eustanquillo (or Eustanquio or Estanislaw or Estanico) Illanes Vargas, but known as Palati, allied with President Eloy Alfaro to forge ties between Amazonia and the Andes. Pierre (1889) and Karsten (1935), who were in Canelos some twenty-five years apart, both wrote that Palati (who died in 1924) was one hundred years old. Faviola remembers the Illanes family well, because even though the Illaneses and the Vargases were related, shamans descended from Palati sent magical darts, *tsintsaca,* at her and Marcelo, endangering their entire family and influencing their decision to return to the greater Puyo area, where the shielding shamanic powers of Virgilio offered sanctuary. Powerful shamans in Canelos today are still known as *alfaros* within some families, and the knowledge passes through *ayllus,* as we shall see.

In 1967 Marcelo and Faviola moved to the Comuna San Jacinto to participate in the nucleation of a section of the *comuna* and to join the growing hamlet of Puma Llacta. They were given a generous portion of Virgilio Santi's land, established a *chagra,* helped to clear a plaza on top of a hill overlooking the rain forest to the east and snowcapped Andean peaks to the west, and built a home on the east edge of that plaza. Marcelo and Faviola often trekked to the site where he had lived with Corina and where he continued to maintain close friendships, bolstered by kinship and ritual coparent ties. In the late 1970s three of his adult sons, with their spouses and children, moved to this area near the Putuimi River to establish residences and gardens to live an essentially subsistence life. In 1982 Marcelo and Faviola began a *chagra* there, as well, near the site where Marcelo and Corina had lived some fifty years ago. Shortly thereafter Marcelo, Faviola, and their sons, daughters, and in-laws founded a new hamlet there, Cushi Tambo.

By this time manifestations of growth and development in Puyo were ubiquitous, and economic pressures led to a twenty-mile-long roads being cut through the site of Cushi Tambo and other comuna hamlets. By 1984 Cushi Tambo had the largest school in this sector of indigenous territory, a complete plaza, and its residents were traveling from Puyo to Quito in search of authorizations and funds to build an electric plant and to acquire other accouterments of modernization. In the midst of such transformation, Marcelo became a traditional shaman; many of his clients came from Otavalo, and eventually he traveled there too, to share and exchange knowledge of control of power with other healers at his level of development. The year 2001 found Marcelo nucleated with his sons and in-laws on the roadside by Cushi Tambo. He became *yali yachaj,* teaching shaman, and one son and his daughter-in-law are *profesores,* teachers, in the grade school right there in Cushi Tambo, while another son and his wife teach in Sarayacu. Their greater area for *chagra,* hunting and fishing, is still a portion of Nayapi Llacta. In 2007 there are more nearby hamlets, some in Nayapi Llacta, some in other *llactas,* and the boundaries shift and change according to prevailing conflicts and alliances.

Marcelo and Faviola and the Whittens have been *compadre* and *comadre* to one another since 1972. A few weeks before the birth of Orlando Victor Santi Vargas, our *ahijado,* Faviola was bitten by a small, deadly pit viper. Marcelo and Norman had just returned from Canelos, where they had mapped all of the internal divisions, noting especially where Zaparoan and Achuar people (all speaking Quichua) lived and where their trekking (*purina*) territories were. We rushed to the trail leading into Tarqui and encountered Faviola on her way in, with sons helping; we immediately took her to Hospital VozAndes, an evangelical mission-run hospital in Shell. She survived, as did our godson, and Marcelo proclaimed that Orlando Victor would be a *sinchi yachaj runa,* a strong one who knows, because he had survived the attack of a shaman bent on killing the vulnerable while the strong Runa *cari* was away.

He and Virgilio had explained some time back, during a *Banisteriopsis caapi*–induced curing seance, that shamanic darts of evil come from one of malign intent, focus on the victim's *wasi* (household), and then carom off the strong to hit the vulnerable, who, without proper shamanic or Western medical attention (or better, a combination of the two), will die.

Stylized Reflexivities

Moving out of the rivulet trail onto muddy ground, when we are a couple of hundred yards from his house, Norman calls in a falsetto sufficiently loudly so that he, and all in the vicinity of his household as well, can hear, "*juuuuuuuuuuuuuu,*" and after a moment Marcelo answers more quietly: "*whaaay!*" We have cleared an audible path, *ñambi,* between the two of us. His response is an invitation to make his house our immediate and direct destination. By our stylized and well-controlled sounds we signal a reciprocal directionality through the concept of breath, *samai,* that projects health and strength from part of our *shungu* (lungs in this case, but signaling heart and will, as well). Norman walks straight toward him with Sibby behind, and Marcelo sits and awaits our arrival. Faviola remains in the woman's part of the house, out of sight for now. Others who hear the exchange from various vantage points may ask *pí ala pasa?* (*ala* is a mythical bracket fungus), what mythic brother is going by? *Runa tian?* Is it a human? another may ask.

We walk steadily to his house and when we see him sitting on a stool, as always when he is so forewarned of our approach, Norman asks, "*Tianguichu gumba?*" (from *tiana,* to be present), "are you there, compadre?" And Marcelo answers, "*Tiaunimi, gumba,*" "I am here compadre." Then still walking steadily, Norman says, "*Pactamuni, gumba,*" "I am arriving, compadre," and Marcelo immediately says "*Shamui,*" "come;" "*Yaicui,*" "enter;" and then "*Tiari,*" "sit down." The way he says "sit down" is important; by inflection he can make it a kind request, or a stern command. We have been observing an etiquette that is present everywhere in Canelos Quichua territory, and in transformed ways, beyond. The falsetto call, for example, is replaced at times by blowing the barrel of a breach-loading shotgun among the Achuar, in some regions, and during festivals a pottery cornet replaces the voice in cutting across the space between humans and spirits. The soft falsetto human sound disturbs no one. Incoming shaman darts make a hard, fearsome noise, *quish whiaj,* which Faviola heard the night before she was bitten by the pit viper.

We orient ourselves toward one another, each thinking something of what the other must be thinking, and each striving to understand the other's immediate intersubjectivity in mood. Men must be sitting on something that itself is on the floor; the head of the household sits on a carved *bancu,* "seat of power," which may be a *tsawata* tortoise, seat of power of the forest spirit master Amasanga, or *charapa* turtle, seat of power of the water spirit master Sungui. As visitors, we both sit on a long bench symbolizing the *amarun,* boa constrictor, but specifically the huge anaconda constrictor that is the corporeal representation of Sungui. We talk and Faviola serves *asua,* and we drink a good deal of this yeasty, mildly fermented manioc brew from lovely ceramic bowls, decorated on the exterior with designs representing Sungui and on the interior with more embellishment of forest, water, and garden motifs. The sun rises as our bellies become full of *asua* and now we may stand, move around, walk as we talk. If others enter the house we again sit until everyone has drunk, until all are full, *sacsashca.*

The human *wasi* contains us, and into it we have properly brought images of a spirit world that may affect us. The world we see is now our foreground; the spirit world, which may merge with this one, is background, relegated for now to our dreams, our remembrances, and our experiences. We are now rooted, so to speak, by our mutual sitting. We are real, corporeal; we are not "standing appearances" to one another. To be "standing-appearing" (*shayarina,* or *shayarina muscui*) is to be "seen" there, in contrast to "being" there. We are real to one another in a waking world, and one of our subjects for conversation may be a dream, another may be a remembrance. Making things real and tangible comes out of the dream world of images, where one "sees" what one will make before she or he begins. Remembrances come from the process of bringing something into being. Our mutual reflections vis-à-vis our mutual presences are represented in anthropology as cultural ontology, the ways by which we understand the very nature of being. What follows is a composite of many conversations in Marcelo and Faviola's house and on their *chagras* and forest trails.

Marcelo is making a drum, called *caja,* the Spanish name for "box." He is sitting on a wooden stool carved in the form of a land tortoise; he made it from a second-growth "cedar" tree he felled while clearing Faviola's *chagra.* He could have carved a canoe from that tree, too, but he didn't need one. The last canoe he made was for the permanent collection of the Museum of the Central Bank of Ecuador, Quito, back in 1972, and he remembers his trip to see it in the exhibition *Causáunchimi!* in the art gallery of that museum in 1987.

His recollections go back to his childhood. When Marcelo was nine years old, his father took him to collect a couple of tortoises for special food for an upcoming festival. He trussed up the first one they found and strapped it on Marcelo's back, leaving the boy staggering under the weight. Then they found the second, and Virgilio told him to carry both home like the *sinchi runa* (strong person) which he became; by the late 1980s he had become *yachaj runa* (one who knows). "My god," said Marcelo, "they were the size of Galápagos tortoises!" Marcelo also points out to us again that when he was only six years old, Virgilio brought him to see where a one-engine Peruvian plane dropped a bomb about a quarter mile from his current house. This was the "War of '41" when Peru invaded Ecuador and, according to Ecuadorian accounts, acquired one-half of the Amazonian territory of the republic. These events Marcelo remembers, and he wants us to know about them.

After talking about these memories Marcelo returned to his hollowed-out drum frame where he had shaped the outside and inside to a pleasant round form. He was sure to make the walls thick enough so that he could bevel down the rims while leaving the shoulder thick; this gave him a nice, aesthetically pleasing body, rather than the standard flat one that most men make. His son brought him *chambira* palm fiber from Pacayacu for the lacing. A few weeks ago he killed an owl monkey, called *jurijuri* after the fearsome spirit that protects high hills, caves, and monkeys from human predation. This skin, when dried, would be the snare-side of the drum. The beating side was to be peccary skin, and he was burnishing it now with his special *amulana rumi,*

Marcelo Santi Simbaña carves a tortoise stool from a tree he felled in Faviola's swidden garden.

the male stone that corresponds to the female burnishing stone for pottery. It is also called a soul stone, *aya rumi*. Marcelo explained that this stone was Amasangamanda; it came "from" Amasanga to him as a black river-polished stone found in the stomach of a huge catfish.

Quietly, without being asked to do so, Faviola came out and, after she served us steaming bowls of fresh *asua*, she showed Sibby her gardening stones that came to her from Nungüi. These two—one red, one black—had been given to her by her mother while she was still a young girl in Canelos. She had taken them to the headwaters of the Villano River when she and Marcelo were first married, before they came to Puma Llacta to live. *Sinchi rumi tian*, said Marcelo, they are powerful stones. Without the power of the polished stones, which contain the spirit essence of Nungüi for women, Amasanga for men, people are less than fully human, as we understand matters. The living world is one where there is a plane of spirits and a plane of humans, and these planes are crossed all the time, as when we walked up the trail and Norman let them know that we were approaching on a human trail, *runa ñambi*. The fact that this trail, however, was part fast-flowing rivulet over polished stones, escapes no one. The journey from household to household is spiritual as well as human; the two realms are separable but conjoined in multiple ways.

"Amasanga is working inside this drum," Marcelo says, "just as I am working on the outside." When it is finished the snare (*zizirma*) will make people's heads buzz during the upcoming Christmas kinship festival in Nueva Esperanza. "They will call out to me '*cajonero!* (drummer!) *uyariungui!* (make noise!).'" There is a power ritual that is sometimes performed when a man completes a drum, or when he wakes up before dawn with surges of energy flowing through his psyche. He picks the drum from where it hangs in the rafters, and tunes it carefully by loosening and then tightening the side wraps until the drum give a sharp "*ting*" when struck on the head, and the snare gives a nice "*zzzzzzzzz*" sound. This is the pulse-tremolo that awakens the forest and alerts people to a source of energy and power radiating from a particular household. Then the man walks in a circle, beating the drum in a 1–2–3–4 cadence, *ting ting ting ting, zzzz, zzzz, zzzz, zzzz*, about four beats and four buzzes to the second.

The buzzing sound is that of the bees coming to the *wanduj* flower as it opens; this opening in turn signals the opening of the forest spirit master's mind together with that of the questing Runa's mind. $mm_{mm}{}^{mm}{}_{mm}$ thinks the drummer, *unaimanda*, from mythic time-space, *callarirucuguna*, from beginning times-places, *ñucanchi yachai!* Our knowledge! And the drummer continues drumming, sometimes moving to another household, perhaps walking a mile or more in the process, as he drums the fusion sounds of forest and household into his moving center. Marcelo will think of all of this as he finishes his drum; but it is for the upcoming kinship ceremony, not for intra-household power enhancement.

Time-Space

An elaboration of time-space quite uncharacteristic of most Amazonian cosmological systems exists in all the Runa territories. Before the beginnings was *unai,* "mythic time-space." Here all beings, animate and inanimate—*everything*—walked upright, just as humans do today. Humans, though, crawled on their hands and knees, like unbound babies, and spoke only in two-tone hums, $mm_{mm}mm_{mm}$. In beginning times-places, *callarirucuguna (callari* = beginning; *rucu* = old; *guna* = plural) transformations occurred so that the beings, including spirits and humans, eventually became what they are today. The tale of Sicuanga and the liberation of female beauty told in chapter 1 begins in *unai* and shapes a part of beginning times-places. The Runa have a saying that expresses much of this: *ñucanchi callarirucuguna cuti yachaspa, unaimandata cuti yachaspa,* "Learning again from our mythic time-space, we are knowing once more our beginning times-places."

Think of each time-space "epoch" or "period" as a cusp. In our quotidian lives we are at the top edge of the penultimate cusp. Under that cusp—just behind us in time and near us in space—lies the information and events that each Runa knows about and controls in different ways. Each cusp can be brought into memory from its specific plane of existence. When we "see," images, called *muscui,* form. By "see" we follow Geertz (1973:110): "A perspective is a mode of seeking, in that extended sense of 'see' in which it means 'discern,' 'apprehend,' 'understand,' or 'grasp.' It is a particular way of looking at life" (for our general use of such concepts as structure, history, historicity, and myth see Sahlins 1976, 1981, 1994, 1999, 2004, 2005).[2] This is as close as we can come to the ways by which Runa express their concepts of *muscui.* The concepts of times-spaces constitute a large-scale cultural knowledge and imageric system whereby information and structured and inchoate imaginations are stored, brought into memory, communicated to those who are capable of receiving messages, and acted upon.

Let us now clarify these concepts of time-space. To begin with *unai,* mythic time-space, we are in the realm where all things known and unknown are sentient and human-like. We enter *unai* when we dream, when we daydream, when we have an insight or sometimes inspiration. Hallucinogens may help, but are not necessarily crucial. To enter *unai* on a full-time basis is to die from this world. *Callarirucuguna,* beginning times-places, are also always with us on another plane of existence. Times of destruction punctuate our lives. Examples include *Cauchurucuguna,* the Amazon Rubber Boom of the 1880s–1890s that flows into *Alfaro Rucuguna,* the times of national upheaval in Ecuador during the 1890s. More recent times of destruction include the Peruvian war of 1941 and petroleum exploration of the 1920s and '30s and again in the 1970s.

Times of the Grandparents, *Apayayarucuguna* (grandfathers times-places) and *Apamamarucuguna* (grandmothers times-places) punctuate times of destruction. Everyone is clear on some of these relationships, but the knowledge is specific to families, kin systems, and common territories. *Cunan* is our present and our immediate past and *cunalla* is our "right now-right here time-place," the penultimate cusp of quotidian life. Finally, *caya* is the future; our destiny. Information and images can be brought "back" by some, especially powerful shamans and image-making ceramists. With this time-space information, we return to the *wasi,* the workshop of human reproduction, the microcosm where culture unfolds from conception to gestation to birth and on toward death.

Marcelo recollects that in the time of Nayapi there were huge tensions between people of Puyo and those of Canelos. He belonged to both of those worlds, though the principal indigenous leaders were now dead. Palati, in Canelos, and Nayapi, in the Puyo-Pastaza Region, were enemies of one another. Their feuds transformed into descriptions of fighting "between" the Canelos and the Chirapa, the latter led by Sharupe, though Palati, Nayapi, and Sharupe were related to each other in various ways according to different people seeing this from varied perspectives. He also remembers that not so long ago he could exchange his drum for a shiny new blowgun made by Achuar relatives and Cocama trade partners. To do so he would give the drum to a visitor and say *apai,* "take it." At sometime in the future he anticipated receipt of a blowgun. These stories occur in settings that are similar throughout the Runa territories. We turn now to describe one hamlet, to see how mythohistories and quotidian life constitute the stuff of enduring cultural life in a small nucleated and dispersed setting south of urban Puyo in Amazonian Ecuador.

This is a site where magical frogs may signal the coming of machinery, where a powerful shaman's advice is sought to understand the nation's political economy. This is but one of thousands of microcosms of inner power around the rim of Amazonia wherein knowledge and vision of alternative modernities are constantly generated. This is the sort of site from which come leaders of today's indigenous resistance.

Nueva Esperanza and Nayapi Llacta

Nueva Esperanza is a small but modern hamlet lying on the north side of Nayapi Llacta, about two kilometers in from the very edge of a 17,000 hectare communal territory. The existence of Nueva Esperanza—its "being," its "cultural ontology"—concretizes the ideology of incorporation into the Ecuadorian nation-state; in turn, such existence depends on the cultural and environmental resources of its Upper Amazonian Nayapi Llacta. People cannot just "be" in their nation-state; they must also be rooted in their locale, their habitat, their historicities, their collective and individual stylized actions, the ensnaring consequences of those actions, and their quotidian present.

Nueva Esperanza features a school with fifteen students; it is considerably smaller than it was twenty years ago. Then they were taught by outsiders who lived in Puyo and commuted to the school. Today they are taught by a bilingual young man and his bilingual wife, both of whom are from Runa territories. They are taught in Spanish, but they lose nothing of their own language. In school they learn to read and write Spanish. There are experiments in bilingual education from time to time, but the rendition of Quichua is so different in the texts that are prepared that learning declines. In school they learn about the rhetoric of national culture; elsewhere they participate in their Runa world and speak Quichua.

At home there are fundamentals of life that are learned from the cradle onward. Words we have used to this point must now be explicated; they are basic to Runa knowledge and to the image system that constitutes their cultural ontology. Nayapi Llacta is rooted in tropical forest ecology, two key concepts of which are *sacha* and *chagra*.

Sacha and Chagra

Sacha means "rain forest" in the Quichua of the Amazonian region. In the Andes it means "bush" or "wild, untamed land" among some Quichua-speaking people. *Chagra* is inextricably related to *sacha;* it is the garden part of the forest. The *chagra* is the swidden garden, the segment of forest that is removed by men who cut the trees. Restoration of domestication of the forest is by women, who clear nicely and who plant manioc in what is called the *chaquichishca panga allpa tucungawa* (dried leaves turning to soil). This is the leaf mat described by ecologists as essential to the vitality of rain-forest fecundity (see Jordon 1982; Janzen 1986).

Sacha and *chagra* are complex, complementary cultural and natural realms unified by cosmological and ecological principles. Many anthropologists who follow structuralist Claude Lévi-Strauss experience an epiphany when they find a contrast between what they take to be Nature and Culture. Unfortunately, such a western contrast does not work in Amazonia, and probably not elsewhere either. A dynamic series of transformations pervade Runa thought. We could express the series as a cycle. On the "wild" side we have male predation. This occurs when men hunt and when they clear the forest for the garden. On the other side is female domestication, where women grow the crops that sustain life. From the domesticated garden the forest again begins to grow, and things become "wilder," or "feral." In the forest itself men and women learn a great deal, they make small alterations, and as the forest becomes "theirs," it becomes part of a *llacta* territory and is tamed.

Lévi-Strauss would label the left side of this cycle "Nature" and the right side "Culture," losing, in one fell stroke, the cultural and natural significance of human dynamics in their environments. The *chagra* is shifted periodically and allowed to grow back to forest. It is shifted as it becomes more diverse, and when its diversity reaches the point at which it is neither garden nor forest it is left to continue growing. Such old, second-growth garden sites—new forest sites—may be called *mauca chagra* (used garden); as they become increasingly indistinguishable from the forest they may be called *mauca sacha* (used forest), again ripe for male predation and female planting. The

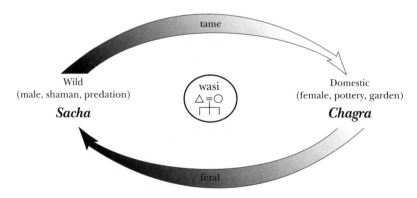

Chagra-sacha dynamics.

entire temporal fallow from the "feral" to the "tame" in the above diagram is sometimes referred to as *mauca llacta* (fallow territory). The fallow areas are known to be good hunting zones. They are said to be a domain haunted by spirits and inhabited by souls. Two of the prominent spirits to be found there, often taken to be souls of the deceased, are deer and owl. As the shade in the old garden forms a high canopy the *chagra* becomes devoid of manioc. More and more diverse plants begin to grow there. These resemble garden plants, but they are different. They are neither of the garden nor of the forest. They are Nungüimanda, "of" or "from" Nungüi, spirit master of garden soil, and her original crops, known as *pachina* (contraction of *aparichina*). Nungüi gives each woman a *pachina* (e.g., *lumu pachina, papaya pachina*) to help her domesticated plants, especially manioc, grow in the human garden.

Two markers of old gardens are the *chontaduro* peach-palm trees (*Bactris gasipaes*) and the *huayusa* (*Ilex guayusa*) trees, both planted by men. As time passes and the *chagra* reaches its thirty-year climax phase, these trees are nested among new forest growth and they take on special significance that evokes memories of the Times of the Grandparents in their continuity and Times of Destruction in their prior abandonment.

Stories of the origin of the *chagra* spiral and twist. They are told in segments. But the elements of their reality come together in this way. A dangerous fructiverous bat-widow, *viuda tutapishcu*, lived alone in the middle of the forest with her six daughters. Her husband had been killed in a war. Her oldest daughter is Sapallu, Squash; the rest, in birth order, are Manduru (*Bixa orellana*), Widuj (*Genipa americana*), Sara (*Zea maize*), and Chucu Purutu (unidentified, inedible nitrogen-fixing beans). They go to look for men, because living with just women is only half of life. They are also looking for *chagra* makers. They encounter men in one segment of this spiraling story. Four are animals, and they each are making special material artifacts before going off to war; these same men know how to transform some growing things into edible foods. They also find four more animal-men who seem to be clearing space for a *chagra*. Two of the men are called Ardilla and Wichingu (names that refer to different species of tropical-forest squirrels), one is Machin (Capuchin monkey), and one is called Chichicu (a species of marmoset). They also encounter two birds making gardens: Hummingbird (Quindi) and Hawk (Acanga).

At this point the reader needs to know that a transformation has taken place from daughter Squash woman to Nungüi in some stories and to Jilucu in other stories. We return to this in chapter 7. Squash woman, as Nungüi, is walking in the forest with Junculu, who may be her sister or her daughter.

They come upon three men, Quindi, Acanga (who is also called Atatatau), and Sicuanga. Somehow Sicuanga always disappears from these tellings. They hear the sound of what they think is a great man cutting trees: *crash, wham, crash, wham*. But when they come upon the scene Acanga is picking up huge rocks and boulders and heaving them into the forest, laughing all the while. The crashing and banging of boulders sounds like the felling of trees, but nothing is being cleared; the forest is just being aroused. They too are aroused by the sight of the big handsome man, but they reluctantly move on, still thinking about his virility.

Hummingbird is the next mythical Runa encountered. He is clearing a forest site, clearing and clearing. Junculu becomes alarmed: "How can we make a *chagra* in such an enormous space," she asks. Nungüi tells her that there is a way: "we must get bundles of manioc," she says. And she and Junculu go and get lots of manioc sticks, hundreds of them. They pile them up and then, with the color of sister Manduru, they paint the sticks red, and then they paint themselves. This red color comes from the Viuda Tutapishcu bat-mother; it symbolizes blood. Once Manioc and the women know each other as of the same blood all are safe; Manioc will not suck the blood out one's own human children.

Then they begin to dig with a wooden *tula,* a big digging stick shaped much like a male fighting stick, *macana*. Nungüi digs and digs and becomes exhausted. Junculu says, "I'll now dig for you," and she does so with gusto. She too becomes fatigued. "When will we ever finish," she asks, "I can't work any more." But they do continue work and again attack the cleared area with the *tula, whack, whack*—a great hole is made. Down goes Junculu into this hole, digging and digging. Seeing this activity in his cleared space Hummingbird becomes furious. "You make fun of me; you do not respect me or my work," he says. "You are in love with Acanga," *piz, piz, piz,* he spits at them. *Tiucasha rin!* He sends a transformative missile at them. *Yumingai!* He curses them. In total anger he blows on Nungüi with his magical breath and creates the spirit as she is today, with a corporeal form of a small black coral snake with coffee-colored throat to live forever in leaf litter or forest and garden undersoil. Nungüi in turn blows on Junculu and creates her present form as an edible frog who lives in a great hole in the forest or garden. Then with a fury Nungüi turns to Quindi, and she blows her magical breath on him, *suuuuuuuuuuuuuuu,* Quindi *cari,* she says, stay this way. And in a tremendous burst of energy Hummingbird is transformed into the sun or into dangerous sun beams that can and do burn the leaves of domesticated crops.

Unlike maize, squash, or beans, manioc must have strong solar illumination to begin to grow, and to continue to grow. Quindi, as transformed to Indi, the sun, now provides that illumination. But the more desirable illumination that provided radiation in the time of *quillu pachama*—the yellow-spaces-times of fertility and fecundity of crops during the great transformations of Beginning Times-Places—is now gone. This lost illumination was once provided by the full moon, Quilla, the older brother of Hummingbird.

The story of the garden origins has spiraled from the actions of Squash, Maize, and Bean women, to that of Manioc spirit woman Nungüi. In this region maize is a male crop, but women know more than men of all this. For maize to grow women must control the growth and distribution of the nitrogen-fixing inedible black beans, the *purutu pachina*. And, in some areas, they must burn the area before planting takes place; they must control fire, which is analogous to and associated with the sun. In the stories of beginnings of these crops women control the power of the male sun, and of the forces of *chagra* nutrients, especially nitrogen. Nitrogen, by the way, is fixed by lightning within the canopy of the tropical rain forest, and it, too, is associated with the sun and with fire. Lightning then is a feminine manifestation of Amasanga, while thunder is male; together the thunder and lightning are controlled by Rayu Runa, or Rayu Supai Runa, an Amasanga transformation. To add more power to this picture, the special Datura of Amasanga is *rayu wanduj*, lightning Datura.

Sacha is overseen by spirit master Amasanga, also called Sacha Runa, forest person. He is Amasanga *supai,* and he is sometimes called *pasu supai.* Pasu is a tropical tree fruit much like the zapote. Amasanga may be male, female, or androgynous. Amasanga is dressed in shimmering blue-black. His or her corporeal representation is the great black jaguar. As male, Amasanga sits on a tortoise seat of power or on an iguanid seat of power; he is forest shaman. As male he carries a blowgun over his shoulder, and a *chambira* knotted net bag on his other shoulder. He wears a toucan feather headdress. His mascot is the bush dog, *sacha allcu.* When one hears the bark of the little short-legged and short-tailed dog, *hau hau hau,* one knows that Amasanga is near. Thunder is the voice of Amasanga in his male dimension; he crosses the water on a cayman canoe, which is also known as *apamama* (grandmother) or on the giant black anaconda.

In the transformation from *unai* to *callarirucuguna* Amasanga (male and female) divided into two parts: one became associated with the high regions of the forest—the area from where the great limbs of trees begin to

Amasanga, left, and Amasanga *warmi,* festival drinking vessels. Apacha Vargas.

radiate outward to the canopy itself. As the association of Amasanga as an androgynous being who walks among the tree limbs emerged, Amasanga and Amasanga *warmi* also began to transform into a fearsome, underearth, androgynous spirit, Jurijuri *supai.* Amasanga became associated with "our forest," and "our game." S/he oversees the course of male predation of rainforest game animals and game birds, and he oversees visionary experiences of lone, questing Runa on Datura-induced journeys, when he is known as Wanduj *supai.*

Jurijuri *supai* became an underearth spirit of *other people,* of the monkey people, the *machin runa.* In the beginnings times-places teeth grew from a mouth that developed in the back of Jurijuri's head (or neck). With his front mouth he would eat monkeys, just as humans do; with his back mouth he would eat humans, and all beings that smell like humans. The beginning times-places divided Runa territory, overseen by Amasanga, from other peoples' territories, associated with monkey abundance and overseen by the Jurijuri master spirit. Human territory and foreign territories abutted one another, and each produced dangers for the other.

Jurijuri *supai* ceramic effigy. Rebeca Gualinga.

Cosmology and Ecology of Spirit Power

Transformations of master spirits abound in the forest and near the garden. All spirits have, from one time or another, corporeal features. They can be seen and felt. They also all have souls, just like humans do. Huge trees with flying buttresses such as the kapok and Ila (unidentified) tree are Amasanga transformations. But near their bases, during heavy rain and thunder storms, the danger of the Jurijuri manifests itself as the Amasanga-Jurijuri forces again merge. The Urcu supai, the Amasanga of the mountain or big hill, also may merge with Jurijuri, especially where there are caves (wherein live *juctu supai*) and streams that run through the hills. The Amasanga spirit forces of "us" and the Jurijuri forces of "others" and "monkeys" are perilously close to one another.

Through garden dynamics Nungüi controls Amasanga, the rain forest. If people were to cut nothing, the forest would lose some of its diversity, but if the men cut too much and the women plant too extensively, they could weaken the power of Amasanga to control the weather, and flood and erosion would occur. Amasanga controls the dynamics of the water world, domain of Sungui. It is in the dynamics of the tame and the feral that these interactions are most apparent. This is why the "contrast" between *sacha* (nature) and *chagra* (culture) dismisses all of the force of indigenous knowledge and thought.

Sungui is the master spirit of the hydrosphere, all of the water systems in

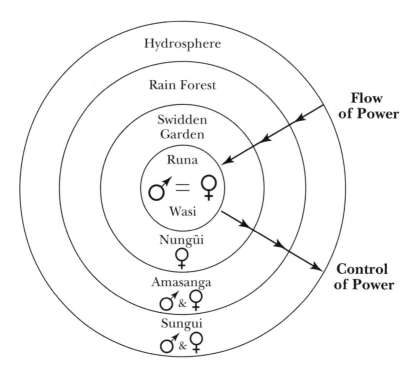

Spheres of power and control.

Sungui, left, and his soul, ceramic effigies. Apacha Vargas.

the world. Sungui may also be male or female, or be androgynous. As male he sits on a turtle seat of power, the *charapa;* the Sungui *wasi* is constructed of chonta poles that are really living anacondas. The corporeal manifestation of Sungui is one of the two great water boa constrictors: the black anaconda, or the rainbow anaconda. In the latter manifestation Sungui, when angry and fierce, may become *cuichi,* the rainbow that spans the sky after a storm or shower. Women control the symbolism of blackness, through their blackware pottery, and of color and beauty, through their polychrome pottery.

The forest nourishes itself; it depends on the water and waterborne nutrients for continuous nourishment while at the same time providing its own source of that very water. It is forever perilously close to the domain of Sungui. The garden centers the forest system and draws it to the household, the *wasi,* wherein Runa live and out of which they move to garden, forest, and water systems. People in Nayapi Llacta depend on the above dynamics in their quotidian lives, and transform the symbolism to a montage of powerful and moving imagery in their ritual performances. The workshop of cultural reproduction is the household, deeply embedded in a myriad of times-places, but present "right now and right here" in a small hamlet. The bonds that connect the immediacy of the household are those of *ayllu* and *llacta.*

Wasi

This is the household. In the 1960s most of these were great oval structures that encompassed a Runa-constructed universe of male and female divisions (see N. Whitten 1976a, 1985). The male head of the house would sit in the middle on a wooden stool carved in the form of a water turtle, *charapa*. Guests would sit in the male side on a long bench that symbolized the anaconda. Women would serve from their side, closer to the pottery shed and cooking area. Today there are many house forms, and the symbolism is more difficult to "see" though it endures in indigenous discourse. However the household is constructed today, the etiquette that opens this chapter is observed, unless the outsider is ignorant of it, in which case the intruder is regarded as less than human.

The *wasi* is a specialized social edifice wherein its Runa inhabitants reproduce their social order. *Wasi* is the center of the concentric circles represented above. Power flows from Sungui to Amasanga to Nungüi into the household; control of such powers radiates from *wasi* to garden to forest to hydrosphere. Straight up (*cusca*) is from the center of the house, and straight down (*ucu*) is there, too. The cardinal point orientation of the house plus its up-down symbolic poles gives us the well-known *axis mundi* of Amazonian cosmology (e.g., Sullivan 1988; N. Whitten 2005).

Ayllu

With the *ayllu*, the core of the kinship system, we come to the unity of segmentary oneness that binds the correspondences of *chagra-sacha* and *wasi* into one social formation. A powerful analogy is employed here to evoke the fundamental trope that unites the cosmos and biosphere and places kinship and shamanism in their most enduring, mystical dimensions: *Runa ullu amarun tian* (The Runa penis is anaconda). A myth segment, regarded as obscene by the Runa and hence often told in somewhat circumlocutory formats, expresses this analogic trope that connects the natural world of sexual relations and indigenous kinship with the spirit world of Sungui, the water world, predation in garden and forest, and contained power.

Older and younger brother were on a *chagra* in the afternoon; in the evening they were talking and the younger said he wanted a woman. As the brothers later slept, a green frog came to the head of the younger, by his right ear, and perhaps its name was Piripiri. *Yucuna!*—the young man was having sexual intercourse with the green frog, against the warning of his older brother. The frog hopped; again and again it hopped. Younger brother's penis remained in the frog as it hopped and hopped away with the half-erect, half-limp penis still in it. The young man was *ungushga,* sick; the sickness was his penis because it had been pulled so long that he could not walk. It became *cauchullu* (*cauchu ullu*—rubber penis). Then the older brother went home to get help, but before he could get back Yacu puma (river jaguar—giant otter—also known as *yacu lubu,* river wolf) was passing by in the river. He came to the younger brother and said, "What's happened?" And the youth said, "*Suni ullu saquirín*" ("large [long] penis stays that way") and sobbed, tears flowing. Yacu puma cut the penis with his machete; he cut it at just the proper length for humans to have. Then he cut up the rest of the elongated penis and put the pieces into his *ashanga* (basket). After that the younger brother went home to his *wasi,* while Yacu puma went downriver in his canoe, throwing the segments into every stream, every lagoon, each side of the big river, into the mouths of rivers and into the oxbow lakes. There the segments became and remain *amarun.* In the household the penis remains *ullu.* The male *ullu* in each *wasi* corresponds to the *amarun* of each river.

Anaconda today comes out of the encompassing water domain—out of stream, river, lagoon, or mud; as boa it comes from soil or trees—to penetrate *sacha* and *chagra,* to hunt humans and other animals, and to devour them. The water domain itself is segmented into distinct rivers and lagoons that often swell tremendously in rain-caused flood. Men kill anaconda-boas and use their fat, brains, and jaws to "make friends"—to prevent an enemy from expressing anger or to prevent one in authority from exercising his power. They never eat an anaconda, boa, or any other snake, however. Shamans call the anaconda to the *wasi* during healing sessions when cosmic ruptures have occurred and when diagnosis is needed. To control the anaconda is to control power, to unleash the anaconda is to unleash flood, to destroy the earth world and its inhabitants.

Once material of this nature is elicited, people readily say that this story of *cauchullu* explains the origin of the *ayllu,* the kinship of the Runa. The Runa are one people, one system of male transmission, but the segments of the oneness have been cut by time and by distance. One Santi segment lives here, in Nayapi Llacta; another lives over there, in Río Chico; still another right nearby, at the Tashapi headwaters. Others are distant (*caru*), in Pacayacu, Sarayacu, and Teresa Mama on the Bobonaza River and Curaray on the Curaray River. Still others exist on the Villano, Conambo, Corrientes, and Capahuari river systems to the east, fanning north and south and even on into Peru. Wherever the *amarun* is found there too is our *ayllu,* for the human penis is anaconda.

Are there female *ayllu* too? The answer is yes, but people have to discuss the epistemology embodied in this question, and it is generally agreed that the *ayllu* must come by men through women. A man, with his penis, places an egg (*lulun*) in a woman, and the egg grows in its watery female womb into *lulun wawa llucshin*. That baby inherits his soul substance from his father and from his mother's father. A man calls his wife's father *yaya*, just as he calls his own father. A constant constructionist occupation of the Runa is being sure that the soul substance (*aya*) from one generation to another is a replication, at least in part, of the segmentary unity through marriage occurring in past generations (see N. Whitten 1976a; N. Whitten and D. Whitten 1984). The male child is extended into the *wasi* by the male substance of mother's father and child's father. As he grows he extends his soul substance out of the *wasi*, maintaining the *ayllu*. As the *ayllu* is maintained, so too is the *wasi* structure reproduced.

One can elicit at times, but not always, that *warmi ayllu* is *sapumanda ayllu* (woman kinship is "from frog kinship"). Sometimes *junculumanda* is offered, sometimes not. Usually, the idea of explicit female kinship becomes mysterious, and analogies to evoke it just drift off. Tales from ancient time-space are called *ñaupa shimi rucuguna* (early ancestors' talk). A teller of such mythic texts is likely to jump to stories of regeneration involving fungi (*ala, calulu*) when explaining the origins of men and women, and the fungi allusions can lead in many directions.

Partimanda

In its eternal and incessant endeavor to reduce the population of indigenous people of Amazonia into manageable aggregations, the Catholic Church created *reducciones,* nucleated clusters of indigenous people. Within them they created *partidos,* divisions, of each *reducción.* Each *partido* (they were sometimes called *barrios,* sections of a reduction) answered separately to the priest or friar making an official inspection visit, *visita.* Through time the Runa of the greater Canelos region appropriated the term into their own concept of *partimanda,* which came to refer to where one's ancestors come from. This, as we have seen, is where one may be said to have his or her "proper" territory.

Dispersal of populations in the face of intrusion and death was a common Upper Amazonian strategy of survival and resistance (see Santos-Granero 1993). Dispersal of people led to intermarriages with people speaking different languages and sharing different systems of knowledge. As these processes went on new identities of widely flung aggregates of people unfolded.

Processes of *ethnogenesis,* of coming into being in history (Whitten 1976a, 1976b; Hill 1996) emerged.

What westerners call "marriage" is conceived in the Runa territories as a three-year process that culminates in *warmiyuj,* possession of woman by a man, and *cariyuj,* possession of man by a woman (N. Whitten and D. Whitten 1984). This mutual reciprocity is part of a structure where people often marry a near relative from distant social and cultural space. The term *partimanda* is closely related to marriage ideas and marriage practices. It refers to where an individual's parents are said to have had their *quiquin llacta,* their proper territory. *Partimanda* is a geographic designation with cultural-ethnic-kinship implications. Some bilingualism and biculturalism exists in every geographic territory of the greater Canelos region. Because of this such people as the Shiwiar, Achuar, Záparo (even though Quichua speakers), and Quichua-speaking people can recall their common roots from time to time, and unite for collective action. Once such dramatic action is described in some length in chapter 8.

Ayllu continuity is also represented by segments in every territorial division. For example, Nayapi's grandson today says that he is from Nayapi Llacta. This is his *partimanda.* He has a large *ayllu* there. But his father (Nayapi's son) claims that Canelos is his *partimanda,* and that, moreover, his mother is Achuar *partimanda* and his father's mother is Napo *partimanda.* Everyone in Nayapi Llacta, and in adjoining and distant territories, can trace parentage to some Achuar territory, to some Napo territory, and to a site on the Bobonaza River where peoples from the Napo and from the Achuar areas intermarried as *runapura,* humans among ourselves. Farther north, in the Curaray region, Záparo-Runa, as *runapura,* is the dominant concept (Reeve 1988a).

Marriages in the times of the grandparents and in times of destruction conjoined *ayllu* segments to create small, complementary, segmentary units interrelated with other similar units. Among these intermarrying humans of the Bobonaza River system were other people speaking other languages. These include, in terms of language families, Zaparoan-speaking people, Jivaroan-speaking people, and some Tupian and Candoan speakers. As Christianity made tenuous inroads there developed a duality of ethnic patterning between the native person of the hamlet, of "civilization," of Christianity—Alli Runa—and the person of the forest, of the spirit-filled sentient universe—Sacha Runa. Alli Runa/Sacha Runa is one and the same. The former is of the world of Christian conquest and state domination. It is from whence destructive powers emanate. Sacha Runa is of the world of spirit control of life-giving and life-taking powers: the garden, the forest, the waterpower system.

Llacta

We have used this term since the very beginning of this book. We can now pull things together by understanding it more thoroughly. *Llacta* is the artificial geographical division of a territory. As *ayllu* is a reference term for kinship, *llacta* is a term of the Andean social world that refers to territory. But *llacta* does not mean nucleation; it refers to a broad territory. The Achuar have an implicit concept of such a dispersed, demarcated territory for hunting and swidden horticulture (Descola 1981, 1994), but the Runa name such a territory. They associate it with an intermarried group of peoples linked by *ayllu* segments, and they attribute its characteristics to mystical events involving shamanic activity and to occupational strategies adopted and deployed by interrelated, intermarried peoples.

A *llacta* is often named after its founder (e.g., Nayapi Llacta). It is regarded as a present, demarcated spatial sector grounded in earlier events, called *ñaupa llacta,* or *ñaupa rucumanda llacta.* People know just what living people are there, or should be there. These are the people who are now "of" the *llacta;* they are *llactamanda.* Before traveling to an area people quietly ask those who know about the present composition of a *llacta.* Information such as this is widely distributed whenever there is a need to know. As indicated in the first chapter, only by actually traveling to the places where real people live can one understand the commonalities of composition that constitute a region of diverse peoples.

Some people who belong to a given *llacta* are related to those who have their *ayllu* ties there; these are the roots to antiquity. Other people are new to the *llacta;* they have no relatives with *ayllu* ties there. They are *masha* (male) and *cachun* (female) in-laws. The concept in this region of *llacta* is fundamentally that of a set of linked *wasis.* Members of a *llacta* share the resources of the territory it encompasses. It is linked by *ayllu* bonds and by marriage bonds. It is an artificial cultural division of an Upper Amazonian ecosystem and social system. Dispersal of resources and consequent dispersal of technoecological strategies is essential to productive and reproductive life in this region.

One mechanism of such dispersal is *purina.* Here some people belonging to intermarried *ayllu* segments journey together to a distant territory where they maintain another *chagra,* and where they hunt and fish and gather for part of the year. In the new millennium of Ecuador, Runa are intensifying their activities in their parent's *purina* territories. We return to this in the final chapter.

Urbanity

The Puyo Runa belong to two worlds of urbanity: that of Puyo, the Capital of Pastaza Province, and that of the *caserío,* the small hamlet, or the "little community." The hamlet justifies the existence of any territory of indigenous people to the national, regional, and local governments. Settlements get put on maps; territories of dispersed people who wrest their lives from Upper Amazonian resource systems are declared "uninhabited." Where the concepts and deep knowledge of *sacha, chagra,* their natural, social, and spiritual forces are crucial to indigenous subsistence among the Puyo Runa and the other indigenous inhabitants of Amazonia, they are excised from the cultural life of urbanity; they become remnants of folklore to be collected, and their exegetes become relics, fragments of lost cultural worlds (N.Whitten 1978a, 1978b). The *caserío* is poised between the gnosis of livelihood and spirituality, and the required knowledge of the urban scene through which their articulation to an imagined future is channeled. Nayapi Llacta belongs to the world of Amazonian ecology and cosmology; Nueva Esperanza, its modern transformation (but not replacement), belongs to the world of national nucleation, hierarchical bureaucracy, and capitalist enterprise. People live in both systems, both worlds.

The *caserío* is usually on the fringe of a *llacta.* Virgilio Santi founded the hamlet of Río Chico in 1967. In 1985 Marcelo Santi and his sons founded the hamlet of Cushi Tambo. Marcelo only joined the nucleated hamlet, though, in 1998. He preferred to reside on top of the hill in his known territory, and he can move back there at any time if he so chooses. Concentrated hamlet life is hard; people are very close together, and their ideas and expressed needs seem to conflict more when they are close than when they are distant. But if the Runa want to live productively in the late twentieth-century and early twenty-first-century world of Ecuador, they must have a nucleated base. The hamlet replicates feasible corporate features drawn from national culture and national society with an eye to increasing incorporation into regional administrative structure. Casual visiting is not any more common in the hamlet than in dispersed dwelling settings. When visiting takes place the etiquette that we indicate at the beginning of this chapter is followed.

What is different about social transactions in the hamlet is that they take place in informal settings that follow national patterns. It is also in the hamlet that national patterns receive critical scrutiny. It is here that alternative modernities are enacted. In such en-actions novel symbolisms are generated. Eventually, these may coalesce into coordinated systems of actors across many

hamlets and spread into the human territories. What may be taken, erroneously, as vestiges of "tribal culture" are actually innovative features that may
come to influence huge systems of collective action.

Puyo

Puyo (*puyu*) means fog or cloud in Quichua. It is with fog and rain that
the domains of Amasanga and Sungui may merge, and it is through and by
clouds, thought of as sky rivers, that songs are communicated to their re-
cipients. Fog and cloud are cosmic prisms. Indi, the sun, who has a strong
mythical association with the toucan and with the hummingbird, shines
through fog or mist to create the spectrum symbolizing ultimate power of
previously unleashed water, the 'amarun.

Power of the nation-state and of the global economy flows into and radiates
out of Puyo to affect much of the life of the Puyo Runa, and through them to
their Achuar and Runa congeners eastward. The Puyo Runa are of Puyo, in
all of its urban dimensions, just as they are of their greater riparian–swidden-
forest environment. Puyo is a familiar place. It is the site of *el gobierno,* the
government, to whom many Runa turn for assistance in the development of
their hamlets. The road from Shell reached Puyo in January 1947 and immediately began moving northward, toward Napo. *Caserío* life on the Comuna San
Jacinto began then, too, as the president of Ecuador, Dr. José María Velasco
Ibarra, established the Comuna in the face of foreign intrusion through tea
plantations (Ledesma Zamora n.d.a; N. Whitten 1976a).

In 2006 the population of Puyo was estimated as over 45,000. During
the 1970s, as we began to undertake research in this area, Puyo and Shell
became staging areas for petroleum exploration (N. Whitten 1976a). In 1978
the Federación de Centros Indígenas de Pastaza (Federation of Indigenous
Centers of Pastaza, FECIP) was founded there, its leaders alternating between
reunions there and in Sarayacu (see N. Whitten 1985:228–30; Reeve 1985). In
1981 FECIP transformed into the Organización de los Pueblos Indígenas de
Pastaza (Organization of Indigenous People of Pastaza, OPIP). Its charter
states, in part: "The ends of the organization of indigenous people of Pastaza
(OPIP) [are to] . . . defend and represent the rights and interests of the native
peoples, participating in joint actions in the development of the nation col-
lectivity of which [the native indigenous people of Pastaza Province] form a
part" (chapter 1, article 2A, Organization of Indigenous Peoples of Pastaza,
October 1981).

OPIP officers and their affiliates have worked with municipal authorities to gain wider recognition of their constituents locally and, later, nationally. They have sponsored their own candidates for offices in municipal and national elections, with varying degrees of success.

An indigenous "recolonization" of Puyo, in an extensive outlying area, also began about 1981 and continues today, highlighting a strong Runa presence in Puyo (described in chapter 4). With the establishment of these little communities on the fringe of Puyo, indigenous life returned on a regular basis to the town out of which the Puyo Runa left, beginning in the 1940s. Now relatives and acquaintances from distant regions visit them in the urban center itself.

* * *

Everything set forth in this chapter is usually implicit knowledge, only occasionally becoming explicit in our mutual intersubjectivities. Every item, every element, must be learned through experience with a minimum of "telling" by knowledgeable Runa. Some of the most elaborate and complicated explications of mythohistorical events, places, and transformations come from someone with whom we are trekking, when we are moving so as to make time, eating ground (*sacha runashina puriáun*). "*Mana intindinguichu gumba?*"—"didn't you understand compadre?" is asked from time to time. For one to "tell" about such cosmic-ecological-mythohistorical features as the story of Nayapi, or segments of it; of the origins of maize and beans; of the Nungüi transformations; or of the raw anger of Hummingbird, is to be situated in, or more often moving through or across, a terrain where the real markers of the story exist—hills, ravines, depressions, hidden streams, the lattice vine snaking upward into the canopy, an area of danger where a boa constrictor's head and body were separated by an historical Runa, and so much more. We move in and out of these events, places, times, transformations, and we share what we can, distributing such knowledge and information sparingly but in an enduring manner, so long as our individual memory serves us and others.

Etiquette, as set forth in pages 34–36, plus shared trekking are extremely important; without such simple conformities on the part of the guest, the host in an encounter moves into the realm of other cultures, other knowledge systems, as he or she strives to imitate the ways of the newcomers, who, devoid of Runa etiquette, are intruders to be tolerated, not people with whom information is shared and exchanged. We have tried hard not to intrude, and think that in our efforts our learning reflects commonalities of culture worth inscribing in this ethnography.

What comes next sets out dimensions of our understanding, one that many Runa comprehend as our side of their world. Whether or not they "see" things in just the same way is essentially moot; we have learned to "see" as we did not before, as well as we can through Runa eyes and sensitivities, and we seek to express the resultant images, *ñucanchi muscuiguna,* as best we can.

Notes

1. This is probably the same Ramón described by Pierre (1983:233) as a "friend" of Palati, with whom the latter would stay en route to war against his Chirapa enemies, led by captain Sharupe.

2. Reflexivity, as we wrote in *Imagery and Creativity* (D. Whitten and N. Whitten 1993b:7–8), stems from the work of George Herbert Mead and Charles Horton Cooley. The former stressed affectivity and taking the role of the other to understand the positioning of the self in social interaction and transactions. He called this "reflexivness," the turning back of social experiences of others upon oneself. Barbara Babcock (1980, 1987) expanded this sense of reflexivity as did many others. We elaborate on reflexivity along with imagery and creativity (D. Whitten and N. Whitten 1993a, 1993b, 1993c) and apply the definitions and conceptualizations throughout this book, with illustrations in every chapter and specific definitions tied to the literature on enacted symbols and metaphors in chapter 5. Reflexivity as we employ it leads to what is now called cosmological perspectivism (Viveiros de Castro 1998, 2005), aesthetic perspectivism (Kohn 2002b), or cultural perspectivism (Uzendoski 2005), ideas that had their first glimmerings in the writings of Clifford Geertz (1973, 1983), which we introduce in this chapter. We also develop these ideas throughout this book. Since the mid-1980s another definition of reflexivity, stemming from the dictionary definition of "reflexive" to refer to an emphasis on the self (I, *myself*), has been used by many scholars. By contrast with our usage, the dictionary definition of reflexive leads to increased consciousness of ego, sometimes bordering on narcissism (I, myself, and me; or more recently, me, myself, and I). We do not use the latter sense of reflexive in this work.

3

Empowerment, Knowledge, and Vision

We have discussed knowledge and vision in several places. We turn now to a synthesis of concepts without which indigenous thought, expressed in *runa shimi,* cannot be understood.

Empowerment

The verb *ushana* in Canelos Quichua means to be capable, to be able to respond to contingencies in life. "To empower" is a good translation. Among the Napo Runa *ushai* can be glossed as "power" (Uzendoski 2004a, 2005b), but the Canelos Quichua do not use this term. *Utipana,* a synonym for *ushana* in the Napo dialect, is sometimes used in the sense of cosmic empowerment. When Lluwi died in Nayapi Llacta in the late 1970s, there were clear rifts in social and cosmic orders that lasted for some time. In the course of a brief stay there a month after his death, I reported to my friends (the shaman's kindred and affinal survivors) occurrences that ranged from strange noises and vibrations to a brief period of possession while dreaming; *utipanamanda* was given as the source of such disturbances, and people said that they came from "beyond," where fire and water merge. A couple of years later, I was unable to elicit *utipana* as a term for anything other than *shuj shimita,* another word in another language. People knew the term, but they didn't want me to use it.

Ursa (or *jursa*), from the Spanish *fuerza,* is the most frequently heard positive term of capability, and the adjective *sinchi,* strong, is affixed to a noun denoting capacity. To have capacity is to prove oneself; the term for proof is *camai.* Proof must be tangible; one must not only succeed in a task but produce something that another can feel. For example, one who says he senses a beauty (*sumaj*) within himself can prove this by playing a flute or by singing. In both cases another concept enters—*samai,* breath. One's *samai* carries with it something of the force of one's will, *shungu,* and something of the invisible (to humans when awake) yet tangible proof of inner strength. The proof of the strength of one's breath for communicating musically through a flute can make the person receiving the musical beauty reflect on the evocative meaning of the unsung words and the heard melody, which may create sad or nostaglic emotions, or perhaps a happy mood. When one plays a poignant song, its beauty evokes love, sadness, or melancholy.[1] A woman may "send" a *llaquichina* song to make a man suffer or long for her, or love her. When the man feels one of these emotions, the song is said to be *llaquirina.* When a "to-make-one-happy" (*cushiyachina*) song is played, the recipient who becomes happy is *cushiyarina. Camai,* proof, a tangible manifestation of *samai,* breath, and *llaqui,* also as proof, are concepts that imply reciprocation in interaction. They must be recorded by alter from ego and ego must be aware of alter's reception.

For another example, a shaman's corporeal heart-throat-stomach area (his *shungu,* his will)[2] contains especially sharp and dangerous objects that protect him but that can also be blown out as projectiles. These are the *tsintsaca* or *supai birutis.* When one gets hit with such a projectile, it is proof of the strength of a shaman; the *tsintsaca* is in a shaman's class, in a shaman's *sami.* When a shaman dies, a certain sort of small snail, when found near his grave, constitutes hard proof of the strength of his tangible breath (these snails-as-proof are *samwai*). Because a shaman's class projectile is stronger than a non-shaman's class projectile, proof exists of reciprocal asymmetry. A shaman of the same or higher class must be consulted for a cure and for redressing the wrong of the reception of a missile from another. Shamans also keep many stones (*rumi*). Each *rumi* in the shaman's class, *yachaj sami rumi,* contains the life force, *causai,* of a deceased shaman, of a spirit, or of a soul (or of some combination of these). One proves that a *rumi* is shaman's class by blowing gently on it with one's own breath—*ffiuuu, ffiuuu*—if condensation appears on the shiny surface, the stone "has breath; it is powerful shaman" (*samai tian sinchi yachaj*). Such stones are "like soldiers" (*soldadoshina*). The shaman with his phalanx of animated shaman's class stones is like the center of a military formation.

For a third example, a woman making a pot must control the breath of the fire, *nina samai,* as this heat leaves a pot after firing. If she does not do so, the fire's *samai* will cause the vessel to crack or burst as it cools. The completed pot is her *camai,* her proof of ability to control clay, water, fire, and breath, and also, with the forces of clay, rock, fire, and water, to produce color, design, and form.

Finally, for a fourth example, actual song unmediated by a musical instrument projects a particular synthesis of mythic time-space, beginnings and other times-places, knowledge of *sacha* and *chagra,* interpersonal-intersubjective reality, and skill into the cosmos across space and through time. Songs are received by those to whom they are sent, by souls and by spirits, and by powerful shamans. Rending beauty and power into the universe places one in a matrix connected to everything about which we have written to this point.

Knowledge, Vision, Thought, and Reflection

The conceptualization of power among the Canelos Quichua is paradigmatic. There is a consistent patterning to certain key concepts; the patterning is anchored in a social status; and the social status is named. Moreover, the semiotic paradigm—the patterning of sets of concepts that helps us understand the conceptualization of power in Canelos Quichua culture—deals with the dynamic relationships between "our" culture and "other" cultures, as well as how the threshold between ours and other can be moved or crossed while maintaining the dynamic relationships. In Western cosmology, us/other is seen as a binary opposition, a contrast; "we" as anthropologists, it is said, are fixated on "the other" (Fabian 2001, 2002; Bunzl 2002, 2004). As noted at the very beginning of this book, a lesson from the Canelos Quichua people of Amazonian Ecuador is that to know other cultures is to know one's own; own and other are dynamic and reflexive concepts. We now move more deeply into the ways by which otherness and selfhood are understood as dynamic relationships to which all humans are culturally connected (for cognate perspectives on Tucanoan indigenous people of Amazonian Colombia, see Goldman 1963, 2004; Reichel-Dolmatoff 1971, 1975, 1976, 1996).

We begin with the concept of *yachaj,* one who knows. For men, we enter the realm of shamanic knowledge. A shaman is one who moves regularly between the here and now, where he is "rooted," and other realms, to which he travels. The shaman moves the threshold between our culture (and the plane of existence of our quotidian world) closer to the edge of other cultures and other worlds. He passes from our culture and our world to others, and he returns, thereby exploring the other while maintaining and enriching the dynamic inner integrity of ours. "One who knows," among the Canelos

Quichua, is a person who has mastered the art of forging concepts of beauty to the bidding of an unusual power to heal. The shaman is also the node of the *ayllu* and *llacta* system, a human broker between indigenous culture and the outside world.

The word *yachaj* derives from the verb *yachana*, to know, to learn. To know and to continue to learn through one's growing mastery so as to respond to the vicissitudes of ordered and disordered worlds, one must balance the concept of *yachana* with another concept—*muscuna*—which means to dream, to envision, to be insightful. *Yachana*, as knowing, has a real "depth" to it, and this depth manifests itself through various forms of "proof." For example, if one sees a deceased relative in a dream, one may, or may not, "know" what the vision is. Is it a soul, or a spirit taking the form of the soul; or is it the relative? The question is important, and it has many levels of interpretation. A *yachaj* "knows" by degrees; and the more he knows, the stronger he becomes.

One of the proofs of increasing strength of a shaman is acquisition of a special shaman's song, *taquina*. The *taquina* is his alone, and it communicates beauty and power to the world of spirits. Only when the shaman is strong enough to ward off incoming projectiles of all other shamans can he actually sing out the song (send it out through his *samai*). When the beauty of the *taquina* is received by other shamans, they blow (*shitana*) back at the singer to test his strength. This is not the tangible blowing (*pucuna*) of, say, a dart through a blowgun. Rather, it is a dangerous blowing of unseen tangibility. If he is now "strong one who knows" (*sinchi yachaj*), he may sing his shaman's song without harm to himself or to *wasi* members; the fearsome beauty of the heard song proves the shaman's strength. He then may continue shamanic activities privately, within his own family, or more publicly, by curing others from his *ayllu* and, eventually, as he becomes stronger, people from other *ayllus* and from other cultures.

Ricsina is another verb that deals with knowledge in a somewhat different way, in a more immediate sense. It means to know, to experience, to perceive, to comprehend. This sort of knowing is experiential, and it must be backed up by depth and balanced with vision. One who is central to the reception of information—a *curaga* in the past—could be known as *sinchi ricsij runa*, a sort of strong know-all, see-all person. Although Eliseo Vargas and Javier Vargas would seem to fit this description, people deny that any of them were *sinchi ricsij*. No one, they say, "knows it all."

There are a number of terms that develop agglutinatively from *yuyana* in Quichua, one of which is the reflexive *yuyarina*, which means to think, to reflect. As Sibby and I came to understand more, and as our questions began to reflect paradigmatic relationships, our friends and colleagues commented on what they took to be our understanding of their understandings. We had entered a realm of sustained reflexivity, a realm in which we continue to exist. Some of our friends found our questions to be compatible with their own thoughts, and they sought to clarify for us what they took to be our thoughts. However, they found some of our ideas about their ideas to be utterly erroneous. Now and then, some of the questions we asked so we could be "clear in our own minds" about what we thought might be in "their minds" made an odd sense to them. Reflecting on our reflections, some said, made them rethink some of their ideas and ask others about relationships that made sense but were far from their consciousness. As the process went on, a few people who had studied us said we were *yuyayuj runa*—sort of professional students. A true insider, however, balances his thoughts and reflections with his immediate and deep knowledge, and—always—with his or her visionary activity.

People who reflect on Canelos Quichua cultural things, actions, and ideas (as we do) may be classed as *shuj shimita yachai* (or *yachan*), other speech knowledge. To so reflect and work within the semiotic paradigm of Canelos Quichua culture one is *ñucanchi yachai* (our cultural knowledge) or *ñucanchi ricsiushca runa* (our people's perception). The relationship between these two realms of knowledge—ours and others, or ours and theirs—is dynamic.

The model given here helps conceptualize the systemic relationships we've discussed. In the model, the *yachaj,* or more properly *sinchi yachaj,* has at-

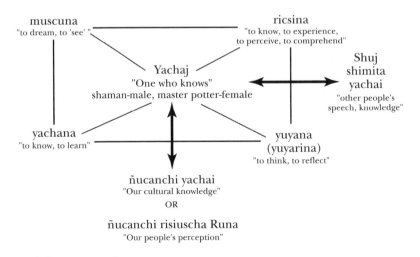

Knowledge, vision, and power.

tained a level of control such that he is sufficiently powerful to balance his knowledge with his visions, to relate his visions to cultural knowledge, and to relate his thoughts and reflections to knowledge and to his visions. To know more about what is within, the shaman must increasingly know more about what is without. The shaman becomes a paradigm builder. He continuously reproduces cultural knowledge, continuously maintains the distance between our culture and other culture, and continuously transcends the boundaries that he enforces by traversing the distances he builds. His work must, in part, be based on experiences with other peoples, past and present, who speak other languages and dialects. Such people (Achuar, Quichua-speaking peoples of the Napo area, Quichua-speaking people of the Sierra, other indigenous people of coastal Ecuador, and nonindigenous people) give to the shaman "other speech-knowledge" (*shuj shimita yachai*). At the same time, the shaman maintains native paradigms and expands the paradigms by drawing from his knowledge of other cultures. The shaman controls the process of syncretism.

Master potters, all of whom are women, do the same thing. Although it is less common to hear this, one may refer to a genuine paradigm builder—a woman who is able to evoke both inner cultural knowledge as a synthesis of vision and experience, and one who can also evoke systematic relationships between such knowledge-vision integration and other forms of integration—as *yachaj warmi*. It is also the case, as far as we know, that every master potter is related closely to a powerful shaman. In some cases the shaman is a father, in some cases a father-in-law, and in many cases there is a complex of shamanic males and master potter females. An example of the latter occurs, for example, when a woman who is the daughter of a powerful shaman marries a man who is the son of a powerful shaman. Her mother and mother-in-law are both master potters and she learns from each. Her husband, in turn, could be an incipient shaman, or a local political leader, or perhaps both.

Yachaj qualities exist in most men—perhaps in all. Most men must be able to "see" that there is something wrong within a *wasi,* and may actually "see" embedded projectiles when they take soul-vine brew. However, at a certain point in obtaining shaman's class status (*yachaj sami*), one must acquire a *taquina* from another shaman. His breath (*samai*) then must be balanced with proof (*camai*). He becomes *sinchi yachaj,* powerful one who knows, and he both anchors and expands a cultural paradigm. Few men reach this level. Two sons of the late powerful shaman Lluwi privately regard themselves as *yachaj;* they cure within their families and have close relationships with shamans equal to them and somewhat more powerful. These men have acquired a *sinchi yachaj taquina,* but only one is strong enough to sing out, and he does so only occasionally, and only within his own house.

Some daughters of Lluwi are potters, and one is a master potter. Unlike men, who place themselves, their *wasi,* and their *ayllu* in danger with *taquina* songs due to their built-in system of potentially uncontrolled, reciprocated "proof," women's proof lies in the control of the breath of fire, in the control of color, of water, of clay, of form. Ceramics emerge as a tangible form of beauty, and the designs and colors evoke and motivate dynamic and syncretic syntheses of deep and immediate knowledge, thought, reflection, and vision.

Parallel Transmission of Cultural Knowledge

One could visit Nueva Esperanza repeatedly and never realize that shamanic activity took place there, but one could never enter a household and overlook the Upper Amazonian ceramics used to store and serve *asua.* Finding a woman who is a master potter gives one the first clue about where to find a nodal relationship with respect to kindred continuity and broker relationships with other indigenous cultures and with the urban system radiating out of Puyo.

The woman's role in paradigm building faces inward and outward, drawing sustenance from ancient knowledge that has been imparted to her by instruction, by demonstration, through impartation of secrets, and through extensive impartation of private imagery drawn from myth and song by other women. The potter works in her own site, often in the middle of the house, but her supplies—which include various clays that may be mixed for different purposes, black rock, clay dyes, and tree resins—come from a number of sources. Female-to-female networks of exchange that range widely, some across territories where men are hostile to one another, have their material manifestation in the ceramic product of the master potter. Seated on a split-bamboo mat that faces away from the Andes, she creates an array of ceramic pieces that represent the cosmos, the mythic ordering of social life, imparting always something of the novel, something of herself, and something of the insights that link private thought and reflection to acquired intracultural knowledge. She works from dawn to dusk, thinking songs and sometimes singing. Within a few days of such sustained activity she is managing a very complex system that includes the building of a large storage jar, several delicate drinking bowls, an effigy jar, and a figurine. As she works—coiling, scraping, burnishing, painting, firing, working clay—she reflects on the complete array that she is making, and she imparts something of this reflected universe to other women who watch, help, and learn. Ceramic manufacture is especially elaborate in preparation for a festive event, when a deliberate rift is made in the fabric of *ñucanchi yachai* in the form of invited intrusion from the right side of the semiotic paradigm given on page 63.

An internal disjuncture of *ñucanchi yachai* within a cosmic network from human to spirit, through cosmos, and back to human triggers the activities that create a situation in which prominent male paradigm building takes place. Here a shaman, working in the woman's sector of the household, faces both inward and outward. His paraphernalia includes a split calabash shell for drinking the *Banisteriopsis caapi* hallucinogen *ayahuasca* (soul vine); a smaller container for snuffing tobacco water; a cigarette or cigar for blowing cleansing smoke on whatever he wishes to "see into"; and an array of stones that themselves contain the life force (*causai*) of contained spirits, each with its own soul. Within him exists an array of hard spirit substances that form a shield (*lurira*) to protect his body. These substances are brought into his throat to help him diagnose the cause of illness, and they may be projected outward on his breath if he chooses to blow harm at an enemy. When these inner substances are blown as projectiles, they are *supai biruti,* spirit darts, or just *tsintsaca* (from the Jivaroan *tsentsak,* dart). One who has felt the hard, living proof of sent evil (*shitashca*) approaches the shaman and asks for help in exchange for pay.

The shamanic seance takes place just after dark and may go on until dawn. The shaman is seated (*tiarishpa*) on a carved stool that symbolizes the Amazonian water turtle, *charapa.* While he is seated and after he has drunk, master-spirit forces come to him in their corporeal manifestations. Then other spirits come to him and a spirit shaman appears standing (*shayarishpa*). As spirits appear standing to the shaman seated on his stool, he travels to other lands where he appears standing to the spirits. To appear standing is to be poised, to be ready, to be capable, to feel power. While still seated, the shaman sings of where he is going, where he has been, and of the power to see and to cure that he has obtained. He identifies the cause of illness as an object (perhaps a spider encased in blue mucous within one's kneecap) and as culprit (the shaman living on the Llushín River) and the client of the shaman-as-culprit, who claims to be a friend of the afflicted one's father. If he is paid to do so, the shaman who makes the diagnosis calls a demonic spirit, often the *pasuca* (from the Jivaroan *pasuk*). While seated and in a state of possession, the shaman sends forth a harmful projectile of his own.

The system of cultural transmission is a parallel one. Taking the master potter female (*sinchi muscuyuj warmi*) and powerful shaman male (*sinchi yachaj*) as the conjoined affinal and household node of a kindred, it seems quite clear that cultural paradigms are built in one way by pottery manufacture and in another way by shamanic activity. In such cultural constructions, shaman and potter evoke, mystify, and clarify in complementary ways. For example, a man may look at a diamond design around the shoulder of a pot and say simply that it is an anaconda. But the woman who made it may wish to evoke a particular *amarun* manifestation that suggests to her and to her daughter or daughter-in-law a whole series of relationships involving territoriality, ethnicity, and kinship. Similarly, when after taking *ayahuasca,* which is prepared by a woman, the anaconda appears to the shaman, he cannot see it well; women working with him snuff tobacco water and clarify the image, even speaking for it: "I am Yacu Mama person." In their activities the shaman and the potter face both outward and inward (in terms of our culture–their culture).

The force field created by the shaman protects the people while at the same time drawing additional strength from the outer world. For example, when a shaman flies to the right bank of the Pastaza River to engage the killing spirit force of the legendary Chirapas, he makes them different as he crosses the boundary between them and us, and takes the power of them back to us. If a woman trades today with people from that same area for her clays and her dyes, then she makes them like us, for potential marriage and kin ties are culturally constructed so that material flow in the female domain is a manifestation of existing social ties. Today in Nayapi Llacta and its nucleated Nueva Esperanza, we can still describe the system of cultural transmission as a parallel one.

In the creation of a *llacta* a clear shaman node exists. But as the *llacta* grows in personnel and nucleates into a *caserío,* the strong shaman node eventually disappears. Few such men currently reside on the Comuna San Jacinto. Most powerful shamans today are of the *ayllus* of Nayapi Llacta residents, but they live in other places, some of them in Puyo, or in one of its satellite towns, some in Achuar territory, some in Canelos, Pacayacu, Sarayacu, Montalvo, or Curaray, some in the Napo region. *Yachaj* status, however, has been achieved by two brothers and one brother-in-law in Nayapi Llacta; each of these men has also taken over important brokerage functions between Puyo and Nueva Esperanza, working in very different ways and often in conflict with one another. The wife of each of these men is a potter; one is a master potter. Until about 1995 each of these women also made pottery for sale in Puyo, and tried, in competition with other women, to attract exclusive patrons from Puyo, Baños, Ambato, Quito, and more recently from Tena, Ahuano, and other sites on the Napo River.

As women and men transmit traditional culture and ancient syncretisms in a parallel, mutually reinforcing and mutually reinterpreting fashion, they also transmit—in a continuing, if transformed, parallel fashion—much of the new syncretic formations, as they intensify their own gender-specific ordering of cultural domains, while expanding those domains by exchange and interaction with bearers of other cultures. In the process of expansion, sensory perceptions of "us" and "them" are constantly invoked. This imagery locates the cosmology of Nayapi Llacta solidly within the Amazonian culture sphere, but also with syncretized elements of the ancient Andean world and the world of Hispanic conquest, and the invidious, pernicious exclusion of the peoples of Nueva Esperanza from the national system. To understand this, we turn to three levels of visionary experience to grasp something of the intensity and versatility of the images that form the substance of reproduction and transformation. In this sequence, we focus on one "ordinary" night dream, an *ayahuasca* seance, and a Datura trip.

Visionary Experiences

The Runa of Nayapi Llacta, like people everywhere, dream when they sleep. They actively seek meaning in dreams, using the concepts set forth in the paradigm to guide them. Dream imagery as sense experience (*muscui*) is related to the universe of souls and spirits, to *unai,* to known history, and to cultural, ethnic, and social space. Like many cultural congeners of Amazonian South America, the Runa also gain visionary experience by use of a soul-vine brew. In this use the Runa are either guided by a shaman or take the shaman role themselves. Unlike most Amazonian peoples, but in concert with many Andean, Mesoamerican, and North American native peoples, the Runa of Nayapi Llacta also use, in a culturally prescribed manner, one of the most dangerous hallucinogens in the world—Datura (specifically *Brugmansia suaveolens* cultivars).

Our intent here is to sketch the cultural patterning of visionary experience by contrasting *ayahuasca* and *wanduj* trips. Such structuralist reduction is not an end in itself but rather a strategy of description that allows us to perceive the means by which ordering of visionary experience, which articulates correspondences from coincidental planes of existence, provides the information necessary to understand the ordering of chaos in Nayapi Llacta/Nueva Esperanza.

Dreams are part of life. As such they are manifestations of life. They are real but not tangible under ordinary circumstances. Their origin is problematic, and they provide the stuff from which creativity and imagination born of reflection are made. One's *causai* exists in corporeal and noncorporeal dimensions. It is reflected, as *aya,* by one's shadow and in one's eye. These reflections seem to be homonyms, not soul images. The fundamental mystery of simultaneous existence of both flesh and soul is not transcended by any sense of soul detached from body. Detachment and attachment are complementary facets of life processes. The *aya* (soul) / *aicha* (flesh, body) contrast is analogous to the *shayarina* (standing-appearing) / *tiarina* (sitting-being) contrast.

If our bodies remained well, if interpersonal tensions did not cause us to be suspicious of our neighbors and friends, if we lived in a static world where the pattern of life was not disrupted by births, deaths, loves, hatreds, alliances, or vendettas, then, perhaps, there would be no need for radical readjustment. But today we are flesh as well as soul; our *ayllus* contain real people. The visions we encounter in today's world, and the difficulties we encounter in bringing our knowledge into line with our thought and reflection, require trips beyond the earthly confines of *sacha, chagra, wasi,* and *caserío.* We go as we are, and we hope to return stronger. There are two mind-altering vehicles for such a trip: the first is Banisteriopsis; the second is Datura.

Ayahuasca

Ayahuasca is a vine that grows in the rain forest, and shamans plant it near their homes. It may also be called *quilla wasca* (moon vine) or *mucu wasca* (knotty vine). The vine stem is split and cooked, together with leaves from another *Banisteriopsis* species or *Psychotria viridis* called *amarun yaji* (anaconda *yaji*). The word *yaji* is not Quichua; it comes from Tucanoan and is used widely throughout Upper Amazonia for the brew itself (*yajé, yahé*).[3]

A man or a woman is advised to take *ayahuasca* by a shaman. The shaman so advises when, in a discussion with someone who has an illness, the shaman feels the need for a deeper experience with patient, onlookers, and sectors of the cosmos, before making a complete diagnosis and before healing. The shaman always takes *ayahuasca* when diagnosing the illness of Amazonian indigenous people; the patient may take it if he or she is an adult; and onlookers, who never number more than three or four, may also take it.

The shaman, or another in his household, may have black paint on his face or body. After being cooked, this paint, from *widuj* (*Genipa americana*), is painted on in the evening and is not visible until the next day. It lasts for about a week. *Widuj* and *ayahuasca* must be cooked (the latter with the leaf additive); each is associated with the moon, which, in turn, is associated with disorder, and with Runa origin and continuity. With this association, shaman and client enter the disorderly realm of the moon.

Seated on his *bancu* in the woman's part of the house, which is very faintly illuminated by flickering flames, the shaman drinks. He feels intoxicated and begins to "see" as he hears the roar of rain or waterfall encompassing the house. As large inchoate images appear before him, a woman who has snuffed liquid tobacco clarifies the first visions and speaks for or as the apparition: *Yana Puma runa mani* ("I am the black jaguar person"), *Yacu Mama runa mani* ("I am the river woman person"). The woman who "sees" is usually the shaman's wife, herself a master potter, who is known as *muscuyuj warmi* or *sinchi muscuyuj warmi,* and may be called *yachaj warmi.*

Black jaguar and black anaconda each appear, each as a separate pair. First, the jaguar comes as co-shaman from the forest domain; then appears the anaconda from the water domain, the world of Sungui, who is himself the first shaman. *Yacu mama,* in the form of a colorful anaconda or fish, examines the Runa shaman's *shungu,* his will, and silently converses with him. The will has two manifestations: the inner essence that contains the shaman's motivations, strengths, and purposes; and the flesh of stomach, heart, and lungs. The shaman converses with *yacu mama,* and, as he gains her knowledge about his will and about his patient's affliction, his body swells.

Now swollen with visionary potency and still sitting on his stool, the shaman talks softly with the patients. He calls for his leaf bundle (*shingui shingu panga,* named after a rain-forest cat; also known as *wairachina,* wind maker), and it is given to him by his wife or daughter. He drinks again, shakes his leaf bundle to create a spirit wind (*supai waira*), and "sees" snake tongues flickering from its lancelet leaves. After whistling his *taquina* song, he sings it out, and more spirits of the forest come. Spirits of events come, too—some are other indigenous peoples in action, some are animals marching as soldiers in the Peru-Ecuador war or as a karate expert who taught soldiers in Shell before the Cenepa Valley war. As these images come, they dance, swinging left and then right; they are beautiful, and they are strong. While still sitting on his *bancu,* the shaman flies into the air and travels to other lands.

From his *bancu* he sings of his travels through space, which varies in its viscosity. Out of this air come killing missiles sent by other shamans, and he defends himself, swinging from side to side, using a shield of Sungui or a deflective move of Amasanga. He returns to where he is, still singing of where he has been, and he "sees" the evil in the patient in the form of a cutting or stinging creature encased in blue mucous in the patient's stomach. Again he drinks, and he sucks, noisily—and sometimes violently—again and again, taking the evil from the patient into his mouth, holding it, allowing his own spirit helpers from his *shungu* to examine and to take the soul of the evil substance from it. He then blows the evil substance, devoid of soul substance, into a tree or stump outside of his house, and there it stays. He examines everyone in the household and cleanses them with the breeze from his leaf bundle.

If the shaman continues his seance, he next calls the undersoil spirits of the forest in triple, feminine form, and they come to him under the house. There, unified as a single, powerful, killing spirit, they arrive somehow to sit on him as the spirit's *bancu*. The human shaman is now possessed by the spirit shaman; he is now *bancu,* and very dangerous. Through him the spirit attacks the shamanic culprit who sent evil, and the culprit's client who paid him to do so. Now the shaman, as Jurijuri *supai,* soul master of other people from other cultures, sends a killing missile out to rend the air with slight, high falsetto sound, *quish whiaj.* The missile breaks into the biological, social, and spiritual network of the evil client and his shaman culprit—into their bodies, protective shields, and into their *ayllus*—to do killing harm.

The complexities of shaman as killing agent need to be spelled out. When the killing missile is sent, the shaman is *bancu* of the spirit while he is also on his *bancu,* which is now grounded with the undersoil spirit force of the Jurijuri *supai.* The shaman stays seated on his *bancu* but appears standing to the spirits; the spirits appear standing to the seated shaman until, finally, both spirits and shaman are together seated in one cosmic connection to project death. After this violent and frightening episode, the seance rapidly quiets down. There is mild talk, some leaf bundle shaking, and maybe another drink of *ayahuasca.* The snakes are gone; the *amarun* long ago departed, and images fade, but the great black jaguar may continue to rub on those who still "see."

Everyone is home before dawn; the disorder of night created within the *wasi* does not carry into day. Out of the waters to the east, the sun brings order to the commonplace world. Day is a time of its own order-disorder. Ruptures that occur during the day are usually mended at night by shamanic activity, activity that creates its own ruptures that then require repair. Rupture that cannot be so mended demands that one enter the cosmos alone, to risk everything, including one's life, for a secure grasp on knowledge and a heightened ability to "see."

Wanduj

The decision to take *wanduj*[4] (previously considered a *Datura* species but now classified as *Brugmansia suaveolens*) varies greatly among individual men and women, and the drug is usually ingested alone. If a second person is present, companionship is precautionary: there is no guiding helper who is of this world. Both the person taking the *wanduj* and the companion, if there is one, paint their faces and maybe some of their bodies with red, uncooked *manduru* (*Bixa orellana*) dye. The *wanduj* must not be *yacu wanduj* but rather *alli upina wanduj* (good drinking Datura, as opposed to water Datura). The *wanduj* stems have been previously acquired from a close friend from a distant *llacta,* usually someone who is not a relative. The stems are planted and then later "found" in an old *chagra,* where the distinction between *chagra* and *sacha* is difficult to make. A great Ila tree is addressed as *amigo* (friend) in Spanish, and the tree is asked to help the person who seeks to enter the realm of the *wanduj muscui,* Datura vision. The man who is to take a Datura trip places a barked pole in front of a lean-to, clears the forest of brush to make a trail in a particular direction, and sometimes other poles are stripped of their bark and placed there too. The pole and the *ñambi* (trail) help the taker, as does the great tree; indeed, the forest itself becomes a helper. The *wanduj* is drunk around noon, when the sun is high and the world is ordered. It is squeezed from the inner bark and drunk with water taken from a bamboo stem, not from a river or stream.

The taker sits in front of his shelter, looking toward his pole and his trail; within ten minutes he passes out completely and falls back into his lean-to. Oscillating between an extremely agitated state and unconsciousness, the taker sees things that are distant as though they were right there, and he sees people and things nearby as though they were far away. He sees clearly, though, and he converses at great length with friends and close ones. Amasanga arrives, usually dressed in a shimmering black-purple robe; he is in two bodies, a tall one and a short one. (Some say that in this context Amasanga and Sungui are one and the same.) He helps the *wanduj* taker to see rifts in the social fabric and spirit darts in his body. The taker sees his enemies and his friends, and he knows how to differentiate between them. He also sees into the future and takes note of coming crises. Then Amasanga, turning to the taker's body, sucks out the intruding projectiles, cleanses him completely, and gives him counsel on coming crises, opportunities, and misfortunes. There is no danger while one is in the expanded universe, where souls, spirits, and humans, both living and dead, are one; but there is danger when one begins to leave the cosmic theater. By midnight the taker begins to move; he staggers and falls. The spirit master of the rain forest helps him avoid injury, and eventually, as the sun rises the next day, the taker finds his way to his own *wasi,* even though it is a couple of hours away from the site of his *wanduj* experience.

On his return, the person is an absolute disaster within the quotidian household. While others attempt to go about routine tasks, he still sees the world of spirits, of the dead, of the future, and of souls; he stumbles and falls and crashes, laughing when he should say *aiyaów!* (ouch!) and frightening people. Gradually he sees the surroundings as others see them, and he sees the expanded cosmos as well; the latter continues to recede as the former comes into sharper and sharper focus. After about three days in a state of agitation and confusion, the taker goes to the river and bathes, returning to "normal" or near normal, but with a new level of knowledge and a new level of "seeing."

Brief Cases

Discussed here are cases in which a few people of Nayapi Llacta/Nueva Esperanza used many of the elements presented in this chapter to create order from disorder, and in so doing maintained a sense of continuity in a setting of radical change.

THE PEOPLE

Taruga, the son of Sicuanga by a previous marriage (his mother died later in childbirth), is from Nayapi Llacta. It is his *quiquin llacta.* He met Elena in Puyo, where she worked in the house of a *comerciante* (business man, trader) to send money home to a small hamlet outside of Archidona. Her family is part of a large *muntun* that periodically travels between the Archidona *llacta* (the territory of which was then owned by a *blanco*) and a site on the Napo River, just up the Río Payamino, which the members of the *muntun* were trying to acquire legally from the Ecuadorian Institute for Agrarian Reform and Colonization (IERAC), with the assistance of the new National Institute for the Colonization of the Ecuadorian Amazonian Region (INCRAE). In 1973, the whole *muntun* attended Taruga and Elena's wedding in Nueva Esperanza. Tempers flared, fights broke out, and most of the members of the *muntun* departed the same day.

Little by little, though, other alliances were formed by men and women visiting back and forth, and by 1981 three more people from Nayapi Llacta had married into Elena's *muntun*. In fact, Elena's mother, called *jauya mama* (mother-in-law), had a now deceased brother, Rodrigo Andi, who was in the same shaman's class as the late Lluwi (Taruga's grandfather). *Jauya mama* was also a potter, making fragile black pots and eating ware in a different style than that of the Canelos Quichua people. As of 2007, Elena and Taruga are well ensconced in Nueva Esperanza, where Taruga has become an expert in natural medicines, which he sells to Quiteños.

TARUGA'S DREAM

Taruga and Elena live near the center of their two-hectare *chagra,* set in a rain forest that appears virgin to the uninitiated but was partially cut some thirty or more years ago by Sicuanga. They are in their second house now, a large, roomy, quadrangular structure on top of a hill, overlooking the rain forest. There is good, filtered spring water twenty yards from the house and a stream to bathe in at the bottom of the hill.

Sleeping in the upper story on the west side of the house one clear night in 1981 in late May, the time when the *guama (Inga)* tree fruits, Taruga saw, in his dream, a great horse coming to the house. He was looking toward Palora, on the right bank of the Pastaza River, when he saw the horse coming. Palora is an urban area, but not long ago it was the territory of the Jivaroan Chirapas. There had been some strange killings near Palora in the few months prior to Taruga's dream, as poor people from many areas struggled for land on the edge of the expanding tea plantations and cattle ranches.

The horse was coming from Palora, directly toward Taruga. On either side were the troops, and behind the horse there were still more troops, all marching toward his house, and he saw them coming in his dream. The horse was as high as his second story—it could look right at him as he looked at it. Taruga was sitting up, looking at the great horse. It snorted as horses do, with nostrils flared and raised: *pljffff.* Taruga snarled back at the horse like a jaguar, *sssgggghhhh.* He woke up. He had a fever. He first blew smoke where the horse had been, and then went down to the ground and blew smoke all around the house.

Taruga returned to sleep and dreamed of a lagoon where he was paddling a canoe; he crossed to the other side, gave a new hand-operated coffee-bean decorticating machine to an in-law there, and received, in turn, a beautiful headdress of toucan feathers. Also, in that dream he "knew" what his *taquina* song would one day be: *unaimanda sicuanga taquina* (toucan shaman song from mythic time-space). The next day Taruga still had his fever, but Elena said it was getting better. She, too, told of how he snarled like a jaguar, how he blew smoke off the second floor into the air, where the all-too-real horse dream-image, with its flanking and following troops, had stood and snorted, before Taruga descended to the ground to cleanse the entire house and surrounding air with his white tobacco-permeated breath.

Taruga was concerned about the dream all day, as his fever subsided. He told me of many young men in the *comuna* who, like himself, were not shamans but were known to be strong to one another, and were so known to residents of Puyo. He fears no one, he says, not even the great horse coming toward him like the president of the *comuna*, whom he had recently crossed politically in an *asamblea general*. The president might hold the dominating authority of office, backed by regional, juridical, and political control, and be represented as the mighty force of a warhorse, but he, Taruga, the red brocket deer, had the powerful breath of a jaguar and the shaman's song of the warrior toucan with which to blow away the president's formation of authority and control.

TARUGA'S TRIP TO VISIT RODRIGO ANDI

On June 1, 1981, Taruga, Elena, Jauya Mama, Taruga's unmarried sister, and one of Taruga's young cousins decided to go to Ahuano, on the Napo River, to visit the *sinchi yachaj* Rodrigo Andi. Taruga had tremendous confidence in himself, but just too many bad dreams were coming his way, and although his fever had subsided and he knew his future shaman's song, little Carlos, son of Taruga and Elena, had twice been stricken with fever and diarrhea. He had been treated in VozAndes Hospital in Shell, and a powerful shaman on the road to Napo had also sucked a spirit protrusion from his heel. Nonetheless, Taruga was uncomfortable, and after consultation with his father, Sicuanga, he decided to drink *ayahuasca* with another powerful one, at a greater distance in space, culture, and ethnic identity but at the same time closely related to him as a member of his wife's *ayllu*.

This group left Puyo on the 9:00 A.M. San Francisco bus, taking with them the green wooden decorticating machine that Taruga had purchased in Puyo as a gift for his brother-in-law. They also took 450 *sucres* to pay necessary fees. They talked to the shaman all one day, learning that he was now treating not only occasional Andean visitors but also posing for pictures (and occasionally selling bottles of *ayahuasca* mixed with alcohol) to tourists from the United States, Germany, Italy, Spain, and other lands. As evening drew near, all talked quietly in the shaman's house, while don Rodrigo himself rested. Dusk descended over the Napo, with the frogs beginning to peep and the skyline of the mighty Andes standing in black relief before the great red ball as *indi* crossed over to *indiyaicushca,* and the whirlpool that grinds and polishes two- to four-pound stones where the Arajuno enters the Napo swelled in intensity. A motor was heard coming downriver, and all waited to see who would arrive. In ten minutes, a commercial cargo canoe pulled to shore. In it were two North Americans with a great deal of recording equipment. While Taruga and Elena listened, the gringos talked to don Rodrigo, and he agreed to let these outsiders sit in on the curing session and partake in the *ayahuasca* drinking.

By 8:00 P.M. all had drunk, become intoxicated, and talked. The following information comes from the recording made by the two North Americans (Crawford 1979, 2007) and from my extended discussion of a portion of the tape recording with people in Taruga's family, Elena's family, and others interested in this very dramatic event. Years later, on the death of don Rodrigo, we learned that Elena was a niece of this powerful shaman.

* * *

On his *bancu,* seat of Sungui, don Rodrigo chants *sumáj, sumáj, sumáj, sumáj* (beauty, beauty, beauty, beauty). Because he is bottling up his sounds, closing his vowels, and "tightly" releasing his *samai,* it sounds as though he's chanting *tomá, tomá, tomá, tomá.* He also chants *taríriríri ri rí ri rí* (from which comes the term *tariri,* "shaman" in several languages), which demonstrates that don Rodrigo has the killing power of the Jurijuri (Jirijiri in Napo Quichua, Jirijri in Achuar) *supai,* the undersoil, cave-dwelling master of monkeys and foreign peoples, who sends out his *waira samai* (breath of the wind) from his mysteriously lighted inner cave and across the mountainous rain forest.

Don Rodrigo sings that he is pleased with the beauty of the spirit of *ayahuasca* herself and with the merged beauty of the spirit world and the strength to kill. He talks and sings of the appearance of a male rain-forest spirit person, who then arrives. This spirit being is first unidentified as it arrives dressed in red and yellow toucan feathers, with bandolier-like seed-bead adornments. He swings his entire body from side to side, side to side. Don Rodrigo, sitting on his stool, becomes the spirit, singing, playing, seeing, ready to travel beyond to bring more spirits to him. He experiences a flying sensation as though he were a great condor, soaring, going out, coming back, and he sings about this.

Danger exists everywhere for the shaman as he experiences flights; now he must fend off flying death in the form of spirit darts and lances. He chants about what he is doing, singing that he is protected by a powerful shield (*lurira*) of Sungui. As the spirit darts come toward him, first from one side and then from the other, he swings his body and his shield rhythmically, as in a dance; and as he swings he blows out, *suuuuuuuu, suuuuuu*. The darts glance off the shield and are blown away by his *samai* full of its spirit forces. He sings that the shield itself is made up of powerful medicine and spirit substances that come from a drugstore. The shaman is at one and the same time fending off killing missiles with his Sungui shield and becoming a doctor who buys medicines in a spirit drugstore on the Napo River.

This ancient Sungui-modern doctor continues to call the beautiful, killing forest spirit Jurijuri to him as he chants that he has now acquired the power of Sungui, which came to him out of a great lagoon, and that he has strong medicine with which he can cure. The shaman continues to sing that the spirit of the forest is arriving and that it is dancing, adorned with *sicuanga* feathers, *sicuanga* bones, and a beautiful *sicuanga* headdress. This unnamed vision dances and arrives, standing right in the place of the shaman himself, where he is seated on his *bancu*. Now a force field of dancing, warrior-spirit power occupies the same space as the chanting shaman, though they are on different, complementary cosmic planes (one sitting-being, the other standing-appearing).

The spirit brings ten machines (*máquinas*)—among them X-ray, blood pressure apparatus, stethoscope, large bright surgical light—with which to cure the patient, little Carlos. The spirit is making quite a noise, jingling and rattling and laughing, and he is dressed like a beautiful Sicuanga Runa. Now the shaman acknowledges the spirit as Uyarij Runa, noisy person, and as *sinchi yachaj*, powerful shaman.

Don Rodrigo identifies the beautiful, noisy spirit still further as Runga *supai*, water-jaguar spirit (Napo Quichua), or giant otter spirit. As the spirit arrives, he snorts, rattles his teeth like a peccary, and makes the jaguar's cough associated with the Jurijuri spirit. Now, as the Runga *supai* is with the shaman on the *bancu* (standing-appearing versus sitting-being has become ambiguous), don Rodrigo chants of power drawn from the spirit and human waking worlds and from recent history. He chants that he has spirit cannons with which enemies will be killed, and that an ancient hill has been pulverized. Then he sings of airplanes around and above—circling, blitzing, buzzing, making a tremendous noise. There are all types: small one-engine planes and big military ones, company and commercial planes, helicopters and Hercules cargo ships. "Here I am," he sings, "a shaman sitting in the center of aviation control, peaceful with the spirit power, while all this noise and destruction go on around me in the air. And it is beautiful."

"From downriver the soldiers are coming," he continues, referring to the power of invasion during the war with Peru in 1941. "A beautiful line of marching soldiers, all swinging from side to side, left to right, right to left, moves upriver. All are water-jaguar spirits; more come from the south, and I, as *yachaj,* contact them with radiograms. They come here and are with me on my *bancu,* a Spanish seat of pure gold." Now the shaman chants that he is arriving at a high hill where there are many *muja warmi supai,* which are special oblong-shaped, basin-like water spirits. There the water-jaguar spirit comes dancing and singing as Amasanga *warmi,* the forest spirit in feminine form. Then the shaman stops singing; he yawns, whistles, talks a bit to the two foreigners, and accepts a cigarette from one of them.

After more whistling, the shaman takes out a *pijuano,* a vertical, shaman's class flute, and again plays his *taquina,* noting with care that the gringos are still recording his music. Quietly, almost but not quite so quietly that those present can't hear, don Rodrigo now hums two tones $mm_{mm}mm_{mm}$. These sounds, it is said, are the only ones that humans made in *unai.* At that time humans crawled around as babies, and all other life forces were "human." The hum, or whistle, of the two tones is the sound analog of swinging from side to side; each brings the Runa world and mythic time-space into the same cosmic dimension with known history and the spirit domains. With ancient and contemporary now one, and with a unity of history and "now," don Rodrigo has taken the steps necessary to establish a force field around himself and his Amazonian water turtle seat of power; he again begins to sing.

Beauty and spirit-killing powers are again chanted, and then don Rodrigo summons the underwater feminine power as a chief, *curaga.* Again the spirit comes as Uyarij Runa, the noisy spirit, making the sound of the jaguar, which evokes the fearsome Jurijuri *supai.* The shaman is now gathering the power to kill, for only when he possesses this power will he be strong enough to cure his patient of the killing darts sent to him by a shaman working for a malevolent agent. Instead of calling a spirit shield he now summons a spirit lance with a steel tip and refers to himself as a warrior, chanting the sounds of the Shuar peoples to the south, who visited him to purchase spirit darts to use against their own enemies. These Shuar, he chants, were Chirapas who lived just beyond Palora, just south of the Pastaza River. He sings as the dancing water-jaguar spirit and enjoys both the beauty of vision and the noise accompanying the vision. Now there is no longer ambiguity about the seat of power and the control of power from the world of spirits. Don Rodrigo himself is the seat of power for the powerful spirit, and the spirit chants through him. The shaman has become *bancu* for the spirit shaman.

Although those present still see the shaman chanting, he himself knows that the chants are coming from the spirit, and he is now the spirit's vessel and vehicle into the waking world of humans. The spirit chants that he will cure, that he is part of a *bancu* (here the shaman himself has become the *bancu*). In addition to the qualities of noise and vision the spirit now chants of strength. The spirit shaman sings that he is like a sun pope, a spirit force of the sky that corresponds to the Pope in the world of Catholic Christians. Then the spirit sings that he is the Tsalamanga *curaga,* chief of the mystical water spirits of the deep, cold Andean lakes. He descends into a lake of beautiful ice inside of a rocky mountain, where he sits on the seat of power there, still swinging from side to side, dancing and singing. Note here that the shaman, as *bancu,* is still seated-being in his house on a high bank above the Napo River, but now his spirit possessor, who has traveled while seated on the shaman to the Andean lakes, is also seated-being in the Andean lake. The shaman with his spirit is anchored solidly in two domains, but as himself (shaman) he remains anchored where he is. There is tremendous danger in this procedure, for if the shaman loses his grip within his household—loses his ground, so to speak—he will die.

The spirit, speaking through the shaman while still within the icy-cold Andean lake, next asks the Tsalamanga spirit if he can have a horse to ride; he wants one that looks like the sun (a palomino). When he returns to the Napo, he says, he will be riding a dancing horse, rhythmically swinging from side to side, right to left, left to right, dancing. He will also return wearing a sweater and a necktie and be master of all these Andean things that have come from other native Quichua cultures, and also from foreign sources.

Now the spirit, singing through don Rodrigo, chants of his and other powerful, sentient, living stones. Spirits are coming to him from such stones in the form of sharp, dartlike projectiles. He grabs them, first from one side, then from another, swinging rhythmically from side to side, taking from the left, then from the right. Where, in the first *taquina* rendition, the shaman was defending himself with Sungui's shield from the incoming darts, the forest-spirit shaman, working through the Runa shaman, is now capturing the darts in the form of sharp stones and keeping them for future use. Behind the incoming spirit projectile stones, the Uyarij Runa once again appears—dancing—and he is beautiful.

Now don Rodrigo, still possessed by the spirit, sings of the Chirapa Jivaroans from the south bank of the Pastaza River. He says that he is chief of the Chirapa and will take the power apparition (*arutam* in Shuar, Achuar, and Shiwiar; *wandujta upina muscuna* in Quichua) of them however this vision may come. He sings that while he is dreaming, the ancient specter comes to him all dressed in white, black, red, and yellow toucan feathers, with a pure *sicuanga* shoulder-bone adornment which Achuar killers wear. All the Chirapa women are brought to him, he sings, and this is both beautiful and powerful. He alone controls their feminine beauty and forces.

The song ends, and don Rodrigo instantly snaps his attention back to what is going on around him. He says that foreigners have come to record his song, and that he has sung well; he shushes a baby who is crying. Then he turns to Elena, who is holding Carlos, and asks her some questions. Taruga enters the conversation and tells of his dream of the horse. Again don Rodrigo drinks *ayahuasca* and offers more to Taruga. He intersperses playing his *pijuano* with making comments and queries; long into the night the flute sounds and conversation goes on. At about 1:00 A.M. don Rodrigo plays his violin, calling once again to the spirits whose help he will need in his diagnosis and curing. He says that the tape recorder has captured his spirit songs, and that the music is good.

He then asks Taruga to put Carlos on the long *bancu*; Elena does so, and don Rodrigo examines the child with a practiced eye. He sees the source of trouble quickly—spirit dartlike projectiles, many of them, lodged in his little stomach. Taruga vaguely sees them too and sighs, *jaaaay*. He bends over the child's stomach and noisily sucks out a dart, blue mucous and all, taking it into his mouth and rolling it around. His own spirit helpers come up from his *shungu* to examine the inner substance of the dart and to take the essence from it, thereby increasing the shaman's power by the addition of more spirit substance. The shaman himself is left to dispose of the remaining substances, and he does so by blowing them into a rock on the edge of the great whirlpool that can be heard clearly from his house.

Elena now tells the shaman that little Carlos was with her in her manioc garden when she went there to harvest for the evening meal. "A stick broke and hit his side, and he fell," she said; "the wound kept hurting and now he is nearly dead." Taruga asks don Rodrigo, "Can you see the one who would do this?" "Yes," says the shaman, Elena's uncle, "I can see him; now I'll do the same to him."

* * *

The next day the gringos left, and the day after that a number of gallons of blue paint arrived by cargo canoe from Misahuallí, a cordial return of outside material previously requested by don Rodrigo for inside knowledge sought by the visitors. Taruga and Elena stayed a week, helping don Rodrigo paint a new addition to his house, where, he said, more tourists would be received and where he would make more money. Carlos became healthy, and Taruga and Elena felt that now, indeed, their merged *ayllus* were more secure within their *wasi* on the second line of Nayapi Llacta, for they had strengthened it by outside shamanic performance in a distant *llacta* by a powerful one with strong ties to Elena's *ayllu* and to the outer worlds.

SICUANGA'S JOURNEY WITH WANDUJ SUPAI

Sicuanga, María, and their children listened with interest to Taruga and Elena's report of don Rodrigo's curing session with Carlos. They reflected on the northern shamanic power of Napo "ones who know" and on the killing prowess of Jivaroan peoples to the south. Sicuanga quietly said that his father had come from the south before living on the Copataza River. Later, out of Canelos, he journeyed to the Napo area, where he met and married Sicuanga's widowed mother, Mamach, bringing her back to Nayapi Llacta and reuniting there in that new territory the ethnic antipodes of Napo Quichua and Shuar, stereotypically perceived as civilized, subjected, and conquered Indian (Napo Runa) and savage "Jívaro" headhunter in the eyes of Puyo's residents. Sicuanga was pleased that his son and daughter-in-law had been able to cure their son, who himself was the embodiment of the social and spiritual essence of the founding *ayllus,* by recourse to Napo shamanic activity no longer securely available at home. But he was also uneasy, for the reproduction of structure—the tenuous, disordered, transcendental conjoining of opposites—by human volition invariably creates rifts elsewhere.

A month later Sicuanga was clearing a new *chagra,* making a big one for María to plant lots of manioc. He expected to be named *chayuj,* host (convener or carrier), of the festival at Rosario Yacu in a couple of years, and he wanted to do right by guests and participants who would be invited and served massive quantities of manioc brew. He chopped away at a massive tree all one day until his body not only ached with each chop, but also took him at times to the edge of visionary experience with the combination of exertion and lack of solid food. He had drunk two gallons of strong *asua* (*ucui yacu*), the pale drippings that María made for him by putting a screen inside the shoulder of the pot, placing fermenting manioc mash on the screen, and taking the drippings from the bottom of the pot. Just as the tree began to fall, images flashed before his eyes of a world asunder; the forest resounded and the great tree crashed, taking four smaller ones and a mass of vegetative tangle with it. A large sector of a palm log from a smaller tree flew up into the air and came crashing down on him, rendering him unconscious.

He thought he had died, but he became increasingly conscious of still being in the forest that he sought to fell, and being pinned there by the *chonta* section and other sylvan limbs that the huge tree carried with it. He was sure that both of his legs and arms were broken, that he was useless, that he had been felled there along with the forest trees to become the home of beetle and fly larvae. María was there with her machete; she cut and cut and dragged him free, but he still hurt and he was frightened. For two weeks he lay in his bed at home and dreamed, thought, and reflected on life. His bones, it seemed, were not broken; but still they hurt. He decided to make a journey beyond the quotidian world, not one controlled by a powerful shaman human, but rather one controlled directly by the forest master spirit,

One Sunday in late August, while most of the residents of Nueva Esperanza were in Puyo to shop and visit with peoples from all over the Oriente and elsewhere, Sicuanga walked westward on the nearly invisible trail that cuts through the forest between Rosario Yacu and the second line of San Jacinto that fans out from Ishcai Tucushca Chingosimi. There he cut south, and in twenty minutes he arrived at the bottom of a high hill. Thirty-five years before, on that spot, Lluwi had given him one dart for his small, new Achuar blowgun, obtained in trade by Lluwi just for him, and had told him to kill just one bird with that dart to "prove his breath" and to return the bird to him. Sicuanga had been afraid of failure. He had walked around quietly until he saw a dozen birds, a small flock of small, lovely chattering finches. They alighted ten feet from him and suddenly he felt strong and accurate. He raised the blowgun, focused on one finch, and blew strongly (*sinchi pucushca*). The dart went straight through the little bird. He went to it and held it gently by the beak, slowly smothering it, the dart still through its tiny body, until its little eyes rolled up, its eyelids closed, and its living force with its soul departed. Then he took it to Lluwi. All this Sicuanga remembered at the base of the hill that Sunday in August. Then he climbed the hill thinking of other hills to the east, north of Canelos, near Villano, where the wooly monkeys would now be growing fat in the tops of the trees, for it was that time of the year when cool misty drizzle (*wira tamia*) came, and when they gorged themselves on a particular palm nut, becoming nice and fat.

Arriving at the top of the hill, he decided to cut his special spirit or soul trail southward. He gently trimmed the trees of their low vines, epiphytes, mosses, lichens, and parasitic plants to make a swath about ten feet across and thirty feet long. When he was satisfied with his *supai ñambi* (spirit trail), he made a lean-to facing due east. Then, taking another trail through the forest, he walked home, taking care to follow the ridges and look for signs of game. He passed through the rear end (*chagra siqui*) of María's and his *cha-*

gra, where his brother had discharged a cash debt to him a decade before by planting plantains, and wandered a bit in the second-growth forest. There, in about ten minutes, he found his *alli upina wanduj* that he had brought with him from Canelos in 1969. The last time he had drunk Datura was in 1967, deep in the forest just south of Villano, where María's father and mother and their family went on *purina* each year. After that drinking journey, María and Sicuanga had decided to migrate from Canelos back to Nayapi Llacta. There had been too many malign influences coming their way, and Sicuanga decided that he needed both the safety of a stronger residential *ayllu* structure and the security of a *llacta* founded by his powerful shaman father.

The *wanduj* was still growing, although it hadn't been cut and replaced for some time now. He continued home, arriving there in the late afternoon. As the pickup trucks arrived from Puyo and Tarqui, one by one, unloading his brothers, sisters, and in-laws in groups reflecting current alliances and oppositions, he listened to the conversations, chuckling at the various voicings of rights and wrongs, of knowledge and ignorance, of the urbanized Runa returning from Sunday market, some with new wares, some with a belly full of *trago,* and all with stories to tell about the bustling national activities so prominent in the urban center at the doorstep of Nueva Esperanza. He drank *asua* and talked softly, María and his children listening. "On Wednesday I will travel with the spirit of Datura. I'll go alone, without a helper; I will go far, to distant gardens, distant forests, to waterfalls, rivers, and faraway cities. I will not go to the United States to visit my *compadre* as my father's soul did when he died, but I will go far and learn much, and then I will return here to my *wasi.*"

Sicuanga spent Monday and Tuesday walking in the forest; he bathed in every stream and river within a nine-mile radius, thinking and reflecting, alone in the forest he knew so well. Twice he checked his lean-to, chuckling over the fact that he could have made a much sturdier one—but the hut wasn't for him, it was only to protect his flesh from rain, and perhaps from failing branches when his body thrashed around in the throes of the uncontrollable powers that would be released within it as he, as his *aya,* traveled with the spirit master of forest substances.

Tuesday afternoon his sister Marta came to see him, and Challua, his brother-in-law, accompanied her, playing his three-hole transverse flute as he approached the house. Both Marta and Challua had painted their faces with *Bixa orellana* for the visit since they were to enter the household of one about to enter the world of the forest-spirit master. The everyday ritual of arriving and being seated over, Marta asked if Sicuanga would like a small *mucawa* from which to drink *wanduj*. He thought about it and declined. "Give it to my *compadre* and *comadre,*" he said. "Maybe they will exhibit it." This trip would be his alone; he would make his own drinking cup from forest materials. Totally relaxed—at peace with themselves in the knowledge that a loved one, socially entwined in more ways than they could count with each of the people drinking *asua* in Sicuanga's house, was soon to journey from setting to setting through a network connecting them right there to other seen and unseen aspects of the cosmos—Marta, Challua, María, Sicuanga, and their children passed the evening away and then retired in their respective households.

Sicuanga arose at 4:30 A.M., bathed, painted his face with *manduru*, and left his house at 5:00 A.M., walking steadily, eating up ground and making time; by 5:30 he had broken off eight nine-inch segments of Datura, each about the size of a nickel in diameter. He replanted three of the sticks and took the other five with him, arriving at the site where he would drink Datura at 6:00 A.M., just as the sun rose. The rain forest was very misty, evanescent light coming in through the canopy the way it flickers through tiny windows and peepholes that are opening and closing. Many birds were around, but the sweat bees hadn't appeared because no exertion had been expended.

Everyone always says that one drinks *wanduj* at noon, but Sicuanga knew that this was silly—one begins the trip at noon, so he would drink soon. He checked the *sacha wasi*, swept inside it and then swept the ground outside, going on down the trail that he would soon travel with the forest spirit. He fashioned a drinking cup (*purungu*) from a palm leaf held together with palm spines. Then he turned to the great Ila tree and embraced it, saying in Spanish, "Help me, friend; help me, friend." He split the Datura stem, taking the inner green pulp, and put this, as mash, into the drinking cup, and set the cup on the frame that he had constructed especially to hold it. María appeared, together with her youngest daughter; both of them had painted their faces with *manduru* as well. It was 8:30 A.M. now, and they were on their way to the *chagra*, María said. Sicuanga accepted her explanation, even though she was about three miles off course. "Go ahead to the *chagra*," he said gently, "and then go home." He spoke softly; she looked at him and left, walking steadily, quietly, peacefully. She passed through the *chagra*, not exerting herself by working that day, and went home.

Sicuanga brushed himself off and checked his clothes. They were the ones he liked the best, those that he wore to Puyo on Sunday: red and black checkered dungarees with flared bottoms, white shirt, dark blue jacket, dark socks, and polished leather shoes. He made a cut in some nearby bamboo, catching a cup of pure water in his *purungu,* mixed the water with the *wanduj,* and drank it. Then he sat down on some palm leaves, looking eastward in front of his lean-to, and composed himself with open mind and peaceful soul. Suddenly he remembered that he'd forgotten a couple of things. He jumped up, put the barked pole six feet out in front of him, and put the *purungu* back on its rack. "How could I forget something so important?" he asked himself. Sitting down again, now slightly harried and not so composed, he remembered the time that he had organized a hunt for a special festival; rented a Datsun pickup truck; bought powder, caps, shot, fish line and hooks; and got all the way to the town of Diez de Agosto, seventeen miles from Puyo—with eight men and provisions—and ready for a two-day trek into the forest, before he realized he had forgotten his own gun! He chuckled over the memory of how he'd rushed back home, borrowed money from his *compadre,* and rushed back again to the taking-off point.

Then Sicuanga died. He fell backward into a black abyss. His body twitched, like one suffering a dreadful poisoning, and then ceased its movement. It was now 9:30 A.M. Marta and Challua arrived during the first few minutes and stayed behind a tree near the lean-to, watching. They saw Sicuanga try to get up, thrash around, and then, at 10:20 A.M., they saw him lurch up violently, crash into the frame, wham into his pole; a tree branch crashed down on him. This worried Marta and Challua tremendously. Challua lifted him, talking to him the way one speaks to a drunk in Puyo: "You're drunk on Datura, *compadre*; you're in the forest drunk, *compadre.*" Sicuanga fell again, and Challua put him in the lean-to, but Sicuanga thrashed out of it and began to giggle and look at his fingertips as though grasping tiny things. "It is good," said Challua; "he is seeing spirits." Marta examined his head and found that the skin had not been broken by the fall. "*Alli man,*" she said. "It's good." For an hour, until about 11:00 A.M. or shortly thereafter, Sicuanga alternated between complete unconsciousness and hallucinations. Flesh and soul were separating and reuniting frightfully. School let out in Nueva Esperanza for an hour, and three of his children came racing to the spot, their faces painted red; they too watched from a distance, and Sicuanga saw them, even though they were hidden. But he saw them as though through the wrong end of a telescope.

Everything described in the Datura trip to this point, I witnessed. From this point on, the description is as Sicuanga later told it repeatedly—as the story became a public discourse about a private trip—the imagery refined and transformed into exegetical text.

The pole in front of Sicuanga spoke to him shortly before noon. In Spanish, it said, *Ya viene gente,* and when he looked it said again, in a mixture of Spanish and Quichua: *Gente shamunchi* ("People are coming"). People were indeed coming, and Sicuanga could see them. His friend the pole stayed in front of him. The *gente* wanted to carry him but he couldn't move. His body was dead. *Wanduj supai* appeared before him. He looked like a great tree, but he was human, a person. He was the owner and chief of the Datura. There were now two of these *Wanduj supai,* and the pole, his friend. During the day, Sicuanga saw many things, and he moved, thrashed, fell, and was dragged back to his lean-to by Challua. Sicuanga sent Challua home before dark; like a drunk, he said in Spanish, "*Vaya no más compadre, déjeme aquí*" and Challua went home.

At midnight the *Wanduj supai* returned and said, "Walk like a jaguar." Sicuanga grasped the ground with his fingers, nails deep in the leaf mat, like a jaguar, clawing. He sat up and looked around, snarling; the *supai* said "*Jacu*" ("Let's go"). He walked a while and came to a lagoon in which there were many anaconda—Jatun Jitamare was the name of the lagoon. Then he came to another lagoon, and another. He came to three lagoons, one after the other. Whenever he stumbled, *Wanduj supai* would steady him; there were two of them helping him. He found himself walking around a lagoon, and the spirit said, "We'll go under the water here," and Sicuanga went under the water in the lagoon and came out again, peacefully. *Wanduj supai* said, "You do well." He invited Sicuanga to go to another house, a great one, almost a city; it was Sacha Runa *wasi* (rain-forest person's house). Sicuanga went into this great house and sat on a long *bancu.* The spirit was talking; it said "Here are peccary," and a tremendous herd appeared. He said "Know them," and Sicuanga did. Monkeys, game birds, jaguars, and anaconda appeared, and Sicuanga knew them. "Good," the spirit said, "*jacu.*" And they left.

Mundu puma (world jaguar, from the Spanish *mundo* and Quichua *puma*) was inside a cave in a high hill, wherein dwell the dangerous *jucta supais.* There were lots of big cats there: jaguars, cougars, and more. All of the animals were there. The spirit said, "Your friend [the Ila tree] made this. We old ones—the *capitanes,* the *curagas*—live here." Then Sicuanga returned; he wanted to drag a big tree trunk with him, back to his little lean-to on the hill, because the *supai* had ordered it. He staggered and fell, but he did not hurt himself. The *wanduj* was passing, but he could still see as *Wanduj supai* sees.

He looked at Curaray, seventy miles away, on the edge of Waorani territory, and he saw that some people there were doing bad things to him, making him ill, making trees fall on him when he cut them. The spirit showed him the exact person sending evil his way to harm him, and said to him, "You will be well, the other who is sending evil will be hurt. The next day he will die. You will live peacefully." Then *Wanduj supai* again said *"Ya viene gente,"* and María appeared. She asked what he was doing, and he said "Walking." She made him sit down while she examined his body—the *supai* agreed that she should do this. Flesh and soul were together, and he'd been falling everywhere in his state of extreme agitation.

As María examined his body, the *supai* did too, and Sicuanga saw as the *supai* saw: he saw round, golden worms, a great many of them, in his right leg. "He" (it is never clear at this point in such telling whether "he" refers to *supai* or Sicuanga—the ambiguity is deliberate) took them out by hand and put them in a tree. The *supai* said, "Let's use a machete and scrape them off," and they did; they chopped them all up with a machete. Then they inspected the other leg and did the same with the worms in it. María watched all this, though she couldn't see the golden worms.

Sicuanga and the *supai* returned to where he had drunk *wanduj* and the *supai* said, "You are peaceful and well; take your things and go home," and Sicuanga did, with María helping. Many *sacha supai runa* came too, and they arrived at his home well before dawn. But then the spirits took him back to the forest. They took hook and nylon fish line, and he tried to put a worm on the hook, to fish, but he couldn't do it. The *sacha supai runa* encouraged him. They picked the worm up again and again, but he was too drunk to put it on the hook. The spirit put the worm on the hook for him, threw it in the water, and told Sicuanga that a fish was coming, that it was biting the worm: "Pull!" Sicuanga did pull, following instructions, and he caught a fish. He caught fifteen fish of all kinds—pike-cichlids, other cichlids, characins. Then the *supai* said, *"Ya viene su compadre* Osvaldo, *vamos."* Osvaldo said to him, "You're walking now, let's go below." And they went to another lagoon and caught more fish, almost thirty of them.

Wanduj supai said, "Enough, let's go." They returned home. Then the *supai* said, "Your wife is arriving," and María came into the house carrying manioc roots from the *chagra.* The spirit went farther away, farther and farther; now Sicuanga could see his surroundings more clearly, his soul and body were returning to waking life, to everyday reality. The spirit spoke again, clearly: "You are a strong man, but no one has the power to live in *unai* where you are now." Then Sicuanga knew that he was well, that the *wanduj* was passing, that he had emerged from *unai* to live strongly in this world. If he had the capacity to live in *unai,* then he would have emerged from the *wanduj* world dead. By exercising control over the *wanduj* power of death, Sicuanga would live on.

Now Sicuanga reflected back on the conversations. The *supai* had told him: "You want to blow darts at enemies. Don't do this; repress your urge." And Sicuanga did this. Some people had already come to Sicuanga's house to be cured, even though he could not yet sing his *taquina* song. The *supai* said to him, "More such people will come and they will pay you; don't charge too much." Then the *supai* said, "Come back and drink *wanduj* one more time." And Sicuanga will, eventually. He was healed, his limbs were perfect, there was no more pain, he was strong.

Then, as an afterthought while emerging from the *wanduj* world, he saw the wife of Nueva Esperanza's schoolteacher robbing him. But he also saw his own wife enter the room just as the professor's wife grabbed his pants and shirt. María was wearing two revolvers with a cartridge belt of bullets to frighten this wife—the *zambita*. Sicuanga saw the curly-headed darker woman hide, so María took care of Sicuanga without having to kill her. Sicuanga thinks that it was really the *causai* of his wife that arrived like that and scared the professor's wife's *causai,* because María can't remember doing it, even in a dream.

Public Dimensions of Private Imagery

Selective and selected facets of Taruga's dream and his visit to his wife's shamanic uncle, and of Sicuanga's trip with *wanduj supai,* are known to everyone in Nayapi Llacta. The condensed stories that individuals and small groupings there construct of such events are in turn elaborated. The semiotic structure of knowledge, vision, thought, and reflection—which create the thresholds and portals between our culture and other cultures—together with the "negotiated proofs" of the capacity to respond that develop out of such a structure, provide a symbolic template that can be endlessly elaborated. Condensation and elaboration are complementary facets of an ongoing process of social reproduction and cultural transformation.

Sicuanga's visionary afterthought while on the threshold of emergence from the *wanduj* world has a personal significance, and a public one. María's two oldest daughters were not sent to the school in Nueva Esperanza; they "accompanied" her to her *chagra* and were well schooled in garden maintenance and in feminine fundamentals of Canelos Quichua life. Under Ecuadorian law, which increasingly governs life in Nueva Esperanza, these girls must go to school. Today in Ecuador, illiteracy is illegal where educational facilities exist. By maintaining the structure of feminine relationships at the core of Nayapi Llacta, María was breaking the national law governing Nueva Esperanza. María belongs to both worlds; she lives in a realm of ongoing antinomy.

In 1980 the teachers in Nueva Esperanza were from the Coast; they were from poor families, friendly, accustomed to living in a rural area, and got along well with the Runa there. They even brought their father to many festivities, and he, too, got along well with the Runa. Gently, by persuasion, María agreed to have her second oldest daughter enrolled in the school in 1980, so that she could gain minimal literacy. After all, she still had her oldest daughter to "accompany" her in the *chagra*. Privately and publicly all agreed that it was best now to have girls formally schooled, so "they would not be ignorant like their parents."

But privately and publicly people were also very pleased to hear of Sicuanga's afterthought. Many chuckled over the story, and retold it a number of times. The *causai* of María, a woman who as yet knows little Spanish, "saw" what the teacher's wife was really doing to María, and by extension, to all of them. She was exercising a new control, thereby taking something from them. Moreover, this *causai*—this living substance of the Runa woman—frightened the *costeña* living among them. As long as the dynamic tension expressed by the verbs *callpachina* (to make run) or *mancharina* (to make tremble) radiates outward from the allusive symbolism of insider-outsider relationships, the antinomies that permeate lifeways and social organization in Nayapi Llacta/Nueva Esperanza are tenuously contained.

The Runa here also reach out to the outside, expanding their horizons. In the next chapter we see this process from the standpoint of some prominent potters.

Notes

1. The meaning of *llaqui* may overlap with *camai* in some senses in which the receipt of the emotion of sadness constitutes "proof" of the sender's intention.

2. Specifically, though there is some variation, here are the parts of the body labeled "*shungu*": *shungu* (stomach), *causai shungu* (heart), *puscu shungu* (lungs), *rullaj shungu* (outer coating of lungs), and *yana shungu* (liver).

3. Technical botanical and chemical aspects of *ayahuasca* and its medical analysis may be found in Schultes 1972 and Schultes and Hofmann 1979.

4. The "classic" monograph on Datura is Conklin 1976; see also Schultes 1972. It is rare for any outsider to accompany a Runa from this region on a *wanduj* trip, and equally rare to be told of the entire trip. We have such depth only from men, not women. For women the experience seems less structured, and we know of cases of women taking *wanduj*, with supervision and help, in house, garden, and maybe forest (see chapter 9).

4

Connections:
Creative Expressions of Canelos
Quichua Women

DOROTHEA SCOTT WHITTEN

On a hot, humid September day in Southern Illinois, Estela Dagua and Mirian Vargas, a mother and daughter team from Puyo, Pastaza Province, Amazonian Ecuador, were giving pottery demonstrations to forty-two high-school art students from Pinkneyville. They were teaching traditional Amazonian techniques of hand coiling, burnishing, and decorating thin-walled bowls and jars. The next day they continued to show methods of painting and firing to more art classes from Belleville College and Sesser High School; about one hundred students traveled to the Southern Illinois Arts and Crafts Market Place, Rend Lake, to learn from the Amazonian potters.[1]

These demonstrations, as well as five previous ones at Southern Illinois University, Carbondale, and John A. Logan College, Cartersville, were done using materials shipped from Ecuador: nearly four hundred pounds of pottery clay from three different mines, chunks of rock-hard clays for paint pigments, big slabs of resins to lacquer and waterproof, smooth special stones for burnishing, dried bottle gourd and calabash scrapers and paddles, and tiny hair brushes to paint fine lines.

The potters are bilingual in Quichua and Spanish. They gave their explanations and answered questions in Spanish, translated by Norman Whitten. Camcorders and flashing cameras did not appear to faze them, although neither had ever experienced such public scrutiny. They had flown only in a single engine Cessna, once or twice, yet they thoroughly enjoyed the jet ride to the United States, the onboard breakfasts and lunches, and the movie *The Babe*, about Babe Ruth. Traveling with our party—Estela, Mirian, Norman, and Dorothea (Sibby) Whitten—was a young man, Sergio Gualinga, from Sarayacu, Pastaza Province. This is the territory where Estela was born and where she spent her formative years. Sergio was on his way to assist Dr. Janis Nuckolls in her translation of Quichua material and in her Quichua classes at Indiana University, Bloomington, Indiana (Nuckolls 1996:viii).

Both mother and daughter were sporting newly permed hairdos and traveling with sensible wardrobes of jeans and T-shirts. Far from the popularized images of feathered and painted Amazonian indigenous people, they in many ways resembled and blended with their student audiences. After they answered questions about what they liked about the United States, particularly Southern Illinois—and seeing deer emerge at dusk from the Shawnee National Forest was a high point—one Pinkneyville student exclaimed, "Why, they're just like us!"

During their two-day sojourn at Rend Lake, they met the Regional Director of Tourism for Southern Illinois; were taken on a tour of a nearby fish hatchery, which was opened after hours just for them; visited a new tourist facility where the gift shop interested them greatly; and received VIP treatment at the local coal mine. After the tour, the manager presented a specimen of Illinois coal to each of them. The remnants of the only gift they left behind in Urbana are still visible below my office window as I write. On the way to the coal mine, our hostess (manager of the Arts and Crafts Market Place) stopped by a Sesser High School football practice to introduce the potters to her son and other players, including a Norwegian exchange student. Mirian learned to throw a forward pass, but more importantly, they got an up-close look at football uniforms. They had been intrigued by this gear, particularly the heavy padding and the strange helmets, ever since they attended the University of Illinois football opening game against Northern Illinois University, four days after their arrival in Urbana. The next day, Sunday, they studied the Chicago Bears' televised game, and by Monday (Labor Day) they were sitting on our back porch watching the birds and squirrels and busily creating the first known pair of Amazonian pottery football players.

Estela and Mirian were accompanied on their Southern Illinois tour by Norman and Sibby Whitten and their arthritic black cocker spaniel, Charger, all traveling in a University of Illinois van packed to the ceiling with buckets of clay, a huge pile of bamboo that had been trucked to Urbana from Miami, other pottery paraphernalia, clothing, and picnic supplies. After meeting the director of the Department of Ceramics, SIU-Carbondale, and unloading bamboo and clay, we visited the University Museum. The current exhibition, *Causáunchimi!* "We are Living!" Ceramics from the Canelos Quichua (March 1–December 18, 1992) contained around one hundred pieces of ceramics, traditional and innovative, made by a number of women from Pastaza Province. Although only women make ceramics or pottery, terms used interchangeably here, the painted decorations may be derived from male shamanic visions and knowledge. The exhibition also featured works by Canelos Quichua men: decorative bead and feather headdresses and necklaces; musical instruments; and wood carvings—traditional hardwood stools, large flat bowls and pestles for pounding cooked manioc, shaped boards for rolling pottery coils—and carved and painted balsa birds, a recent commercial enterprise that draws on the vibrant imagery of the rain forest.

The potters first studied their own contributions before moving on to examine and discuss every other item on display. Ceramics by Estela included an elaborately decorated *tinaja, asua churana manga,* a large round-bellied jar in which cooked manioc pulp is fermented and stored before being mixed with preboiled water and served in delicate painted bowls, called *mucawa*. Her contributions also included two glistening, smoke-blackened cooking pots, one made to cook manioc roots, the other to brew *Banisteriopsis caapi,* the hallucinogenic drink known to Quichua speakers and others as *ayahuasca*. Additionally, she had created over the past several years a number of figurines designed explicitly to teach us and the outside world about mythical and spirit beings that are significant in Canelos Quichua cosmology. Among them were the mean monkey person, the embodiment of outside disruption; water spirit people and fish representing the power of the hydrosphere; *cachi amu,* overseer of salt, and a bracket fungus, which respectively portray symbolic elements of the myths of the origin of salt, sun, and seed beads, and of soul restoration and resurrection of man. A segment of the exhibition, labeled "Control of Power," displayed shamanic paraphernalia and items that symbolically depict facets of shamanic power. One was Estela's figurine Wanduj Warmi, feminine spirit master of the hallucinogen Datura (*Brugmansia suaveolens*). A shaman's ability to send deadly spirit darts to enemies was represented by a ceramic scorpion, its stinging tail arched high over its back, made by Denise Curipallo (Apacha) Vargas, Estela's *comadre* from whom she first learned her pottery skills in the hamlet of Unión Base. I return to design motifs and symbolism later in this chapter.

Mirian lingered over her shaman's set, a group of small figurines that depicted a patient and his supplicant or intercessor, the shaman's assistant, and the shaman, sitting on his seat of power, surrounded by his cleansing and curing tools: a leaf bundle, a rolled up cigar of native tobacco, several spirit stones, and a gourd bowl for drinking *ayahuasca*. She created her shaman's set to instruct others about Canelos Quichua peoples' abiding belief in the powers of shamanism, just as Alfonso Chango intended when he wrote and illustrated his book *Yachaj Sami Yachachina*, Shaman's Class Knowledge (Chango 1984).

By the end of the eleven-day tour, the women had given six eight-hour-long demonstrations in five locations, and they produced some thirty to forty pieces of pottery in spite of having to adjust to faster drying conditions, improvising with use of local woods to supplement the thin Florida bamboo, and repeatedly packing, unpacking, and repacking everything, including greenware. We were all tired and relieved to get home to Urbana, but after a day's rest the potters graciously accepted invitations to give a few demonstrations at the Ceramics Studio and the Department of Anthropology, both on the campus of the University of Illinois at Urbana-Champaign.

Before these sessions were completed, however, a friend and buyer from California came to Urbana and flew them back to Berkeley to give a lecture and demonstration at her mother's gallery. After a quick tour of San Francisco and a moonlight champagne dinner cruise on San Francisco Bay, they were back in Urbana within three days, bringing with them their champagne flutes. The prairie winds of late September were getting stronger and colder, practically ruining their last two attempts at outdoor firing and strengthening their feelings that it was time to return to their tropical Pastaza homes.

* * *

Pastaza Province, larger than the Republic of Haiti, or the U.S. state of Maryland, is the second largest province in Ecuador, but one of the least populated.[2] It is bordered by the turbulent Pastaza River, gushing from its sources near the Andean Cordillera de los Llanganatis to its juncture with the Marañón in Amazonian Peru. From its western backdrop of Andean foothills, the territory gradually descends to the low-lying, true Amazonian rain forest in the areas of Montalvo (on the Bobonaza River) and Curaray (on the Curaray River), and other sites further east. The province is home to seven indigenous cultural groups—Shuar, Achuar, Shiwiar, Canelos Quichua, Záparo, Andoa, and Waorani—who identify themselves as separate *nacionalidades*. Canelos Quichua constitutes the largest population; the few remaining Zaparoan speakers are teaching their language, more people are reclaiming their heritage, and they are recognized nationally and internationally.[3] A few dedicated Shiwiar are undergoing a sort of cultural revival and struggling to be recognized as their own people, distinct from Shuar and Achuar (Kunchicuy and Tsetsekip 2003). Both indigenous and nonindigenous populations maintain a strong identity as residents of Pastaza.

The major indigenous language of Ecuador, Quichua, is spoken throughout the Sierra and the Oriente, as the Amazonian region is often called. It constitutes many Ecuadorian variants of Quechua, language of the Imperial Inca, which is spoken by millions of people in Peru and Bolivia, and by some people in Colombia and Argentina. Canelos Quichua take their name from the early mission base of Canelos, which moved its locus east of Puyo several times (see chapters 1 and 2), and the speakers also identify themselves by the place-names of their *quiquin llacta,* place of origin of their ancestors. Hence, people from riverine sites such as Puyo, Pacayacu, Sarayacu, Villano, Curaray, or Moretecocha could call themselves Puyu Runa, Pacayacu Runa, Sarayacu Runa, and so on. The place name denotes the site, and *runa* means human, human being. Their language is called *runa shimi,* human speech. Quichua speakers live in hamlets and dispersed settlements in these and numerous other sites scattered throughout much of the province, but the majority live in an arc surrounding Puyo, capital of the province, and within the city and its ever-growing outskirts.

According to the official history publicized by the municipality, Puyo (from *puyu,* "fog" in Quichua) was established on May 12, 1899, as a Dominican mission to Christianize indigenous people living along the eastern banks of the Pinduc River (also Pinduj, now Pindo River) and to offer them refuge from marauding, bellicose peoples who invaded from the southern and western areas.[4] Because of its location, Puyo provided a convenient midpoint stopover for missionaries who traveled from Andean Baños via the Pastaza Valley to Canelos and from Canelos to Baños. The trip was two or more rugged days of riding on mules for the missionaries and walking for the native cargo bearers, a rest, then two more days of harsh travel in either direction.

Although there are different versions and interpretations of the data and circumstances of the founding of Puyo, there seems to be general agreement that the original hamlet consisted of a cluster of indigenous homes and the mission building (or buildings). Alfonso Chango has drawn a map, based primarily on the recollections of his mother, Clara Santi Simbaña, that shows eighteen or nineteen indigenous families living around the plaza and the priest's buildings in earliest Puyo.[5] Colonists from the Sierra were arriving in the early 1900s, and by 1931 the population of Puyo reportedly included seventy-eight indigenous and thirty-one colonist families (Ledesma Zamora [n.d.]a:74). The trickle of colonists became a flow as a road inched its way

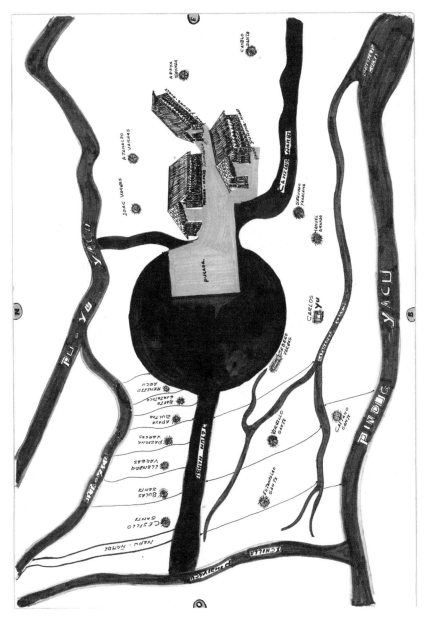

Map of early puyo. Alfonso Chango.

from Baños to Puyo, following the old foot and mule trail high over the Pastaza gorge. Begun in the late 1920s, the road reached Puyo in 1947, the same year that President José María Velasco Ibarra established the Comuna San Jacinto del Pindo several miles south of Puyo. He did so in response to a petition from indigenous leaders who expressed their constituents' need for their own territory in which to live their own lives free of now overwhelming colonist presence.

Clara Santi and Apacha Vargas, both master potters and daughters of two well-known men who were among the original founders of Puyo, have shown the Whittens the locations of their own and other families' homes around what is now the Central Plaza of Puyo. They have done this repeatedly over the years; their histories are complementary and unchanging. Apacha poignantly recalled, in a 1982 interview for a local publication, how she lived in Puyo as a child, when there were no roads or cars, people worked with machetes, and missionaries knew how to walk from Baños. Then came white colonists, gradually taking over the land with the help of government decrees and agencies (Ruiz n.d.:25–26).

Having survived progressive waves of intrusions that came and left, indigenous people finally succumbed to permanent colonization: by 1955 virtually all of them had relocated to the Comuna San Jacinto del Pindo. By 1990 a reverse process was underway due to two major factors. With every ensuing generation, pressure for land in the Comuna became more intense as each family's designated area eventually had to be divided among their children (frequently six, eight, or more) and then subdivided among their heirs. As tensions and conflicts over scarce land in the Comuna increased, the Dominican mission in Puyo was persuaded in 1981 by a few indigenous families to "loan" land in a largely uninhabited territory between a Dominican school and the Pindo River, just south of Puyo.

Before long the first residents began to rent or sell parcels of land to a number of *comuneros,* and the process of buying, selling, and reselling was underway. More indigenous families were soon moving in, obtaining lots by whatever means they could and building small houses, but still maintaining their swidden gardens in the Comuna for sustenance. A number of them were engaged in the popular ethnic art–tourist art industry of carving and painting balsa birds.[6] A pattern of an ongoing collective enterprise eventually appeared. As more family members joined the wood-carving industry, their increased (if slight) prosperity allowed them to secure adjoining lots, build houses, and bring in still more relatives. Within six to eight years, a number of extended families had recreated a small-scale version of their traditional kindred-based *ayllu* and territorial-based *llacta* systems. This area on the edge of Puyo continues to expand and now (2005) is home to an estimated several hundred indigenous people, from both the Comuna and from other parts of Pastaza, and a number of mestizo families.

The indigenous, family-based tracts of land are organized as mini-*barrios*, each with its own name such as Ñucanchi Allpa (our land), and Santo Domingo. The area has running water, electricity, phone service, and city bus service. Televisions and cell phones are common and regarded as necessities by some people. A few indigenous people there also own cars or pickup trucks.

Several Waorani families have lived in and around Puyo for years. Recently a well-known family established a nucleus in the midst of Santo Domingo. They and others working in the Puyo-based Waorani office, gift store, and museum exchange visits with relatives still living in their territories to the northeast.

Puyo today probably has the most dependable supply of electricity in the country; its source is the Agoyán hydroelectric dam, located just east of Baños and powered by the Pastaza River. Telephone, television, and electronic communications link Puyo to the rest of the nation and hence to most of the world. The steadily increasing infrastructure of roadways and air strips has greatly increased the mobility of people from outlying areas: Canelos is now two hours from Puyo by car or three by bus; and an hour's flight from Shell in a one-engine plane will take one to the farthest reaches of the province.

Access to Puyo via road was greatly expanded in 2005 when the last of seven tunnels, blasted through shear rock and constantly oozing, sliding earth, was completed. In anticipation of a flood of tourists, a huge water park was constructed behind the bus terminal, and numerous hotels and lodgings sprang up. As of 2006 the water park was popular for day-trippers, but tourism otherwise fell far short of expectations.

* * *

Four months before Estela Dagua and Mirian Vargas traveled to the United States, a different sort of journey was launched from Puyo. This was the *Caminata* of 1992, a peaceful march from Puyo to the national capital, Quito, by Pastaza Runa (used here to refer to the collective *nacionalidades* of the province, including Achuar and Shiwiar) to petition the president, Dr. Rodrigo Borja Cevallos, for the rights to their own lands and hence the right to control their own livelihood (Whitten et al. 1997). This is the subject of chapter 8.

According to *El Comercio* (April 23, 1992), as reprinted in *Kipu* (1992b:79), representatives of 148 communities of indigenous people of Pastaza Province took part in the "March for Land and Life." Among them were Apacha Vargas; Clara Santi and her husband, José Abraham Chango; two of Clara's brothers, Camilo Santi Simbaña and Marcelo Santi Simbaña; and Marcelo's wife, Faviola Vargas Aranda. Children accompanied their parents, many of whom have shared their lives with the Whittens since 1968 and the early 1970s. Once they safely reached Quito, mayor Rodrigo Paz directed them to the Plaza San Francisco, in "old," central Quito, for their meetings, and to the Parque El Ejido, in north-central Quito for their encampment, which lasted for twenty days. Their original destination, the central Plaza de la Independencia, was undergoing restoration and was closed for security, as were the surrounding buildings and the presidential palace.

While awaiting results of the drawn-out negotiations with government officials during this period, a number of marchers engaged in dialogues with curious onlookers from all walks of life. They talked a great deal about their history and their environment, which they hoped to bring under indigenous control through nationalist legal commitment, action, and compliance. They tried to communicate the meaning of mythic time-space (*unai*) and its transformation (*tucuna*) into beginning times-places (*callarirucuguna*) and through times of destruction and ancestral times into the future (*caya*), and how the future, which they were now trying to take into their own hands, is bound through these transformations to enduring indigenous history. Speakers patiently explained male shamanic power and female visionary power, the latter manifest in women's creation of songs and fine hand-coiled Upper Amazonian ceramics.[7] Clara composed songs about the March, and she and other women gave demonstrations of their pottery-making skills, using clay and mineral paints brought from Amazonia by leaders of the Confederation of Indigenous Peoples of Amazonian Ecuador (CONFENIAE).

Pastaza Runa had established themselves as an active force in the national political scene, but some, particularly Clara Santi, felt that other people did not understand the message she and her brothers had tried to convey about their culture and about the very nature of indigenous concepts of territoriality. To understand Clara's concerns, we must turn to the pottery tradition, because it embodies the symbols and knowledge that link environment to people, and people to cosmos. Today Canelos Quichua potters continue to demonstrate their remarkable adaptability to modern life, on the one hand, and a strikingly apt reference to their enduring traditions, on the other. The integration of tradition and modernity, of continuity and change, is graphically represented by their thin-walled, coil-built ceramics. We return to the power of music later.

Production of *asua* is basic to the production of their decorated vessels. *Asua* is a mildly fermented food beverage that is fundamental to the Canelos Quichua diet. Women cultivate and carefully prepare the manioc from which they make *asua* by boiling cleaned, peeled roots of this earth vegetable, which is also known as cassava, or *yuca*. Cooked roots are pounded into a pulp in a large, flat wooden bowl. Some of the pulp is then gently chewed to provide the proper yeasts for fermentation, which is necessary for storage in the moist tropics. An enzyme in the saliva, ptyalin, converts starch into dextrine and maltose. Yeasts that cause fermentation also supplement the scant vegetable protein of the starchy root.

Both spheres of activity—making ceramics and making *asua*—are the exclusive domain of women. Their array of polychrome vessels includes large jars in which manioc pulp ferments and is stored, bowls to serve *asua* every day to household members and guests, and special bowls and figures to serve *asua* during periodic ceremonies and festivals. In addition, they make blackware pots to cook manioc, other foods, spices, or drinks, and blackware bowls to serve cooked food. Unlike the polychrome ware, blackware came to be replaced by aluminum cooking pots and enamel plates and cups. By the early 1970s, it was made and used only in some fiestas.

One woman in particular undertook the task of teaching the Whittens about the old ways, about the black vessels her mother and grandmother used to make. This was the late Soledad Vargas, daughter of the famous territorial founder Javier Vargas (Nayapi), and wife of Camilo Santi Simbaña. She patiently created one after another form and explained its purpose: larger pots for cooking manioc (*yanuna manga*) and the traditional Amazonian "Pepper pot" stew (*uchu manga*); and *huayusa* [or *waisa*] *manga*, a small bowl with extremely wide flaring wall and rim to brew a tea called *huayusa* [*wayusa*], which is an *Ilex* species similar to *mate* in Argentina. She also made different styles of *callana*, eating bowls for serving cooked food; tiny bowls to hold salt and cooked hot pepper sauce; and even a *cachi manga*, a salt jar. Soledad's ancestors trekked to salt mines on the Huallaga and Marañon rivers, filled these jars with the slushy, semiliquid brine, boiled it down, and then broke the jar to obtain a molded chunk of solid salt.[8]

In 2000 people began to insist on the use of traditional blackware at their festivals and for their own participation in national festivals. Women responded by remembering how their mothers had made such ware, and older women joined the movement of cultural restoration by teaching their daughters and granddaughters these techniques. The technology of ceramic production is described by Kelly and Orr (1976), N. Whitten (1976a, 1985), and D. Whitten and N. Whitten (1978, 1988, 1989, 1993c).

Three spirit masters are dominant symbols to the Canelos Quichua and in one or another transformation come to be represented in ceramic art. These include Sungui, spirit master of the water domain; Amasanga, spirit master of the rain forest; and Nungüi, the spirit master of garden soil and of pottery clay. The first two may be male or female or androgynous, but Nungüi is strictly feminine.

Peak creativity occurs when a woman prepares an array of pottery for a festival. She draws on her cultural heritage, her ecological knowledge, and her personal observations to re-create ancient images. The festival is a time of conceptual expansion, when *everything*—animals, plants, spirits, and souls—is regarded as existing in the contemporary, living, sentient, indigenous world. Many life forces are represented by special effigy jars made with spouts to serve *asua*.

Music is integral to the festival, for it is through music that people transcend everyday life to communicate with the spirit world. Men play flutes and beat drums; the pulse of their nearly synchronized drumming represents the thunder of Amasanga, just as the tremolo buzz of the snares signifies the spirit bee-helpers that come to a shaman entering seance. Frequently, a woman makes a ceramic trumpet and fills it with *asua* to serve to the festival host or another important man. After he finishes drinking all of the contents of the trumpet, he blows it, replicating the echoing sound of *yami,* the tropical bird known as trumpeter, *Psophia crepitans.* While other men continue to drum and play flutes, the host again blows the trumpet—creating a long, honking sound—as he leads the procession of guests from one main festival house to the other, then back to the first, and so on throughout the ceremony, which may last three days. He also honks away while sitting on the bench in his own festival house. People tell myths and exchange songs, evoking imagery of the past while incorporating their experiences of the present. Sometimes, people sing silently to themselves, just as women often do when making pottery.

In addition to the household and ceremonial uses of pottery, we have mentioned several instances of women who want to communicate their cultural values to an outside world by making ceramics for museum display. There is also an important commercial value involved. Potters and their husbands have long sold bowls, figurines, and even jars left over after a ceremony. Any number of women currently produce items to sell in the ethnic-art market, either sporadically or regularly, to supplement the family income. Quite a few women sell or trade their ceramics to obtain modern medical care for themselves and their families, especially for their children. Women and some men have participated in a medical-care delivery program since 1976 (D. Whitten and N. Whitten 1985; D. Whitten 1996). Their trust in contemporary Western medical care coexists with their belief in shamanic practice.

Unfortunately, certain commercial pressures emanating from Quito are forcing some pottery production into a mold. This results in crudely made items that sell for low prices and in economic exploitation of the potters who are not fully paid until their work is sold. Potters placed in this predicament must make two or more trips to Quito, at their own expense, to be paid. Their situation is explored further in D. Whitten (2003).

Until fairly recently, all women of Canelos Quichua culture were expected to make pottery for their families' needs, but this is no longer the case. A number of young women are extending their education beyond the mandatory six primary years and are going on to complete secondary school, technical and professional courses, and college programs which qualify them to work as secretaries or teachers or to take active leadership roles in indigenous organizations. Others may spend a few years in domestic service for nonindigenous families, both locally and in the Andes, before returning home to marry and rear their own children. Pressures to migrate—economic needs, internal conflict within kin groups, and shamanic feuds, to mention only a few—may place a woman far from a source of good pottery clay. This is an incomplete list of factors that have contributed to a gradual decline in basic pottery skills of some women. The Organization of Indigenous People of Pastaza (OPIP) has attempted to remedy this perceived problem by hiring a few master potters to give courses in areas it deemed lacking in knowledge of pottery making. How successful such courses were, and are, remains to be seen. If production of ceramics has seemed to be disappearing in some places, it has been flourishing in Puyo and its immediate environs for over twenty years. The rest of this chapter deals with women who have maintained their skills and who balance traditional knowledge with modern experience to create outstanding ceramics.

A girl may learn to make pottery at her mother's knee, or she may learn later from her mother-in-law or another close female relative. The actual production of pottery varies according to immediate circumstances, which change as a woman moves through her life cycle. Creative ability is different for each woman; the highest level of skill is achieved by those whose mastery of knowledge allows them to control and project the symbolism of their universe. A potter of this stature is generally regarded as *sinchi muscuj warmi,* a woman of strong vision or images. A woman who expresses powerful images through her songs is also called *sinchi muscuj warmi*.

Amazonian pottery impressed early European explorers, particularly Francisco de Orellana and Hans Staden, in the 1500s. Some three hundred years later, the British naturalist Richard Spruce traveled through the heartland of the Canelos Quichua people and noted the constant use of delicate ceramics, even during canoe trips. On the basis of his field research in Upper Amazonian during 1916–19 and 1928–29 and additional museum research, Rafael Karsten (1935) identified the various ceramic styles of indigenous people in this region of Peru and Ecuador. He noted the fragility of the clay and added that "certain magical or animistic ideas seem to be associated with the very material used." He thought that the Canelos people in particular brought their ceramic art "to a remarkable degree of perfection" (Karsten 1935:99–100).

We now turn our attention to several *sinchi muscuj warmiguna*, women who have brought their ceramic art "to a remarkable degree of perfection."

Estela Dagua has survived a difficult early life to become the best known Canelos Quichua potter to date. Her ceramics are sold, among other places, at several prestigious galleries in Quito and at a few locations in the United States. One of the Quito shops has a second gallery in Cuzco, Peru, and in both sites Estela's creations sit next to elaborately decorated Shipibo-Conibo pottery. In her home, she has received numerous visitors from the United States, Germany, Switzerland, England, and France. Often attracted to her and her work through the publication of *From Myth to Creation* (D. Whitten and N. Whitten 1988), they come to study with her for a few days, to place special orders, or just to watch and purchase two or three pieces. A guide from Baños periodically stops at her house, unleashing a van load of curious, gawking, questioning tourists. She takes all this in stride, just as she has done with more serious trials in her life.

When Estela was quite young, probably in her early teens, her ailing father died, leaving the family without a strong kin network or solid territorial base. After several years of unsettled living, trekking from place to place, her mother remarried a Shuar, and Estela and one brother moved to Unión Base, a hamlet of the Comuna San Jacinto del Pindo, in about 1970. Shortly thereafter she married Luis Vargas, who had recently returned from working in Ambato to reside with his uncle, Severo Vargas (the second). His sister, Apacha, was currently living there and became Estela's first mentor in ceramics. Another master potter, the late Pastora Guatatuca, was also a strong influence in Estela's acquisition of knowledge and skill. Pastora, whose photographs were featured in an article in *Natural History* (D. Whitten

Estela Dagua and Mirian Vargas apply resin (*shinquillu*) to a small fired storage jar, 1993.

and N. Whitten 1978), decorated her bowls and jars with strong anaconda designs. While working on her swidden garden in 1988, she was struck in the neck by a huge fer-de-lance and died before she could receive medical attention. She did not live to see her son, Antonio Vargas Guatatuca, rise to political prominence as president of OPIP, leader of the Caminata, later as president of CONAIE, as a member of the brief governing junta of Ecuador in 2000, and as minister of social welfare for several months during the administration of Lucio Gutiérrez.

Within four years, Estela and Luis found themselves in the same situation that she, her mother, and siblings had suffered through, with no land and no strong kindred support in Unión Base. They trekked through the rugged, hilly rain forest to Canelos and then to Villano, where they eked out an existence for two more years. When Luis took a job with a petroleum exploration company in 1976, Estela returned to Puyo to live and work. Unable to find a residence, she went to live with her mother in the Shuar hamlet of Kunguki, on the Sigüín Range south of Puyo. In 1980 she obtained a five-year "loan" of a tiny plot of land in Puyo in exchange for the free, part-time labor of Luis. They built a small wood house. Luis continued to take contract jobs to cut lumber in the rain forest, and Estela dedicated herself to making and selling pottery to feed, clothe, and educate their five children.

In the spring of 1987, the landlady sent a bulldozer to knock down the house. She claimed it was to make way for a new street, but Estela firmly believed that the woman was jealous of her because she was successful in selling pottery and "had too many visitors," some indigenous, some foreign. As the bulldozer roared closer and closer to the house, Estela tried desperately to finish firing a large *tinaja* in spite of a drizzly rain; from the radio still playing inside the house came the strains of the sign-on tune of the Catholic radio station's classical music hour: "Ode to Joy."

To interfere or intervene in the conflict would have only heightened the tension between Estela and the landlady; we had to leave the scene and help later, in other ways. On our way home, we stopped by the house of Rebeca Gualinga, another master potter, originally from Sarayacu, who was noted for her vast repertoire of myths and for figurines representing the spirit world.[9] We intended to tell her about Estela's misfortune, but she already knew. She just looked at us and said "Tractor *wá!*"—the equivalent of "the tractor cometh." After Estela and children settled temporarily into the cramped quarters of Apacha, then living in Puyo, she told us "*wasi wañui, Estela wañui*"—"when my house died, Estela died."

Within days Luis returned from a logging job; he and Estela obtained permission to build on another small lot, and they quickly constructed a small wood house with a zinc roof. She had already entered the domain of *sinchi muscuj warmi* by creating representations of dangerous spirits such as *wamaj supai*, a fierce female spirit who lives deep in the thicket of giant bamboo (*wamaj*) and jealously guards it from robbers who try to steal her spiny stalks. Now, more determined than ever to succeed in her pottery-making endeavors, Estela turned out arrays of blackware, small effigies of nuts from forest trees, sets of figurines representing shamanic practice (the forerunner of her daughter Mirian's specialty), and large models of toucans, giant anteaters, deer, and tapir, accurately portrayed and embellished with the symbols of iguanid, anaconda, tortoise, and turtle.

Estela constantly strives to innovate, to incorporate something new into her basically traditional designs. On the body (*wicsa*, belly) of one large storage jar she painted a horizontal, symmetrical anaconda motif embedded in two rows of symmetrical turtle motifs which, in turn, encapsulate asymmetrical representations of spirit stones (*supai rumi*). She painted the neck (*cunga*) with vertical, alternating rows of anaconda and zigzag patterns. She also produced a series of what she called her "*ollas fantásticas*," fantastic jars. This is an apt description of their decoration. The design painted around the belly of one jar is composed totally of horizontal, stylized segments of various motifs, all floating on a soft coral-pink background. The segments combine basic symbolism of the rain forest with references to Estela's personal experiences.

While she was in Urbana, Estela made a large blackened cooking pot with a rippled or corrugated exterior surface that suggested a woman's long, flowing hair; the pot was adorned with the face of Manga Allpa Mama, master spirit of garden soil and pottery clay. She also has been technologically innovative, at one time using an old oil drum, cut lengthwise, to fire bowls and figurines. This pseudokiln burned less firewood than aboveground firing, and gave some protection against shifting winds. In 2004 she began experimenting with a small gas-fired kiln brought to her by another potter from the United States, and she continues to use it regularly, often with the help of a son and daughter-in-law.

For a number of years, a Quito gallery that specializes in Latin American art has placed orders with Estela for her ceramics; a request might be for twenty very large bowls, perhaps eighteen inches in diameter, or for a set number of figurines or *tinajas*. Estela hires assistants to help fill these orders. She may have from one to four helpers, young indigenous women who come to Puyo from Canelos, Pacayacu, Sarayacu, Montalvo, and other sites to look for employment. Estela does all the basic work for each and every piece. She coils and shapes the form, brushes on the slip and burnishes it, and then lays on the *mama churana,* the guiding lines of the predominant motif. The assistants (currently including two daughters-in-law) elaborate this, filling in the design with smaller lines, called *paiba aisana,* "its decoration," adding contrasting colors and details with tiny brushes made of a strand of a woman's hair tied to a sliver of wood.

Since 1988 Estela and family have lived on a sloping lot near the center of Puyo; from the highest spot one can look south to see the hills and small mountains rising from the Comuna San Jacinto del Pindo. On a clear day, the permanently snow-covered volcanoes Sangay and Altar stand out against the Andean cordillera to the west. As some of the ten children have grown up and married, they have settled on land adjoining their parents' home. Mirian Vargas lives just to the north, her younger sister Marta to the south. Both Mirian and Marta make pottery to sell in the tourist market, but Mirian must do her work on weekends and during vacations from her full-time job as secretary in an indigenous-run school within the Comuna.

Until recently, her brother Juan and his family lived between Mirian's and her parents' houses. His wife, Gloria Machoa, learned as a young girl to make pottery from her mother, Alegría Canelos, who in her prime was a recognized master potter from Curaray. But Gloria did not have a chance to do serious work until she and Juan settled here. She has become skilled in producing beautifully decorated small jars, *sicuanga manga,* and is venturing into larger and larger *tinajas.* Some of her ceramics display a striking continuity of designs created by her mother in the 1970s. Gloria explained that when she was a child her mother showed her a *tinaja* and told her to "remember the design." She did remember it. She re-created it when she saw a photograph of her mother's original jar in *From Myth to Creation;* she nodded and said, "This is the design I was told to remember—and I remembered." She is becoming a master potter, and as she acquires more experience and more visions of the cosmos, she should become a *sinchi muscuj warmi.*

Another blossoming potter, Guadalupe Alexandra Martínez Ampam, learned from Estela only a couple of years ago, after she married Estela and Luis's son Pedro and they joined the family compound. By the summer of 2005, she was creating *mucawas* with exquisitely painted renditions of basic Shuar and Canelos Quichua motifs.

A very well-known master potter, Apacha Vargas, learned to make ceramics primarily from her mother, Andrea Canelos. Her father, Severo Vargas, was a strong *curaga,* a Church-appointed leader who could rally his own people as well as mediate between Church-state authority and indigenous dissidence. He was a legendary traveler throughout the Ecuadorian and Peruvian Oriente, and he acquired a vast knowledge of the flora, fauna, and indigenous peoples of the rain forest. He was a noted guide for other travelers, including the Swedish anthropologist Rafael Karsten and the German anthropologist Udo Oberem.[10] The knowledge Apacha gleaned from her father was amplified by her own experiences in the Amazonian rain forest, particularly in the Comuna San Jacinto del Pindo where she and her husband, Dario Vargas, established their home and reared their many children.

During a 1982 interview with a local investigator, Apacha reflected on her experiences growing up in Puyo and witnessing its transformation from indigenous hamlet to colonist settlement to village and later to town. Her father

Apacha Vargas with Estela Dagua being interviewed prior to their departure to Quito to view the *Causáunchimi* exhibition, 1987.

had two houses on the plaza, where all indigenous people then lived, where the church now stands and "*blancos*" live. As the road inched toward Puyo, colonists arrived, became friends and *compadres* with the native inhabitants, and gradually acquired their land by giving little gifts and obtaining titles to "*tierras baldías,*" supposedly uninhabited land. Apacha experienced the pain of the newcomers' ridicule of her people as being dumb and illiterate. "Even the priest turned against us, while the colonists could all write and through writing got what they wanted from Church and State . . . they had a blanket deed. Such is history" (Ruiz n.d.:25–26). These early impressions surfaced later in her ceramic expressions.

Her creative powers are grounded in her deep knowledge of history, mythology, and natural and supernatural beings, and in her existential experiences. She has made figurative representations of powerful forces of the cosmos, such as Amasanga, master spirit of the rain forest, and Sungui, the first shaman and master spirit of the water domain, and the soul of Sungui. Her ceramic images include every conceivable life force of the rain forest, from jaguars to rattlesnakes, from tapirs to turtles. During the 1970s she made a series of insects—rhinoceros beetle, mole cricket, various larvae, and many others—that were so accurate they could be identified by an entomologist from the Smithsonian Institution who was doing research in the area. Her pottery statements about contemporary life are compelling: a worker's hard-hat, decorated with the flower of a large rain-forest tree; two ticks, one thin, one fat from engorging the blood of cattle now pastured on land cleared of the forest; and Godzilla, Apacha's interpretation of the monster that arises from the Sea of Japan to combat the destructive forces of "civilization."

Apacha's self-confidence as a powerful woman was apparent in a brief, significant event that occurred during the Caminata of 1992. As a delegation of indigenous leaders and government officials escorted the president from the Palace to the Plaza de San Francisco, he hesitated before the multitude. Apacha, her face painted as jaguar woman (*puma warmi*), took the president by the arm and, speaking in Spanish and Quichua said, "Don't be afraid of us, we are all your *churis* and *ushis*" (sons and daughters).[11] By acting as a mediator between cultures, as her father had done before, she confirmed her identity as a bona fide indigenous person and a proud citizen of the Republic of Ecuador.

The life history of Clara Santi is in many ways similar to that of Apacha Vargas. Clara spent her early years in the tiny village of Puyo and often accompanied her parents on periodic treks to dispersed settlements along the Conambo, Curaray, and Copataza rivers. Her father, Virgilio Santi, originally from the Copataza River region, acquired shamanic powers, which increased as he gleaned more knowledge of the worlds of other people through his own travels and from strangers who came to him seeking treatment. He became a widely known *sinchi yachaj*, a strong shaman, one who could "see" the cause of an illness and remove it from the patient's body. Clara learned by listening to his shamanic music and his telling of mythic and historic episodes and of his own shamanic travels. She incorporated this knowledge of distant worlds into her increasing familiarity with her rain-forest environment and her everyday experiences. From her mother, Antonia Simbaña, her grandmother, and the mother of her close sister-in-law, Soledad, she learned the art of pottery making and, additionally, the heritage of women's songs.

When Clara was about fifteen, Virgilio moved his family from Puyo to the newly established Comuna San Jacinto, and he also contracted her marriage to an Achuar youth, José Abraham Chango, better known as Paushi (currassow). They settled in the Comuna and moved periodically from one location to another. Their most stable residence was in the hamlet of Río Chico, where Virgilio and four of Clara's brothers lived. Here they reared many of their ten children as well as Clara's niece, whose mother died in childbirth. Later, after the death of their eighteen-year-old daughter, they "adopted" and reared her two daughters. They currently live on the edge of Puyo, in the recently settled territory formerly owned by the Dominicans, where they are surrounded by many of their adult children, grandchildren, and great-grandchildren.

Living among his wife's kindred, in their territory, Paushi mastered the Quichua language while retaining his own native Achuar. Clara's knowledge grew as she learned more of her husband's language, customs, and myths from him and through visits with his relatives from Capahuari, a dispersed settlement midway between the headwaters and the mouth of the Capahuari River.

Clara's experiences bridge three cultures, those of the indigenous Quichua and Achuar peoples, and of the nonindigenous colonists. The expansiveness of her knowledge and the depth of her observations over time inform her status as *sinchi muscuj warmi*. She has the rare ability to express her visions in ceramics and in songs. Her repertoire of songs includes some she learned from older female relatives and others she composes herself. Many of them merge poetic descriptions of nature with ancient mythology and with her own personal experiences. In almost all of her songs, Clara reveals a multi-vocalic reflexivity through which she takes the role of actor while observing his or her behavior, with references to herself and comments to other family members who may or may not be present. Clara sings a lesson in ecology when she enacts the role of the wife of the mythic toucan person: "I'm toucan woman, eating only nuts . . . I don't kill in eating this way . . . don't eat my flesh" (see chapter 1, pp. 13–14).

In Yacu Lubu (river otter, *lubu* is "*lobo*"), Clara sings "I'm river otter woman, I'm river otter woman," who travels the fast currents, dives deep for fish, and defends herself against threats. She continues:

> Why do they want to domesticate this otter woman,
> living, swimming in the water?
> You shall never be able to silence me.
> I shall endure saying "you can't do it to me."

Clara takes the role of Big Black Amarun (anaconda) woman in another song:

> I lie in the river, I lie in the deep river.
> I watch people, I seem to be watching people.
> I shall make the river swell up and roar.
> I shall lose the people, saying I am an existing woman.
> Very angry anaconda, very angry anaconda, I shall get very quiet.
> You come into the house, just thinking, you just come here.
> Don't you know how to lose everything?
> Everything seems to be lost.
> Losing half of the territory, I won't say it wasn't lost,
> you remember, you remember . . . it seems to be lost.
> Why shall I come to this territory like this, just saying I'm lost—you
>   remember—
> This *amarun*, black *amarun*, was angry, didn't you know?
> Now, just like this, you are lost.
> Who, who will bring, just bring you?
> Just now you lie down becoming unseen.
> Therefore, I shall return if you forgive me,
> I shall never return if you don't defend me.

On a descriptive level, this song delivers an accurate report of anaconda behavior: it lies below the water surface, watching and waiting to capture its victim. Symbolically, the song alludes to the Canelos Quichua belief that the anaconda is a corporeal representative of the master spirit of the hydrosphere, Sungui, and when this mighty power is unleashed, chaos and destruction follow. On a personal level, Clara is referring to terrible conflicts over her father's land after his death, disputes that troubled her greatly as she saw her brothers and sisters pitted against one another.

Over her lifetime, Clara has made innumerable pieces of pottery, ranging from very large storage jars to a tiny bowl from which her brother drank

Ceramic anaconda effigy made for a festival at Rosario Yacu, 1972, Elsa Vargas Santi.

Datura during a vision quest. During a disruptive period in the 1970s, when economic pressures forced Paushi and many other indigenous men to take jobs with petroleum exploration companies, Clara, her face painted (like Apacha's) as black jaguar woman, composed a song about the big monkey person, Jatun Machinmi:

> Big monkey, big monkey, big monkey, from just here he will call, from just here he will call.
> They say if the big monkey comes, he will stay, dying in a big trap, he will stay, dying.
> If the big, big monkey just comes, he just stays, remains, dead.
> What are you saying to me, little sister, what do you say to me?
> Perhaps he didn't die, perhaps he will come—we'll just see, little sister.
> Perhaps the monkey person isn't dead.
> My dear husband, my dear husband was a monkey person, perhaps in vain he became dead.
> He will come, little sister, we shall see, little sister, we shall see his face, little sister.

Ceramic oil boss, in form of a monkey person, shouting orders to workers. Clara Santi Simbaña, 1975.

She also made two figurines that reflect the dual meaning of *machin*, monkey or stranger. One is a straightforward representation of a woolly monkey, with his face blackened and his tail resting casually on his shoulder. A spout protrudes from his back, for this *machin* was designed to serve *asua* at a traditional kinship festival. The other figure has a round head placed on a body shaped like an edible gourd. One hand is raised to the baseball cap shoved back on his head, and his mouth is wide open. This monkey is the epitome of *machin* as stranger. He is the oil boss shouting orders to his indigenous workers, orders that they must understand emotionally if not literally. To Clara, the oil boss represented entrapment. His ceramic image was made to sell to tourists for much-needed money.

As previously stated, Clara and Paushi participated in the Caminata of 1992. Clara, her face again painted as black jaguar woman, composed the following song, which she sang in El Ejido Park:

> I am puma woman, I am black jaguar woman,
> walking through the mountains, walking through the rain.
> From my territory, I am just walking, walking to Quito.
> Puma woman, standing here in Quito, singing ¡hoo hoo, jijiji, meeoow!
> Standing here before the palace, I am not afraid.

Clara's father, Virgilio, was such a powerful shaman that he could transform himself into a jaguar and travel as one. According to Canelos Quichua cosmology, jaguars are corporeal representatives of Amasanga, and are sometimes

Clara Santi Simbaña and Abraham Chango reenact their performance during in the *Caminata* of 1992.

Great black jaguar effigy. Rebeca Gualinga.

known to be the mascots of Sungui. Clara sings here as black jaguar woman, Amasanga *warmi,* feminine counterpart of the master spirit of the rain forest, not afraid to confront the national government for her land and her life.

* * *

Travel is integral and essential to the lifeways of the Canelos Quichua and other rain-forest peoples. Travel is defined as movement between places, motivated by the intent to accomplish or attain something. It may be as simple as one woman, with her young children, walking to a nearby stream to fetch water for her household, an act I once timed at seventeen minutes, or as complicated as making all necessary preparations for a family to make the long trek to its *purina* grounds.

The Caminata of 1992 had a history of other journeys from Pastaza to Quito to petition the national government on behalf of indigenous citizens. One was the visit to President José María Velasco Ibarra in 1946–47, to request the establishment of the Comuna San Jacinto del Pindo. According to Simón Espinosa, some years earlier, in the late 1870s or early 1880s, people traveled from "Andoas" to Quito to negotiate a road. After marching in Quito in the civic-military parade to celebrate *diéz de agosto,* Ecuador's independence day, they returned to their rain-forest homes with promises never fulfilled (Espinosa in *Kipu* 1992b:129).

The two journeys discussed in this chapter, the Caminata to Quito and the potters' trip to Illinois, could not have been more different. One involved thousands of participants in a politically motivated, peaceful demonstration of citizens confronting their national government. The other was a low-keyed intercultural exchange, two potters teaching something of their culture to varied community and academic audiences and learning from them as well. Both trips elicited considerable expressed interest and curiosity, blended with understanding and misunderstanding, and in the case of the Caminata, intense national and international media coverage.

An article in *El Comercio* (April 25, 1992; *Kipu* 1992b:107) described the scene in El Ejido: a mixture of indigenous people, their tents and cooking equipment, with students, children, bureaucrats, workers, music and theater groups, and street vendors. Many came to observe, to learn, even to ask for autographs. Large numbers of high school students came "armed with recorders, paper and pencil, to dialogue and ask the reason for the march, or the significance of the painted facial designs." Some expected to find bellicose, naked savages. Others came to understand the marchers' necessities, to help with tasks, and to offer solidarity. Many Quiteños got the message that all Ecuadorians need to defend their natural, "pure" environments. Others did not.

In Southern Illinois, the potters seemed to relax and enjoy sharing knowledge in the collegial settings of the Southern Illinois University pottery studio and the outdoor workshops in Cartersville, Rend Lake, and Mt. Vernon. A number of North American potters, including students, amateurs, and professionals, asked well-grounded questions, exchanged information about their own work, and in general expressed amazement at what they saw being created before their eyes. Others voiced skepticism: were these women truly traditional if they wore jeans and T-shirts and made the occasional football player instead of an effigy of a mythical being or a jaguar?[12]

Similar queries about authenticity arose during the demonstrations at the University of Illinois' Ceramics Studio. Here, Estela and Mirian were impressed by the results of the potter's wheel and by a large professional kiln. Mirian experimented with both and, with the help of the ceramic art professor Ron Kovatch, "cooked" a bowl in the kiln, knowing by the color of its glow exactly when to remove it.

Appreciation far outweighed skepticism, but the burden of questions sometimes gave the women severe headaches. One day they finally asked us, "What does *whayont* mean?" The next day, after we listened carefully to questions, the answer became clear: "Why don't you paint other designs? Why don't you use other glazes? Why don't you use a kiln? Why don't you use wood instead of bamboo?" The challenges to the authenticity of Estela and Mirian in Illinois, and to Apacha, Clara, and many others in El Ejido Park, reflect the binary assumptions of the questioners. Tradition versus modern, authentic versus fake, static versus innovative, always opposites that cannot be bridged in the minds of some.

* * *

The changes taking place in the lives of Canelos Quichua people, and other Ecuadorians and South Americans in general, are part of the worldwide process known as globalization.[13] In his analysis of the contemporary transformations of "traditional" creative expressions of Australian indigenous people, Robert Layton states that he wishes to make a distinction between creative action and its consequences in the world:

> On one hand, those who are competent in a cultural tradition use its intellectual resources to build outwards into the world. They construct metaphors, similes and other tropes that play on congruencies between different orders of experience, and they construct causal hypotheses about how the world "works." Deployed in practical settings, these become assertions about the social order. On the other hand, such creative actions are produced into a world beyond their creator's control, which determines their fate as others take them up or reject them according to what is desirable or possible in particular social circumstances. . . . In a connected world, the social and natural environments promote or inhibit the effects of creativity but do not determine what the creative urge will produce. (Layton 2000:49–50)

The Canelos Quichua language has no word for art, yet Canelos Quichua people recognize beauty in the objects they create. Regardless of how others may label their creations, they have widespread aesthetic appeal. Women and men, guided by a deep-rooted cosmology that integrates shamanic beliefs, mythology, legend, history, ecological knowledge, and personal experiences, make ceramic, wood, feather, and bead objects that are imbued with meaning. When a man carves a hardwood stool, it is not merely something to sit on; its shape and decoration signal that it represents the *charapa*, water turtle, seat of power of the first shaman and ultimate source of shamanic power. A woman forms a thin-walled drinking bowl and paints a small face on it to represent the master spirit of pottery clay and garden soil.

Belief in the transition from mythic time-space to beginning times-places rests on the concept of transformation, *tucuna*. Through transformational processes, mythic time-space and beginning times-places, which span mythology, lore, and history, are projected into contemporary life. Virtual travel, through dreams, hallucinogenic experiences, and shamanic seance, are as essential to transformational processes as physical travel is in contemporary life.

The potters described in this chapter, and many others, have proved their ability to animate their beliefs and integrate them with their knowledge and experiences as they participate in an ever-changing modern world. Some ceramists travel abroad as goodwill ambassadors and give demonstrations of pottery making, as did Estela Dagua and Mirian Vargas in their trip to Illinois and California. Others tour the United States, Canada, and Europe to raise funds for their indigenous organizations. There is a strong feminine presence in indigenous organizations and in conferences that deal with indigenous rights on local, national and international levels. To date, no Canelos Quichua or other lowland indigenous women have achieved the political visibility of several Andean women, most notably Nina Pacari, former congresswoman, former vice president of Congress, and former minister of foreign affairs for six months in the Gutiérrez administration.

Through their creation of songs and ceramics, women reflect the multiple, connected and interconnected worlds of the Canelos Quichua people. They participate in many versions of modernity on their own terms and by their own choices. As they do so, they contribute a sense of enduring aesthetics to the world in which we dwell.

Acknowledgments

This chapter is an expanded and revised version of a chapter published in *Crafting Gender: Women and Folk Art in Latin America and the Caribbean,* edited by Eli Bartra. Copyright © 2003 Duke University Press. Published by permission. I am indebted to all of the ceramic artists mentioned in this chapter. They have shared their knowledge and time with us over the years, as have many others. Absalóm Guevara has added to our knowledge of both indigenous and nonindigenous people of Pastaza. I wish to thank don Felipe Balcázar R. for his gift of the book *Pastaza: Manifestaciones Culturales,* a valuable source of information that is exceedingly difficult to obtain.

Notes

1. The potters' trip to the United States to give demonstrations in five facilities in southern and south-central Illinois was supported through the Illinois Humanities Council, Grant #11273-1492, "Culture and Ceramic Art." Supplementary funds and in-kind assistance were provided by the following units of the University of Illinois

at Urbana-Champaign: Center for Latin American and Caribbean Studies, Program on Ancient Technologies and Archaeological Materials (ATAM), Department of Anthropology, and the School of Art and Design. Additional support was provided by the Sacha Runa Research Foundation, a not-for-profit corporation.

2. Areas are given first in square kilometers and in parentheses in square miles: Pastaza, 29,520 (11,398); Haiti 27,749 (10,714); Maryland 27,394 (10,577).

3. Naranjo (1977) and Reeve (1985, 1988a, 1988b, 1993–94) present the known histories of the Záparo. Some of their current revitalization efforts are described in *El Comercio* (July 7, 2005:D3).

4. In addition to N. Whitten 1976a, see Ruiz et al. n.d. and Ledesma Zamora [n.d.]a, b.

5. Chango's original map drawing and explication of it are in the Whittens' files. The map is reproduced in Ledesma Zamora ([n.d.]b:195).

6. The term "ethnic art–tourist art market" is derived from Graburn's (1976) definitions and refers to arts that are based in ethnic cultures and are sold in the tourist market.

7. Shamanic music has been recorded and documented by Crawford and Whitten (1979); the importance of women's songs among various Quechua-Quichua cultural systems is demonstrated by Harrison (1989). Uzendoski and colleagues (2005) demonstrate the power of Napo Runa women's songs.

8. The antiquity of salt jars in China, to about 4,000 to 3,750 B.P., as well as early widespread use of salt-production pottery, is reported by Flad et al. (2005:12618–19). Salt production from sea water by boiling it in pottery vessels during the Late Classic Maya (600–900 A.D.) is discussed by McKillop (2005:5630–32).

9. Carlos Viteri contextualizes the Runa spirit world by explication and illustration of the mythical ceramic creations of his mother, Rebeca Gualinga (Viteri 1993:148–57). His chapter includes an autobiographical statement by her. A number of her figurines are shown in D. Whitten and N. Whitten (1988).

10. In preparation for his 1928–29 expedition to the Aguaruna in Peru, Karsten (1935:72) paid Acevedo (Severo) Vargas US$100 to obtain a canoe and crew and to guide him down the Pastaza to the Marañón through the territory of the hostile Muratos (Candoshi).

11. A photograph of this event was published on the front page of the prominent Quito newspaper *Hoy*, April 24, 1992. For a broad survey of women's participation in political events in South America, see Kellogg (2005:127–42).

12. Perceptions of authenticity and the contradictions they evoke have been and continue to be all too familiar to Native North Americans (see, e.g., Deloria 1998; Rahimi 2005:B15). Well-documented North American cases, including debates over the Native American Graves Protection and Repatriation Act, are beyond the scope of this chapter (see Fine-Dare 2002 for a comprehensive review of this material).

13. The multidimensional "waves" of events leading to globalization and the varying rates of progression are discussed by Santos-Granero (1996:23–36); see also Smith and Ward (2000).

5

Imagery and the Control of Power

Symbolic Action and the Construal of Social Expressions

Imagery constitutes a tripartite construct of mental processes that develop in human interaction and that characterize the human psyche (D. Whitten and N. Whitten 1993b:7–8). Imagery is the corpus of images—concrete and allusive, stable and changing, patterned and chaotic, mimetic and inventive—developed by individuals from many sources in the course of their interpersonal and intersubjective interactions. People draw on this corpus to create; creativity is the execution of expression of imagery, the communication of inner imagery to others. Reflexivity is the inward-looking process that involves the incorporation, integration, and interpretation of social interaction experiences (e.g., Babcock 1978, 1980, 1987). It is a mediator between inner imagery and the outward expression of creativity and is central to the highly complex, continuous feedback that occurs in self-other interactions. Through reflexivity, social experiences of others are turned back on oneself.

We have used these concepts in other chapters, but now further elaboration is necessary as we move toward a full-scale cultural performance—the *ayllu jista*—and its attendant complex and transformational dynamics. The Canelos Quichua engage annually or semiannually in the production of certain symbols that, though they permeate quotidian life, gain a power through ritual that becomes a full-blown cultural performance (Geertz 1973; Guss 2000). In this ritual, considerable creativity and innovation occur, but the structure itself is clearly recognizable over time and across territories of the contemporary Canelos Quichua people and their ancestors. With stylized behavior, ritual context, and cultural performance, people enact the meaning of symbols and deploy metaphors, some of which, in the words of James W. Fernandez (1974), "move people to action." There is no style, no ritual, no performance, without action. It is symbolic action, symbols in action, action in symbols, symbols enacted, that we seek to understand. "Ritual action is capable of transforming the relationship between context and human subjectivity and, consequently, of transforming the ways in which messages can be interpreted and by whom" (Abercrombie 1998:421–22).

Symbols are the keys to understanding cultural associations and the construal of social expressions (Geertz 1973:5). According to Victor Turner (1973, 1974) the fundamental properties of symbols are multivocality, associational unification, condensation, and polarization. *Multivocality* means that symbols may stand for different things. *Associational unification* occurs when actors perceive seemingly different meanings as connected; processes of analogy, such as when we use a metaphor, are common when meanings are unified (see, e.g., Fernandez 1973, 1974; Sapir and Crocker 1977). *Condensation* refers to the symbol as a vehicle that represents many things all at the same time. A *"vehicle"* here is a cultural mechanism that "abridges a lengthy statement or argument" (Turner 1973:179). *Polarization* occurs especially in political confrontations and cultural performances when the meanings of an important object are grouped at opposite poles: one pole is institutional, the other is laden with emotion. As we move into style, ritual, and performance, we move to the realm of incessant, condensed, multivocal symbolic action; some of this action is "standard" or "institutional," but as it is "played with" it takes on emotional meaning, and considerable innovation occurs.

Among the first actions that constitute style are those that bring something into existence. Ordinary and powerful men must make their own drums and their transverse three-hole flutes; powerful shamans must make their *pijuano* bird-bone flutes or transact an exchange with another powerful shaman to acquire one. Women must make their blackware and polychrome-decorated pottery; they must also plant, harvest, and process the food. Men and women must think of their special songs, bring into consciousness the times and places that inspire their compositions, and compose them. All, in other words, must draw on the template of tradition to create a meaningful and evocative corpus of imagery. Creativity is fundamental here, but so is continuity with the pasts and places of enduring cultural features.

In chapter 2 we encountered the authors and Marcelo Santi Simbaña as Marcelo was making a drum. We return to this now. Any man who has made his drum can initiate a series of activities that unfold, up to a point, with remarkable consistency. He tests his drum head and snare by beating on it with a stick cut and scraped from peach palm hardwood: *ting, ting,* the pulse sound of the drum head. With his left hand he adjusts the snare until he gets a nice *tingzzzz tingzzzz* from it, the tremolo sound. The sound then is the *ting ting ting ting, zzzz, zzzz, zzzz, zzzz*—the pulse-tremolo—that he and others desire. The sound delivers an evocative imagery; it removes mundane thoughts and invokes other moods. He stands, walks in a circle drumming, and strong symbolism enters. The drum beat itself stands for the thunder of spirit master Amasanga; the buzz of the snare signals spirit movement. It is the buzz of bees coming to the opening of the pendulous, trumpet shaped *wanduj* flower; it is the opening of the human psyche to *unai,* analogous to the two tone shamanic hum. The ritual context intensifies as the man changes direction, his beat becoming stronger and stronger, *1-2-3-4 / 1-2-3-4,* with the fourth beat either absent or distinctly diminished to allow the snare to "sing" out its buzzing *muscuyuj,* soul-dream, sound. As the man moves and makes these sounds, a power force emanates from his circle, and a power shield, *lurira,* builds up there too.

Women now enter, usually a wife and daughters. They unpin their hair to allow it to flow freely, and as they toss their heads it moves back and forth, left to right, right to left; they too evoke mythic time-space; the rhythmic tossing of their hair is analogous to the two-tone shamanic hum, which is the sound of the humans in *unai,* when all other beings were humanlike. They dance to Nungüi and as Nungüi, as *chagra mama,* and *manga allpa mama,* spirit masters of garden soil and pottery clay. For both men and women thoughts of distant living and dead relatives come to mind, as the time-space scape unfolds to *unai* and *callarirucuguna,* to times of destruction and times of the grandparents. The here and now, our quotidian space-time, is transformed to stylized space-time; our inchoate everyday world partakes of pasts and futures; spirit life joins us. Men and women think-sing or sing in falsettos; the beginnings, times of destruction, and times of the grandparents all blend. The universe opens, and people play (*pugllana*) with the forces of nature, su-pernature, and culture, which merge and diverge. The play incorporates that which is "fun" and that which is "tense." The signals polarize to letting go and holding in. Inner controls become strong as outer forces are drawn upon.

This kind of stylized activity often occurs when a man returns with game from hunting. First he drops the uncooked game rather rudely in the female part of the house, an area that is now more like a rustic western kitchen. Then he walks to a resting place, a hammock or seat, drinks the warm *asua* served to him by his wife. He drinks and drinks, and when he has rested and is satiated, and while she is preparing the game as human food, he begins his *yachajuí,* festive knowledge-enactment. The souls of other animals awaken and also sing their own songs, which the man and woman think-hear. The woman may, individually, sing one or another of the songs, beginning with the phrase "I am the owl woman," "I am the trumpeter woman," or "I am toucan woman." When women do this, they clarify the experiential relationship between the predator human male hunter and the game birds or game animals, just as they clarify the vision of the predator shamanic hunter-warrior during curing seances.

Empowerment, *ushana,* is evoked and enacted in this ritual context. It refers to cultural capability, the ability to carry through a task, to make something come out as one intends. Cultural capability is aesthetic, *sumaj;* it is pleasing to the maker and to the beholder. It is nicely made, *sumaj awashca.* Empowerment also refers to the ability to break bonds of domination, to allow the world to open and unfold as it is, to release humanity, spirituality, and animality to their unconstrained conditions. *Ushana* also denotes the ability to constrain what one releases, to build the spirit shield, *supai lurira,* around the performers so that which is opened and released will not do harm to those within the circle created by the force field of ritual activity. Power may be unleashed, but it must also be controlled. The stem *ushana,* human capability and empowerment, then, brings us to the control of power.

Domination and Hegemony in Antiquity

During the period of Spanish conquest of the Americas, priests from various orders sought to "reduce" populations into manageable sites and to empower certain individuals at these sites to serve as brokers between the Church and what was known as the *república de indios,* the republic of indians. The Spanish belonged to their *república de españoles,* and they left no room for the Africans or for those who represented the Americas through "mixed blood." Later, as "mixed Americans," called *mestizos,* "hybrids," "half-castes," or "mixed bloods," emerged as dominant, the priests and curates continued to segregate the *indios.* In the Upper Amazon of Ecuador, as in the Andes and deeper Amazonia, the men and women of the cloth garbed a few indigenous leaders in power roles: *alcalde* (mayor), *alguacil* (sheriff, governor), *fiscal* (attorney), and *capitán* (captain). They also organized people into *barrios,* or sections of the territory, each the site of its own *reducción* (reduction). Each of the officers of each *barrio,* or *partido* (part, division, sector) as it was also called, was given a *vara* (staff of authority) by the reigning priest. The staffs were given out annually in church, following a sermon against savagery and for civilization. The *varayuj* (possessor of the staff), as each staff holder was called, was to oversee the governance of his mandated territory and hold the indigenous people as subalterns. When a *varayuj* was a powerful person among indigenous people, like Nayapi in Puyo or Palati in Canelos, he was called *curaga* (*curaca*). Since at least 1877—through the epochs of republic revolutions, the emergence of nation-states, and into the globalization of economic forces—the Dominican Order of the Roman Catholic Church has tried to maintain this system.

* * *

The most dramatic example of the manipulation of the imagery of the *varayujs* and the people occurs on Sunday in the set of sites located in Sarayacu. I remember being puzzled once when Marcelo Santi and I were preparing for a trip there. Trade between visitors and hosts is customary everywhere in this territory, and we were making a collection of cultural artifacts for the Museum of the Central Bank of Ecuador, and for a research collection in Urbana, Illinois. After choosing nylon fish line, fish hooks, cotton dress material and other items from Puyo shops, and glass seed beads and other items that we had purchased in Chicago, Illinois, Marcelo showed me the new black shoes and black pants and white shirt he was bringing with us. I asked him why. We would be walking from about 5:30 A.M. until 7:30 P.M., from one site to another, stopping for an hour or more in some houses, where people from other houses would visit before we were off again, likely accompanied by one or more of our hosts. The walking was hard, grueling, and always extremely sweaty; moreover, most of the time we would be carrying from twenty-five to sixty-five pounds on our backs. There is almost no flat area; we either go uphill or downhill. So, why, I asked, was he taking his finest clothes with him? "Because we will be there Sunday," he said.

He and I arose by 4:00 A.M. that Sunday, washed in Achuar Yacu, just south of the airstrip, crossed the Bobonaza River in a canoe we had borrowed the night before, and walked quickly and steadily across the plaza, past the chapel and schoolhouse, to arrive in Sarayaquillu as dawn was breaking. There Tariri (Otoñen Escobar), so named because he was a powerful shaman whose chant often ended in rhythmic onomatopoetic sequences *taríríririririrí*, had already begun drumming, *ting ting ting ting, zzzz, zzzz, zzzz, zzzz*. Soon he was joined by his wife, and then people from the Canelos family and the Gualinga family joined in. Marcelo sat quietly drinking his *asua*, as did I; he in his finery, I in my grubby jeans, rubber boots, and sweaty cotton work shirt. This is great, I thought, as similar sounds came from the distance, louder and louder, with women's cries of glee, *jijijijijiiiíiiii.*

Then as a group from halfway between Sarayacu and Sarayaquillu, an area known as Curasiqui (rear end, or ass, of the priest), arrived, a *varayuj* appeared. He began to order people around while accepting reluctantly his portion of the *asua* that was flowing liberally. He had challenged our arrival a few days before by one-engine plane and then said he would "order" the time of our departure. Maybe the *guiringu* should not be here, he said, referring to me; maybe he should stay locked in the schoolhouse until he ordered the plane to come for me. I sat quietly while the people whom we had now come to know quite well, having visited them (alone) the first time back in 1970, negotiated our continued presence. Marcelo and I kept drinking *asua,* but the *varayuj,* an *alguacil* in this case, refused the drink. He held his staff of authority on high, conducted himself like an outsider, and said "we will see about all of this when the plane arrives. I may confiscate the plane."

This was quite a jolt to me, but Marcelo and others said "don't worry about him; he is just behaving as he is supposed to on Sunday." "He is an authority of the Church." We moved from place to place that Sunday, drinking *asua* and talking, and in every site the same thing happened. Some years later, the tension went through a transformation from ecclesiastical power to secular power as an organization known as the "Federation of Indigenous Centers of Pastaza Province" (FECIP) formed. Another anthropologist who was unattached to the power fields of Sarayaquillu and without an accompanying figure such as Marcelo Santi was indeed placed under lock and key in the schoolhouse but allowed to come out on Sunday. But this is another story.

This play between strong and austere authority and the ritual contexts described here produce a weekly tension in Sarayacu that comes down through history from the tension between the Church (and later Church and state) and the powers of the native peoples. A polarization is played out every week when people are not on trek: on the one side is the hegemonic *varayuj* garbed in institutional authority; on the other is the growing play of the *yachajuí,* the force field and spirit shield of one important set of stylized behaviors to be attached to special festive knowledge. The tension becomes one within social formations of the people themselves. The forces of the eternal Roman Catholic Church meet those of the forces of the people. Native people enact and play with (*pugllana*) institutional ecclesiastic and secular hegemony, and the *varayujs* come face to face with the counterhegemony of ritual context development. The tension endures and has been transformed from the local level to the national and global political realm to sustain a defiance of petroleum and government personnel (see chapter 9).

Ayllu Cultural Performance

Once a year, or sometimes twice a year, in every setting and hamlet with a manifestation of the Roman Catholic Church, this tension is played out in a large-scale cultural performance, often called the *ayllu jista,* festival of the kin system. This festival is, by traditional anthropological theory, a centrality of Canelos Quichua culture. Aspects of it are enacted during national celebrations in Puyo and elsewhere, and the drumming and dancing associated with it—including the plays with empowerment (discussed later)—are now included on national theatrical stages where indigenous and Afro-Ecuadorian people publicly perform as an affirmation of appropriate cultural variation in the plural nation-state of modern Ecuador.

In 1976 I published this generalization, and it seems borne out by subsequent research over the past thirty years. Back then I called this a "ceremony," but I now prefer "cultural performance":

> In this ceremony distant and local ayllu members from separate llactas group together to create a mutual mystical power field devoid of spirit darts. The men are visited by Amasanga, the women by Nungüi, and both are visited by the souls of dead, distant ayllu members, and eventually by the Yacu Supai Runa. Men conjoin their souls with those of animals. Women sing or think-sing flower songs, especially of the *lumu sisa,* manioc flower, and open their minds like the opening of flowers of food-giving plants to the female-owner spirit bees. Such mind opening allows for integration with mythic time and enactment of mythic structure. While enacting such structure women pour huge quantities of chicha, fungus chicha, and *vinillu* into (and onto) the participants. Both men and women cross [gendered] domain boundaries and play with animal souls and with spirit souls and mystical presence. (N. Whitten 1976a:167–68)

This may sound pretty romantic, and it certainly is essentialist, but that is what cultural performance is all about. Back in 1973 Clifford Geertz put it this way (he was writing about "religion," a concept I now subsume under "cosmology"): "In a ritual, the world as lived and the world as imagined, fused under the agency of a single set of symbolic forms, turn out to be the same world" (Geertz 1973:112; see also Geertz 2005). He writes, "Cultural acts, the construction, apprehension and utilization of symbolic forms, are social events like any other; they are as public as marriage and as observable as agriculture" (Geertz 1973:91). Here I deal with what is public and observable, and also with what is theoretically abstractable. Reflexivity is central; the aim is to come as close to indigenous theoretical abstractions or association as I can.

The macro structure of the *ayllu* cultural performance is always the same. It may be more elaborated or it may be simpler, but the structure—the invariant reference points of a social formation that remain relatively constant after a series of transformations (Lévi-Strauss 1954; N. Whitten 1981)—is describable in this way. Agentive activities—what people do and the effects they have on the lives of those around them, and to history itself—are framed by their relationships to the reference points of this structure (see, e.g., Trouillot 1995:1–30).

Spatial Structure and the Construal of Social Expressions

The entire cultural performance is divided into two distinct parts. One part is that of the Quilla Jista, the moon festival. It is overseen by a male *chayuj*, host (or convener or carrier, also called *amu chayuj,* head or boss host), called *prioste* in Spanish. This festival is the *cari jista,* the male festival. The other part is the Jilucu Jista, the Potoo bird festival. This is the *warmi jista,* the female festival. The *chayuj* here is also a strong male. The noun *chayuj,* by the way, comes from the Andean Quichua verb *chayana,* which does not exist in the quotidian Canelos Quichua lexicon. The Quilla Jista is said to be "above" and the Jilucu Jista "below." This represents the relationships of mythic incest of the Quilla-sky and the Jilucu-earth.

The strong men who are to be *chayuj* for the coming year are supposed to be chosen by acclamation of *llacta* and *ayllu* members vis-à-vis an authority of the Roman Catholic Church in the preceding year. The ways this choice is made vary greatly. If the structure of the cultural performance described here is reduced, there will be only one *chayuj,* but his house will be divided into *cari* and *warmi* (Quilla and Jilucu). Nueva Esperanza now has a one-house, one *chayuj* festival. To expand this structure, as occurs in Canelos, Pacayacu, and Sarayacu, the male/female, Moon/Potoo dualities are simply doubled. It is also possible, as I have seen in Pacayacu and heard about elsewhere, to have both the simplified and doubled structure operating simultaneously in a Runa territory.

In creating the relatively invariant reference points, people organize themselves into groupings that are not those of quotidian life. They consist of peoples intricately interrelated with one another, but the actual organization into a cooperative *jista* group is unique to the *jista.* The relationships that emerge from the *jista* depend on many factors. The structure of the *jista* is known to all, and the activities that take place during it are highly stylized. But the relationships that are part of daily life at the end of the *jista* are unknown; sometimes they are strengthened, and sometimes they are weakened. New solidarities may emerge, but social groups may also fissure and detach from what seemed previously to be a stable organization.

For example, Sicuanga was *chayuj* of the Quilla festival in Rosario Yacu in the mid-1970s. Challua, his brother-in-law, was the host of the Jilucu festival. Sicuanga drew his assistants (Spanish *ayudantes*) from the hamlets of Rosario Yacu and Unión Base, as well as from dispersed settlements farther down the Puyo River, all the way to just upriver from Nuevo Mundo. Challua drew from Río Chico and Putuimi, as well as from dispersed settlements at Cacal Urcu and Rayu Urcu.

While Sicuanga and Challua dealt with the men of their assembled group, which aggregated people with all sorts of consanguineal, affinal, co-parent, and ethnic ties and divergences, their wives, Marta and María, were bound for a year to the wives of the men chosen by the conveners to constitute the two *jistas*. All the women so bound would be known as the *jista mamas* (or *jista mamaguna*), the festival women. This ability of people to radically alter their social ties from year to year to create a mutual power field is remarkable. Sicuanga and Challua, in this case, were in-laws, as of course were Marta and María. By dividing themselves into ceremonial factions that are mythically representative of consanguinity, affinity, and incest, the symbolic bonds of unity are confirmed in multiple ways, and those ways extend to all participants in the two opposed but united *jistas*.

Spatio-Temporal Structure

Linear time structure, as we think of it in the West, is also quite clear and well articulated. As the year moves toward its festival conclusion, which is different in different locations, but is often at or near Christmas, certain events must occur. The *chayujs* should (but they do not always do this) build a new festival house, the Moon house to the west, the Potoo house to the east. The locations reflect a territorial division into upriver and downriver, and they carry the connotation of "superior wife taker" and "inferior wife giver." The houses are supposed to be traditional, very large, oval, and arranged with ample female-side space for the eventual placing of dozens of huge decorated pots for the storage of up to hundreds of gallons of *asua*. The conveners must also clear a large *chagra* for the women to plant ample quantities of manioc. In addition, they must each plan where they and a selected group of their assistants will hunt, and they select subsidiary regions where other assistants will trek to hunt and/or fish. Territories of *other people* are chosen; in this sense the planning is similar to planning an invasion, a raid, an attack. As women plan for manioc domestication prior to the *jista,* men plan their predatory strategies.

One month before the great cultural performance, male activities stress the acquisition of powder, caps, and shot. The muzzle-loading .410-gauge shotgun (called *chiminea*), owned by every man, is checked, as are the Achuar-made blowguns and small gourd of curare dart poison, which most men also have. Men make drums and play them, as in the power field and *lurira* stylized activity discussed previously and in chapter 2. Men also play their transverse three-hole flutes with greater frequency, and shamans play their *taquinas* on their six-hole bird-bone flutes. Women, with the help of men, trek to clay mines and return with hundreds of pounds of gritty clay for pottery making. If they are lucky, they hear the song of the Potoo at night, when the moon is full or near full, *jiluuuúúú-cucucucu,* she sings. If the hearer can then dream of the site of the sound, she will then "see" a new source of clay, which will be her *jista mama*'s clay. Pottery and the rock and clay dyes come from sources that are relatively wet or relatively dry. The former are known as *yacumanda,* from the water, and the latter *urcumanda,* from the hill. Each is associated with powerful spirit forces, which women must "know" if they are to exploit these resources that bring beauty into the festival through the manufacture of pottery. This knowledge connects the woman to the feminine dimensions of master spirits Sungui and Amasanga, the latter in dangerous transformation as *urcu supai* (hill spirit), inside of which are the dangerous *juctu supais* (cave spirits).

As the two-week buildup occurs, eight named episodes emerge. Each of them features some sort of gender or territorial reversal of quotidian human roles. These are, in sequence: (1) *yandachina allu cusana,* amassing firewood on the *chagra;* (2) *allu mucuna,* masticating roasted manioc permeated and encrusted with fungi; (3) *sachama rina,* going to the forest to hunt; (4) *shamuna sachamanda pactamuna,* to come back from the forest, to arrive (hunter's return); (5) *upina shamunguichi,* you come to drink; (6) *sisa mandana,* ordering flowers; (7) *camari,* feast; (8) and *dominario,* "control," from the Spanish verb *dominar,* "to dominate." A description of these named periods, some of which occur simultaneously, help us understand the symbolic powers of Puyo Runa life that sometimes radiate into events that may, in time, even change the overall structure of domination within the nation-state of Ecuador and beyond.

Amassing firewood on the *chagra* takes place about three weeks before the actual *jista,* about a week prior to the formal two-week sequence to which all people refer. Normally, all work in the *chagra,* once the trees are felled, is woman's work. Only when plantains and maize are planted do men claim the work and crop as "theirs." In the maize planting, however, women plant black, inedible beans, *purutu pachina.* Prior to planting they burn the area selectively, thereby controlling the ash and the nitrogen fixation process. Men plant plantains. It is desirable to have huge quantities of manioc and plantains for the *jista* and, if possible, some maize. More often than not, however, the maize is harvested and eaten in advance of the *jista,* a treat for all collaborating with the *jista mamas.* During this period of festival buildup men carry firewood from different parts of the forest to the *chagra.* The quotidian sequence is for women to carry the firewood from the forest and manioc from the garden to the house; but now the men not only bring the firewood, but they also help roast the manioc, with the skin still on it. Since most of the prussic acid is in the skin (corticus), the people are consciously selecting what they know can do damage. They play with the poisonous dimensions of their staple food.

During the period of masticating the manioc with fungi, the men and women on the *chagra* "chew" the roasted manioc and put the results in a large *batea,* where both men and women pound, chew, pound, chew. The roasting of the manioc produces an orange fungus, which in a couple of days the men and women "find" growing on stumps of charred wood and on the manioc itself. They put all they can find on the roasted manioc, leave it for another day or two, covering the manioc with balsa leaves. They then take off the leaves to find a orange and white fungal "infection" throughout. This manioc is now again pounded, and the men leave the women to finish the process. They gather together in various households, play drums and flutes, enact repeatedly the stylized activity associated with drumming, and talk of the coming hunt. The women, in turn, carry the fungal manioc to the house. There they have built a filter out of bamboo, and they fit it three-quarters of the way down in the storage pot and place the fungal manioc on the filter, filling the pot to the brim with fungal manioc mash and then covering the mouth of the pot with plantain or haleconia leaves.

In about a week, drippings from the fungal manioc fill the bottom of the pot. The drippings are called *vinillu,* from the Spanish *vino* (wine). This liquid is put in bottles. The remaining *asua* is called *allu asua,* mold or fungus *asua,* and it is stored back in the decorated storage jar from which the *vinillu* has been removed. Within a day or two the fermented mold *asua* becomes literally alive with tiny orange and white maggots, and little pseudo-scorpions wriggle in it too. In addition to the *vinillu,* the women (with no help from men) choose a very bitter manioc, make *asua* in the usual way, but also filter the drippings through a screen to produce *ucui yacu* (deep or inner water), to increase alcoholic content.

Vinillu has the effect of a sherry, partly because of its enhanced alcoholic content and partly because of its cyanotropic effect. That effect, by the way, always reminds me of the "hard cider" that my grandfather in Maine would make to serve to men helping in the hay fields; a nice high occurs up to a point, and then one can become quite sick. In hard cider it is the ground-up apple seeds that provide the cyanotropic effect.

The night before the departure of the hunters is celebratory. The drumming, dancing, shouting, and laughing go on to about midnight, and then people sleep, some in the Moon house, some in the Potoo house, and some elsewhere. Important here is that the hunting groups are organized so as to overlap the two divided, or dual, festival houses. Over the next two days, the hunters leave in different groups and go in different directions. The overall strategy is to send at least three hunting groups into different territories where someone in the group knows enough from past experience to maximize game acquisition for the festival. Especially sought after are monkey troops, peccary herds, and large catfish. Stories are told here, as elsewhere in Amazonia, about how the hunters would line up, and at dawn the women would put red pepper or fire ants in their pants and shriek in glee as the hunters, now shouting, would leave in a run for their destinations. The usual ceremonial departure goes like this:

> Before dawn the hunters line up in their hunting groups, each with gun slung over left shoulder, tslambu ditty bags with soul stones, powder, caps, and shot, over their chests and on right hips, shigra net bag with fishing net, wrapped chicha, and plantains secured on the back with head tumpline, machete across right arms and blowgun in right hand. The women, decorated with black face paint force chicha on them; they drink and drink and then the women smear red achiote paint on their faces. The hunters shout *juuuiiiiiiiiiii,* and as they do the women switch the backs of their legs with stinging nettles and the men go roaring off, shouting. They usually run the first mile or so before settling into a trot for about five hours. (N. Whitten 1976a:172)

This send-off propels the men into the first day's trek, which is truly Olympic in terms of endurance.

With their bundles (*wangus*) of *asua,* some may even carry a pottery drinking bowl, especially if they are to travel by canoe. The hunters arrive in the territories within two days, establish a base camp, and begin their hunting and fishing. All game so caught is brought back to camp and "smoked" at once. Actually, this smoking involves thorough cooking by men. The meat is blackened all the way through and often is as hard as leather. Such cooking is essential because there is a tropical forest botfly that invades fresh meat and will create a maggoty mess within six hours. Sometimes the hunters encounter fishermen or other hunters (remember, they are in other territories). They explain that they are on a hunt for a festival, and if the fishermen have catfish, the hunters may trade for the fish while inviting the fishing people to attend the festival. Although such attendance is not normal, it does occur. Those who engage in these exchanges may visit each other later. Out of such contacts—festival exchanges and the subsequent generation of new knowledge of a distant territory—can come a petition for marriage or an agreement to ally if either group is threatened.

About twenty-five years ago, as we arrived back in the Puyo area after nine months in the United States, Sicuanga couldn't wait to tell us about the Rosario Yacu festival for which he was primary aide to the host. He asked if we had ever driven on the road from Quito through Papallacta to Baeza, and then on northeastward toward Lago Agrio. We said we had not, that we drive through Baños, but we had been on the Upper Aguarico years ago. He remembered that we had been there and proceeded to tell us of his trip from Puyo through Baños, to Quito, where he and four festival assistants caught the bus for Lago Agrio. He said they were hassled by police in Quito because all were carrying *chimineas* at the bus station. But they told the police they were from the Oriente and going to hunt in the forests of their ancestors in Quijos territory; the police then gave them their blessing, and Sicuanga and his comrades didn't even have to bribe them. He told of going through Papallacta in the middle of the night, through Baeza in the wee hours, and then getting off the bus at dawn and trekking north toward Cofán territory.

Listening to this story, the veracity of which we corroborated, another old friend, "Cuarenta y Uno," so known because he fought in the "war of '41," chimed in and told how he and his aides flew the Caribou (a Canadian cargo plane) to Loro Cachi, way down the Curaray River, where they trekked north to find woolly monkeys and spider monkeys in great abundance. He spoke of the danger of strange people living in the area, but not until 2003 did we learn that this region was and is, indeed, inhabited by the mysterious Taromenane, thought by many to be mythical beings (Cabodevilla 1994; Cabodevilla et al. 2004; N. Whitten 2004). Since the 1980s, treks to hunt for a traditional festival involve the modern infrastructure. The expanding knowledge of hunting and questing Runa is thereby, through native people's own creative agency, carried deeply into that infrastructure and through it to hunting territories of others, with whom alliances can and are made.

Danger exists in these hunts because not only do the hunters "invade" the territory of others, but they are also in an area of unknown spirit forces. They invade the domain of Sungui in strange waters where anacondas, caymans, piranhas, electric fish, and sting rays live; the hills they climb in search of monkeys are the dominion of the Jurijuri spirit, and the Urcu spirit. The former is a guardian of monkeys, and the latter is a humpback with thousands of magical darts to send out. Hunters sometimes become lost or disoriented, seeing things in their fatigue and confusion that, on this plane of existence, they know cannot exist. But they also know that harm comes from the unknown. All this they later report, as the festival activity keeps them in the mythical and beginning times-places where they are joined by their ancestors and the spirits they evoke.

While the men are in the forest the women settle down to make pottery, to think and think-sing about their husbands and loved ones, and to actively think about where they may be. The women work to imagine what is transpiring for these *sacha runa,* people who are in Amasanga's forest but out of their particular territories. They think of people they once knew, of areas to which they too trekked, and the markers of space and time throughout the area now brought into memory through song and conversation.

Because people from Puyo and elsewhere know that women are making pottery in earnest, and because pottery is now popular on the ethnic-arts market, outsiders come to them. Let us pause in this description to visit a scene previously described. We go to Marta's preparations, while Challua is away on a hunt with his brother-in-law Sicuanga.

Marta Prepares for a Festival in Nuevo Mundo

Before sunrise on November 12, 1981, Marta sat down on a split bamboo mat and reached for the cool, damp clay at her side. She had dreamed of water, rapidly but gently flowing around bends in a river, and of her husband, Challua, trekking north with Sicuanga to hunt game. She would rendezvous with her husband two weeks from Friday at Nuevo Mundo, six hours' walk due south, where her brother Sicuanga is *prioste* to the upcoming festival. She had come to the second line of Nayapi Llacta to get away from the *bulla* (escalating noise), as she called it, of the bulldozers and road scrapers now working only a few hundred yards away in an adjacent *llacta*. Pungent smoke from the glowing wood fire penetrated the swirling, chilly predawn mists rising from the surrounding canopied hills. She relaxed as she studied the handsome faces of her children and those of Elena—who had invited her to work in her house since Taruga was off working on a forest-clearing contract with a local *hacendado*. She looked especially at little Carlos, now healthy after his long bout with various illnesses, and she thought about don Rodrigo's house, which she had never visited, on the hilltop above the Napo River where the entry of the Arajuno River creates a great and treacherous whirlpool. She concentrated on her dream visions, seeking to integrate them with her environmental knowledge. She thought of Papaya Llacta on the upper Conambo River, where her stepmother, Blanca, had once lived. She thought of the great oval houses she had visited there on the edge of the fast-flowing, crystal-clear river filled with rocks and cut by ledges, under which lived abundant armored catfish—so delicious when cooked in a black *uchu manga* with manioc, fiery red peppers, and salt obtained by trade with the Achuar from the lower Río Huasaga region.

Segments of mythic episodes came swiftly to mind, as did images of life in forest, garden, river, and household, and she knew what she would make. As she thought and studied her surroundings, she decided she would also teach Elena, her son's wife, to make ancient blackware. "*Cachun*," she said, "would you like to make something new?" And without waiting for a response, Marta began to talk rapidly, to laugh, to imbue the entire household with the unleashed enthusiasm of a massive creative effort. Elena joined her in the center of the house; both of the women faced east, their array of clays, paints, water, and little brushes—each crafted from a bit of hair tied with cotton onto a tiny stick to make one size of line only—spread throughout the household. No longer was there a female and a male side; the entire interior of the house was feminine.

Marta spoke of mythical events, and from them she selected images to guide her pottery making: mature Quilla, the roguish moon, and Jilucu, moon's sister-lover. Looking at Carlos, whom she dubbed Sicuanga Runa Carlos, Marta said she would make *cagun*, a mythical forest monster with joined tails and two heads that eats people. She would now play with and shape strong cosmic forces in her graphic imagery, just as her father Lluwi—the bright orange-red cock-of-the-rock associated with waterfalls of the Andean slopes—had done in his shamanic trips of magical flight. She would also make an Amasanga figurine and put a little pottery baseball cap on his head as the Jurijuri *supai* of the North American oil company bosses who shouted orders that no one could understand. And in addition to drinking bowls especially decorated in imagery that conjoined her special Gualinga *ayllu* with the feminine dimension of Challua's Vargas *ayllu* via her own personal knowledge and reflection, she would make a couple of unusual red *callanas,* as the old Achuar and Zaparoan women she had known in Papaya Llacta used to do. She might take the *callanas* to the festival and serve food out of them at the *camari* or she might just keep them here.

Her special array of ceramics would be completed on the eve of Challua's return, when he would, she told little Sicuanga Runa Carlos, drum the thunder of Amasanga to begin an enactment joining soul substance that she would impart to the ceramics with known and unknown thought systems—"ours" and "theirs." Moreover, she said to Elena, she was going to make three plant pots for don Valverde, the bank official to whom Challua was indebted. She would sell the pots to don Valverde at a low price, "to make friends," but not to bind him to her as a gift does. She would also put very special decorations on these pots reflective of Challua's life situation. *Jiijiijiijiiiii* she laughed-sang, "I'll make that pot first."

Working quickly now, coiling, hand-building, directing Elena, and talking, Marta completed a small pot in the form of a *sicuanga manga.* "Years ago we used to put toucan feathers in pots like this," she said to no one in particular, and she sang a song, Urcumanda Yao Sicuanga Warmi Mani, the words to which are in chapter 1. "This is what don Valverde calls an *olla*" she said to Elena, making the harsh, voiced [*zh*] sound for the [*ll*]used by most *serranos.* "Look how I'm painting it." Around the rim of the pot she put *quingu,* zigzag, and Elena knew what Marta was thinking. The zigzag represented, in this case, bends in a river symbolizing Marta's husband, Challua (the *bocachica* fish), as he was going downriver with Sicuanga in a borrowed canoe somewhere near the headwaters of the Curaray River. Then she filled in the zigzag, and explained to Elena that the fillers were hills, *urcu,* that Challua would traverse—implying the overcoming of obstacles, the conquering of the Jurijuri, and the sheer physical strength and endurance of her dear one (*cusacú*), trekking and hunting so very far away and yet symbolically so very near. Underneath the rim Marta painted a design that Elena had seen and that she knew different people thought of in multiple ways. She looked at Marta, questioning with her eyes and lips. "*Lica ñawi,*" said Marta knowingly, referring to the eye of a rectangular fishnet used for catching *challua* when they come down feeder streams of larger rivers. And under the *lica ñawi,* in her mind the net of bureaucratic entanglement within which her husband had psychologically struggled several months ago, and which continued to hem them in from day to day, she painted the diamond pattern of the *amarun.* She looked again at Elena and said, "It is a mud anaconda, the one who comes to eat us."

The motif of Challua the fish caught in the net of a bank loan and now compelled to utilize the most powerful of destructive, devouring forces known to the Runa provided a poignant beginning to what would be two weeks of sustained activity within this household, itself symbolizing a contained universe. Marta continued talking: "We used to put toucan feathers in such pots," she repeated, "and when we had enough of them men would make special headdresses and the women would put some of the red and yellow feathers onto white beads and wear the beads as we made pottery. We called this our *tawasamba watarina* (headdress to get tied into—symbolizing here the tied-up red woman and black woman and their liberation by the toucan). The men would wear their red and yellow feathers together with noisy bird-bone and seed adornments to visit one another and carry the headdresses outward to other peoples. Sometimes they would give the feathers to a powerful shaman as payment for curing; sometimes they would trade with storekeepers in Puyo, "for a good deal of money."

The next morning Marta was busily sculpting and painting. That night she had thought about money and decided to forestall her array for the Nuevo Mundo *ayllu* festival and make even more plant pots. "I'd better feature a face of Sacha Warmi," she said to Elena, "and why don't you make a few, too. The pots with these faces bring the best price now at the Hotel Alemania in Puyo, especially when we tell don Roberto a good story about rain-forest spirits. The trouble, though, is that he only pays part of what he owes us." As she worked Marta continued to muse over her commercial production. Again she wound the diamond *amarun* motif back from the face (painting that face as she had previously painted her own, with *widuj,* the evening before) and around the pot, where it failed to join with the diamonds coming around the other side. *Ayllu shina,* she said, looking at the disjuncture, "like an *ayllu.*" Then she filled in the diamonds at their top corner, saying that the fill was *jista sisa,* festival flowers, referring to the arches that would be set up at Nuevo Mundo for the dancers to weave through.

And then she softly whispered, *sinchi amarun runa mani,* using the first-person form of the verb *to be* as the powerful anaconda speaking: "I am powerful anaconda person." Then, briefly, she began to cry as she thought simultaneously of her dead daughter, of her brother Jaime who is "oh so modern with his black shiny shoes, and oh so nasty to me when big officials from Puyo come to Nueva Esperanza." She sang a terribly sad song that made Elena cry too. "*Chaiiii,*" she said, "my house, my *ayllu,* my dear husband, my sons, my daughters; maybe someday I'll go under the water and die and live like a fish." The day wore on, the pottery array developed, and as she worked Marta came to be increasingly at peace with herself, with her life situation, and to feel increasingly in touch with the vast resources she controlled. Meanwhile, Elena sculpted a little canoe with another head in the prow. "*Aaaaiii,*" said Marta when she saw it; *uraimanda yacu puma!*

"*Buenas tardes,*" someone yelled in Spanish, and the dogs and turkeys set up a ruckus. She and Elena looked up from their tasks and saw two men and a woman coming down the hill. She and Elena sat watching until the people had come to the door, the children running first to corral the dogs. "*Buenos dias,* don Valverde," she said to the banker, *venga, descanse*—"come in, rest." The threesome tromped up the notched log-ladder. They were breathing hard and sweating profusely. With don Valverde were two blonds, a young man and a woman, each with a camera. "This couple has come from Germany just to take pictures of pottery making," said don Valverde, "and the monseñor who is educating your daughter in Puyo sent them to me." Don Valverde also drives a taxi in Puyo and knows a good deal about the Runa and their ways, being the son of one of the town's first settlers.

Reluctantly, because she knew what would probably happen, Marta got up, filled a calabash shell and a large enameled cup with *asua* mash mixed with clean, previously boiled water, and handed the cup to the strange man and the calabash shell to the banker–taxi driver and tourist guide. Sure enough, they all began to discuss her *asua* right in front of her, and then the stranger put down the bowl without drinking and started to take pictures of her, his flash popping. After about ten minutes of picture-taking and inane commentary Marta asked don Valverde if he would like to buy some more plant pots. He said he definitely would, and she said "fifty sucres each." Don Roberto at the Alemania paid from one hundred to two hundred sucres for this quality, but he would give only a part of the payment and she'd have to hound him later, or agree to paint more bark cloth that he got from a gift-shop owner in Quito (who in turn got it from evangelical missionaries working with the Chachi in the coastal province of Esmeraldas). After she painted the bark cloth it was sold in two elegant shops in Quito and at the Hotel Alemania in Puyo as Záparo art.

By asking only half the value she placed on the pots she could sell to someone to whom she was in debt at a lower price than usual and gain more immediate cash than she could by selling at the higher price. Don Valverde paid her two hundred fifty sucres for five exquisite little pots, and he and the two gringas made their own comments about what the faces must be. At least don Roberto asks, thought Marta, though he doesn't usually remember. Marta quickly took the money, went into the back room, took out a Nescafé coffee jar, and put the money in it, placing the jar back into a wooden suitcase where she kept such valuables.

Don Valverde and the couple then took leave, and Marta went back to work. In the distance she could hear the buzz of a chainsaw as Tselctselc cut logs north on the trail to Putuimi. A road was cutting in from that side of the Comuna too, and big money was soon to be made, everyone agreed. An Atlas Hercules roared overhead, just beginning its descent to Shell. Elena said, "Perhaps Ramón and Rosa are on that flight. They said they'd be visiting about now." Ramón and Rosa are Shuar, Achuar, or Shiwiar from the Río Bufeo, northeast of Montalvo, who speak Quichua as a second language and are very fluent in Spanish. Marta hoped that they would arrive today or tomorrow, because Rosa was also a master potter from another culture, and her inner universe constituted in Elena's house would thereby continue to expand right up to the *jista,* when the entire Runa world would be situated on Sungui's threshold of *tucurina,* ending everything.

For two weeks Marta and Elena worked on their pottery array. Different clays were mixed for the *tinajas* (large storage jars), *callanas* (eating dishes, both red and black), *jista puruwás* (festive bowls in the form of animals), *mucawas* (traditional drinking bowls), and cornets.

Over one hundred different designs were integrated, their explicit motifs noted, and the evocation and multiple meanings of their unfolding symbolism discussed as these women made their artistic statement with regard to the known and unknown, their world and other worlds. Over fifty songs were sung, and one night after Rosa and her husband had arrived, Rosa and Marta sang together, one in Achuar, the other in Quichua, intertwining their melodies in an intricate and lovely manner.

The private workshop of symbolic reproduction—Marta's centralization of ceramic production within Elena's house—rapidly became something of a public event. The bishop of the archdiocese of Canelos, together with two young, attractive nuns, visited there about three days before the women were to trek to Nuevo Mundo. The threesome was formally greeted, the room quickly swept clean, and they were served from excellent *mucawas.* Monseñor Calderón told Marta that her daughter was doing well in her work for the nuns and progressing reasonably well in her seventh-grade education. "She can be the *catequista* for Nueva Esperanza in another year," said the monseñor. "*Sí padrecito*" said Marta. "Moreover," said the monseñor, "we are thinking of educating her more fully in Baños so that she can return here in five years as the bilingual schoolteacher of Nueva Esperanza." Marta readily agreed that this would be fine and quickly asked, "How much money will she make?" The monseñor did not answer her, but the *madrecita* spoke up and said, "We are now negotiating with the director of the Ministry of Education. We have every reason to believe that the True Church, which has been civilizing all of the indigenous people in this zone for centuries, will be in control of all education soon. Then your daughter will be paid well for her work right here in your own community of New Hope." "*Sí, madrecita,*" said Marta. "*Bueno,*" announced Monseñor Calderón, "will you please bring me fifty *mucawas,* small ones, after the fiesta of Nuevo Mundo. They are payment for your daughter's education. We want you to learn the meaning of money. You can make these in a *minga* with other women; that way you won't forget how."

Marta had heard this lecture many times before and pondered once again the exchange system whereby she gave her daughter to the church and gave pottery to the Church so that the Church could sell the pottery at a very low price (ten sucres was what she had seen for one of her bowls worth one hundred in Puyo, when she visited the Dominican wholesale outlet store in Baños) and direct her *ushi* to do the Church's bidding. But she agreed because she and her daughter Ermilinda wanted the outside knowledge, which to now could be gained only through the formal educational system. She was paying her *jucha* (sin), she thought, just as the old ones from Canelos had to pay the *dominicanos* for their intervention in the killing disputes erupting in this zone. So she quickly countered with "Twenty *mucawas, padrecito;* I need to sell more in Puyo to help Challua pay off his bank loan."

The monseñor and his youthful escorts departed, each of them helping him up the slightly slippery path heading back to Puyo, each with the gift of a fine *mucawa* from which they had drunk. "Poor woman," said the young blond German nun, "she really doesn't know what money is."

The next day, contained in the still-expanding *wasi* universe patterned by all the elements of spirit force and inside and outside knowledge systems, Marta began to relax, secure in the thought that the life of her cherished ones was proceeding such that all would survive the coming changes. Her brother Jaime—the one with the "black shiny shoes" who had been frightened by spirit frogs long ago—and his wife stopped by to talk, having heard of the monseñor's visit. They were returning from their daughter's *chagra,* which is also on the second line of Nayapi Llacta. Shiny Shoes had had a severe drinking problem a few years before. He overcame it by becoming an *evangélico* and allowing a Runa from Riobamba to baptize him in the Putuimi River. Afterward he stopped drinking *trago* anywhere and cut back on drinking beer in Puyo or at public events. Marta told him forthrightly about the monseñor's plan for Ermilinda and how good it would be to have their own teacher in Nueva Esperanza. Shiny Shoes thought for only a second and then said softly, but brutally, "No, she will not be our teacher; let her go teach in Baños."

After that statement Marta bore up well, talking to brother Jaime's wife, her cousin whom she now called *cachun* (sister-in-law), about the pottery she had made. But later, when they had gone, after consuming a good deal of rich, yeasty *asua,* Marta cried again, *Sinchi chijnij* (such strong envy), "so many bad words." Life would be intolerable for Ermilinda if she tried to return here and take over the role of the *zambu.* Again, Marta felt the force of external control, this time applied from the inside, from our cultural knowledge. And she looked to Elena and explained: "Those from whom we learn outside ways," she said, "must come from the outside." Sighing, Elena replied, "*Así es, comadreiiiiiii,*" letting her terminal vowel trail off like a phrase of a song.

On November 26, Marta, Elena, and Rosa, accompanied by five children, bundled up all of their ceramics and trekked overland to Nuevo Mundo, arriving just before dark. They had sent fifteen *wangus* of *asua* ahead over a several-day period with in-laws who were coming and going between Nuevo Mundo, Puyo, and Nayapi Llacta, and all of this *asua* was fermenting nicely—really bubbling—in huge, decorated *tinajas* made previously by Marta in Nuevo Mundo, working with her husband's sister there. The women also carried four rum bottles full of *vinillu,* which they had obtained from the drippings of the *allu asua* by placing a screen just below the widest girth of the shoulder of the *tinajas.*

They began walking purposefully, talking, backs rigid with the weight of sixty-five-pound baskets laden with cargo, including pottery wrapped in clothes, and the bottles of home brew *vinillu.* Arriving about midday, they immediately hid most of the ceramics about half a mile away from the festival site, taking only a couple of *mucawas* to the *cari jista wasi.* They would bring forth some of the collection bit by bit, but they intended to sell most of it after the *jista* right there in Nuevo Mundo to the *comerciantes* who would come only for that purpose Sunday afternoon, before the *dominario.*

In this chapter we encounter a series of micro rituals undergirded by symbols with varied and shifting properties. Quotidian life and the break into stylized activity flow into and out of the other. We turn now, in chapter 6, to the more general description of festival and performance in cultural space, where quotidian life and ritual structure and performance become quite sharply differentiated, and where innovation within performance enhances the continuities and transformation of full-blown cultural performance.

6

Cultural Performance

Cultural performance is the culmination of stylized activity that generates a ritual context (Geertz 1973:112–14; Guss 1989, 2000). A ritual context is a setting for stylized behavior that is no more, and no less, than people coming together to perform in ways somewhat different than those of everyday life (e.g., Falassi 1987). Individual or collective drumming, or seance participation, or wailing at a wake or funeral, all constitute stylized behavior, and the particular sets of symbolic action establish a ritual context. Cultural performances are full-blown ritual contexts performed on a larger stage. The difference is that of degree, not kind (Wibbelsman 2004, 2005). This chapter continues the description begun in chapter 5 and offers interpretations in line with our observations and research and the research and serious ethnography of other scholars.

The Ayllu Festival Unfolds

While the men are away the *asua mamas* have all been busy working with their mothers, sisters, nieces, and other female friends. Marta's experiences illustrate this. Symbolism is uppermost on people's minds. If one wants to learn he or she need only hang around at this time, pay attention to what is said or sung, and perhaps ask questions now and then about what someone is thinking about or on what subject reflection is taking place.

We offer here a few examples of what we learn when we listen to songs, and later reflect on them with the help of the singer. Marta sings a song about the sun going into the river and turning it red; she does this as she looks at a sunset over the Andes and reflects on its blood-red glow through the amassed cumulus clouds that passed over Nueva Esperanza earlier in the day. She sings or thinks about songs of a great flood in which the humans were swept eastward toward the sea, and songs that belong to deceased women. In everyday life the sun is yellow, male, and symbolizes affinity, whereas the color red symbolizes consanguinity, blood, and conflict. Red is also connected to the water domain as Sungui's central color of the rainbow-angry-boa manifestation of the Yacu Supai Runa. When one thinks of the toucan colors of red and yellow, continuity through blood, conflict with others, warmth and friendship, and the treachery of the hummingbird who became the sun all come to mind. Sun yellow is the opposite of rainbow red; the former dries water, the latter is associated with rain. By merging these affinity-consanguinity colors and the attendant male-female, sky-river domains, women establish the essential quality of the ceremonial universe: a reversal of everyday opposition, segmentation, and alliance.

After the departure of the hunters the women take over the entire household, establishing themselves at the center of the world, the place from which due east and due west is reckoned, with straight up and straight down as an *axis mundi*. North, which symbolizes safety, and south, which symbolizes danger, are "either side," *chimbajta*. Facing east or "either side," they work in this center in groups, creating through ceramics an opening cosmos of mythic time-space and all of the forces of their contemporary and historical worlds. Hilarity often reigns in this realm, especially for the first week or so.

The hunters' return is filled with relief. For the past couple of days and especially the last few hours, the women in the hamlets have grown increasingly silent. And now, just before the anticipated return, there is no sound. People think of the worst that could happen: that the hunters have died or fallen on ill luck. The return is timed for arrival in the hamlet on Friday. Usually the timing is excellent, even when coordination involves treks by foot, canoe trips, bus trips, and even a safe landing in Shell in a military plane. A half hour or more before the hunters arrive a distant falsetto—*juuuuuuuuuuuu*—rends the air. Worry and fear instantly vanish. Women call back in their own falsettos, and young men rush to the edge of the hamlet or to the riverbank to receive the hunters and carry their loads of broasted meat on to the appropriate festival house. Most of the smoked and thoroughly cooked game and fish go to respective festival houses, but each hunter gives some fowl to his own wife for their own consumption. None of this meat is ready for eating. Over the next couple of days the women will chop it up and boil it thoroughly, and then chop and sort and think about later allocations. Only when women complete their work of recooking is the meat fit for real humans to eat.

While in the forest the hunters made baskets by which to carry the meat back, and they also made basket hats on which an elaborate headdress is constructed. One lucky enough to kill a toucan makes a headdress of its entire skin, with beak point forward. With parrots the gear features the ring of bright feathers. If a man has killed a monkey he uses its skin as a tie from the headdress around his chin, making him look out at the world as a feather-bedecked *machin runa*, or foreign (now victim to the hunt) person. Monkey skulls may also be taken from the skin and the head skin reduced to form a *muqui* (Quichua, from the Shuar word *mucu* or Achuar word *muuk*) or *tsantsa* (Jivaroan). These are used to adorn the hunter, and sometimes one or two are placed on a center pole of the festival house and verbally abused. Women in the festival houses store peccary and tapir meat in the kitchen area and hang smoked chunks of fowl, peccary, deer, and tapir from the ceiling of the house center. Men drink strong (*ucui yacu*) *asua,* made especially for the festival, *allu asua,* and a little *vinillu.* Becoming tipsy doesn't take long. The men laugh loudly, beat drums, and play flutes. They tell fragments of tales from the hunt. Emphases in such tales are placed on the high hills they climbed, on the rushing waters they crossed, and in the great ox bow lagoons they fished. Crucial here is the verbal portrayal of near disastrous encounters with the spirit protectors of their domains: waterfall spirit, cataract spirit, hill spirit, cave spirit, tree spirit, and so many more. They weave these spirit tales in with those of how they conquered an area and captured and killed their adversarial game for humans to soon eat.

As they tell these tales, one or two of the most successful hunters hang blackened monkey meat and the monkey-head *muquis* from the center poles and make fun of them. They abuse the acquired souls believed to remain in the area of the charred, smoked bodies. Other men join in, making crowns for the monkeys, placing cigarettes in their mouths, and otherwise treating meat and souls of the killed *machin runa* with the opposite of normal respect for the game animals. This is not meat given by Amasanga but the bodies and souls of foreign people taken from the Jurijuri. With the storage of meat and the taunting of the hung *machin runa* the stage is entirely set for the annual cultural performance. Some cry out in a falsetto *juuuuuuui;* others answer from different houses, *juuí juuuí.* And a host yells *parijú, parijú, jistata ranúuuu* (togetherness, togetherness, the festival begiiiins!—literally, "is constructed").

In each festival house, a man picks up his drum and begins to circle counterclockwise, beating the standard rhythm (usually some men in other houses do the same). Immediately other men shout the falsetto *juí, juí,* and cry out for "*asua, asua, asua!* Bring me *asua, mama!*" (*asua, asuatapamui mamuuuu*); immediately the *asua mamas* appear before the drummers with large (quart capacity or more) *mucawas* brimming with *asua.* The men drink and drink, first from one, then from another—taking in a half-gallon of mild brew with large gulps. If a man can't swallow it all he may blow out a cupful or more, in order to gulp more offered from another *asua mama's* bowl. Usually he can't drink it all down fast enough and then he gets the remainder from the bowl smack on his headdress as the "chicha shampoo." *Jijijijijijijijiii,* cry the women, as they rush back to the storage jars for more and more and more. As the drumming picks up, people shout *cajonero uyariungui,* "drummer, make a great sound." At this point a man may come forth with a small friction drum made of turtle carapace and black bee's wax to add a *breep, breep, breep* sound to the crescendoing din.

The *chayuj* takes a seat at the far end of the male side of the house as this behavior proceeds, and his wife gives him a two-quart bowl of strong *vinillu* from which he drinks a little now and then. He sometimes hands this bowl to other men or women, and they drink and return it. The women keep it full, nearly to the brim. Normally the host does not play the drum. He just sits and gives his heady drink to others in the far end of his own ceremonial house while the assistant men and the *asua mamas* drive the cultural performance along.

A brief meal break occurs before the full-scale performance really gets under way. Women hastily place cooked fowl, manioc, and plantains on banana leaves on the floor near the center of the house, and all quickly devour the food with gusto. Immediately afterward an aide or two begin their drumming-circling pattern, the host resumes his seat, and other aides of the host arrive bedecked in skins and plumage, drumming as they come. All aides now circle round and round, as their wives urge *asua* on everyone else. Other members of the *chayujs'* families and visiting friends and relatives take seats on the long *bancus* around the house. Women go from one to another, actively pouring rich and varied brews into their mouths. All swallow and swallow to avoid the inevitable splash on their heads and bodies of undrunk *asua.* Sometimes four or five women converge on one person, each continuing her pouring as the selected receiver gulps, blows out liquid, and even stands on the bench in an effort to avoid the inevitable deluge of flying and slopping *asua.*

By dark, identical behavior is taking place in both ceremonial houses, and in other houses as well, in the larger Runa territories. The central aide, who demonstrated great prowess in hunting, maintains his drumming and a calm demeanor in spite of the enormous amounts of drink he is expected to consume. As visitors to the house begin to outnumber the *asua mamas* and their daughters, other male helpers begin to serve *asua* as well. Their adult married and unmarried sons also help do this, undertaking the woman's primary role as *asua* giver. Now the drummers turn outward, letting the distant and ancient souls of the drum and house sing out. From this point on the circling pattern shifts from clockwise (outward) to counterclockwise (inward) every ten minutes or so.

In about an hour, one or two drummers each invite an *asua mama* to dance. They do this by simply breaking the circling pattern, walking toward the women with a more rapid step—two steps rather than one every four beats—and invited women quickly respond, handing their *mucawas* to other women, lifting their skirts slightly, and with both knees slightly bent begin skip-hopping, a toucanlike-hop dance, throwing their bodies back and forth and their heads in opposition so that their long hair flies to and fro. The drummers lift their knees higher and move forward and backward as the women approach them, moving from side to side, keeping their entire bodies in motion. A woman may sometimes playfully throw her hips or torso in such a way as to knock her male dancing partner off balance, to the delight of everyone.

As the drummers invite other women to dance, other men, both guests and helpers, do the same, and some produce transverse flutes to play while dancing. Each male dancer plays an instrument—drum or transverse flute—and each song played while dancing comes from an ancient soul, or special spirit soul. As the songs are played, thoughts and visions come to other men and women and are said to mingle with the domain-loosened festival house. The women are dancing to Nungüi and think-singing songs to her as well. The men are playing out Amasanga power in the face of the meat taken from the domains of Jurijuri and Sungui. Dressed as animals and birds of the forest and accompanied by the souls of those very beings, men play at assuming other identities, of other peoples, of other places, of other cultures. A dance with a woman lasts only two to three minutes, after which the man moves to another woman or resumes his circling drumming. After the flute players tire of dancing, they also join the group of circling men.

All drumming and flute-playing men are *yachaj* in this context; they represent the accumulated soul power of merged domains. They all have the power to bring visions, just as the spirits of the Datura—Amasanga and Nungüi—Ayahuasca Mama and Yaji Mama—bring visions in shamanic seance. Powerful shamans, the *sinchi yachajs,* may also join the festival pattern. When they do this they play a six-hole flute called *pijuano* or *pingullu.* This flute is normally made from the tibia of a water bird. This "shin bone" (especially the right one) is where the soul born to animal, bird, or human resides. Synonyms in Canelos Quichua for the *pingullu* flute are *rima tullu,* talking bone, and *aya tullu,* soul bone. The powerful ones play their *taquinas,* or special shaman songs, on their flute.

This song is usually whistled in shamanic seance as the breath of the shaman goes directly into the world of spirits. But in the *ayllu* performance the song goes through the flute, leaving its powers in the shaman and his instrument. In this way shamanic power is shared within the force field of the festival performance. The powerful shamans may also adorn themselves with a double *jalinga,* two strings of rattling nuts or seeds slung bandoleer style over shoulders and chests. Some even adorn this with porcupine quills that stab into the clothes and flesh while dancing. This symbolizes the ability of shamans to shed magical darts.

The noise of perhaps fifty to a hundred people talking loudly, from three to five to more than twenty drums beating in unison or near unison, snares resounding with multiple humming overtones, and two or three separate flute songs intricately weaving in and out of one another's patterns drowns out all other sounds in the area. Some women and men sing in falsetto, too, letting their usually thought songs emerge to synergize with the other powers and forces now clearly believed to be within the ceremonial universe in the festival house. Flutes and falsetto voice intricately weave in and out of the individual melodies to create a musical tapestry of counterpoint and reflection juxtaposed to the steady, tedious, monotonous drum beat-snare drone.

About a half an hour after dark, the *warmi jista* group makes its first visit to the *cari jista* group. With drummers in the lead beating away, flute players following, and then others who were in the house—men, women, and children—the ceremonial Jilucu people walk slowly, noisily, to the ceremonial Quilla people's resounding household. The sound from within the Moon house as the Potoo people approach is first that of increased snare buzzing and drum beats, for the incoming group endeavors to match a unison beat with that of the host house. Drummers enter and immediately begin to follow those circling within, matching the beats and steps. They circle counterclockwise once or twice, and then there are many shouts of *parijú, parijú, jista, jista, jistangawa,* "equal, equal, festival, festival, we are making a festival!" The assistants are all given way more *asua* than they can possible hold and the visiting host sits quietly next to the house *chayuj,* each with his quart or more of *vinillu.*

Women and men in the host house rush back and forth pouring *asua,* fungus *asua,* and *ucui yacu* down the throats of male and female visitors. As the drummers go round and round and then turn to allow the merged *cari-warmi,* Moon-Potoo vision-producing snares to resound outwards, more and more shouts and falsetto shrieks are voiced, for now the visiting drummers are leading the host drummers in sending the visions outward. Stylized collective action described earlier takes place: male drumming and flute playing, couples dancing and sometimes singing, female *asua* shampooing, and circling. In about three-quarters of an hour the Jilucu *jista* group prepares to leave, and drummers move toward the door. At this time there is a veritable deluge of brew rushed their way and most, if not all, get a thorough soaking in the life-giving fluid as they finally escape and move back toward their ceremonial house. There they resume their circling, and await the reciprocal visit of the Moon group. In about ten minutes the visit takes place, and the scene is acted out again as above with the roles reversed.

These reciprocal visits go on until about 10:00 P.M. or midnight, when many go to their respective households to snooze a bit and receive vivid dreams. But person after person talks, yells, and some *jisteros* continue to beat drums and come and go from the ceremonial houses until 1:00 A.M. No one can sleep for more than ten or fifteen minutes at a time because of the noise—and no one wants to. Domains are merged, souls are everywhere, spirits are present, and one could easily lose control of his or her own or acquired souls. Dreams or dream images (*muscui*) are received as they arrive (*pactana*), and they are commented upon; jokes are made and drums are beaten and songs are sung. By 3:00 A.M. even those rendered unconscious by alcohol and fatigue are up again, and the noise level rises all over the central Runa territory. Drums are beaten, flutes played, and animated conversations take place until 4:30 A.M. Around 5:00 A.M. a hearty meal and plenty of warm *asua* is served in each house—not the strong stuff, but the good solid nourishing variety. Festival assistants go to their respective ceremonial houses, and the second day of the festival as great cultural performance is underway.

Saturday from about 11:00 A.M. on is the fifth phase of the kin festival, the *shamuna shamunguichi,* "you come to drink." It is followed in mid-afternoon by the *sisa mandana,* "ordering of flowers." By midmorning of Saturday people wind down, having played with the forces of their universe all night and into the morning hours. Word has spread far and wide that a festival is being held today, and visitors dressed in nice clothes will soon arrive.

The first visitors to arrive are usually Runa from territories a few hours away by canoe, trail, or gravel and mud road. Some come dressed as festival participants and move into the circling, visiting activity. Others come dressed for Sunday in Puyo. All are treated the same by the *asua mamas*. They are given huge quantities of *asua* to drink, the *mamas* force and force the milder *asua* down their gullets, pushing the large and small drinking bowls with no mercy. No way can one take a breath or swallow slowly. One must gulp and gulp and breathe through one's nose, and try to drink from three to six bowls almost at the same time. As one slows, the *asua* is dumped on his or her head. The women servers take special glee in dumping *asua* on those who are especially well dressed. "He who walks like Amasanga must be ready to get rained on," they shout. The conveners of the two houses continue to sit on the anaconda bench, each with a huge *mucawa* of *vinillu*. They get up in a tipsy but dignified manner now and then, walk to a man or woman, and hold the huge *mucawa* for him or her to drink. As they do this, the host's wife, as *chayuj warmi*, takes a small *mucawa* that she has made and dips from the big bowl and scurries around serving person after person after person. She is back and forth and round and round. He is rooted, nearly, on the anaconda bench, and moves sluggishly to one, then another, and then sits again.

The pottery cornets are filled with *asua* and given to the conveners by a sister or mother. The man sets his large bowl of *vinillu* aside, takes the cornet and drinks all the *asua* in it, through its bell, which may be shaped as a Datura flower. Then he begins to blow: *hooonk, hoooonk,* and as he does he may get up and circle. *Hooonk, hoooonk,* joins the sounds of *ting ting ting ting, zzzz, zzzz, zzzz, zzzz,* the female shouts of *jijijijííiiiii.*

Some men sing in falsettos; others play their transverse flutes thinking about the words that go with the melody. Women think of those words, too. Some man always grabs the big *batea* used to pound and masticate the manioc and whacks it with a stick that he takes from anywhere. *Whack! Whack!* and then peels of laughter. The wood for the *batea* is cut from Amasanga's forest from one of the huge trees with flying buttresses, either the Ila tree (the one embraced by Sicuanga on his trip with the Wanduj Supai) or the Uchuputu tree, from which "silk-cotton" (kapok) for the blowgun darts comes. During heavy rain storms, the Ila Supai, or Uchuputu Supai, Amasanga transformations, come from the tree and whack it with a great stick.

The playful Runa symbolize this forest spirit within the food preparation apparatus within the festival house. One or two shamans enter, playing their *taquina* songs on their vertical bird-bone flutes, but no curing or killing spirits are summoned. This is not a time of shamanic danger. The universe is open, strangers and friends are arriving, and spirits are already all around. Heads are buzzing. It is full-scale performative tension-filled play time. The play goes on in one house, then the other, then back again. Back and forth between the male and female, Moon and Potoo domains and inside each round and round, first one way, then another, one way, then another. Sometimes, at this point, a man produces a small turtle carapace, the underside of which has been tarred with black bees wax and chicle; this is a friction drum played by pulling the thumb over the tarred surface to produce *breep, breep, breep* sounds, said to be forest spirits in festival mode.

More people arrive to watch and stay on the fringe of the *jista*, on the edge of the plaza of the hamlet. They don't want to get too close to this chaotic event, but they are curious. Some officials from Puyo attend, and come to sit and drink for ten minutes, are reluctant to drink *asua* and are silent. They are given as much as they can hold; then, since they know how to do this from much previous experience, they get up and literally run for the door before they can be doused more than once. Once a visiting anthropologist, thirsty from his hour-long fast walk, let everyone know how much he liked to drink *asua*. "Bring me brew!" he yelled. His enthusiasm to drink more and more rather than the reluctance anticipated by the women presented a wonderful challenge to them. Within ten minutes he had been forced to gulp about a gallon and a half of five different *asuas*, including the foul tasting *allu asua*. He then staggered outside and barfed onto the side of the *cari jista wasi*. *Jiji-jijijiiiiii* squealed the *asua mamas*, "this one was really fun to serve!"

Arriving indigenous people now drop bundles of flowers in a large basket next to the conveners. A very few master potters may have made special large *mucawas* with built-in "shelves" to hold the flowers. They are for the Christian God. Women immediately converge on the male flower giver, trying to make him or her drink several quarts of *asua* and soaking the giver with the sticky, clinging, thick liquid. Women and girls move quickly to the kitchen area to see if they can help, and to hide from the shampooing. As one house, then the other, fill up with seventy-five people or so, the drummers get some respite from the gallons of forced guzzling, for everyone is too busy pushing *asua* on the newcomers to worry about the actual participants.

Things calm down some by 2:00 P.M. or so in the afternoon. Between 3:00 and 5:00 the conveners and their aides go to nearby gardens, second-growth forest, or riverside to cut tarapoto palm fronds and gather their own flowers. The fronds are to construct arches as directed by the Dominican order, and the flowers will adorn them. As they return, women mob them and make them fight their way back into the houses, and even onto the plaza where the arches are to be erected. By celebrating the Church's dominance, feminine resistance is dramatically encountered. Then the arches are set up without ceremony. The festival goes on as described, with crescendos and decrescendos depending on innumerable intrusions and interests. People say they literally dream on their feet, experiencing altered realities in the company of their human, soul, and spirit mates.

Sunday begins with the preparations for the *camari,* feast; it moves toward the arrival of the priest and nuns. The priest will say Mass, he and his entourage—which may include foreign tourists or bureaucrats and Ecuadorian officials—will be fed. In some areas, such as Pacayacu and Sarayacu, there will be marriage ceremonies. Late in the day, from an ecclesiastical point of view, all hell breaks loose as the *dominario* takes place.

Mass and Camari: Celebration of Christian Dominance and Chastisement of Savagery

There are two feasts: one for the indigenous people, the other for the priest and his entourage of outsiders. In the first feast, which may begin as early as 10:00 A.M., banana leaves are laid on long benches with lower benches along each side. Then *callanas* with steaming meat and fish soup with grated plantain mush are put down on the table, and boiled plantains and manioc are laid along side the bowls to present each participant, outsider and insider, with a bowl of chowder and as much starch as she or he cares to eat. People are invited by name to come, sit, eat. Some people insult the food, calling it mutton (sheep meat—*carne de burrigú,* which, according to Pierre [1983:249], the Dominicans once tried unsuccessfully to raise for their own consumption in Canelos). This is a rejection of the feast of the Church and the food of the *curas.* As this goes on, those serving ask each partaker to provide a *jucha.* This is a cash payment for the Dominican Church. It refers to the "blame," or "sin," a condition in which the Church considers the people to exist. People resist this payment and insult the food even more. As they do so, some prominent men and women of the festival reach into the bowls and slap food on the heads of the diners. There is much tension here; hungry people eat quickly, get up, and resume all of the festival activities of drumming, dancing, playing flutes, drinking, and singing.

This feast is interrupted when the priest rings the bell on the chapel, if there is one, to call everyone to Mass. Into the chapel pour the indigenous people, some covered with *asua,* some exhausted, most partially inebriated. Women have previously placed effigies with small spouts on the altar (which may have been hastily made of split bamboo), into which candles have been placed and lit. Decorated pottery jars of flowers are also there, the symbolism on the jars representing the powerful forces of the Runa universe; especially prominent are images of the anaconda, jaguar, and small coral snake. The priest blesses the sacred table and unfolds his apparatus, but before he offers Mass he chastises the people: he tells them they are drunkards and dope takers. They spend time with their *wanduj* and *ayahuasca* instead of working for their wives. He says that the festival is slothful and savage, and that by next year he expects to see some improvement in civilized activity.

The most powerful of the indigenous men, including the conveners of the festival and the shamans, stand at the front and agree with the priest. "*Sí padrecito,*" they say, "what you say is true!" "I am an awful bad sinner." "Who wants to be *varayuj* for next year?" the priest asks, and if he doesn't get an answer he makes his own designation. Then the next year's conveners step forth and claim they will give the biggest *jista* ever, for the Church, if they are named, and the priest names them, making no attempt to note whom

Festival drinking vessel in form of Curaray Chapel. Inéz Padilla.

he is naming. Now the priest sets out his wafer and his wine and begins to lecture about the body of Christ and his blood, including the mysterious reality of transubstantiation and how what we are all about to eat and drink is actually the body and blood of Christ the Redeemer. "This is the great *transformación*," he preaches, "something that you don't understand." At this point most people cringe and move to the rear, and many leave. The entourage partakes, but the indigenous people do not. Eating monkey meat and abusing it as flesh of the foreign monkey person is one thing; eating Christ the dead (and uncooked) *cristiano* is quite another. Over 120 years ago Pierre (1983:198) wrote that Runa told the priest at Canelos that they refused to eat the host of Christ because they were Sacha Runa.

The second feast takes place right after Mass. Usually the priest and his entourage are trying to leave, but the conveners are insistent. "This feast is only for you," they are told. They are seated at a regular quadrangular table. Usually they drink very little *asua* and normally nothing is dumped on them. They are served a bowl of meat or fish soup with grated plantain gruel and some boiled chicken, the latter of which delights them. Then each is given a hunk of blackened meat, just as it came from the forest. This is not meat prepared by women as food by boiling but rather a whole hunk of *sacha aicha* or *yacu aicha,* something to take with them. As representatives of the outsiders, Machin Runa, they get food taken from the outsider's spirit master Jurijuri, from whose territory they come.

As they eat, some of the male festival participants begin to drum around their table, *ting ting ting ting, zzzz zzzz zzzz zzzz, hooonk hooonk*. First they circle counterclockwise, then back clockwise. Flutes are played and cornets are honked. A powerful shaman plays his *pijuano*. A force field is built up between the outsiders at the table and the rest of the festival participants. Any dancing going on at this time is outside of this power circle. The shield so erected by the circling festival men is said to protect all from the contamination of the external powers taking their food at the festival table. For this brief period the outsiders are ensnared and contained by the indigenous festival force of *yachajuí.*

Usually visitors are very polite and appreciative of the food, but they nonetheless manage to insult the hosts in fundamental ways. One way is to ask for, or demand, salt. Salt is to Christians as its absence is to heathens. Even when they receive their salt they often talk about how the *indios* don't use salt, and begin to talk about the distant *aucas* who they say are led by women and don't even know what salt is. "They even eat raw meat," someone says, "and they grow no crops," says another. All such things are said in Spanish in earshot of everyone. The drumming picks up as these conversations go on. As the outsiders eat, they are presented with pottery effigies: Amasanga, Jurijuri, Quilla, Jilucu, Manduru, Widuj, Machin Runa, Sicuanga Runa, and many more. The imagery of the real people is given to the outsiders so that the spirits of their universe will accompany the soon-to-depart visitors back to their territories, which are now part of indigenous territory.

Dominario

Late in the day, as many of the visitors have departed, festival conveners ask the priest for a "benediction" so they may end the festival. Sometimes the benediction is given, sometimes not. Some priests know what will happen next, and seek to prevent it. Others are ignorant, and the events described take place. At first all things seem as the priest might wish, for the festival participants begin to dance on the plaza, in front of the church, moving in and out of the arches of flowers and palm fronds. Soon, however, the mood changes and becomes tense; festival spirit transforms rapidly into something akin to the approach of a monster in a horror show. One sound is heard, *tick! tick!* as a drummer whacks the wooden side of his drum with a palmwood polished stick. The sound signals the emergence of a *taqui,* conductor or spirit conductor.

The *dominario* is about to begin. This word comes from the Spanish *dominar,* to control. It refers both to the control of indigenous people by outsiders, especially until recently by the Dominican Church, and to the indigenous people's ability to play with the force fields of domination (see N. Whitten 1976a; D. Whitten and N. Whitten 1988; Reeve 1985, 1988a).

As the *dominario* begins, an indigenous outsider, a downriver (*uraimanda*) powerful shaman, gently plays a combination of flute and drum associated with Andean masked ceremonies. In this context, the shaman-drummer-flute player is called *taqui,* "conductor" (spirit conductor). The word comes from the root *taquina,* shaman's song. The melody itself is a skillful blend of his private Amazonian shaman's song and a public Andean motif. The visitor has some special relationship with some participant in the festival; either he is "from" the same area or he has made exchanges in the past that led to the visit. With the sound of this special melody and rhythm the indigenous world expands into the continental container of Western power, signaled by the priest's pumping, two-armed assault of his chapel bell, as he rang it earlier to call people to Mass, to chastisement, and to celestial or divine anthropophagy. This chapel bell, Runa say, shakes their very psyches. Perhaps this is why, historically, there are records of this bell being stolen and taken far away.

Church bell and indigenous drum: symbols of dominance and resistance.

Now four men, each representing the mighty black jaguar (corporeal representative of forest-spirit Amasanga), go to the river and remove from it a bamboo pole, into which four copal fires are placed. As the pole with the four fires is brought into the plaza, everyone's breathing becomes labored, for they all know that the anaconda is no longer in the water. When the anaconda is on land, it is there only to hunt people, to crush them, and then to put the crushed person into that mighty, expanded mouth—to swallow and swallow and then vomit noisily, to allow the crushed ones to putrefy, to again swallow and vomit, until at last that which was human flesh and bone (*aicha* and *tullu*) is within the anaconda, the body of which is now terribly swollen. The giant anaconda then returns to its tellurian lair within mud under water to lie more or less dormant for up to a half year, digesting its meal and growing stronger, increasing its size and power for its next sojourn through water and onto land. This is the sort of thinking—as a montage of palpable images—that the emergence of the ceremonial pole with glowing fires inside instantly evokes.

As the four men come forth bearing the pole, festival participants dance through palm-frond arches constructed for the Catholic chapel. Then the great transformation, called *tucuna*, begins. The pole, as *amarun* (anaconda), Sungui's corporeal form, is borne in a lurching manner and almost instantly becomes destructive. The bearers and the pole crash right into and through the split bamboo walls of the chapel, slamming, falling, rising again, running, frightening everyone, going completely out of control while still in a cultural domain characterized by Catholic mission control, or domination. The chapel is symbolically penetrated and crushed by a mighty constrictor, itself homologous with the indigenous *ayllu* system (N. Whitten 1976a), and the people themselves are being symbolically devoured by the manifestation of the release of their own contained power.

The people are acting against domination but they are in a domain of domination. The festival reaches a crescendo that is, quite literally and quite obviously, terrifying to the participants. Women dance with their hair flying to and fro, to and fro, their sideways motion being the feminine analog of the male-performed two-tone hum of shamanic chanting that evokes the imagery of mythic time-space. It is also a fervent dance to Nungüi. Men beat snare drums, circling and circling while producing the resonating pulse-tremolo signifying Amasanga's rumble of approaching thunder and the buzz of approaching spirit-bees as shamanic helpers. The shamans, too, play their *taquinas* through their bird-bone (soul bone) flutes, evoking the powers of forest and water spirits, living and dead. All souls and spirits and beings are indiscriminately summoned as all containment dissolves into a mighty tropical storm that surrounds the entire earth-world. Escalating chaos reigns as nightfall rapidly approaches, and the Church as represented by the chapel is said to be destroyed in one great transformation of the world of forest and garden and earth and mire into an encompassing, rushing, surging, eastward-flowing river sea.

When performing this ritual people say that they fear *tucurina*, ending everything (which is the reflexive of *tucuna*, transformation). The concept *tucurina* is one of the most powerful ones in Runa thought, particularly when applied reflexively to one's own family, group, or people. *Tucurina* means, in this sense, that to truly destroy the hegemonic authority of the Church by the invocation of the ultimate power of Sungui, here portrayed as the crushing, devouring anaconda, the people may also destroy themselves, embedded, however resistantly, as they are—in a revelatory manner through the vehicle of this ritual—in that very domination.

By moving to the brink of "ending everything," Runa in all their Canelos Quichua territories structure the processes of domination that bear down upon them while repelling hegemony.

Feminine Enactment

Marta thoroughly enjoyed the ongoing performance. Challua, Sicuanga, and the rest had arrived in good spirits, literally, for someone in Puyo had given them a bottle of *trago* and they were happily inebriated as they arrived, shouting in falsetto, rending the air with their alcohol-infested breath. Although she had hidden it away to be sold later, Marta brought forth a little armored catfish that first night, filled with *vinillu,* and made everyone drink and drink until their heads reeled.

She kept refilling the little fish's mouth from the big festival bowl (on the bottom of which she had painted a large, stylized Datura icon), held by Challua as he sat on his long bench near the opening of the house. Challua, at least, knew that the fish represented the times enjoyed and the knowledge gained from the stay at Papaya Llacta the year before, and was pleased that Marta had come up with such a charming *jista puru.* Later, during the *camari,* while several tourists were looking for ceramics to purchase and the *comerciantes* arriving in pickup trucks were suggesting higher prices because of the tourists' presence, Marta brought forth the *cagun* she had sculpted and that had been fired beautifully, teeth intact, with only a few hair cracks. She brought it right to the monseñor eating at the table and made him drink from it—twice—and it was strong *vinillu* that she got into him, too. She suppressed the urge to dump a large *mucawa* full of *asua* on him, for this should be done

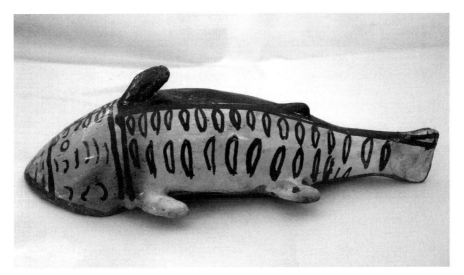

Ceramic catfish drinking vessel. The serving spout is the catfish's wide mouth.

to people one really wants to play with, like the *jisteros,* and sometimes those one wants to mess up a bit while pretending play. The monseñor fit neither class of insiders. But Marta did force four big *mucawas* full of rich, sweet, freshly fermented *asua* on Shiny Shoes when he arrived, and as other women converged on him with his new, strikingly attractive red jacket, she dumped an entire big bowl full of the sticky stuff on his head, making sure that it ran down the front of that expensive coat.

So many things Marta did during that festival event, and she remembered all of them. Halfway through the night, on Saturday, during a lull when Sicuanga was holding forth about the rivers they had crossed and the hills they had climbed, she came forth with the Amasanga image she had made and made him drink and drink from it; the fact that teeth were painstakingly sculpted and painted as growing out of the back of this Jurijuri's head escaped no one. "Sicuanga *mama camwai, ñucanchi muscuj warmi,*" said Shiny Shoes, in genuine, deep appreciation for the work of Marta, his and Sicuanga's sister of Nayapi Llacta, whose daughter's potential role as teacher in Nueva Esperanza he had quietly, but brutally, rejected a week before.

About 11:00 A.M. on Sunday, having drunk the blood of Christ and eaten his body, and having a belly full of meat, plantains, and brew, the monseñor trudged toward the river, where a canoe awaited him. He had to return to Puyo, he said ("for a siesta with two nuns," said Sicuanga, quietly). Marta ran after him. "*Padrecito, padrecito*" she called, and she gave him the Jurijuri drinking bowl with the teeth growing out of the back of its head that she had labored over just for this special *jista.* "*Apai, padrecito,*" she said—"Take it." She pointed with care to the three little Christian crosses painted on Amasanga's nose. Later, she told women in the cooking area that she had made Amasanga as a Jurijuri *supai* in the shape of a squash—ancient food of Jilucu. The bowl also looked like a hill with a magical door at the top where Nayapi had once entered on a Datura trip to make this his land. All the women now knew that a master condensed set of symbols was going into the Catholic Church, and they were pleased. The monseñor really had received a "gift," someone said, a gift of *ñucanchi ricsiushca runa* (our people's perception) bundled into "our tangible proof" by the profound anchoring device of our own image-making woman.

After the Festival

From Sunday night through most of the day Monday, people rest and talk. Exhausted deep sleep from early Sunday night to about 3:00 A.M. imposes quiet on the territory. At about 3:00 A.M. people begin to rise again and to quietly engage in what sometimes is called a *cunchu* festival that refers to drinking up the remaining *asua* and *allu asua*. People slowly drink up what is left of the manioc brews. There is no forcing, no pushing, just quiet, thoughtful consumption. Telling of tales is ubiquitous in this postceremonial readjustment to quotidian life. In some of the popular stories, an analogy is drawn between the accumulation of centralized urban power and the disruption of life in one or another of the Runa territories. For example, it is said that the Canelos Runa and the Puyo Runa would trek with ease to the land of the Salasaca Runa. If bad trails or barriers were encountered in their sojourn up the *montaña,* they would transform themselves into jaguars and bound and leap over obstacles. With the Salasaca, the Puyo Runa and their neighbors would travel on to the Quito Runa territory and would then go right to and into the national palace to make direct petition to the president (or dictator) of the republic. As petitions were granted, local power increased, always in the hands of a *curaga* such as Nayapi of Puyo, or Palati of Canelos (see Pierre 1983 and Karsten 1935 for corroboration of the historical existence of the two great *curagas*).

The same tellers of tales insist that chaos reigned in Canelos due to the activity of the priests there and the alliance and dissidence vis-à-vis these priests created by the powerful ones (such as Nayapi and Palati). In such strife the Virgin Mary, or the Virgin Rosario, is said to have climbed out of her picture frame in the Catholic church in Canelos and fled north to hide in the forest near Huiduj (Huito) at the headwaters of the Villano River. Listening to such tales told by men, women often say, with a sigh, that men seem bent on political moves aimed at the acquisition of power that creates chaos out of the order that power establishes.

Ethnogenesis and Resistance

One of the striking features of everything presented above is that until recently this cultural performance takes place *only* where there is a representation of the Roman Catholic Church. It presents us with the thorny problem of how to understand something seemingly central to the organization and reorganization of Runa lifeways that derives from a superimposition of Western hegemony through the Holy Roman Church. One simplistic explanation is that the Church "imposed" the system of festivals on the people. What the Church imposed, however, was a system of rule through the *varayujs,* a system that was reaffirmed whenever a curate made his "visit." That the indigenous people were required to "celebrate" the *visita* is clear. It led more often than not to attempts to further concentrate or "reduce" the people to a governable territory with indigenous brokers carrying their staffs of authority. But we sincerely doubt that the Jesuit Order (expelled in 1895 by Eloy Alfaro), and then the Franciscan, followed by the Dominican, set out to create anything vaguely resembling what is described here.

People, as cultural agents, create traditions out of conjunctures (e.g., Sahlins 1981, 2005). In this case we are dealing with a colonial-republican conjuncture—the great cultural performance—that draws cultural sustenance from stylized activity and from ritual contexts within the framework of Dominican (and later state) control systems. People do not always create what they wish to create, but the resulting structures of time and space and action are there. Agency brings structure into being, and subsequent agency is framed by formations so constructed. As traditions emerge, they become templates for creative activity, which in turn may severely alter, transform, or reverse the constraints of structure.

Anthropologists often see festival, religion, ritual, and cultural performances as central to the lifeways and sense of cultural being of a people. From the work of Émile Durkheim to that of Clifford Geertz, anthropologists have accepted this canon (see, e.g., Lambek 2002). In accepting this canon we end up centralizing, via a particular set of ritual models for behavior and self-expression, the concepts of "culture" as they have developed over time, beginning with Tylor, Malinowski, and Boas and running through Turner and Geertz. The idea here is that ritual activity generates standards that maintain cultural integrity. Victor Turner (1973), in his important article "Symbols in African Ritual" published in the distinguished journal *Science,* wrote this: "A ritual is a stereotyped sequence of activities involving gestures, words, and objects, *performed in a sequestered place,* and designed to influence preternatural entities or forces on behalf of the actors' goals and interests" (Turner 1973:1100, emphasis added).

Turner saw African people as retiring to a "sequestered place" to perform something to their own centrality, something set aside from the lives under colonial rule. But the Runa play out their ritual (cultural performance) only where there is a manifestation of Catholic hegemony. We must explore this further.

Ethnographer and ethnohistorian Mary-Elizabeth Reeve describes the *ayllu jista* among the Curaray Runa, with whom she worked for eighteen months, in this way: "Runa say that the *jista* is not central to their way of life, that a *jista* would never be held without the presence of European outsiders (*ahuallacta*). The *jista* takes place only at a mission site, and only if *ahuallacta* are present because it is in this context of identity contrasts that Curaray Runa are *runapura*. The *jista* ritual is part of the process of ethnogenesis and has, according to the Runa, no prehispanic antecedent and is not part of the lifeways of *runapura*. *Runapura* refers to 'Quichua speakers among ourselves'" (Reeve 1985:139). After more reflection and more ethnohistoric research, Reeve (1988:20) went on to write: "The concept of *runapura* . . . includes kin and potential kin—those believed to share a common origin in mythic time-space. Runa use stipulated shared descent as a symbolic statement of commonality that unites the several historically intermarrying ethnic groups as one people. This indigenous theory of identity is at the core of Runa historical thought, a theory transmitted and reinforced through the telling of events from mythic time-space and beginning times[-places]."

Runapura, Quichua speakers among ourselves, must have a contrast to emerge in indigenous theory of human ontology. In Curaray Reeve found that Záparo-Quichua alliances radiating out of Canelos and the hinterland of Curaray south of the Curaray River (south of Waorani territory) created a web of kinship and alliance that contrasted sharply with the Waorani people, on one side, and the *ahuallacta* quasi-people, on the other. *Ahua* (*awa*) in Quichua means "high," and in this case is "Andean." *Llacta* means territory, Andean territory. This contrast is with those from Andean territory, including foreigners. The concept "people" is absent.

Ethnogenesis

In the early 1970s I wrote about "Andean ethnocide and indigenous ethnogenesis" (N. Whitten 1976a, 1976b) because, under military dictatorship, the military establishment was focused on obliterating indigenous ways of life among the Puyo Runa. I took ethnocide and ethnogenesis as complementary features in a system of radical change. The people of the Canelos region were among the first indigenous people in the moist tropics of South America to become part of Christendom (Pierre 1983:188). In the new millennium, as before, they sustain a rich indigenous cosmology and cosmogony, and their Quichua language is a fundamental marker of their collective identity.

By *ethnogenesis* I mean the public, historical emergence of culture. This emergence occurs in history, when people become "written in." More often than not, the Canelos Quichua have been "written out," or "silenced," because of the Western focus on savagery and wildness. Historical emergence also occurs in indigenous ideas about the salience of a people. Here we can document ethnogenesis in the mid-eighteenth century, as Zaparoan and Jivaroan people become buffered in the Bobonaza River region and westward to Puyo, with the Quichua language in clear ascendance.

The term *ethnogenesis* was first used, as far as I know, by William Sturtevant (1971), who demonstrated that the Seminole indigenous people of Florida and Georgia emerged into history and became so known because of a transformation of the fifteenth-century Spanish-Arawak term, *cimarrón*, which means "self-liberated." Jonathan D. Hill, in the introduction to *History, Power and Identity: Ethnogenesis in the Americas, 1492–1992* (1996), writes: "Ethnogenesis can . . . serve as an analytical tool for developing critical historical approaches to culture as an ongoing process of conflict and struggle over a people's existence and their positioning within and against a general history of domination. . . . Ethnogenesis can be understood as a creative adaptation to a general history of violent changes—including demographic collapse, forced relocations, enslavement, ethnic soldiering, ethnocide and genocide—imposed during the historical expansion of colonial and national states in the Americas" (Hill 1996:1).

The concept of ethnogenesis refers to the symbolism of "being" as a social and cultural "fact" of history. As such, symbolism looms large. People are remembered or they are written down, or both. What the people or name for a people "stand for" is what symbolism is all about. Edmund Leach (1982:107) argues that "the naming of relationships marks the beginning of moral sanctions." For the early Church in this region—the Franciscans and/or Dominicans in the late 1500s—the symbolism of "Canelos" was that of a *reducción*, reduction (nucleation) to control the "savage" Jivaroans and Zaparoans, among others. These names were preceded by the stigmatized label *indios* applied to all native peoples of the Americas by Cristobal Colón in 1493. By the time the concepts of "indians" and "Canelos" and "Jívaros" reaches history, all "indians" have been separated out of Western development and have been divided into and contrasted as the "reduced Christians" and the "heathen savages." Pierre (1983) documents convincingly that the Dominicans carefully divided the territory of Macas-as-Jívaro from Canelos-as-Quichua—the former as savage and the latter as semi-civilized—and strove to maintain this distinction even though they were using the same techniques of reduction and evangelization in both "savage" and "semi-civilized" sectors of their dominion.

Historicity—high salience given to past events and people in indigenous discourse—enters anthropological understanding. The concept of "Runa," as "fully human being," emerges as focal in several territories of Upper Amazonian Ecuador, as discussed in chapter 1. The fact that territory and Runa ran together through time and that the Shuar and the Achuar people in various locations often use the word *Canelos* to refer to people from the Runa territories leads to a focus on the term *Canelos* as ethnogenetic of a way of life that developed out of antiquity and is projected into specific histories of a nation-state and two vast regions: Amazonian and Andean.

Crucial to the concept of ethnogenesis is that of *contrast*. One language, appearance, or culture as distinct from another is the key feature. It does not matter that cultural features vary considerably among people or that people can move back and forth between areas where different features predominate. What matters is the essentialist character of ethnogenesis: people see themselves as different from, and contrasting with, specific others. Ethnogenesis may emerge during a social movement, when people consciously forge (or try to forge) their futures by making specific reference to their common heritage in order to create or enforce a particular desirable destiny or to avoid a foreseen undesirable destiny.

Ending Everything

The symbolic actions that constitute the cultural performance described in this chapter move toward "ending everything" (*tucurina*). We cannot stress too strongly the culturally produced powerful emotions that emerge publicly when the image of the mighty anaconda lurches toward, into, and through the chapel in Canelos, Pacayacu, or Sarayacu. Even where the *dominario* is not enacted people move toward the river as the sun goes down, and they fear that the anaconda itself may erupt from the water and send them eastward toward the sea. The images of the *dominario* exist in indigenous discourse, and the discourse emerges in symbolic enactment during festival activities, when these activities occur in a setting of domination symbolism. At this time, people speak of, and palpably fear, a movement into or beyond beginning times-places (*callarirucuguna*).

Callarirucuguna

In beginning times-places and in times of destruction, people say, before the times of the grandparents, *tucurina* did occur. With the flood coming and the sky darkening with black clouds, the ancient ones hastily built balsa rafts, put all the manioc on them that they would hold, got their belongings, and were swept away eastward on a great flood as the ground shook and Andean volcanoes erupted, sending darkness into the rain-forest lands.

The people became separated. As they wandered back westward, they found some territories abandoned long ago. They recognized them because of the huayusa (*Ilex guayusa*) trees growing there. They also found them due to the peach palms (*Bactris gasipaes*) planted by the ancestral shamans to establish their human territories. Most significant though in the long treks westward were the experiences with bracket fungi, called *ala*. A young Runa walking with his older brother saw such a fungus growing out of the *mindal* tree, a tree that yields a red sap that can be mixed with *Bixa orellana* and fat of the anaconda to make a lovely deep-red paint known as *carawira*. With that paint one "sees" as the anaconda sees; when one looks at an adversary the person is immobilized. Why do we diverge like this? Because this is the way that stories spiral; they are told in this way, and as such they have significance that we can grasp, if we try.

"I wonder if this fungus is edible," says the young Runa. "Try it," says the older brother. So the young man reaches to break off a piece of the *ala* and it cries out: "*aiyai ala, ama tiushi waichu wauqui; ñuca ringri*" (Don't pinch me like that, brother; that's my ear!). And the bracket fungus transforms into a real brother, and all proceed together westward from deeper Amazonia toward the mighty Andes. When they meet other people they call them Ala, which comes to mean "mythic brother." (Women, too, use *ala* but less frequently, and usually to refer to a man; their special regenerative fungus is the *calulu*, a white mushroom that grows on the forest floor and on logs.)

The image of ending everything evokes at once stories that contribute to a corpus of images that stress regeneration. The world and our spaces-times are restored after they are destroyed. There is a concept in Andean Quechua to express this: *pachacutij* (now often written *pachacutic, or pachakutik*); it is known among the people in the Runa territories but was seldom used until the mid-1990s. When the image of destroying that which oppresses the people—the jaguars carrying the out-of-control anaconda in and through the church while women dance to Nungüi outside the church—is brought into strong and collective consciousness, the complementary image of *regeneration* also emerges. That's why the stories spiral around. They are highly symbolic, and they are *en*-acted. They are not to be found in Western contrast sets of us/them, though the sets exist with great clarity. They are to be found in indigenous thought, which—during, after, and long after the European conquest of the Americas—focused on oppression and indigenous resistance to that oppression.

"Diversionary Activity"

In the words of Lawrence Sullivan, a specialist in comparative religion, the cultural performance sketched previously should not be viewed as a "core aspect of culture" or as a "centrality" or ritual that generates models for cultural endurance. Rather, he writes of "diversionary practices," "diversionary events," or "diversionary entertainment." These, he says, constitute an *eschatological theater,* which itself "is a deliberate diversion from historical experience" (Sullivan 1988:680–81). "Each form of diversion—military, scriptural, choreographic, or theatrical—attempts to pass the time, to end the quality of terrible expectation. Taking their cue from religious rites of renewal, warfare, writing, dance, and drama divert recurrent primordial disaster through the ironic symbolic exercise of reenacting or miming the catastrophic flood, fire, or other violent dismissals of the fully sacred world. *By turning primordial realities off to one side and historical existence off to another, diversionary entertainment rends chaos asunder and stretches open the distance between clashing times*" (Sullivan 1988:681, emphasis in original).

The diversionary festivities, drama, and feasts together with the accompanying traditional play and transformable outcomes that constitute the *ayllu jista* provide a template on which people draw to underscore their commonality, on the one hand, and their sheer difference from others who constitute the structure of oppression, on the other. The stylized behavior and ritual contexts described at the outset of the previous chapter are central to cultural performance. *But the full-blown cultural performance itself is set aside from historical existence to allow reflexive activity vis-à-vis that very experience.* The two principal features that emerge from understanding of the stylized activities, ritual structure, and cultural performance of this event are *ethnogenesis* and *resistance* (see, e.g., Geertz 2005).

The Lancero Festival

To complicate matters, another festival exists, about which I know far less. This is the *lansa jista,* or festival of the "lance" wielders. There is no Quichua word for *lancero.* I have seen it performed during the *ayllu jista* in Pacayacu, during the twelfth of May celebration in Puyo, and have heard about it elsewhere. Mary-Elizabeth Reeve (1985) reports on it as well. She observed it in Canelos, and heard about it elsewhere. Karsten (1935) never mentions it, but Pierre (1983:191–92) observed it over a century ago in Canelos. Most of what I know is published in *Sacha Runa* (N. Whitten 1976a:178–80), but I assure the reader that this performance is alive and well in Canelos, Pacayacu, and Sarayacu, and is still performed, especially by those from Pacayacu, in the twelfth of May celebration in Puyo.

The *lanceros* are in-laws to a special *llacta* in Canelos, Pacayacu, or Sarayacu. When a father and brothers who have been *lanceros* so choose, they present the in-law with a hardwood *macana* made from *Litae vignum*. *Macana* is the verb stem for "fighting." It usually refers to a flattened, two-sided "club." In the case of the "*lanceros*," it refers to a carved wooden "knife." The *lanceros* hold their own hunt and prepare their own festival during the *ayllu jista*. Ideally they build their own house in front of the chapel and call it *mushuj wasi*, new house, or *lancero wasi*, lancer house. The *lanceros* each make a similar or identical headdress that is distinct from all others. It consists of a narrow toucan-feather headpiece woven into a basket head frame. Four tall macaw tail feathers are placed in a vertical position in the frame; each is topped with white bird down. These represent deer antlers. They fasten a band of small bells around their ankles, calves, or just below their knees, and wear bandoleers over each shoulder. Although the bells are common in Andean indigenous festivals, their use in Amazonian cultural performances occurs only in the *lancero* dance in the three Runa territories of Canelos, Pacayacu, and Sarayacu.

They begin their own dance on Thursday night. On Friday individuals may visit any of the festival participants, where they are treated as any other participant. On Sunday it is often they who bring the anaconda from the water and crash through the church. They may approach the feast for the curates where they perform a "war dance" (Pierre 1983:191).

There are four *lanceros* who are led by a flute-playing drummer (the *taqui*). In their own house, and on Sunday in the plaza, they dance in quadrangular patterns to his beat, sometimes disrupting the other festival activities. They enter the Moon house and Potoo house only as individuals, never, as far as I know, as a dance ensemble. *Lanceros* from Sarayacu sometimes perform their dance in Puyo during the twelfth of May celebration, in front of the Dominican church.

Their dance is similar to one performed in the Archidona Region of the Napo Runa during the festival of the Chonta, and also bears considerable resemblance to the Yumbada in Urban Quito during the period of Corpus Christi (Salomon 1981; Fine 1991; N. Whitten 1981). The Yumbada cultural performance celebrates the coming of the "Yumbos," Upper Amazonian people, to Quito, where they are killed and then resurrected by shamanic practice. We shall say more about this in chapter 8, after exploring the dy-

Lanceros from Shihuacocha-Sarayacu perform in front of the Dominican church in Puyo, 1976. *Taqui* with drum and flute is to the right.

namics of aesthetics in the construction of cultural performance systems in chapter 7.

The *lanceros* seemed to have emerged as a dance group oriented toward the attack of the "Chirapa" on the south side of the Pastaza River. Only in Canelos have I heard of these tales of attack when, it is clearly said, the *lanceros* would organize a raid, to be led by the *sicuanga runa* warriors. Such attacks would take place the day after the end of the annual cultural performance we described above. François Pierre (1983) observed this very activity in Canelos during Corpus Christi. Here a prominent *capitán* from Villano, named Salúa, danced with the *capitán* Palati of Canelos. Mary-Elizabeth Reeve learned in Canelos that the dance itself represents a simulacrum of the movements of the mountain lion, *puma,* the steps one will take in enemy territory so as not to be seen or heard. The living *lanceros* are to "move like the cougar," just as a deceased shaman has acquired the powers of *tsumi* by drinking a tea made from the *puma yuyu* plant before his death and learned to walk after death as a jaguar, also called *puma* (see Uzendoski 1999 for *puma yuyu* use among the Napo Runa).

Puma symbolism, which subsumes cougars, jaguars, and other wild and feral felines, is related to predation and attack. The cougar, or mountain lion, is called *taruga puma,* "deer puma" (*japa yawar* in Achuar), because of its color and because it hunts deer. The jaguars, ocelots, and related "jungle cats" all have their own adjectives. To repeat and condense here: the shaman in attack mode may be likened to a jaguar, and Amasanga's corporeal representation is the huge black jaguar, *yana puma.* Deceased shamans who have acquired the powers of *tsumi* may return as black jaguars. As such they are extremely dangerous. Even the great anaconda, as spirit-master Sungui, first shaman and *curaga* of the *yacu supai runa,* the water spirit people, may have as his mascots two great black jaguars (for deep analysis of jaguar symbolism in central Amazonia see Fausto 2000, 2004).

We have spiraled through the symbolism of the *dominario* now in some of its associational complexity, condensation, polarization, and multivocality. These images are bound to the *lanceros* just as they are to the *ayllu jista;* the two coexist from time to time, fusing still further these traditional associations that seem quite outside of ordinary cultural life. Traditional though they may be, they nonetheless stand aside from the stylized activity and ritual contexts of centralized cultural life.

Obviously, there is much more to an annual cultural performance than a mere celebration of togetherness to which outsiders are invited. I introduce the subject of the *lanceros* here, rather than in an endnote, for two reasons. The first is that for insiders, talk of the *lanceros* constitutes a point of reference for the discourses of resistance. The second is that in 1992 during the March for Land and Life the concept of *guerreros* who carried *macanas* as defensive staffs emerged as central to the new organization of a national drama. The *guerrero* (warrior) concept and complex is a direct transformation of the *lancero* as festival performer and from the *sicuanga* as liberator. Together, in today's reality, they fuse to the role of cultural warrior, the epitome of resistance to domination and hegemony. We pursue this in chapters 8 and 9. But first, in chapter 7, let us drop back and examine the antiquity and continuity that undergird the transformations that bring us right up to the immediate present times-places.

7

Aesthetic Contours: History, Conjuncture, and Transformation

DOROTHEA SCOTT WHITTEN
AND NORMAN WHITTEN

Early European explorers of South America were impressed both by the aesthetic quality and by the mundane and festive uses of pottery in widely separated regions of Amazonia. Traveling down what is now known as the Napo River through the Upper and Middle Amazonian areas inhabited by Omagua Tupian speakers, Francisco de Orellana noted the quality of the ceramics produced by the very people his troops were raiding and plundering: "[T]his porcelain [is] of the best that has ever been seen in the world, for that of Málaga is not its equal. . . . [It] is all glazed and embellished with all colors, and so bright . . . that they astonish" (Carvajal 1934:200).

Some thirty years later, Hans Staden (1944:1) wrote of how Tupinambá women of coastal Brazil knew how to make and paint clay vessels that glowed "like hot iron" when fired. They used manioc roots to make flour for thin cakes to be eaten with pounded dried fish and dried game. The women also made drinks by boiling manioc roots, which were masticated and put into special vessels half buried in the ground. These were tightly covered and the masticated manioc-water mixture was left to ferment for two days to produce a strong, thick drink.

> Each hut makes its own drink. And when a village wants to make merry with it, which generally happens once a month, the men first go all together to one hut, and drink out there. This is so carried on in succession, until they have

drunk out the drink in all the huts. They sit around the vessels from which they drink. The women help them to the liquor in due order; some stand, sing and dance around the vessels. . . . The drinking lasts through the whole night; they also dance between the fires, shout, and blow [ceramic] trumpets. (Stade [Staden] 1847:135–36; see also Léry 1990:69–77)

Beautiful ceramics, as we have seen, are still being made today by indigenous people living at the base of the Andes in Amazonian Ecuador. The potters there produce polychrome and blackwares quite reminiscent of Tupian traditions. The origins of these fine, hand-coiled ceramics probably date back 4,500 years and are closely associated with manioc cultivation and utilization. Such pottery developed from still earlier Amazonian traditions that could be the earliest in the Western Hemisphere. According to Anna C. Roosevelt (1995:115), an archaeologist, "pottery began in Amazonia about 7,500 years ago, more than 1,500 years earlier than elsewhere in the hemisphere." She argues that tropical root cropping had spread throughout the Amazon basin and its rims by 4,000 years ago in association with elaborate styles of pottery decorated with geometric and animal designs (Roosevelt et al. 1996:380–81).

The florescence of superb pottery that occurred at the mouth of the Amazon in association with manioc (and later maize) horticulture and intensive fishing endured for more than a thousand years on the fourteen thousand-square-mile island called Marajó. Although Marajó Island was abandoned about 190 years before the European "encounter" and subsequent conquest of the Americas, the pottery tradition spread—presumably in association with manioc—throughout Amazonia and to the base of the Andes. This extended period from 4,500 BP to the mid-sixteenth century was one of great expansion of the Amazonian peoples into many ecological niches through varied biomes. The conquistadors of the Caribbean and Amazonian regions encountered large-scale societies of indigenous people, some of them settled, some migrating. The people of these societies had developed technologies that included the skills necessary to produce huge polychrome pottery jars, effigy (and even monumental) pottery statues, and probably delicate bowls and whimsical figurines.

Peoples migrating by 1492 included Tupian speakers who traveled from different parts of Amazonia westward all the way to the east Andean foothills. Searching for the "land without evil," these Tupians were led by powerful shamans who prophesied the location of the sacred land and made vast treks to find it (Métraux 1927; Lathrap 1970; Shapiro 1987; Clastres 1995; Whitehead 2003). In the early sixteenth century, a Spanish adventurer named

Alejo García traveled with Tupian (Chiriguano) warriors to eastern Bolivia, where the Inca were mobilizing the Yura people to defend a sector of the east Andean slopes recently incorporated into their empire (Rasnake 1988; Rowe 1946:208). By the time Staden made his observations in coastal Brazil, thousands of Tupinambá had already traveled four thousand miles or more to the edge of the Inca empire. "About 1540," Alfred Métraux noted, "several thousands of Tupinambá left the coast of Brazil in quest of the 'land-of-immortality-and-perpetual-rest' and, in 1549, arrived at Chachapoyas in Peru" (Métraux 1948:98; see also Clastres 1995).

As noted in chapter 4, Rafael Karsten was intrigued with the ceramics of Canelos people. "Like the Achuares," he commented, "the Canelos Indians nearly always apply ornamental designs to their clay vessels, but their ornamental art is easily distinguished from that of the Achuares, and even the clay they use is different" (Karsten 1935:102).

The Quichua-speaking people now widely known as the Canelos Quichua still inhabit the Upper Amazonian territories of Ecuador visited by Karsten, and they still make a distinct type of fine pottery for storing and serving a manioc food beverage (Kelley and Orr 1976; D. Whitten 1981, 2003; N. Whitten 1976a, 1985; D. Whitten and N. Whitten 1978, 1988, 1989). Today strikingly beautiful traditional ware is flourishing in the most modern setting in this region. In this chapter we examine the "perfection of their ceramic art," first through the imagery of one potter and then more broadly through the imagery of other potters who work in the contemporary scene centered in and radiating from the town of Puyo, capital of Pastaza Province in Amazonian Ecuador.

Strong Visionary Woman

"*Yachaj awashca,*" she said, picking up a piece of ancient thin-walled pottery with a smooth, shiny surface. *Mana yachaj awashca, mana sumaj,* illustrating her description with a thick-walled, rough-textured sherd, a remnant of an old cooking pot. *Yachaj awashca* literally means something made by the most knowledgeable one, therefore master-crafted, well made, and imbued with knowledge. *Mana* is negative; *sumaj* is beautiful. *Mana yachaj awashca, mana sumaj* refers to something not knowledgeably made and not beautiful; if it is not knowledgeably made, it lacks significance, and if it is insignificant, it lacks beauty.

Clara Santi Simbaña had come to a point in her pottery making where some bowls and jars had to be air dried before she could paint them. Three monkeys and a couple of coiled snakes needed to dry before their separate halves could be spliced together. It was time for a break, and she needed some nourishment from the manioc food beverage (*asua*) and relief from sitting in a fixed position for hours. Before serving *asua* in a decorated drinking bowl, she brought a small bundle from her treasure trove in the bedroom, put it on the dirt floor, and untied the corners of the cloth. Spreading it, she laid out an assortment of valuables collected mainly from the Copataza River region during visits to her husband's relatives and from the river regions of the Upper Conambo and Curaray during recent treks there to renew old bonds of friendship and kinship.

Her first concern was with her stones, some with explicit purposes, others with obscure functions. A smooth, flatish black *lumu rumi* (manioc stone) helps her manioc grow. She does not need to talk to it; she just holds it against her body to make it work. She bought it from her son-in-law's mother, who lived in the Copataza River region. She sorted the stones into *warmi rumi* and *cari rumi* (female stones and male stones), then put aside only the manioc stone and an egg-shaped white alabaster one, a tourist item from the Cuenca area that had been given to her "for luck" by a North American to whom she sold pottery. She needed to keep her two female stones, but she indicated that she had no need for the polished black and red male stones, including a long, thin red one called a "tongue." Perhaps some tourist would like to buy these, she hoped.[1]

Turning her attention back to her collection of sherds, she explained that she had found all of them in one ravine off the edge of the small airstrip at Copataza during visits to her husband's relatives. Through her combination of Jivaroan, Quichua, and Spanish, she interpreted sherds as fragments of strange bowls made by outside or foreign women of ancient times. She singled out the sherds that she associated with drinking bowls as *yachaj awashca, sumaj,* because the inside surfaces were well scraped and burnished, and the rims were clean and smooth. Some had punctate designs, "painted or decorated with a stick"; others bore traces of painted designs, said to be *sumaj pintashca* (beautifully painted). The *sumaj* sherds were quite distinct both from those identified as eating bowls by their folded-over rims, and from cooking pots, which were thick walled, coarser grained, unpainted or undecorated, and not beautiful.

A round, chunky object that at one time might have been a rudimentary anthropomorphic figurine had been given to her by a relative, and she did not know much about it, except that it was ancient. She identified a small spindle whorl with punctate marks as *algudunta tisana,* literally cotton disentangler, a spindle whorl used for working cotton. She was more interested, however, in the punctate designs on the *sumaj* sherds. She interpreted diamond shapes as *amarun* (anaconda), zigzag lines as a twisting river or the skyline silhouette of the Andes, a series of U designs (U U U U) as *shiwai cara* (centipede shell), and a flattened diamond form as an anaconda skin shed during molting. Some circular punctate designs puzzled her; she sighed and said, "We don't know these designs now," and went on to add that she would like to learn them, but they were made by "the other women long ago."

The contents of the plank shelves in her small pottery-making shed revealed the extent of her knowledge and skill. A row of toucan jars (*sicuanga mangas*) and drinking bowls lay in various stages of completion. Their thin walls were slipped in cream, red, and rose tones and burnished to a soft sheen with a special water-polished stone. Brown, black, and white line drawings on some vessels took the shape of diamonds, zigzags, or five- and six-sided geometric designs. After the monkey- and snake-halves had been joined into whole figurines, and after the array had been slipped, air dried, burnished, and painted, each piece would be fired and then covered with resin to fix the colors and decorations under a brilliant lacquer-like coating to make the piece waterproof. The final results bore an uncanny resemblance to the *yachaj awashca* fragments of antiquity in Clara's collection.

She attributed much of her knowledge to her mother and grandmother, and to the mother of a close sister-in-law. As a child, she would hang around while her mother made pottery, watching closely and then practicing rolling out coils of clay on a flat board, just as her granddaughter was now doing at her side. Through continued observation and practice, she gradually became more adept at handling clay and turning it into little animal figurines and small bowls. She had long worked the plastic clay intuitively. Now, as she held a bowl on her lap to scrape its walls thin, it changed from round to oval; when she put it down on her flat board, the slight, sure pressure of her hands restored its roundness.

Her horizons constantly expanded as she accompanied her parents on periodic treks (*purina*) from their home in the village of Puyo to the dispersed settlements in the river regions of the Conambo, the Curaray, and sometimes the Copataza. Strangers seeking cures for their ailments from her shaman father (Virgilio Santi) came from other parts of Amazonian Ecuador, as well as from the Andes to the west. Her father also traveled to these areas, gleaning knowledge of the worlds of other people, diagnosing the causes of their illnesses, and bringing home reports of his travels and, sometimes, special gifts from his patients. One prized gift was a violin from the dispersed settlement of Chapana near the headwaters of the Curaray and Oglán rivers on the very edge of Waorani territory. It was hand-carved and was fastened together with palmwood nails. She remembered listening to him play shamanic tunes and sing his special shamanic songs, communicating with the world of spirits and distant and foreign others. Through his music and the telling of mythic and historical episodes, she came to understand the meaning of *unai* (mythic time-space) and *callarirucuguna* (beginning times-places). She incorporated this knowledge of distant worlds into her increasing familiarity with her rain-forest environment and with the customs, histories, and myths of her people.

Clara's knowledge expanded even more after her marriage to Paushi (see chapter 4). Through visits with Paushi's female relatives, she became familiar with their distinct pottery styles. She admired their skill in making very large drinking bowls and considered the cooking pot for *Ilex* (*huayusa*) tea beautiful, with its dramatically flared rim and gleaming black inside, but she preferred her more elaborate polychrome pottery to theirs.

During her childhood, Clara witnessed the transformation of Puyo from a largely indigenous village with some mestizo settlers into a frontier town swelled by waves of Andean colonists. Later, her husband shared her observation, but from the perspective of his Achuar background and culture. Being an outsider brought inside to help his father-in-law, Paushi had tentative control of some land because the oldest daughter has permanent rights to swidden garden territory, and this becomes part of her husband's right as well. But in practice such rights of usufruct depend on sustained alliances with recognized kin. The couple moved periodically as alliances shifted in the face of ecological factors, on the one hand, and national and international pressures, regionally defined, on the other. Eventually it became necessary for Paushi to accept sporadic contract labor for petroleum exploration companies.

Paushi was not alone in seeking outside work, for practically all the *comuneros* were being thrust into the booming capitalist economy as it became more and more difficult to balance subsistence work, trade, and religious and commercial patronage. During the early forays of foreign petroleum companies into the eastern rain forests of Ecuador, Paushi worked alongside some of his wife's brothers and cousins. In later explorations, many of the same men and their older sons and sons-in-law were hired for the labor force that cleared passages through the forest, strung dynamite wire, built base camps, and cooked for the crews. By the 1970s the men were being flown to work sites that earlier could be reached only by foot and canoe, near land that Clara's father had cleared during the 1930s in anticipation of the grand scheme to build a railroad from Andean Ambato to Amazonian Curaray to connect with the lines running between the Andes and the coast.

The nation's early twentieth-century dream, shared with Brazil, was to link the Pacific and Atlantic Oceans. The Amazonian, Andean, and coastal railroads would be coupled with the Amazon and tributary ports to serve both nations. The Ecuadorian and Brazilian vision was shattered in 1941 when Peru invaded Ecuador during what Jaime Galarza (1972) called "the Petroleum War" (between Royal Dutch Shell in Ecuador and Standard Oil of New Jersey in Peru). Peru seized half of Ecuador's Amazonian territory and carved out a sovereign swath across the region of imagined international collaboration. Ecuador's desire to link its coast with its eastern forest was renewed in the 1970s, this time by an oil pipeline that would fuel an anticipated epoch of new industrial expansion and wealth.

Once oil was flowing from the northern Amazonian region, petroleum interests temporarily abandoned the central and southern sections and shifted their exploration to the coastal side of the Andes. In July 1980 a labor recruiter held interviews at a local hotel in Puyo (on the site where Clara's father had sold land to a German colonist and his Ecuadorian wife), and Comuna men flocked in, hoping to be part of the thirty or so chosen. While waiting their turn for an interview, they talked to some of the hotel guests, including an ethnobotanist from Harvard and two herpetologists from the University of Kansas. On the Fourth of July they were treated to a North American-style barbecue and picnic, stayed around awhile to watch the assembled gringos gyrate to thunderous disco music, and then took bags of leftover hamburgers and hot dogs home to their families. They were back the next morning for the final selection, and at 6:00 P.M. a busload set out for the area near Santo Domingo de los Colorados, where they would run dynamite lines through a region dominated by African palm and sugarcane plantations. Paushi and one son signed on with the recruiter. Another son wanted to go but decided to stay home to complete his paramedical training, tend his twenty or more cattle, and help his wife through the impending birth of their sixth child.

Watching the excitement of the busy hiring scene, Clara's older brother reminisced about his experiences in the Ecuadorian-Peruvian War of 1941, when he was about sixteen years old, and about his subsequent work trips for petroleum companies. He was eager to join this group but lacked some necessary permits. His wife was not well and wanted him to stay home anyway. He said his good-byes to several nephews who were leaving on the bus and returned home to the Comuna. The next evening he was back in Puyo, this time to report that he had just taken his next-to-youngest son to a nearby hospital. The sixteen-year-old youth had fallen from a tree while hunting, and his shotgun had discharged, sending two small pellets into his head. They penetrated the upper eyelid, moved into the brain through the eye socket, and continued all the way to the back of the skull, leaving massive damage. Death came to him in thirty-six hours. During the following days, the wake and funeral were crushing for the immediate family and close kin.

Unable to provide the required military release forms, Paushi returned from Santo Domingo the next day in time to help his brother-in-law with wake and funeral arrangements. The occasion was triply sad for Clara and him, for they mourned the loss not only of their nephew but also of their last-born child, who had died before he turned two, and of their eighteen-year-old daughter, who had died just a few years ago. During the wake, the mothers cried out their stylized death wails, male relatives of the deceased's father served alcohol, and guests not related to the deceased's immediate kindred played traditional funeral games (see N. Whitten 1976a:136–37) through which the opposite of grief—uproarious humor—is expressed. Clara's daughters continuously served manioc food beverage from delicate ceramic bowls that they and their mother had made.

While Clara, like other Canelos Quichua women, makes ceramics for the basic purposes of producing, storing, and serving *asua,* the quality and variety of vessels far exceeds the demands of necessity. Her own store of knowledge and ability to integrate this with her participatory and visionary experiences are the sources of her creative expressions in pottery and in songs. Because these expressions reflect her control of powerful imagery, she is widely regarded as a strong visionary woman (*sinchi muscuj* [or *muscuyuj*] *warmi*). This figure of speech is one of respect and admiration, but it is also tinged with envy when used by some of her fellow master potters. When Clara sings the song *Sacha Allcu Warmi Mani* (I am a bush dog woman), which she learned by listening to her grandmother, she takes the role of the little bush dog, wandering around through a palm thicket in the forest, seemingly lost but trying to return, looking very sad and barking *hau hau hau* as she walks, stands up, then walks some more. Clara's small *sacha allcu* figurine has small, rounded ears and a short snout. To an outsider, the song and the figurine are unremarkable depictions of an animal that exists deep in the forest but is seldom seen. To Canelos Quichua people, they evoke the image of Amasanga, master spirit of rain-forest dynamics, for *sacha allcu* is his mascot; it accompanies him on his travels, barking *hau hau hau* at any sign of danger. When Clara enters the spirit domain of Amasanga, she takes on the role of Amasanga *warmi,* female master of rain-forest knowledge.

Included in her repertoire are songs about other animals and birds, nuts and trees of the forest, and mythical figures such as the Toucan person, a symbol of liberation "who doesn't kill in eating nuts." Some of her songs tell of personal experiences in going to Quito, capital of the Republic of Ecuador, where her mother had never gone, and walking the streets in black, black shoes. Other songs draw on imagery and events from mythic time-space and apply them to present circumstances, as in Jatun Machinmi (big monkey). Two versions of Clara's pottery monkey figurine are described in chapter 4 (p. 112–13). One is realistic; the other, representative of monkey as stranger, foreign person, *machin runa*. In mythic time-space, *machin runa* tried to ensnare two beautiful women, but they were liberated by the forest-dwelling *sicuanga runa,* toucan person. Clara's husband was an outsider brought into a system where he was nearly trapped by another external system, the capitalist economy. The oil boss was seen as a figure of entrapment, and the ceramic image of entrapment was made to sell to tourists for much-needed money.

Imagery and Art Worlds

In historical times, nonindigenous middlemen traded Canelos Quichua ceramics eastward toward central Amazonian markets at Iquitos and Manaus, and westward toward Andean markets. Within their own region, Canelos Quichua people themselves exchanged ceramics for favors from patrons, offered them as gifts to prestigious visitors, and sporadically sold them for extra cash. Some pieces found their way to exclusive shops in Quito, in North America, and in Europe. A few were included in a batch of largely lowland Peruvian ethnographic art auctioned by the Parke-Bernet Galleries in 1970. The catalogue for this sale included notes provided by the North American collectors about when and where pieces were collected; use of the item; from whom the item was acquired, meaning the "tribal name" and previous Western owner, if any; and the condition of the "tribe"—for example, "completely assimilated," "impoverished" with no tribal tradition, or "entirely Christianized." The lack of complete information about every item did not distract from the lure of exotica created by this and many other galleries and shops.

The message of salvaging the last examples of the art of destabilized, and preferably savage, "tribes" suggests an ancient heritage lost to the consciousness of fast-disappearing peoples of dark, alien worlds. After cloaking the art of indigenous others in mystery, dealers then situate it within the framework of contemporary Western art worlds: "the ideas and shapes of primitive art fit well with modern design." Alas, "original Tribal Art came to an end around the turn of the century in Oceania, and in Africa a few decades later. . . . Because the usual medium of primitive art was perishable, little exists from previous centuries, so a time shutter before and after the nineteenth century limits supply. Collectors can now buy beautiful craftsmanship cheaply in a market that is likely to appreciate the art over the next few years" (*Anthropology Today* 1989:26, quoting from *Bonham's Auction Guide* No. 10).

Pressures toward exclusivity in the art world are countered by efforts to promote mass production. During the 1970s, some Peace Corps volunteers, in trying to increase the cash flow to Canelos Quichua peoples, encouraged potters to produce ashtrays, coffee cups, saucers, and plates in large quantities. When enough stock could be accumulated, they said, a full-page advertisement in the Sears catalog would be purchased, and successful sales of "Indian pottery" would allow the potters to purchase "good" commercial clays, paints, glazes, wheels, and kilns. Potters could transform their traditional art into a growth industry and become prosperous, if only the Sears venture were to succeed. It did not. The few potters who experimented with the new forms—most of whom lived in Rosario Yacu and Unión Base—tested local and national markets and soon learned that there was from time to time aesthetic appreciation for a beautiful, knowledgeably made object. The manufacture of Canelos Quichua ceramics has thus far survived pressures toward the two extremes of exclusivity and mass production, and it continues in the face of rapid modernization.

For more than a half-century, external development forces have contributed heavily to the growth of infrastructure within Ecuador, with consequences reaching from the national political economy right down to the basis of local indigenous livelihood. Near the headwaters of the Pastaza River, in an eastern Andean gorge, a huge dam, financed by an international consortium, is the source of electricity for the Amazonian Pastaza Province. Old roads are constantly being improved, and heavy machinery is used to decimate forests and construct new roads through the heart of indigenous terrain. New schools springing up alongside the roads serve as meeting halls for assemblies organized by anyone wishing for contact with local community members. On the edge of indigenous territory, a complex of large wooden buildings has been constructed by another international consortium and given to the indigenous confederation of the Amazonian region to conduct various training courses and eventually to house a high school. Three indigenous organizations now have their own airplanes and foreign pilots to fly leaders to outlying areas, and perhaps to train them to fly. Puyo had an official population of eighteen thousand in 1989 and according to its mayor "is a city in permanent growth" (*El Comercio,* Crónicas section, December 29, 1989). Today it has grown to over forty-five thousand inhabitants.

In the face of this constantly modernizing situation, Canelos Quichua women continue to make pottery for their own everyday household use, for ceremonial occasions, and for sale. As indicated earlier, sales of ceramics have evolved from local to national and international markets. During the late 1970s and early 1980s, the sporadic but pervasive commoditization of ceramics was surpassed by the rampant commoditization of a newly introduced art form: balsa wood carving and painting. This strictly commercial enterprise fulfilled a consumptive urge of the outside world and an economic need of the indigenous world. Completely externally directed, this new art form could not have become successful without the woodworking skills and ecological knowledge of the indigenous carvers, primarily men, and the technical input of a North American artist-entrepreneur. The manufacture and sale of wood and pottery art have become important sources of income for many Canelos Quichua people and have involved them in a myriad of collaborative, sometimes hostile, and crosscutting relationships and negotiations that are both intracultural and intercultural.

While the wood carvings caught on very quickly in the tourist-oriented ethnic-art market, the ceramics limped along, frequently under the misnomer of "Jívaro pottery." Finally, however, these ceramics have gained national and international recognition, in part through publications about them, and the appreciation of them in their own right has enhanced sales far more than did the earlier promotion of them as objects made by "pristine savages" best known for their head-shrinking skills.

Recognition and appreciation of the ceramics by participants in the art worlds of others eventually led to exhibitions, which in turn triggered another kind of feedback. When potters looked at photographs of their works on display and heard the words of praise from others, they responded by creating pottery for a new purpose: to be exhibited in order to educate outsiders about Canelos Quichua culture. Juana Catalina Chango and her brother, Alfonso Chango, were forerunners, or pioneers, of this movement to create in order to educate. In 1975 Juana made a large ceramic tapir with thick walls and no serving spout. It was unlike festival figurines but realistic enough for North American audiences to visualize this tropical rain-forest animal. Alfonso works with paper, pens, and paints to portray the cosmology of the Canelos Quichua. His drawings and descriptions of shamanic practices

Drawing of Manga Allpa Mama. Alfonso Chango, 1987.

have been published and distributed in Ecuador and the United States. In Amazonian Ecuador, his booklet *Yachaj Sami Yachachina* (Shaman-class teachings; Chango 1984), has been used in a course for training medical auxiliaries. Eventually, through drawings and explanations based on songs of his mother and tales told by his mother and father, he clarified the picture of the mythical origin of pottery clay that had been emerging from many people over a number of years.

Prelude to a Myth

Two exhibitions in 1987 framed an outpouring of lore, including the mythical origin of pottery clay, conveyed through songs, stories, and ceramic figurines. The exhibitions took place during our residence in Ecuador in 1986–87. The first was invited by the director of the Museum of the Central Bank of Ecuador, to be held in Quito to commemorate February 12, 1542, the day that Francisco de Orellana purportedly discovered the Amazon during his search for the land of the Canela (*ishpingo*), worth more in Europe at this time than the price of gold in Spain (Latorre 1995:121). The second was invited by the mayor of Puyo and was to be held in that city in conjunction with the annual celebration of its legendary founding on May 12, 1899, by Friar Álvaro Valladares. Four hundred and ninety-five years after its "discovery" by Europeans, the Amazonian region—itself declared a myth by President Galo Plaza Lasso in 1948 and revived as a nationalist emblem by President Velasco Ibarra in the early 1960s ("Ecuador has been, is, and will be, an Amazonian Nation!")—was receiving national and local recognition through the artwork of its indigenous people. The title of both exhibitions was *Causáunchimi!*—We are Living!

Initially, the Quito exhibition was intended to display ceramics from the museum's own collection, to be complemented by some new acquisitions. As planning progressed, it became clear that the museum's holdings did not include representations of important facets of Canelos Quichua culture revealed to us after we made the collections in the early and mid-1970s, and the director authorized us to acquire new items. Even before a date was confirmed, we began to spread the word of a probable exhibition later in the year, in Quito. Both the time and the place seemed remote, and responses were fairly casual except for the intense interest of a few potters.

One of these was Estela Dagua, who had been living in urban Puyo for several years and who was dedicating herself to pottery making full-time in order to support her eight children. Before long she had turned out a series of large-scale animals and birds, smaller figurines, intricately painted storage jars, and a blackware cooking pot so big that she had to have help from her teenage son when she fired it. Between the sequences of coiling, drying, decorating, and firing large pieces, she found time to make a number of significant small items. Among these were figures of edible palm larvae, edible flying ants, turtles, and turtle eggs, all of which were indicative of human dependence on a tropical ecosystem for protein to supplement the basic carbohydrates from cultivated crops. She also made figures of inedible bracket fungi with faces painted on one side, symbolic of mythic transformation and regeneration, and realistic wild cacao nuts, representative of the natural festival drinking bowls of human-like monkeys in mythic time-space and in beginning times-places. She gave special attention to a pair of ceramic cornets to be presented to two important men to blow during festival activity. In addition to rounding out the museum's collections with her own work, she helped to obtain pottery from women who were visiting Puyo from outlying areas of Pastaza Province, and she brought to our attention another Puyo household of potters who were producing ceramic art for the national and international ethnic-arts market.

Little new information about myths and mythic beings was generated during the period of collecting in the fall of 1986, with two exceptions. Soon after we began work in Puyo in 1986 we accompanied Estela and her son to cut and gather bamboo firewood for her pottery making. The next day, as she was working her clay, Estela asked if I (Sibby) saw something and became frightened while in the bamboo thicket. Not knowing that I had stepped on a long and very sharp bamboo thorn, she became frightened after seeing me leave hurriedly but said nothing at the time. She now said she thought I had seen the bamboo spirit (Wamaj *supai*), a fierce female spirit that lives in the thicket and that jealously guards it from those who come to steal from her. After Estela confided that she cuts in that thicket only when the owner is in Quito, she showed us a pair of bamboo spirits (male and female) that she was fashioning. This was her first movement into the rare potter's universe of actually creating representations of dangerous spirits. She was becoming *sinchi muscuj warmi,* a strong visionary woman.

A few weeks later, during a trip to mine pottery clay, Estela and several friends explained to us, as had other potters in the past, the different qualities of clay needed to make fine bowls, large storage jars, and cookware, and where these clays could be found at distant mine sites. The mine near the Shuar settlement of Pitarishca on the Sigüín road, for example, yields the smooth gray plastic clay (similar to Kentucky Blue in the United States) with evenly distributed fine, sandy granules that is ideal for making thin-walled drinking bowls. The mine near the colonist settlement of San Pedro on the road to the headwaters of the Bobonaza River contains the heavier grade yellowish clay with more grit and minute pebbles, suitable for the pots that have to withstand high cooking temperatures.

Storage jars must have strong walls to endure the heavy bulk of fermenting manioc pulp, but their exterior surface should be beautiful, smoothly burnished, and decorated. If an ideal clay is not found, a mixture is made from the gray and yellow clays to produce a sturdy paste with a balance of grittiness and tiny pebbles that feels right to the potter's touch. Although they know about the use of sand, ash, and ground-up sherds for temper, they prefer naturally tempered secondary clays to which they add nothing. As the women discussed clays and mines, they repeatedly mentioned *Manga allpa mama* without explaining what this meant. We knew from previous remarks by other potters that the name referred to a master spirit of pottery clay, but at this time we had little understanding of it other than that it was a transformation of the spirit master of garden soil and pottery clay, Nungüi (see, e.g., D. Whitten 1981; N. Whitten 1976a, 1985; D. Whitten and N. Whitten 1988).

Activities escalated in the spring of 1987, with a concomitant flow of information. *Causáunchimi!* opened in Quito on March 10 (about a month later than originally planned), and several weeks later we returned to see it with a bus load of the artists who had contributed to it. After first checking their own individual works on display, the thirty-one people went systematically through the entire exhibition, commenting on every concept and component, going over the myths that were represented, and explaining all of this to a Quichua-speaking guide from Otavalo. She could read the Spanish labels and texts, but many of the artists could not. Later, when she took them through the archaeological museum in the same building, her explanations and the lively questions and discussions were again in Quichua.

Shortly after this trip, city counselor César Abád informally invited us to "bring the Quito exhibition to Puyo." When this turned out to be impossible because the Quito exhibition was scheduled to run through June, we immediately set out to re-create *Causáunchimi!* with new materials. The artists who went to Quito, having interpreted and absorbed two professionally mounted exhibitions, were well prepared to help, and enthusiastically spread the news that *ñucanchi yachai*, "our cultural knowledge," would be displayed in Puyo. Suddenly preparations were underway for an exhibition that would feature an array of significant indigenous ceramic portrayals of myth, history, and modernity. Everything had to be produced in a very brief span of time.

Pottery making was especially intensive and expansive in the household that specialized in fine pottery for the market. Rebeca Gualinga, originally from Sarayacu, seemed to attract other potters from that Bobonaza River settlement—noted for its exquisite ceramics—to her Puyo home, where she had lived for years. She was working collectively with two other potters from Sarayacu, Amadora Aranda Canelos and Santa Gualinga, whom we had known since 1971. We had visited Rebeca's home several times in recent months to see the women's pottery, usually finely decorated drinking

Ceramic effigy of Manga Allpa Mama. Rebeca Gualinga, 1987.

bowls and shiny black eating bowls. To this point, most of their products had been sent to Quito with indigenous and nonindigenous entrepreneurs as a strictly commercial venture. Now, a week after the Quito trip, Santa had two figurines to sell for the exhibition; one was Indi, the sun, and the other portrayed Nungüi, the master spirit of garden soil and pottery clay. Rebeca, holding Santa's Nungüi in her hands, spontaneously rendered the Manga Allpa Mama myth and then asked if she and the others could see "the video" we had previously invited them to watch.

A few days later, the three women and Estela came to our house, and after being served sodas and cookies, settled down to watch *Our Knowledge, Our Beauty.* The festive atmosphere and initial joking and giggling quickly turned into intense concentration as they watched the unfolding of scenes of familiar places and people, listened to the songs, and commented under their breath about the juxtapositions of ceramics and wood carvings. Santa squealed with pleasure as she saw her Black Woman figurine, made in 1975, blow her magical breath on Toucan person (made by Alicia Canelos, Amadora's mother, for a *ayllu* cultural performance in Sarayacu in 1976) to transform him into the long-billed bird we know today.

Estela beamed when she was shown making pottery, and they all commented in Quichua on whatever concept was being portrayed even though the narration was in English. Before long, another master potter, Apacha Vargas, and her husband joined the group to watch a tape made earlier that morning of the final burning of a dugout canoe—to make it buoyant and impervious to water—and to see portions of the video of the indigenous artists going through their exhibition in Quito. Among those artists was a man affectionately nicknamed Rucu, "The Elder," who was now completing this canoe for the Puyo exhibition, and his wife, Pastora Guatatuca, a well-known potter. "Rucu" is none other than Venancio Vargas, the father of Antonio Vargas.

During the same week we acquired more ceramic figurines, bowls, and hardwood carvings, accepted the formal invitation for the exhibition from the mayor, and submitted a brief article about the vitality of the indigenous people to the municipal review (*Pastaza: Un municipio al servicio del Pueblo,* N. Whitten and D. Whitten 1987) to be distributed on May 12. We were shown the city architect's plans for a huge concrete *mucawa* already under construction in the center of town. His model for the monument—a delicate bowl from Sarayacu with a striking anaconda motif—was on sale in a music and ethnic-art store in Puyo. After the architect copied its design he had no further use for the piece, and neither he nor the officers of the municipio could see the relationship between the indigenous piece and the cement monument to the art form being erected.

An interlude followed in the form of a short business trip to Quito, during which we arranged for the Abya-Yala Press to set up a book exhibit in the forthcoming exhibition and saw the Quito version of *Causáunchimi!* dismantled two months early. Back in Puyo by May 1, we found the bases for the exhibition nearly finished and the women potters with a bevy of new creations. Estela had completed a large standing anteater, other animal figurines, and a very large cooking pot covered with thumbnail impressions that simulated an armadillo's skin. At Rebeca's house, the women brought out an astounding array of figurines: Amasanga, master spirit of the rain forest; an iguanid, his seat of power; a jaguar, his corporeal representation; Jurijuri, a dangerous spirit master transformed from the Amasanga associated with "our rain forest" into an underearth spirit of others, the *machin runa,* monkey person; and two representations of Nungüi, one as spirit master of garden soil and the other as spirit master of pottery clay. Seemingly inspired by all of this, Rebeca held Santa's Jurijuri figurine before our video camera and told about this peculiar creature, with his dog-like feet and with teeth in the back of his head or neck, then went on to repeat the myth of Manga Allpa Mama, illustrating with her own Nungüi-pottery clay figurine, and finally sang a song about Jayambi, an iguanid, while demonstrating its undulating movements with the ceramic likeness she had made.

Wedged in between the opening of *Causáunchimi!* in Quito and the return to see it with indigenous artists was a full day's video "studio" work with Alfonso and his mother, Clara, to document various segments of the Manga Allpa Mama myth: the moon, the Squash woman, Potoo bird (a member of the Nightjar family), and different manifestations of the spirit of pottery clay and garden soil. In the past, Clara and her daughter Juana, among many others, had rendered myth segments as both encapsulated and continuing parts of a larger emerging story about these transformational beings. Alfonso was now drawing graphic representations of his mother's stories, while she explained his drawings through song and narration. The day yielded volumes of songs and tales to be transcribed and translated at some future date and two large, colorful paintings—soon put to use—of the spirit of pottery clay and an affiliate, the spirit of drinking bowls.

As Alfonso's paintings were being hung in the Puyo gallery (the converted municipal library), César Abád became fascinated with the interplay of ceramic and painted images. He rushed home and returned with his contribution to the exhibition: two intact archaeological urns. They were about two and a half feet high and were painted with deep-red and white diamond and circular designs. They appeared to be transitional between Marajó pottery, various manifestations of Tupian pottery, and contemporary Canelos Quichua pottery. They had been found recently by residents of Charapa Cocha (Turtle Lake, or Lagoon), a settlement on the Pastaza River near the Peruvian border, forty-five minutes, flying time southeast of Puyo. This territory had been settled in 1980 by an extended kindred group of Achuar people seeking refuge from escalating feuds in their former home, Capahuari, which was the original home of Paushi, husband of Clara and father of Alfonso.

By 1985, Charapa Cocha had an airstrip, a school, and a meeting house for the rapidly growing population of about a hundred. César Abád had worked unstintingly to bring the school and bilingual education to the settlement, and for this he was presented with the first two urns discovered in a section of riverbank that had fallen after floodwaters receded. They were given not only to express appreciation and for safekeeping from would-be looters, but also because they did not fit the self-identified cultural heritage of the Achuar, who wanted to know what outsiders thought about the urns they regarded as inherently beautiful and powerful, but "of others," not "theirs."

The *Causáunchimi!* exhibition opened on schedule the evening of May 8 after two final days of putting up texts and maps, securing objects to bases with monofilament fishing line, moving in the full-size canoe recently made by Venancio Vargas, fetching newly made wooden items from outlying hamlets, escorting a local photographer through his video coverage, and setting up television and audio systems. The activity and mood of excitement approached the frenzy of final preparations for an indigenous festival. Space had to be found for last-minute spontaneous contributions, including large storage jars and cooking pots and a small-scale pottery canoe Rebeca had made after she saw the real one on video at our house. Impressed by the beauty and significance of the ceramics (which represented virtually all major myths and mythical beings), a crowd of indigenous and nonindigenous people alike lingered over displays, the former frequently becoming enthusiastic interpreters for the latter. Indigenous appreciation was reflected by Venancio Vargas (Rucu), the canoe maker, a longtime friend who strode around the room, looking carefully at everything, apparently reliving memories. Rubbing his palms, he repeatedly said "I like it, I like it."

Drawn to the urns, a cluster of indigenous women gathered around Abád for a serious discussion. They were fascinated with the designs and with the idea of beautiful antiquity extending from beginning times-places, perhaps from mythic time-space, down through the times of destruction to the times of the ancestors and into the present. Compared to their own delicate, thin-walled pottery, the thick walls of the urns were "like cement," but they were beautiful in their near indestructibility. The women wondered where the ancient potters got their clay and what kind of clay it was. Abád admitted that this also puzzled the women and men of Charapa Cocha. They had no source of clay as strong as cement, and they were sure the urns were not made by their ancestors.

The Achuar relegated the urns to the domain of Tsunki, their master spirit of the water world and first shaman, whose power is often related to outsiders. The Canelos Quichua discussed whether these giant vessels had been made to store *asua* or to hold the bones of deceased humans (some are found with human bones in them), a practice several women had heard of from their grandparents. There was no doubt in the potters' minds that the diamond-patterned mazeway painted on one urn represented the anaconda, but the swirling circular motif of the other could not be clearly interpreted, though it evoked a great deal of speculation about the Charapa Runa, the mythical spirit person who is believed to inhabit the area around Charapa Cocha and to steal Achuar women.

The Charapa Runa is said to have special relationships with the Canelos Quichua people of the Bobonaza River region. The design itself was unknown in the contemporary potters' iconography but was obviously important to the ancient ones who made the urn. By the time the exhibition ended ten days later, it was generally conceded that those ancient pottery makers could safely be claimed as ancestors of the contemporary Canelos Quichua people but not of the Achuar Jivaroan people, with whom they intermarry. The source of the clay, however, remained a deep mystery, as did the meaning of the spiral designs.

The sad, empty feeling that comes with dismantling an exhibition was not only shared but poignantly expressed by two friends. Rebeca and Rucu stopped by at different times to take a last look and to offer assistance in packing. When we arrived home to unload, Rucu was waiting, and he stayed to watch, commenting in a melancholy way on each item—who made it, where it came from, and where it was in the exhibition. We stopped by Rebeca's house later to purchase her pottery canoe and to say good-bye to Amadora, who was to return to Sarayacu the next day.

Suddenly Rebeca was telling us how sad the big kinship performances used to be. Hundreds of people would come, they would have a wonderful festival, then everybody would go away, leaving only three or four families in the place where all had been together—very, very sad. To some, at least, the massed spirits in the exhibition evoked the expansive sentience of a festive cultural performance, with its merger of intrusive outside forces and inside, indigenous knowledge and empowerment. The end of the exhibition signaled a return to the reality of the mundane world.

A new outside force soon appeared in the hubbub of everyday life in Puyo in the form of the United States Army. Through an agreement between President León Febres Cordero and Vice-President George Bush, the troops were sent to Ecuador to build a new road between Archidona and the Agua Rico River. Construction began only fifty miles north of Puyo in the area of Napo Province that had been very badly damaged by an earthquake on March 5. In Quito the National Congress refused to allow the United States armed forces to land on sovereign territory, but after heated debate among Ecuadorian military leaders and legislators, the agreement with Bush prevailed and the troops moved in. The airport at Shell, eight miles west of Puyo, was readied as a staging area for Hercules fixed-wing aircraft and Blackhawk helicopters. United States army pilots, officers, and key personnel were housed in Puyo hotels, while field troops set up camp on the outskirts of Archidona. Almost overnight, prostitutes driving late-model Troopers appeared on the streets of Puyo, and cases of Bacardi rum were stocked by enterprising store owners. In Archidona, a reported thirty booths were set up by artisans from Otavalo to sell their famous handwoven woolens as souvenirs, and thousands of cases of Budweiser beer were airlifted from the United States and stocked in the temporary PX.

While the military was becoming entrenched amid continuing national debates on the question of sovereignty and on the danger of the introduction of HIV virus by U.S. troops, Estela's world was shattered when her landlady decided to bulldoze her house into the abutting creek with only a few hours' abrupt notice, as described in chapter 4, (p. 104). Within a few days, however, she had relocated her family to a new site where her husband was building their house with materials bought with her earnings from pottery sales, and she was once again busy at work. Within a month she had assembled her first pottery shaman group, made figurines based on one she had seen in the archaeological museum in Quito, and created a representation of Cachi Amu, spirit master of salt. In 2003 this figure became the iconic motif for the permanent South American exhibition of the Americas Gallery of the Spurlock Museum of the University of Illinois at Urbana-Champaign.

During this same period, Alfonso volunteered to translate into Quichua the Spanish version of the script of *Our Knowledge, Our Beauty*. Before he tackled that job, however, he decided it was time to review some of the abundant materials we now had. It was important, he carefully pointed out, for him to *interpret* what had been given to us so that we and others might better understand the nature of the indigenous incorporation of thought and knowledge. In Spanish he used the exact cognate, *interpretación,* that one would expect. In Quichua, he explained, "we call this *cuintaushcata ricuchina quillcaushcata. Cuintaushcata* means spoken or told; *ricuchina* means to show, teach, or explain; *quillcaushcata* means written or inscribed. His phrase for interpretation, then, means "narrative written to explain." Specifically, he wanted to interpret the myths recently written, drawn, sung, and narrated by his mother and him. Part of the process of interpretation must involve full explication (*explicación*) of the text. That which is obviously implicit among sharers of indigenous knowledge must be made explicit in an interpretation to outsiders. The prelude had ended, the myths were recorded, but only through indigenous interpretation based on reflexivity could others, such as us, understand something embedded in Canelos Quichua mythology that is usually left unsaid.

Explication of a Myth

From the extensive, expansive, ongoing spiraling and mythology of the Canelos Quichua presented to us over a number of years, we extract here only those segments that have immediate relevance to Alfonso's interpretation. His reflexive explication is based on his deep cultural knowledge and his awareness that others do not share that knowledge. We have encountered some of these stories before, and we condense them here. It is the flow and the indigenous explication that we seek to impart.

In the transition from the earlier mythic time-space into beginning times-places, Jilucu was a beautiful woman whose handsome lover came to her only at night. After becoming pregnant she wanted to see the father of her child, so one night before his arrival she cooked a seed from the *widuj* tree and later painted her lover's face and body with beautiful designs, telling him that it would make him feel "fresh" (*Genipa americana* is an astringent). Much later, in the predawn hours after he had left, she looked at the sky and saw the full ("ripe") Quilla (Moon Man) in his complete masculinity. Clearly, he was her brother, and his face and body were covered with the lovely black *widuj* designs she had painted on him.

She knew then that she had committed incest, that her children would inherit male and female soul substances from the same consanguine source. Her sisters, including Red Woman and Black Woman, were also living in

Ceramic Moon Man. Alicia Canelos, 1975.

the sky at this time. Seeing that their brother, Moon, and their sister had enjoyed an incestuous union, they painted their faces black with the same paint, and they cried and cried. Their tears fell to earth and seeded the *widuj* tree in all of the areas where the contemporary people now live and where their ancestors lived.

All the stars cried too, producing the dreaded merger of rain, earthquake, and flood. The rivers swelled, volcanoes erupted, high new hills appeared, and the earth shook and shuddered. The earth people, descendants of Jilucu and Quilla, were caught up in a great river that swept them eastward into the (Amazonian) sea. Out of this river came Indi, the sun, who had been living in a cave at the base of the Andes. He ascended to the sky to begin his regular course and to bring the orderly east-west axis to the earth world. As Indi exploded out of the Amazon, thousands of tiny colored bubbles flew outward, as did thousands of white ones. The colored bubbles became seed beads, to be found later by deep Amazonian peoples such as the Achuar Jivaroans and Cocama Tupians, who traded them westward to the contemporary people.

The white bubbles became salt that lodged in eastern mines to which the indigenous people would trek for this desirable flavoring for their native foods. Some would travel for a year or more to the Marañón River area, where, many say, they had to appease not only Jivaroan, Cocama, Candoshi, and other residents but also the Cachi Amu. Cachi Amu is an undulating, sentient overseer of salt. Many women, especially master potters, say that Cachi Amu is strictly feminine, but men, whose fathers made the trips to collect salt, say that Cachi Amu is androgynous.

While humans and animals were becoming what they are today in the transformations occurring from mythic time-space to beginning times-places, spirit masters, too, were transforming. Nungüi, a beautiful spirit woman dressed in shimmering blue-black, was a sister of Manduru Warmi (Red Woman) and Widuj Warmi (Black Woman). As Nungüi walked in the forest with her daughter, Junculu (who in some variants of this myth may also be her sister), three men—Quindi (hummingbird), Acanga (hawk), and Sicuanga (toucan)—competed for Junculu's hand in marriage by trying to clear trees for a garden plot. We offer a variant of this story in chapter 2.

In beginning times-places there was a voluptuous unmarried Squash Woman (Sapallu Warmi) who was having an affair with Moon Man (Quilla). The woman planted a swidden garden with squash, and in the middle of it she lived with Moon Man in a huge oval house with a thatched roof. Before the squash matured the only food in the house was that captured by Moon Man from the forest with his blowgun. When the squash ripened, Squash Woman wished to deceive Moon Man, so she stitched up her mouth, saying that she did not like squash. The stitches were to show that the squash was reserved just for Moon Man.

One day when he came home from the forest Moon Man found that Squash Woman had "prepared" raw green squash for him to eat instead of the ripe squash she had previously served. He demanded cooked ripe squash. The woman mumbled through her closed mouth, "There are no ripe ones in the garden." And then, implying that he had accused her of eating the ripe squash, she asked: "How do you think I can eat with my mouth sewn shut?"

The next day, without saying anything, Moon Man went to the garden and found nice ripe squash there. He brought them back to Squash Woman and said, "Please cook these for me and have them ready when I return." He pretended to go off to the forest, but after his woman went to her garden he returned secretly to hide on the roof. Soon, Squash Woman brought more ripe squash to the house and cooked them. Opening her stitched mouth wide, she ate all of them and began to prepare green squash for her man. When she left to fetch water for cooking, he came down from the roof and left. Later he came back from the forest and was served cooked green squash. He said, "The squash is green." He became angry and vexed and told the truth: "You say that you don't like to eat squash, and you say that you don't eat ripe squash in order to deceive me. All right, then," he said, "I am going back to the sky where I belong."

Playing sad songs on his three-hole transverse flute, he moved away toward a vine ladder called *jilucu chaca*, jilucu ladder, he had left in place when he descended to visit Jilucu earlier. He now climbed the ladder linking sky and earth. Hearing and seeing this, Squash Woman believed that they both would go live in the sky. She tarried in gathering all of her things, including everything needed to make pottery, but then she filled her basket and set out for where her man had gone. When she arrived at the ladder she could see that he was halfway up it, and she began to climb. When she got halfway up she could see that her man was now in the sky. Moon Man turned back to see that she was now halfway up the ladder, and he said, "You defamed me when you tried to deceive me." He cut the vine holding the ladder and she and all of her household and garden belongings fell to earth. Then Quilla blew on the woman with his magical breath, "*Suuuuuuuu* Jilucu," and said, "You become Jilucu [the common Potoo bird], and your feces will become special pottery clay." (For information on the Potoo see Scutch 1970.)

Jilucu, who in this story, with the use of the concept *chaca*, epitomizes the concept of *axis mundi* so prevalent in Andean and Amazonian cosmology and topography (e.g., Sullivan 1988; N. Whitten 2005; Wibbelsman 2004, 2005).[2] In such renditions, Manga Allpa Mama, connected to pottery clay through Jilucu's feces—a transformation of Squash Woman who tried to climb the *chaca* and created the *axis mundi*—is the master spirit of pottery clays for eating, drinking, cooking, and storage vessels. The final part of the story of Squash Woman, to the best of our knowledge, had always been implicit in previous tellings but was made quite explicit at this time by people stimulated by the festive atmosphere of the exhibitions, the melancholy letdown after

Jilucu *chaca* growing near Puyo, 2005.

Ceramic festival vessel in form of Jilucu. Erlinda Manglla, 1972.

the Puyo exhibition, and their reflexive interest in communicating to others their own indigenous interpretation of imagery portrayed through narration, song, and ceramic art. Clara, Alfonso, Rebeca, and others self-consciously told us complete stories so well known among themselves that customarily they are told casually, in segments, and their content expressed by allusion.

Aesthetic Forces

Through indigenous peoples' explication of their imagery, we came to appreciate the aesthetic force of mythology as a sort of transformational tunnel through which lore and history are projected into contemporary life. For example, at one point in the tunnel, Jilucu and Quilla were the mythic ancestral mother and father, and the seed beads that were eventual transformational consequences of their incestuous relation became a medium of exchange connecting early to contemporary Amazonian peoples. In a series of transformations, Jilucu became the master spirit of pottery clay (which needs no temper) for contemporary women potters and presumably for their ancestors. As such, she is a counterpart of Nungüi, the master spirit of women's agriculture.

The strictly feminine force of domestication, seen in the pottery clay-garden soil spirits of Jilucu-Nungüi, is complemented by the master spirit of the rain forest, Amasanga, an androgynous, predatory force who controls the ultimate power of the hydrosphere, Sungui (Tsungui). Amasanga's foreign counterpart, Jurijuri, went through a series of transformations to become the underearth spirit of other people, known as the *machin runa,* monkey people. Mythological beginning times-places are brought into contemporary life in Canelos Quichua festive activity, which plays out and for a time overcomes the contrast between fully human territory, overseen by Amasanga, and other peoples' territories, associated with monkey abundance and overseen by Jurijuri.

Nowhere is the set of complex and dynamic relationships between the self and the other in mythic and experiential realms more apparent than in the human enactment of kinship festivals, the subject of chapters 5 and 6. It is here that the aesthetic forces of creativity become *en*-acted in an expanding universe that includes all humans, souls, spirits, and other beings. This is a time of continuity and transformation signaled by the rich integration of performance, narration, melody, rhythm, cacophony, play, innovation, creativity, and a bevy of highly significant ceramic representations.

The festival allows participants a profound "diversionary activity" (Sullivan 1988) during which they stand apart from Roman Catholic and state dominance over indigenous people. They play with the dominance and take themselves and their universe to the brink of ending everything. The *ayllu jista* continues to be held once or twice a year in every Canelos Quichua hamlet where there is a tangible manifestation of Catholic control, such as a chapel or a niche with a saint. Over the past twenty-five years or so this festival has been held whether or not a priest or friar is present, often in recent years at a time and place selected without consultation with church officials.

Clara Santi tells of how much the people *like* to sing, that it is the "custom" to exchange songs (literally, "to catch each other's songs"). These include the beginning times-places' songs, our mothers' songs, and our grandmothers' songs. People sing songs for each other, and their hearts become sad (*llaquichina*). As they sing and tell myths, imagery of the past and present is evoked by the forms and motifs of pottery from which women serve, drink, and play with *asua*.

Aesthetic Conjunctures

The indigenous cosmology signaled by the Canelos Quichua kinship ritual performance shows remarkable commonalities with other Amazonian and Andean societies past and present, as analyzed recently by Lawrence Sullivan (1988; see also Brown 1984; Santos-Granero 1996; Salomon and Schwartz 1999a, 1999b; Schwartz and Salomon 1999). We are tempted to compare this contemporary festival with activities of the Tupinambá described by Staden four hundred and fifty years ago in a region four thousand miles east of Canelos Quichua territory. But we are restrained from this by the knowledge that, until recently, contemporary Canelos Quichua perform their richly lived and deeply felt kinship festivals *only* where there is a manifestation of Catholic dominion. Their ritual performances clearly reflect this tradition as it is now embedded in the historical and contemporary structure of domination and as it expresses counterhegemony in its final, dramatic phase, the *dominario*.

When large numbers of people are gathered for a kinship festival, a priest has an opportunity to celebrate mass and perhaps perform marriages. Before a priest's scheduled visit, whether or not he actually arrives, wives and female relatives of the hosts place pottery chalices and candlesticks on the crude split-bamboo altar in the chapel, and visitors present these women with candles just as they do during a wake. On the final afternoon, the priest and his entourage are served a special dinner at tables set in each festival house. Otherwise, the structure and enactment of the festival is entirely indigenous, though Christian symbols are embedded in pottery decorations derived from powerful indigenous images. In addition to chalices or candlesticks, women may shape small pottery chapels or decorate bowls with a cross motif. Explication of the cross is difficult to elicit (though people commonly use the Spanish word *cruz*), but one woman finally and firmly identified her striking design on several bowls as the *cura cruzashca*, the symbol of the priest's blessing as he makes the sign of the Christian cross.

After the hordes of guests depart, quotidian life begins anew before dawn the next day, often with women using up their supply of clay by making more jars and bowls for their home and increasingly, today, for fluctuating ethnic-art markets and for exhibitions. A number of women had quite a large stock of pottery ready and waiting for the annual May 12 celebration in Puyo in 1989. Several of these had a copy of the book *From Myth to Creation: Art from Amazonian Ecuador* (1988) opened to a page showing their earlier creations, to validate their status as master potters.

Among them was Estela Dagua. Because of her urban residence in Puyo, she is removed from the everyday routine of indigenous life, but she nevertheless keeps track of activities (including festivals) through a stream of kith and kin to her home. They, as well as other indigenous cultural resources, past and present, provide inspiration for her continuing creative production of pottery for sale and for exhibit. After her ceramic portrayal of a series of master spirit beings—of salt, fire, and bamboo, among others—she created several Banco Central men, based on her memory of an Andean archaeological figurine she had seen during the museum excursion to Quito. Her little figurines, however, were rendered as lowland people carrying deer and other rain-forest game animals with tumplines. She then turned her attention to making several sets of figurines portraying shamanic practice. The sets include the shaman, his patient, the person who negotiates treatment for the patient, the shaman's special curing stones, and even the canoe used to transport the patient to the shaman. Every set is complete with the names of the shaman and the patient, and each of the stones is named.

Some of her more recent innovations are drawn from the imagery of indigenous architecture. She has produced her version of the Curaray chapel pictured in her copy of *From Myth to Creation* and a portrayal of a festival house from Sarayacu, where she spent her younger years. Her most elaborate and beautiful construction to date is her Charapa Cocha *wasi*, Turtle Lagoon house, made after seeing a photograph of the traditional oval house with thatched roof and open sides built by the Achuar elders and founders (*uunt*) who live today in Charapa Cocha.

The geometric turtle and tortoise designs she painted on her roof do suggest thatch, and they represent the seat of power of forest spirit-master Amasanga. She enclosed her house with walls decorated with the powerful anaconda-embedded-in-water-turtle motif, symbolic of the first shaman, Sungui (as anaconda), and his seat of power (Amazon water turtle). As she did with her Central Bank people, she appropriated a theme of another indigenous cultural technology but embellished her creation aesthetically through the imagery of her own culture.

The arts of the Canelos Quichua demonstrate, we think, that reflexivity enters and reenters the creative process to incorporate and integrate imagery

Achuar house at Charapa Cocha.

Estela Dagua's recreation of the Charapa Cocha house.

projected in multiple ways. As artistic representations by native peoples are introduced to and accepted by participants in the outside art worlds, the artists seek to explicate their sense of meaning, and their explication is capable of influencing the tastes of those strangers who come increasingly to their territory to learn about or to purchase something inherently beautiful and knowledgeably made. Robert Plant Armstrong wrote about this process of aesthetic forces and their reflexivity across cultural distances many years ago. He called this force an "affecting presence," which he described poetically in this way:

> The complete, total affecting presence is a web of tension—tension between form and formlessness, intension and extension, continuity and discontinuity, physical conformation (spatial or temporal) and emotion, media and metaphor, and the ordinary and the extraordinary. Further, it is a complex of metaphoric levels, all coming simultaneously to focus in the work—the universal metaphor, the cultural metaphoric base, the space/time metaphor, the objective metaphor, the formal metaphor, and the objective correlative. It is a wonder, but no surprise, that the affecting work may be described as a presence, an entity which though it is native to a time and place, is not the prisoner of either. At the same time, however, the affecting presence is as subject to misunderstanding—or, indeed, understanding—out of its own culture as its creator himself [or herself] might be. (Armstrong 1971:196)

Native arts, we argue, may "speak." The artists of Canelos Quichua culture join the voices of a multitude of artists of the Americas who continue to create beauty amid ceaseless and relentless change. Neither they nor their works are "prisoners" to time, place, or encounters with the art worlds of others (D. Whitten and N. Whitten 1993a). Their interactions *on their own terms* with representatives of these art worlds suggest that their creativity may be enhanced by reexamining tradition against a backdrop of change, to produce aesthetic expressions that transcend time, space, and cultural barriers.

The story does not end with festival activity and the ethnoaesthetics of ceramics and music, however. Nor are these dynamic cultural forces contained by region or by tradition. Protest movements, led by indigenous people, now sweep the nation of Ecuador on a regular basis. In 1992 a particular dynamic event began in Puyo and moved out westward to the Andes and on northward to the capital city. Elements of everything we have written about thus far permeated the drama of the ensuing cultural performance with significant social, political and economic affect. We turn now to that event: The *caminata*, or great trek, from Puyo to Quito, known generally as the "March for Land and Life."

Notes

1. Brown (1980, 1985a, 1985b) describes remarkable similarities in the importance and uses of stones among the Aguaruna (who are Jivaroan speakers) of Amazonian Peru.

2. *Chaca* is rendered *chacana* among the Napo Runa. It can also mean "bridge" when it is horizontal. The *Jilucu chaca* (a *Bauhinia* species known as "monkey's ladder" in many places of Central and South America) is a legume that fixes nitrogen in the tropical forest, thereby furthering the nurturing work of the microrizal fungi in the leaf litter on top of the soil. Plants acquire most of these nutrients from mycrorhizal fungi that fasten to roots and exchange minerals for sugars produced by their plant hosts. Some trees and vines form associations with bacteria in their roots and benefit from a supply of fixed nitrogen. These symbiotic relationships underpin the luxuriant growth of the tropical rain-forest ecosystem. For an excellent presentation of the concept (here *chakana*) in the Otavalo region of northern Ecuadorian Andes see Wibbelsman 2004 and 2005. When the concept is opened up as vertical and horizontal transitions, whether as bridge, ladder, or crossroads with dangerous underworld below a central point (see Corr 2000 for Salasaca), or as a combination of all these transitions, the *axis mundi* concept is broadened to mesh nicely with Amazonian and Andean cosmology (e.g., Guss 1989; Sullivan 1988).

8

Return of the Yumbo:
The *Caminata* from Amazonia
to Andean Quito

NORMAN E. WHITTEN JR.,

DOROTHEA SCOTT WHITTEN,

AND ALFONSO CHANGO

"We are . . . in Quito; . . . all nations are here."

On April 24, 1992, the phone rang in the Whittens' home in Urbana, Illinois. *"Causanguichu gumba?"* (Are you living, *compadre?*), asked Marcelo Santi Simbaña, our longtime indigenous associate in Amazonian Ecuador. He went on to say, "We are here in Quito; we, the forest people, have arrived here. We walked here and we have arrived. We are many; all our brothers are here. All nations are here: Pastaza Runa, Salasaca Runa, Chimborazo Runa, Cotopaxi Runa; Yana Runa are also here, *compadre;* all nations have come to be within Quito." Marcelo; his wife, Faviola Vargas; and many of their relatives had just completed a peaceful protest march undertaken by indigenous people from their Amazonian homelands to Quito, the capital city of Ecuador. They had walked for thirteen days.

In this chapter we draw attention to the unfolding dramatic structure of this event (the Caminata de Pastaza a Quito, later called the March for Land and Life), and to the symbolic processes of its enactment. By so doing, we contribute to an ethnology of practical activity and symbolic efficacy. We seek to portray, understand, and explicate aspects of the suasive cultural forces that created an aura of empowerment that energized the pragmatic success of one of the most dramatic indigenous events in Ecuador's turbulent history.[1]

We begin by placing the Caminata in the context of recent indigenous protest movements. We then present a chronicle of events as a composite description drawn from firsthand accounts by participants and other observers. These descriptions have been collected over several years from marchers themselves and from accounts in the national media. We then move to the symbolic affinity of this pragmatic march with a north Andean ritual festival, the *yumbada*. This festival enacts the story of a group of Amazonian people, collectively known as "Yumbo," coming to Quito. Through the course of the article, the multivocality of the concept of the Yumbo as "shamanic healer from the forest" unfolds. The public narrative of the *yumbada*, as it was reported in the national media, was important because the marchers became increasingly aware of the mass audience reaction to their moving theater of empowerment and because they commented specifically on the perceptions of their march by others after the Caminata itself had ended. Finally, we discuss the political aftermath of the indigenous movement in Ecuador through June 1996.

"1492–1992": Recent Symbol and Protest in Ecuador

Ecuador contains a number of nationalities (*nacionalidades*) (CONAIE 1989), long called *naciones* in the vernacular of indigenous peoples. Since 1990 representatives of some of these nationalities have accomplished feats of political persuasion unprecedented in Ecuador's colonial, republican, or modern history. The public displays of force, unity, and peaceful tactics contradicted a number of assumptions and beliefs held by many Ecuadorian nonindigenous people and significantly affected the nationalist discourse about the structure of the nation-state itself.

The prevailing mood in Ecuador from about 1989 through mid-1992 was one of desire for radical change in the republic as a whole and for its nationalities in particular. For indigenous people in the Andes and Amazonia the rallying cry was ¡*Después de 500 años de dominación, autodeterminación indígena en 1992!* (After five hundred years of domination, indigenous self-determination in 1992!). The year 1992 was chosen as the symbol of a cultural, political, and economic uprising, a choice made to highlight their opposition to the elitist rhetoric of the quincentennial celebration planned for the same year: the commemoration of the European "discovery" or "encounter," the conquest of ancient indigenous territory, and the eventual establishment of nation-state hegemony over indigenous people.

Indigenous efforts to gain self-determination occurred in various regions of the country at different times. In early May 1989 indigenous people and national representatives held a confrontational meeting in Amazonia, which produced the highly controversial "Acuerdo de Sarayacu" (Agreement of Sarayacu). This was followed by a sit-in and threats of a hunger strike by Andean people in the Santo Domingo "Temple" in Quito in June 1990. The Levantamiento Indígena (Indigenous Uprising) of 1990 was, without question, the greatest mobilization of people in Ecuadorian history, and it publicly established an indigenous power source that could not be denied.

Over the course of 1990 and 1991 the symbol of "1992" and the Levantamiento Indígena conjoined imagery from the highest level of Ecuadorian society with the antipodes of Ecuadorian blackness and indigenousness. Much of the public rhetoric of the Levantamiento Indígena focused on making 1992 the year when the Euro-American conquest would be publicly challenged and a new nation of indigenous peoples would regain its lost freedom and assert its cultural and political autonomy. In July 1990 a dramatic encounter between indigenous leaders of North and South America again emphasized the commonality of experience of five hundred years of external domination and the ideal of transforming societies and cultures of the Americas in 1992 into lands of indigenous autonomy (N. Whitten 1996).

As October 12, 1992, approached, a number of marches and other forms of indigenous protest took place throughout the Sierra. According to Lynn Meisch (1994), the climax of all "Five Hundred Years of Resistance" demonstrations was to be a huge, peaceful march and rally in the historic colonial center of Quito on the day that Columbus initiated his "encounter" with the people of the Americas. Thousands of indigenous people and supporters, including "Afro-Ecuadorians, white-mestizo students, *campesinos,* members of the clergy, and workers" (Meisch 1994:67) turned out for the rally, festive in mood but tightly controlled by military and police in full riot and combat gear. Many would-be participants, possibly thousands, were blocked by military and police at all points of entry to Quito and at strategic departure points from many provinces.

The Levantamiento Indígena of 1990 challenged nation-state control systems. There were clashes with police and military, and the military subsequently occupied large sectors of indigenous land in the Sierra. The Caminata underscored and reaffirmed the challenge. Taken together, these two events emphasized the inner powers and externalized forces of politically conscious indigenous people on the move. *Doce de octubre* demonstrations had the potential of expanding the forces of the Levantamiento and the Caminata but, just before and during the October 12th rally, nation-state officials moved decisively and with a massive show of armed force. The display of force against the indigenous and Afro-Ecuadorian liberation movements enacted the very core expressions of the 1992 symbol of ethnic oppression.

It is significant that both the military and police actually facilitated the Caminata once it was underway and that they refrained from actions leading to bloodshed in the Levantamiento after the initial clashes. From its beginning in Puyo to its arrival in Quito, the Caminata was accompanied by the police; no marchers were officially impeded although some individual conflicts and skirmishes took place. The minister of government, César Verduga Vélez, committed the government to helping the marchers maintain their integrity and make a case for their pragmatic goals. The president of the republic, Dr. Rodrigo Borja Cevallos, is often credited with issuing orders to the military and police leaders to protect these events from the violence of armed confrontation. "This is not against us, nor against our Government, it is against five hundred years of injustice," he is quoted as saying (Rangles Lara 1995:195). This stands in stark contrast to the tragic crushing of Asháninka people by military forces in Peru described by Brown and Fernández (1991).

The Caminata began in Puyo on April 11, 1992, and ended there on May 14. Approximately two thousand indigenous people left Puyo in a driving tropical rainstorm; by the time they reached Salcedo their number had grown to between five thousand and ten thousand. They spent two days in Salasaca, in an unprecedented festive and religious sharing of Andean and Amazonian symbolism. The marchers trekked 180 miles and arrived in Quito thirteen days later. The camp-out in El Ejido park in Quito and negotiations with the president's "social front" matched the drama of the Levantamiento and resulted in the promise of significant accessions of land from the nation-state to indigenous organizations of Pastaza Province.

The Caminata was a powerful pragmatic and political event undertaken as a last resort after the participants had exhausted all other efforts to gain usufruct to their Amazonian territories. It was one of many such manifestations ranging from Mexico through Central America to Colombia, Ecuador, and Bolivia that preceded the quincentennial year 1992. In its general form, the Caminata may be taken to be a microcosm of similar international activities. To the best of our knowledge, the inner symbolism of an emergent movement and the pragmatic externalization of such symbolism has not been described in Latin American settings. This chapter deals with these two phenomena—inner symbolism and pragmatic externalization—as they are embedded in the discourse of those who marched and those who listened to the tales of the marchers.

The Sociopolitical Stage of the Caminata de Pastaza a Quito

Throughout the Caminata, and subsequently, the polarized issue of indigenous leaders as bona fide representatives of indigenous movements on the one side, and as co-opted figureheads for national political powers and international non-governmental organizations on the other, was (and is) salient. No set of preconceived oppositions can help one to understand the pulling and tugging of political, economic, and ideological forces that themselves become intertwined in enduring paradoxes, contradictions, and antinomies (see N. Whitten 1985, 1988, 1996).

In late 1991 and early 1992 officers of OPIP held a series of meetings with representatives of affiliates to evaluate policy regarding territory and politics. The resultant decisions were: to eschew national elections and, instead, to support indigenous candidates for local offices; to march to Quito to negotiate territorial claims with the government; and to seek funds (specifically dollars) from the exterior.

The president of OPIP, Carlos Antonio Vargas Guatatuca (known generally in Ecuador as Antonio Vargas), left Ecuador under the sponsorship of the U.S.-based Rainforest Action Group to raise international funds to save indigenous people and their rain forest. Electronic mail networks carried messages urging supporters of the proposed march to send money in Vargas's name to a bank in Berkeley, California. Other accounts were allegedly set up in Seville and Brussels. After an apparently successful fund-raising drive, Vargas returned to Puyo, according to some accounts, with suitcases full of money.

Rumors about the success of the fund-raising became coupled with confusion and misinterpretation of the initial OPIP goals. Some people thought, or hoped, that the march would also promote the indigenous candidates of the the National Liberation (LN) party for mayor of Puyo and prefect of Pastaza and raise money for their campaigns, while others said that the foreign money from the Caminata fund was being usurped for party-based campaign expenses. This polarity of rhetoric resulted in intraindigenous charges of embezzlement and wider accusations that the march was being financed by or for a political party or a coalition of parties. This verbal jousting did not diminish the ultimate success of the march and indeed was completely muted among indigenous people until the Caminata ended.

The four "historical proposals for the future" (*planteamientos*) resulting from the assessment and evaluation of the indigenous position in the nation in 1992, and for which the Caminata was initiated, were

1. the establishment of permanent territorial rights for indigenous people;
2. the derivation of rights to wealth from territorial commerce, including subsurface exploitation;
3. the final resolution of 117 specific conflicts registered by indigenous people over land rights; and
4. a national constitutional reform to make Ecuador a multicultural, multinational nation-state.

The fundamental purpose of these history-making demands was (and is) to claim all indigenous territory legally controlled by the Ecuadorian nation-state through the agency of the Instituto Ecuatoriano de Reforma Agraria y Colonización, IERAC (Ecuadorian Institute of Agrarian Reform and Colonization), and to place the land occupied by indigenous people under the effective control of formal indigenous organizations.

Organizational plans for the march were drawn up during an OPIP meeting in early March 1992. At least eight commissions and a general coordinator were appointed, and the instructions to participants were issued. Among these were

- that each community should send as many delegates as it can—men, women, children, and elders—and should send powerful delegates, including holders of staffs (in communities where the Catholic Church maintains this system), shamans, "strong ones" who can give orders, and elderly women with special knowledge;
- to bring your own plate, gourd bowl, and spoon;
- to bring your own wrapped chicha (manioc mash), dried rations, and dried meat;
- to bring your own blankets and warm clothes;
- to bring musical instruments, including hand-coiled pottery cornets, drums, slit gongs, flutes, violins, and musical bows; and
- to bring lances, shoulder adornments, and headdresses and come painted as warriors.

After Antonio Vargas returned to Puyo, he held a press conference on March 27 to announce the Caminata. OPIP leaders called on indigenous people throughout Pastaza Province to undertake an arduous journey by river and land to assemble on April 10 at the headquarters of CONFENIAE. The organization's buildings are on a hill overlooking the indigenous community of Unión Base, home of Antonio Vargas.

The appeal to the people was based on the clear message of an earlier (1991–92) pragmatic assessment and evaluation by assembled indigenous leaders: "We either go to Quito now to present our proposals to the president of the republic, or we lose all our territory, and hence our livelihood." OPIP leaders specifically requested the Achuar Jivaroans (Descola 1994), the multicultural Shiwiar (Seymour-Smith 1988), and all Quichua-speaking people of Pastaza Province to unite with people from Canelos and the Comuna San Jacinto del Pindo and to march together from Puyo to Quito. According to *El Comercio* (April 23, 1992, in *Kipu* 1992b:79), representatives of 148 communities of indigenous people of Pastaza Province took part in the march.

On April 8, three days before the march was to begin, the Brigada de la Selva (Brigade of the Rain Forest) #17, based eight miles from Puyo in Shell (named after the Royal Dutch Shell Petroleum Company), militarized the Puyo-Napo and the Puyo-Macas Roads and occupied Unión Base, including the bilingual school there. Troops guarded all gas stations and other waystations on the route of the Caminata, in Amazonia and in the Andes.

On the rainy morning of April 11, roads were jammed with people walking from Unión Base into Puyo to join many others who swarmed into the central plaza. When nearly all were assembled a pottery cornet was blown from somewhere in the crowd. People stood in the downpour to listen to leaders from provincial, regional, and national organizations give speeches. The most moving of these was by Dr. Luis Macas, president of CONAIE.

After they spoke, Macas, Valerio Grefa (president of CONFENIAE), and the other leaders joined the serpentine mass of people, which was colorful with the feather headdresses, bead and bone necklaces, and black and red face paints worn by marchers (*Punto de Vista* in *Kipu* 1992b:5). They crowded into the cathedral for a special mass celebrated by Monseñor Victor Corral, bishop of the Andean city of Riobamba and head of the indigenous ministry of the Catholic Church. The bishop blessed the march as a sacrifice "worthy of being justly examined by the Government and by the Ecuadorian people" (Punto de Vista in *Kipu* 1992b:5). The people reciprocated by presenting a feather headdress to the bishop.

On the other side of town a counter-march organized by FEDECAP—Federación de Desarrollo Campesino de Pastaza (Federation of Development for Small Farmers of Pastaza)—was underway to protest the right of OPIP to speak for the entire province. These protesters were accompanied by cars belonging to a bank and municipal, provincial, and national government agencies. As the Caminata participants left the cathedral to begin their journey, Antonio Vargas addressed the largely colonist counter-marchers, asking them not to see indigenous peoples as their enemies, and assuring them that this fight would be for the good of all Pastaza habitants.

The town became quiet and empty: "not one indigenous person was left in Puyo," wrote Alfonso Chango in 1992. Approximately two thousand Shiwiar, Achuar, and Canelos Quichua left the outskirts of Puyo that rainy afternoon, not knowing how long they would march, what dangers lay ahead, or when they would return. They were led by residents of the Comuna San Jacinto del Pindo, officers of OPIP, and representatives of independent communities loosely associated with OPIP. They marched under a rainbow-colored banner bearing an artist's rendition of the face of Inca Atahualpa with the bold emblematic statement *Allpamanda, causaimanda, jatarishún!* (For land, for life, rise up!).

The march was composed of men, women, and children. Alfonso Chango's expanded kin participated. We have known many of the adults for over thirty-five years. During our research in Puyo and its surrounding areas in 1992, 1993, and 1994, one of the most salient issues of discourse among women and men was their participation in the Caminata. Our role was to listen to what they had to say, ask some questions for clarity, and record discussions on audio- and videotape for later transcription. Alfonso Chango took notes during the Caminata itself and wrote them up in Quichua and Spanish in June and July 1992. Together with Luzmila Salazar, Alfonso's wife, we worked with all of the marchers who took an interest in the project.

The Caminata was undertaken to provide Ecuadorian leaders and the general Ecuadorian populace with a modern, radical alternative to nation-state power over frontier territories in Pastaza Province. Its spokesmen and spokeswomen suggested that, in lands where the nation-state had no colonists, control of such noncolonized regions be ceded to indigenous organizations representing people who knew how to wrest a living from their rain forest and riparian environment. To live productively in the rain forest is to live with the power systems generated by the forest itself and by the encompassing hydrosphere. The concept of "environment," they affirmed, is not something easily transformed into nation-state discourse and bureaucratic management. From their point of view, it would seem, ecology is cultural and the way to understand political-economic demands on the environment involves explication and interpretation (see, e.g., Chango 1984; Viteri 1993).

In their public dialogues speakers made ceaseless mention of male shamanic power and female visionary power. The latter has been manifest in women's creation of songs and hand-coiled ceramics, which are both contemporary renditions of ancient traditions and knowledge (see Chango 1984; D. Whitten 1981; D. Whitten and N. Whitten 1988, 1993).

The Unfolding of a Ritual Drama of the
Caminata de Pastaza a Quito

To the men, women, and children who participated in the Caminata, the march was politically persuasive; it sought legal, ethnic-nationalist control over indigenous usufruct. It was also an aesthetically suasive manifestation of counterhegemonic empowerment. Beauty and ethnic strength were seen to generate a fount of internal, indigenous power that complemented the ideological, political, and economic forces on display. Bolstered by this aesthetic force people talked continually about their environment, which they hoped to bring once again under indigenous control through nationalist legal commitment, action, and compliance.

They talked of mythic time-space (*unai*) and its transformation (*tucuna*) into beginning times-places (*callarirucuguna*) and through times of destruction and ancestral times into the future (*caya*). The future was bound through these transformations to enduring indigenous history. People were clearly conscious of their role in making history, of taking the future into their own hands.

The march proceeded as a dynamic event and as a system of discourse of empowerment on the move. A ritual drama unfolded, which involved the use of a large array of symbolically charged materials. These included foods from native gardens, forests, and rivers; special headdresses, necklaces, and arm bands; carved palm-nut containers for spirit substances; plant dyes for body and face adornment; musical instruments; pottery items; and palmwood lances. In 1992 and 1993 some people brought items they had worn or carried to show us the details of every one of these ritual symbols, and Chango made drawings with notes on the significance of each piece. Many people recalled the specific items that they had previously traded, given, or sold to the Whittens for further study or for use in exhibitions, underscoring the imaged efficacy of such signifiers. We see these ritual objects as constituting a cultural map of signifiers of specific markers of social and material indigenous endurance (e.g., Turner 1974:239).

Three ritual items—pottery cornets, face and body paints, and headdresses—illustrate the symbolic embeddedness of these objects in the drama of the Caminata. Cornets, sounded at the beginning and then blown throughout the march, are made only by women, usually for special kinship festivals held in indigenous hamlets and geographically remote areas where the evidence of the Catholic Church is typically reflected in the presence of a crude chapel. When the festival atmosphere escalates into chaos, a woman who made

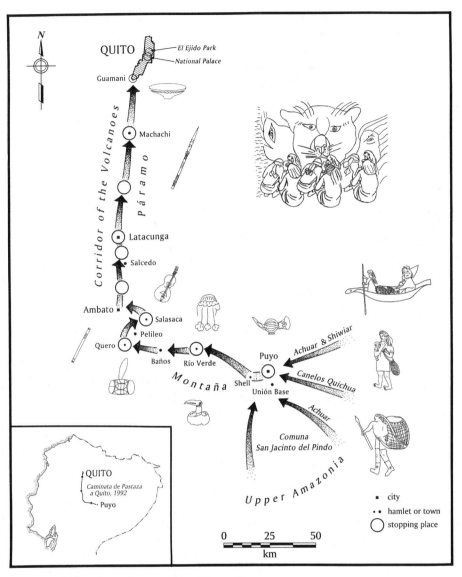

Map of cultural signifiers. Icons by Alfonso Chango.

a cornet presents it, filled with *asua,* to an important man. He sits on a long bench that symbolizes the anaconda, drinks the *asua,* and then blows on the cornet while other men beat drums, play flutes, and dance with women.

The cornet makes the haunting sound of the game bird Trumpeter who, in mythic time-space transforming into beginning times-places, comes as a forest warrior to rescue two beautiful women in distress. He fails. Other game birds as warriors arrive to liberate the two women and they also fail. Finally Toucan (Sicuanga Runa) arrives and frees them. The women then turn the warriors into the game birds of the forest and create the basic colors of red, yellow, black, and white to give beauty to the world (see D. Whitten and N. Whitten 1988 for more of these elaborations). Stories such as this one were told repeatedly, with much elaboration, by the marchers during 1992, 1993, and 1994.

Symbols of representation—face painting, feather headdresses and special shoulder slings, necklaces and arm bands—are ancient practices nowadays mainly relegated to the ritual kinship festivals. The black and red paint (from *Genipa americana* and *Bixa orellana,* respectively) symbolize the beauty given to humans by the two mythic women (Widuj Warmi and Manduru Warmi) who transformed themselves into these trees. Men and women make special nut and gourd containers for their paints. The most treasured of these paints is *carawira,* made of *Bixa orellana,* red sap from one of several trees, and anaconda fat. The mixture itself is one of many substances called *sima-yuca.* Men and women paint a little of this along the edge of their eyelids before facing danger. By then looking directly at one's foe, one "sees" as the anaconda "sees." Foes are neutralized in that their vindictive will (*manalli shungu*) is suppressed. In this aesthetic action, if the self in its mystic as well as human dimensions is correctly presented, the foe cannot injure the person so painted.

The headdresses worn by men constitute our third illustration of the ramifying and intersecting cultural map of signifiers. Each headdress must have a direct relationship to birds, reptiles, amphibians, and mammals the maker or wearer (headdresses are often exchanged and traded) has encountered. Each man who makes a headdress must first encounter the being he is to kill in a dream and "know" in a transcendental way that this creature will be "his." Bird feathers, once woven into a headdress, represent the colors and sounds of the spirit world because each feather exhibits flashes and streaks of color usually visible only to spirits. When a human being takes soul-vine brew, however, the colors and sounds of the spirit world may be revealed to the taker. Attached to the back of a headdress are pieces of cloth, bone, nut, or other tangible things. Each of these represents the transformation of a spirit with which the maker of the headdress is comfortable. Each spirit so represented has its distinct sound—*breep, breep, breep, breep*—and, when it moves, a distinct motion, usually in a directed spiral—*wshhh wshhh wshhh wshhh*. These sounds and motions can be heard and seen by spirits.

The moving performances of the Caminata included dances and songs by women taking on the personae of powerful spirit-animals and birds (black jaguar woman, hawk woman, owl woman), of master spirits in feminine manifestation, and of other people of the rain forest (*Llushtirunaguna,* unclothed forest people). Focal women were called *sinchi muscuyuj warmi* (strong visionary women or women who "see").

Many men took on the personae of ancient warriors of mythology and history, including *sicuanga runa* (the liberator person) and *curaga* (ancient heads of different Quichua peoples) (see N. Whitten 1985). They called themselves *guerreros* (warriors) and *guardianes* (guardians). They were overseen by shamans called the *sinchi yachaj runa* (strong men who know) and motivated by the *sinchi muscuyuj warmi* (strong women who "see"). During the summers of 1992, 1993, and 1994 the Whittens worked closely with several *guerreros* and *guardianes* and with one of the *sinchi yachaj runa,* and also with several of the *sinchi muscuyuj warmi*. Several of Chango's relatives were among these special people; one of his brothers was (and is) a *sinchi yachaj*.

Spirits (*supai*) cannot be brought directly to a march; to do so would be to introduce a monster into the midst of the crowd. (The Achuar and Shiwiar call such a being *iwianch*.) The mystical works of spirits are recognized as essences. It is the essences that constitute the signifieds. Quichua speakers think of these essences as living force (*causai*) or breath (*samai*). They are said to have an inner proof and on occasion to manifest a special tangibility. These essences were brought into the march, where they were named and identified, and the forces they manifested were incorporated into what all described as a sustained emotional experience. The spirits included Amasanga, spirit master of the rain forest and indigenous territory; Jurijuri Supai, the dangerous underground spirit of other peoples' territories; Urcu Supai, the dangerous spirit of hills and their hidden caves; Waira Supai, the spirit of wind that brings torrential rains; and many others.

It was on April 12 that the ritual drama brought together the spirit forces of the rain-forest and riparian habitat of the native peoples of modern Pastaza Province. That night, in their camp at Río Verde on the Puyo-Baños road between Amazonia and the Andes, shamans gathered. The marchers were now in the veritable *montaña* (sometimes called the *yunga* by Andean Quichua speakers), the legendary topographical and ritual site of the Yumbo. By drinking soul-vine brews the shamans sought mystical union with powerful legendary forces. As the shamans entered into collective and individual trances, moving between the spirit world of the forests and the hills of this familiar environment, women sang and danced and the guardians and warriors prepared for whatever intrusion might occur.

On Monday, April 13, the two thousand marchers moved out before dawn toward their first Andean destination; from there they would begin their northward trek toward Quito across the immense Andes through the Corridor of the Volcanoes. They marched together rapidly and robustly, making loud noises—calling in falsettos, beating drums, playing flutes, blowing cornets, and shouting slogans. Past the hydroelectric plant and beyond Agoyán Falls, they moved through a long dark tunnel that eerily echoed their calls, songs, drumming, and cornet sounding. They forced their sounds to an even greater crescendo as they poured out into the sunlit Andean world and moved across the bridge over the huge dam near the headwaters of the Pastaza River.

Passing Baños late in the afternoon, they quieted as they veered off to the indigenous community of Quero (southwest of Pelileo), where they were met clandestinely by representatives from Salasaca. Thus the march entered the escalating drama of Andean theater on its third day, establishing what Victor Turner (1974) called a "charged field" wherein cultural paradigms emerge, are tested, and acquire a cultural life that transcends the dynamics of the social movement itself.

Passage into Liminality-1

By the end of the day on Monday a feeling of uncertainty shrouded the marchers. Many of them had injured their feet on gravel, cobblestones, and macadam. They were treated by shamans and by a physician using Western medicine. People wondered what would happen next, and they decided to see what would transpire with anticipated new allies in enemy territory. Now the people were "betwixt and between" (Turner 1974:13)—out of their known environment and far from their destination.

The liminal period that began in Quero became transformed ceremonially into a remarkable series of events in Salasaca. Salasacans said that the Yumbo had arrived in the Andes and the marchers said that they took no offense with the use of the word in this context. At this point everything changed; the shroud of uncertainty was removed. Salasacans came from all sectors of their territory in ceremonial dress associated with Corpus Christi, beating huge painted snare drums, playing flutes, and dancing as they do during the major festivals that punctuate the ritual year. Salasacans gave an abundance of food—corn, beans, potatoes, and fruit—to the marchers (whose own food, backpacked from Puyo, was by this stage depleted) and also loaned them warm clothes. As other men, women, and children from Amazonia and the Andes continued to arrive, the shamans of the lowlands drank soul-vine brew and received council from the Salasacan shamans about the mountain and weather spirits of the Andes.

Narrators later said that an integration had taken place, uniting contemporary worlds that had once been conjoined but had long been divided. Andean and Amazonian peoples united with Andean and Amazonian spirits. In trances the lowland shamans "saw" that the frigid Andean winds would not blow, that rain, sleet, and hail would not fall as they crossed the *páramo* (11–16,000 feet elevation), and that Indi, the sun, would shine during the entire trek to Quito. They also foresaw that their powerful adversaries throughout the Amazonian and Andean regions would be overcome or circumvented as they marched forward, and that more and more compatriots would come to their aid. They saw victory in their immediate future *(cayamanda)*.

The Salasacans spent that night and the next day partaking in festivities that had not been celebrated in many years. They were joined by even larger indigenous groups from various other parts of the Sierra, while still more indigenous people from the lowland rain forest arrived by bus and truck. The doubts the marchers had harbored on arrival in the Andes were now dispelled. Reinvigorated, they prepared to move out together on April 16.

Puriáun! (Trek on!) At dawn, spiritually, psychically, and physically fortified, they resumed their advance toward Quito, still far to the north. The marchers described their undulating procession as *amarunshina*, "like an anaconda."[2] During annual or semiannual kinship festivals that celebrate the oneness of a people, the Canelos Quichua walk in circles and dance to the pulse-tremolo of many snare drums, creating a cultural force field (see N. Whitten 1976, 1985; D. Whitten and N. Whitten 1988). Alfonso Chango and others saw the Caminata as creating this same force, here in the form of movement evoking the powers of the spirit master Amasanga—*tan, tan, tan, tan, tan, tan* (blows on the head of the drum); *ween, ween, ween, ween, ween, ween* (buzzes of the snares)—and heading northward toward the national capital.

Danger lay ahead, for the marchers had to circumvent the third-largest city in Ecuador, Ambato—a treacherous urban zone known to be replete with residents who hated and feared indigenous people and their social movements. A hub between north and south Andean cities and towns, located between the coast and the Andes and between the Andes and the Amazonian region, Ambato had been virtually closed down for five days in 1990 by participants in the Levantamiento Indígena (see N. Whitten 1996).

Passage into Liminality-2

As the Caminata approached and passed through Ambato early on Thursday morning, hundreds of indigenous people joined it. Now heading due north toward Salcedo and the first night beyond Andean indigenous territory, three thousand to five thousand people were on the move—shouting, laughing, singing, beating snare drums, flourishing palmwood (*chonta*) lances and knives, and calling out names to people watching from a respectable distance, "Hey you, monkey person; look here at us, the *indios*. We are on trek; be careful of us; we are the powerful ones."

North of Ambato, high above the Yambo Lagoon, marchers met with the parents of two "disappeared" youths (the Restrepo brothers, victims of alleged police atrocities; España Torres 1996). At an emotional end to the encounter, they collectively cast a palmwood lance into the lake as a symbolic petition for justice for the Restrepo brothers. Following this ritual protest of injustice, the marchers took stock of where they might be in relation to their eventual destination. The longest period in ever-higher and colder climes lay ahead. No one knew how many days the march would take. The sick were healed with medicines provided by the Red Cross, with "popular" medicines brought by Andean healers, and by shamanic performances and ministrations. Warriors, guardians, and shamans consulted with one another and all agreed that only the very ill might now turn back. The die was cast. The marchers would now press on to Quito.

The next day—Good Friday—the marchers departed by 6:00 A.M., resolutely heading toward Salcedo. More and more indigenous people from the provinces of Tungurahua, Chimborazo, and Cotopaxi joined, coming from feeder trails and roads onto the Panamerican highway, surging toward a route that would take them through the center of town. The Caminata entered Salcedo around midday, and thousands more turned out to cheer on the marchers. To the surprise of many—indigenous and nonindigenous people alike—not a single negative comment or slur was heard as the marchers went through Salcedo. Everything was upbeat and positive. Firsthand reports indicate that the march was "like a celebratory parade"; people threw flowers from balconies and from the sides of streets and cheered "Long live the march!" and "Go to Quito and claim your rights as indigenous Ecuadorians!"

After camping overnight without further incident, the marchers pressed on to Latacunga and camped just outside this market-oriented city around midday. The ranks had swelled enormously with indigenous people from the *páramo* area of Zumbagua Parish to the west and from other settlements to the east of Latacunga. Here for the first time the indigenous people symbolically reversed the brutality of the colonial and republican rule over native Andean peoples. Nonindigenous people (some allegedly from the military) had infiltrated the march and were trying to elicit information to take to enemies of the Caminata. As word passed among warriors, guardians, and shamans about the intruders, the guardians rounded them up, tied them to trees or stakes, stripped off their britches, poured icy water on their buttocks and genitals—thereby supposedly cooling their *machismo*—and, in some instances, enacted what marchers called *la ley del indio* (law of the indian) or *justicia indígena* (indigenous justice): practical or vigilante enactment of "law." Some press releases called this practice *la ley de la selva* (law of the jungle). When the Whittens discussed this use of language, in Spanish, with people who had taken part in the Caminata, some participants used the Spanish verb *castigar* (to punish) to describe such acts.

The importance of punishing "spies" was underscored by all marchers who chose to discuss the Caminata with us. The guardians and warriors were entrusted with the obligation to arrest (*prender*), to punish (*castigar*), and to release (*soltar*) those found inside the Caminata formation who had not been specifically invited by a marcher. We were repeatedly told by marchers, who spoke in earnest tones and made forceful and persuasive eye contact, that "we also have laws" and "we also have rights."

This sequence of discovering, arresting, punishing, and releasing is itself a social drama within a larger social drama. It is an onstage reversal of the brutal practices of hacienda owners or overseers who tied indigenous serfs or sharecroppers to posts and publicly whipped them for refusing or failing to produce for the owners. Sometimes people died as a consequence of this punishment; moreover, they had no legal recourse. On the Caminata (as in the Levantamiento of 1990) some marchers did take action against captured infiltrators but they released those they had whipped and, as they pointed out to reporters, their whips consisted of single strips of rawhide, unlike those used by the *hacendados,* which were made of multiple leather strips with steel tips on the ends, to lacerate, maim, and scar. Nor did indigenous marchers use their lances as spears. Their lances were only for defense, not for punishment. To spear someone with a lance would be a reversion to the cultural status of *auca,* "savage."

Enactment of indigenous justice on the march was an onstage activity, one of many designed to communicate the sense of indigenous control to a regional and national audience. Only those the marchers considered a threat were placed in the spotlight of punishment. Others, such as Ecuadorian ethnographer Diego Quiroga, who met the Caminata at Yambo Lagoon just beyond Ambato, were invited in, albeit clandestinely. Diego simply walked near the front line of the march until Marcelo Santi Simbaña saw him. Marcelo identified Diego to his brother, Bolívar Santi Simbaña, and together they motioned him to enter their sector of the Comuna San Jacinto marchers and excitedly told him about what they were doing. This backstage activity—also open to selected representatives of the press and some politicians and social activists—carried numerous messages beyond that conveyed by the primary dramatic event. Such encounters always remained backstage and involved at most two or three designated spokesmen who chose their own times and places for formal interviews.

That Saturday afternoon and evening in Latacunga a significant indigenous cultural exchange took place. Spokesmen for different indigenous organizations voiced mutual respect for one another and urged their followers to listen to and try to understand a range of indigenous perspectives. Leaders of various groupings gave formal speeches about their formations, strategies, and goals.

The next leg of the trek was the most arduous. The marchers walked one hundred kilometers through one of the coldest regions of Ecuador and camped at a frigid elevation of eleven thousand feet. Easter night was grim; one child, succumbing to cold and fever, died in her mother's arms.

Broken Barriers

The march from Latacunga across the *páramo* to the outskirts of Quito took three days. As they entered Machachi on the second day, people's spirits were buoyed by the knowledge that representatives of more organizations had joined them in solidarity (*Kipu* 1992b:63). Near the end of the third day, when Quito could be seen from the distance, cars and buses full of counterdemonstrators from FEDECAP blocked the way. These organized anti-Caminata groups, which included some indigenous people, were armed with guns, axes, machetes, clubs, and other deadly implements. As they began to form a roadblock, small groups of guardians and warriors wielding lances as slicing clubs (*macana*) suddenly attacked them. The antagonists had expected a standoff during which the march would stop and the military and police would intervene. Instead the marchers attacked immediately. Those blocking the road retreated quickly with bleeding faces, cracked skulls, and bruised or broken limbs. The route of the march was successfully defended and the Caminata proceeded along the Panamerican highway to the last camp before entering Quito, the old and once-indigenous community of Guamaní, now incorporated into expanding south Quito.

South Quito is a sector where the indigenous/nonindigenous polarity regularly dissolves and reemerges. Despite the potential for opposition here, the march was favorably received by thousands of residents of south Quito. No marcher reported any hostility. People arrived around 5:00 P.M. and rested in preparation for an early departure the next day. At least some residents of south Quito were familiar with the idea of forest people coming to the urban center; a ritual festival called the *yumbada* was performed in 1991 in barrio La Magdalena, not far from the marchers' route. Roggiero's extended commentary of the south Quito *yumbada* urges readers of the popular newspaper *Hoy,* modeled on *USA Today,* to "comprehend and evaluate its profound significance" (Roggiero 1991:3C).

Simón Espinosa (1992a:159) wrote poetically about the political drama unfolding as the Caminata moved through south Quito.

And the Jungle Arrives in Quito:

> Before dawn on Thursday, the inhabitants of the south of the capital awoke frightened [as in a sudden surprise assault that terrifies]. The jungle had arrived in Quito. At four in the morning of the foretold day the march began its final assault. A dark and noisy army of indígenas advanced on the pavement miming monkeys and birds, howling [yelling, crying out], making falsetto calls, beating drums. The lights of the houses came on. The sleeping citizens got up and applauded. The great indigenous serpent encountered the factory workers entering their dawn shift. Two opposed worlds with one destiny crossed.

The marchers departed from Guamaní in the cold darkness well before dawn on April 23. They were now accompanied by indigenous delegations from Azuay, Cañar, Chimborazo, Tungurahua, Cotopaxi, Pichincha, and Imbabura—most of the provinces of the Sierra. Afro-Ecuadorian people who had come from Esmeraldas province on the north coast had also joined them. The march proceeded up the southern Panamerican highway through one urban barrio after another; residents came out just to look and often to cheer. One large elementary school released all its students, and the teachers encouraged them to sing and shout and chant, "Welcome, indigenous brothers." The teachers waived Ecuadorian flags and white flags with "Equality," "Peace," "Love," and "Justice" printed on them (*Hoy* April 25, 1992; in *Kipu* 1992b:110).

The march passed through the Santo Domingo Plaza, surged on to the San Blas Plaza and the Plaza de Independencia, and arrived at the Plaza de San Francisco at 9:30 A.M. The stream of people, now between five thousand and ten thousand strong, moved through streets lined with police in full riot gear and curious onlookers standing ten to twenty deep. There were reports of minor confrontations with police. Shamans, warriors, and guardians wielding chonta lances countered the threats by police to strike marchers with rubber batons or the butts of their rifles. Conscious opposition, said those whose narration we follow, won out over the highly organized, repressive tactics of police.

The Plaza de Independencia and the Plaza de San Francisco are in the colonial center of Quito. The body of indigenous Amazonian and Andean people was now united with the heartland and headship of Ecuadorian nation-state power. This unity provoked enormous social and political tensions that had significant ramifications for that very power.

As the Quichua, Achuar, and Shiwiar crowded into the Plaza de San Francisco, their indigenous leaders—Luis Macas, president of CONAIE, Valerio Grefa, president of CONFENIAE, and Antonio Vargas, president of OPIP, along with many others—accompanied by police, prepared to meet with the president of the republic, Dr. Rodrigo Borja Cevallos. As the president left the national palace accompanied by indigenous and national leaders, he hesitated. Up stepped Apacha Vargas; she took his arm, and told him not to be afraid. She asserted that the marchers are all his *ushis* and *churis* (sons and daughters of the *patria*), that all was peaceful. Together they walked to the plaza where the president addressed the assembled mass of people. The president offered them their land, and Grefa and Vargas publicly thanked him gracefully in Spanish and in Quichua. Then the leaders turned to the people in the Plaza de San Francisco and announced that usufruct would be ceded to indigenous people; the crowd cheered and shouted at the news.

The mayor of Quito, Rodrigo Paz (founder of the largest chain of money-change houses in Ecuador, and presidential candidate in 1996), offered the marchers space to set up camp in El Ejido Park. They readily accepted and the Caminata proceeded northward out of the colonial sector and into the modern one, past the Central Bank of Ecuador and to the park, which is surrounded by the House of Ecuadorian Culture, the Hilton Colón Intercontinental Hotel, several international banks, and other corporate and government buildings. Here, as thousands of marchers settled down, President Borja again spoke, sketching the details of the "gift" of Amazonian land to its indigenous inhabitants. The speech carried these chilling messages:

- The president could do nothing about changing the constitution to make Ecuador a multinational state; only the Congress could do this.
- With regard to the request that government-owned land be transferred to indigenous people, the president promised that a "positive dialogue" would be opened between the two parties.
- The government would set up a fifteen-day period of "study" to be undertaken by a "social front" composed of representatives from the Ministry of Government, the Department of Defense, the Program for Welfare, and the Ecuadorian Institute for Land Reform and Colonization (IERAC).

With this speech the president made it clear—as it had not been hitherto—that the government would talk and delay. The marchers, however, had come for immediate results. To remain too long in Quito could be deadly for the Amazonian people. The conflict pitted indigenous against bureaucratic concerns.

The marchers were now out of liminality; they were no longer "betwixt and between" (Turner 1974:13). They had arrived at the antipode of their origins, the sacred center of the republic—urban, urbane, sophisticated, white, powerful, Catholic, stratified, and Iberian-oriented Quito.

During this period supporters arrived from many parts of the Andean highlands, and another delegation of coastal black people from Esmeraldas Province also arrived. More people poured in from the south, heading for the park, and downtown Quito was heavily guarded by police outfitted in protective gear, including helmets with face protectors, shields, rubber batons, and canisters of tear gas. Few, however, carried firearms. Onlookers reported that it was exceedingly difficult to get through the police to speak to, or even see, the marchers. And if they did penetrate the police barriers they were met by guardians and warriors wielding palmwood lances that constituted the ultimate perimeter of defense of the March for Land and Life.

The Yumbo, many onlookers said, had returned. A new but ancient body of power was pulsating within the city. *Los selváticos nos interpelan* ("The savages [forest dwellers] implore our [Quiteño] aid") announced the prominent headline of one editorial of the April 26 newspaper *Hoy,* written by the historian Galo Ramón Valarezo (*Kipu* 1992b:118–19):

Are We Interested in Their Visit?

[It is] a novel consequence that the Amazonian indians, those "yumbos of the jungle," address in the first instance the Quito Runa [runa quiteños] in a demand of solidarity. We remember the *yumbadas,* these famous festivals of Quito in which the indians from yumbos visit to celebrate this type of encounter. [It] appears interesting that they seek solidarity from numerous different groups to share the destiny of a subaltern sector [of people] of Ecuador [who are] ignored and segregated.

That Ecuadorian journalists and other writers turned to a north Ecuadorian Andean festival is significant. From the entry to south Quito onward, the collective consciousness of marchers and the massive Ecuadorian audience following the moving theater through radio, television, newspapers, and magazines increasingly focused on the symbolism—explicit and implicit—of this *yumbada*. For Caminata participants, the space they now occupied represented centuries of cultural terror for native peoples; in the eyes of elite and other Quito residents, a reciprocal cultural terror might now, in turn, be imminent. Quito had become a living embodiment of what Michael Taussig (1987) calls "the space of death." And ironically, much like Taussig's description of such developments, out of this space of death came powers to heal. Using a common ideological body metaphor for the Ecuadorian nation-state, Ramón Valarezo enunciates the new disposition:

> We Ecuadorians will gain more if we "permit" the selváticos [those of the forest, implying "savages"] to continue managing the [Amazonian] region that they have managed for thousands of years. Conservation is the lung of Ecuador and the world is going to believe in the traditional science of the selváticos. (Ramón Valarezo 1992:118)

We now turn to a north Ecuadorian ritual of reversal in order to ground such discourse in symbolic structures that emerge during a collective crisis involving encounters with Amazonian peoples.

Cultural Representation and Ritual Reversal

The symbolic evocations of the Caminata bear dramatic resemblances to the Andean ceremony *yumbada* performed in north Ecuador during June and July, as a parallel to the Catholic festivals of Corpus Christi. Throughout the Ecuadorian Andes, Quito is described as the "head, heart, and soul" of the Ecuadorian social body. Members of the Quito elite and upper classes often use such lofty figures of speech. Although only a small percentage of the population of Ecuador lives in the Amazonian territories, Quiteños nonetheless think of Amazonia as inextricably bound to the past and future of its special society. More than half of this Amazonian body was severed from its

Andean head in 1941 during a war with Peru, prompting the charged nationalist motto "Ecuador is, has been, and will be an Amazonian country!"

In north Quito, as in other areas of the Ecuadorian highlands, the *yumbada* is held by people who strongly identify themselves as Quiteños and indigenous. During the festival, the identifying emblem of "Quito Runa" (indigenous person of Quito) emerges. This figure reverses the hierarchical polarity of white over "Indian" and white over black, and negates *mestizaje* redemption. To be Quito Runa in the *yumbada* ceremony is also to evoke the power of the Yumbo people from the eastern tropical rain forest of Upper Amazonia (N. Whitten 1988).[3]

Yumbo is a multivocalic term with its origin in the northwest rain-forest slopes of the western Cordillera of the Ecuadorian Andes (Cabello de Balboa 1945; Fine 1991; Lippi 1986; Salomon 1981, 1986; Weismantel 1988). Some time after the Spanish conquest, the Catholic clergy and indigenous people of the Ecuadorian Andes and elsewhere began using it to refer to powerful indigenous healers (including human healers and mystical, spirit healers) on either side of the Andes. Upper Amazonian rain-forest dwellers, or inhabitants of the designated area of origin, were particularly inclined to use the term (Oberem 1971; Salomon 1986). The term Yumbo is often used by indigenous Andean people as a synonym for *yachaj* (Quichua) or *sabio* (Spanish), both of which mean "one who knows," "shaman."

It is also a pejorative term in the Andes for Quichua-speaking people who come from Amazonia. Such people self-identify as Runa, a term by which they mean fully human. Today, when used nonpejoratively in the Andes, Yumbo carries the connotations of spirit power, mystical founts of Amazonian knowledge, and shamanic gnosis.

In his chapter "Killing the Yumbo: A Ritual Drama of Northern Quito," Frank Salomon (1981) discusses this extended indigenous performance, which takes place during or near the time of Corpus Christi in urban (and urbane) north Quito. During this drama, Spanish-speaking native urbanites who also speak Quichua celebrate the coming of forest people to the capital city. In this context, the word Yumbo connotes "semi-civilized" (Quichua) and "wild, free, and savage" (Auca), both with the specific designation of shaman. The Yumbos arrive in Quito; the world turns upside-down; and a liminal space comes into being between urbanity and savagery, humanity and animality, city and forest, and head and body. Mediating this creation of reversal are the mountain mothers who stand in an intermediate position between Quito and the coastal rain forest, and between Quito and the Amazonian rain forest.

Salomon poignantly describes an event that occurs early in the ceremony. This is the transformation of a central participant, Segundo Salazar Imapanta, as he "looks both outward, toward the luminous snowcaps fencing the Andean *altiplano* [high plateau] off from the Amazonian and Pacific rain forest, and downward, toward the white skyline of the highland metropolis" (Salomon 1981:162–63). He is an urbane caretaker of the international airport, a true Andean Quiteño, with gray suit and trim mustache. Salomon then quotes Salazar Imapanta's feelings about the palmwood lances that he keeps in his home to explain the difference between collectors' curios and the imagery of life forces that connect what other quiteños take to be the antithetical extremes of city and forest, civilized and savage: "The mountain accompanies the lance, and the lance accompanies me; the lance and I are one single being when we are dancing" (Salomon 1981:162–63).

In July 1979, N. Whitten attended one Yumbo festival with Frank Salomon in North Quito. Whitten had returned from field research with Canelos Quichua indigenous people of Pastaza Province, and it was soon clear to the festival participants that he was not only fascinated by but also familiar with what they were doing and portraying. Parts of the *camari* feast, as well as the dancing of the *lanceros*, bore uncanny cultural resemblance to the *jista* with which he was familiar. Participants wanted him to know, though, that this was a festival, like a theater (*teatroshina*), and that they were miming or "playing with" (*pugllana*) the forces and images of the forest. They insisted that no real shamanic forces, such as those manifest in the spirits of rain forest or Andean mountains, were being summoned: the power to summon spirits belongs to those from or of the lowland forest.

We return now to the Caminata of 1992. As symbolic activities coalesced and expanded amid intense scrutiny by the Ecuadorian populace and press, a transformation occurred wherein the spiritual realm acquired focal salience. Pragmatic activities were not diminished by merging with the spiritual; to the contrary, they were significantly enhanced. The Caminata created a palpable rift in the social and political fabric of the Ecuadorian nation. Unlike the quasi-theatrical ceremonial drama of the *yumbada*, the passages into liminality of the march did establish powerful mystical links between the Andean and Amazonian shamans, Andean and Amazonian spirit forces, and Andean and Amazonian peoples. The marchers expanded their theatricality, but they were not "play-acting": they were *en*-acting.

The entry to Quito forced the nation to consider the reality of indigenous power, which embraced all people; events in the Ejido Park reaffirmed a reality of Quito Runa-Amazonian Runa solidarity that collapsed elite-sponsored polarities and oppositions, already weakened during the Levantamiento of 1990. The Caminata was simultaneously pragmatic and theatrical. It both accomplished a political-economic goal and expanded the conjoined human and spirit spheres of empowerment.

Life in El Ejido Park: Alternative Modernities

Throughout Ecuador it was quite clear that the Caminata was a quintessential political event. It was a dramatic and courageous act that called for radically alternative strategies of Amazonian development. It was also a quintessential ritual metaphor of the kind that is well-known in modern and traditional pilgrimages. It created an affecting presence (Armstrong 1971) that transcended, while also undergirding, the political actions.

Those in the front section of the Caminata, most of whom were residents of the Comuna San Jacinto del Pindo and Puyo proper, described their sense of elation that the event was "like a festival" (*jistashina*) but far more intense. During the Caminata Clara Santi Simbaña composed and sang the song translated and presented on pages 13–14. When she sang this in El Ejido Park, a number of people recorded it and asked her questions about her provenance and her life. One of her brothers, Marcelo Santi Simbaña, was asked to cure Quiteños of many afflictions, including magical fright (*susto*), evil eye (*mal ojo*), and evil or malignant air (*mal aire*). People from humble rural areas, sophisticated offices, and urbane homes alike came to the park and sought out shamans among the campers. Those who came to be cured were respectful; some remembered a trip to the upper Amazon or a sojourn there in the military. Many other Quiteños stayed away and, when passing the park, looked away. For them the Yumbo represented the embodiment of filth and contamination emanating from the distant forest to the enlightened civilization of Quito.

The combination of the female projection of song and the beauty that flows from it with the male projection of shamanic control and its own, complementary beauty provided the indigenous multitude in El Ejido Park with a nationally staged paradigm of indigenous culture. Multidimensional concepts of knowledge, vision, and power were now located in the capital city (see Salomon 1981; N. Whitten 1976a, 1985; D. Whitten and N. Whitten 1988).

Clara, Apacha, Marcelo, and more than two thousand other Amazonian residents of Ecuador had walked to Quito to claim, in an ethnic nationalist idiom, the territory that they said had belonged to their *mayores* (old ones, elders). The national press routinely translated *mayores* into *antepasados* (ancestors). The press often represented indigenous people as bumpkin relics from the past who did not know the Spanish language well enough to express themselves properly. Indigenous people were viewed by many Quiteños as *indios alzados* (unruly indians) and *indios fuera de su lugar* (indians out of place), and they were said to lack consciousness.

Indigenous marchers, however, clearly knew—and stated quite specifically—which of their elders had previously walked to Quito to request rights to their rain-forest territory. Indeed, the late Virgilio Santi (father of Clara and Marcelo) and his brother Camilo (who died in 1994 over the age of ninety), along with other brothers and indigenous leaders, made such a trek in the 1940s.[4] As a result, in 1947 they secured the Comuna San Jacinto del Pindo from the Ecuadorian *caudillo* (renowned leader) and president, the late Dr. José María Velasco Ibarra (N. Whitten 1976a). Perhaps no onlookers realized that, years before, Velasco Ibarra had been healed by a powerful Zaparoan-Canelos Quichua shaman, Eliseo Vargas, grandfather of Antonio Vargas, in the small hamlet of Unión Base.

Clara composed her song while marching with a host of indigenous people numbering somewhere between two thousand and ten thousand. Clara, deliberately colorful in her two-piece jaguar-skin outfit and ocelot-skin hat, sunburned and with blisters on her feet, sang while accompanied by her husband, Abraham Chango, on a three-hole transverse flute (*Hoy* April 22, 1992, in *Kipu* 1992b:69). She was widely recorded and photographed by Ecuadorians, Europeans, and North Americans.

Clara's theatricality in foreign territory showed that she was self-reflexive and that she knew that she and her kin were taking on the role of the ancient Yumbo who traveled to Quito only to be killed and then resurrected by an Amazonian shaman (Salomon 1981; N. Whitten 1981, 1988). But, she later told us, she feared that the people who took her picture and recorded her songs and dances did not understand the underlying messages about the garden, the forest, domesticity, and the awesome danger of uncontrolled power—the very nature of indigenous concepts of territoriality. Nor did they know that she was an accomplished potter and gardener. She was a veritable *muscuj* (or *muscuyuj*) *warmi*—the feminine equivalent of a male shaman. For most Ecuadorians, epoch history in the making still excluded the specific history of women, let alone indigenous women.

Runa Wañungachu?—Will People Die?

In Canelos Quichua thought and cosmology it is expected that people will, from time to time, leave their homes and travel to other territories. Their mythology revolves around two men, or two women, traveling in transforming times-spaces from one point to another. In real life, men and women trek to establish and maintain distant gardens, to fish, or to mine clay; men trek to hunt. People go to visit relatives or powerful ones in distant territories. These are exciting but normal events, and return is expected. Shamans in seance travel in and out of the spirit world and this is very dangerous—to stay in that world is to die in this one. Shamans, dreamers, and powerful image makers may also travel to other times-places; if they do not return, they die (see N. Whitten 1985:106–63). When Marcelo Santi called the Whittens from Quito, he did not say anything about the possibility of being killed, although later, in June 1992, in Puyo, he told them that this could have happened.

On April 23, President Borja had requested a fifteen-day period to study the petition for adjudication of Amazonian lands. As days and nights turned into weeks and the deadline approached, tensions continued to mount among the campers. For most of them, serious reflection and a mood of growing trepidation replaced the excitement that had accompanied the intense activity of the Caminata. It was reported that the cordoned-off encampment had expanded to cover about one-third of El Ejido Park. The city of Quito had set up portable latrines and provided water supplies. Food, medicines, blankets, and clothes were donated by private individuals and institutions and by numerous other indigenous communities. A reporter noticed that the lowland apparel of feathers and skins was being replaced by modern clothing and that some campers were selling Amazonian products, including pure snake oil and even a live boa constrictor for the equivalent of US$35.00. People did not know how, when, or if they would return home. No one could have predicted the series of events that was to unfold as the campers awaited the results of Borja's response to their demands.

The government's efforts to resolve the land claim legally and equitably, without compromising subsoil rights or national sovereignty, became increasingly complicated because of an outpouring of opposition in the form of accusations, counterclaims, and demonstrations by the military, colonists, and sierran indigenous people. The military not only opposed the concept of plural nationality but, under the laws of national security, refused to sanction any decrease in the fifty-kilometer security zone along the border with Peru, where many indigenous people live.

As negotiations stalled, about seven hundred campers marched to the Ministry of Social Welfare on May 5 intending to occupy the building and so increase pressure on the government. The work of the national police security guards was slowed by indigenous guardians who surrounded the building; but, after representatives of the demonstrators talked with the minister of state, all the marchers returned peacefully to the park. After this encounter, word spread that the government had reached a decision, which would be announced on May 6 on national television and radio networks. This advisory informed indigenous people throughout the republic that the administration would grant 1,115,574 hectares of land to all indigenous communities of Pastaza; that the security zone on the frontier would be reduced to forty kilometers; and that the territory of the Yasuní National Park would be extended but remain under government control. Leaders of the march immediately expressed their dissatisfaction with the land offer, which amounted to a concession of about 65 percent of their initial request. They objected, also, to the refusal of their requests to reduce the security zone to two kilometers, and to transfer the Yasuní reserve to indigenous control. Seven members of OPIP carried the protest slightly further the night of May 7 by occupying the IERAC building; they did not resist when they were removed several hours later by a detachment of three hundred police.

Back in Puyo, there was immediate reaction from the opposition organizations, some of whose members had jeered the departing marchers on April 11. In protest to the unilateral land accession to OPIP, they dynamited a section of the Puyo-Baños road, threatened to impede the return of the marchers from Quito, and declared a province-wide strike that would entail, among other acts, blocking all major roads in Pastaza Province.

There were parallel reactions and counterprotests on the coast, where Afro-Ecuadorians demanded the legalization of their land ownership and indemnification for centuries of unjust treatment and for the destruction of their forests and ecosystems. In several Andean provinces indigenous people also stepped up their calls for an end to injustice and for legal rights to the land that they had occupied since time immemorial. The resounding fervor for fair adjudication of land disputes and for civil rights and social justice escalated, and cases that had been under "review by officials" for years were repeatedly cited by indigenous leaders. In Tungurahua Province Salasacans closed major roads; in the provinces of Cotopaxi and Chimborazo indigenous people invaded haciendas. Attacks on petroleum camps in Napo Province were also reported (*El Comercio* May 8, 1992, in *Kipu* 1992a:199).

The apparent escalation set off waves of nervous speculation that another Levantamiento was about to take place. The secretary-general of public administration, Dr. Gonzalo Ortiz Crespo, insisted that these were merely isolated events. As the nation approached the general elections scheduled for May 17, the president similarly assured the populace that peace and tranquility would be maintained, by force if necessary. Because citizens are required by law to vote where they are registered, many must travel large distances. Ecuadorians now learned that disruption of major highways would not be tolerated.

The dialogue between Borja's representatives and the indigenous leaders nevertheless continued until the government announced that it would be ready to sign documents on May 14. This plan was postponed and then rescheduled because the opposition organizations of Pastaza increased pressure on the government to grant them what they considered to be their fair share of provincial territory. The organizations reactivated their strike and renewed the threat to block the marchers' return to Puyo, using any kind of force available. The government was compelled to send high-level representatives in haste to negotiate in Puyo's municipal colosseum. After further "closed-door talks" with officials of IERAC, a committee returned to Quito to talk with the president of the republic (*El Comercio* May 8, 1992, in *Kipu* 1992a:154).

Finally, on the night of May 13, President Borja, in three consecutive ceremonies, delivered titles of well over a million hectares of land to indigenous people. Each of three organizations received approximately one-third of the total allocation: FEDECAP, OPIP, and AIEPRA. The resale and subsurface exploration and exploitation of minerals and petroleum were prohibited, and the rights of colonists living on previously occupied or allocated land were protected.

The weary and partially satisfied leaders of the march returned from the two-hour ceremony to El Ejido Park for a brief celebration of music and speeches. Then they and approximately two thousand fellow campers boarded the forty to sixty buses, contracted by the government, that ringed the park. The honking of bus horns signaled the hour of departure and the long caravan began to retrace the route of the marchers. Protected all the way by national police, the caravan entered the streets of Puyo early the next morning and, by 8:00 A.M., had discharged the last of the travelers in the central plaza whence they had departed thirty-four days previously. After a triumphant march through the main streets, the crowd reassembled in the plaza to hear brief speeches by Valerio Grefa and Antonio Vargas on the themes of peace, unity, and perseverance. Many returned to nearby homes, but, for others, the journey would continue for several more days.

Ethnic Multinationalism and Empowerment

From beginning to end, the enactment of the Caminata conveyed to the nation a message of two profound truths professed by the participants and by many others. First, the Quichua, Achuar, and Shiwiar are indigenous people, *gente indígena,* or Runa—fully cultured and capable, and imbued with ideas, hopes, dreams, and realities of quintessential human beings. Second, as true indigenous peoples, they are also fully human residents of the Pastaza Province of Amazonian Ecuador. Denied their rights to land, health, and prosperity, they are nonetheless full citizens, *ecuatorianos.* The message underscored the fundamental antinomy between an indigenous-based movement for ethnic multinationalism, in which "all our brothers" (Salomon 1981) are represented, and institutional nationalism, in which *mestizaje* ideology manipulated by "whites" excludes those classed as indigenous and black.

The symbolic power of the Ecuadorian indigenous movement gained strength that transformed it from a ritual drama to an active force for genuine change. This power, periodically unleashed through collective, pragmatic actions such as the Ecuadorian Levantamiento Indígena of 1990 and the Caminata of 1992, was circumscribed by the state's nationalist war rhetoric in 1995, but became manifest again in the political movements of 1996.

In the early months of 1996, a strikingly flexible political alliance presented itself to the public as a social movement, *not as a party.* Officially termed "Unidad Plurinacional Pachakutik-Nuevo País," it came to be called the Pachakutik-Nuevo País movement. For indigenous people this was shortened to the Pachakutik movement; for others who did not identify themselves as indigenous or as supporters of the indigenous movement, it was often shortened to "Nuevo País." The Pachakutik segment, organized by Dr. Luis Macas, Valerio Grefa, and other indigenous leaders, sponsored several indigenous candidates throughout the provinces. The New Country segment was organized by its own presidential candidate, the television personality Freddy Ehlers.

Overall the new movement won about 20 percent of the votes in the elections of May 19, 1996. Although Ehlers lost his bid for the presidency, Valerio Grefa (from Napo Province) and other indigenous candidates were elected as provincial representatives to Congress, and Dr. Macas was elected as a national representative—Ecuador's first indigenous people ever elected to Congress. When he entered the legislative palace for President Abdalá Bucaram Ortiz's inauguration on August 10, 1996, Dr. Macas was accompanied by Rigoberta Menchú Tum, the Guatemalan Nobel Peace Prize winner.

The trajectory from the pragmatic march for life and land to the ritual drama of peaceful, mass protest and thence to organized, legitimate political action was—and is still—closely watched by national academic and popular writers in Ecuador. As Raúl Vallejo, who is the former secretary of education, put it:

Six Years Later: Pachakutik

Six years after [the 1990 Levantamiento] the electoral victory . . . accomplished by Pachakutik–Nuevo País should be seen as a logical result of a genuine organizational process and as an important step toward a democratic deepening [profundización] that permits recognition of the plurinational character of our country as a basis of wide political alliances. (Vallejo 1996a: A5)

On Local-Level Ritual Dramas and National-Level Political Transformations

The heart of the organizational process that led to Pachakutik and similar entities is embodied in social movements—paradigmatic cultural processes of organization that move people to action in which the accomplishment of pragmatic goals is often framed by ritual dramas. In the case presented here, the ritual symbolism of rain-forest imagery was emergent during the first camp-out in Río Verde in the veritable *montaña* and was conjoined to imagery of mountain spirits and lowland forces that emerged in Salasaca. In Latacunga the juropolitical domain of appropriated and reversed justice became part of the ritual drama, and, as the Caminata entered Quito, the force of North Ecuadorian *yumbada* ritual was evoked.

The power of ritual symbols in covert as well as overt discourses continues in local-level festivals throughout Ecuador. While the substance and contents of such festivals and ritual activities vary greatly, the ability of such dramatic activity to communicate to those at the social or ethnic antipodes of Ecuadorian life—nearly half the population of the nation-state—seems to be very great. In these festivals to "see" all one's relatives, all one's people—all one's *ushis* and *churis,* as Apacha Vargas expressed it to the president of the republic, or all the nationalities (*tucui naciones*), as Marcelo Santi Simbaña has expressed it to us on many occasions—is to understand the power and efficacy of symbols to overcome adversity. The power evidenced in the Levantamiento Indígena of 1990 and the Caminata de Pastaza a Quito in 1992 synergized with other nationalist cultural forces in 1996 to effect a transformation of the ideological representation of the plural structure of Ecuador. The emergent structure of affirmation of indigenousness and public denial of the nation-state's efficacy in indigenous affairs creates a discourse of multifaceted dialogues, within which the nation-state is bound more and more closely to its representational antipodes of blackness and indigenousness.

Acknowledgments

This chapter is a condensed and revised version of an article published in the *American Ethnologist* 24(2):355–91. Copyright © American Anthropological Association and the University of California Press. Published by permission. Alfonso Chango thanks his wife, Luzmila Salazar; his mother, Clara Santi Simbaña; and his father, Abraham Chango, for clarifying and deepening his understanding of the world powers that can do harm, be deflected, or be used with discretion. Thanks also to the late Domingo Salazar, *sinchi yachaj*, whose insights, sought with care, revealed images not otherwise attainable. The Sacha Runa Research Foundation in Urbana, Illinois, provided fellowship support to allow Alfonso Chango to undertake technical training at the Indigenous Writing School of the Centro Editorial en Lenguas Indígenas Latinamericano, CELIL, in Oaxaca, Mexico. He thanks Jesús Salinas for his painstaking mentoring at CELIL.

Notes

1. An extended note on methodology is given in the original *AE* article, as are very specific notes on use of terminology and sources of information, including detailed ethnographic sources for inner symbolism and the externalization of such symbolism. (For more information see Acosta et al. 2001; Almeida et al. 1992; Almeida Vinuenza 1995; CONAIE 1992; Macas 1991; Vallejo 1996a, 1996b.)

2. The significance of the body of the anaconda moving toward the head is described and analyzed elsewhere (N. Whitten 1981, 1985, 1988). The rainbow-colored banner chosen as the emblem for the march is a visual manifestation of anaconda imagery, although the specific flag was appropriated from the 1991 indigenous Bolivian march from Bení to La Paz.

3. Other festival representations of the Yumbo also occur in Ecuador. For example, there are Yumbo dancers during Christmas festivities in Zumbagua parish, Cotopaxi Province (Weismantel 1988). Painters from the dispersed community of Tigua in the same province portray Yumbos as shamans from the Oriente (D. Whitten 2003), or a Tsáchila from Santo Domingo de los Colorados in the western rain-forest *montaña*.

4. In the 1890s a renowned *curaga* from Canelos, Palati, is said to have trekked to Quito from Canelos. On the way to Quito he meandered through the Sierra to gain indigenous support from one Quichua-speaking community after another. In Quito he is said to have gained tremendous concessions of land from the liberal *caudillo* Eloy Alfaro Delgado. For a nationalist rendition of this history see Ramón Valarezo 1992; for indigenous tales involving such treks, shamanism, and human-jaguar metamorphoses, see N. Whitten 1985:193, 221. There are remarkable similarities in Andean tales of the treks of Alfaro and the Pastaza Amazonian tales of the treks of Palati.

9

Causáunchimi!:
Processes of Empowerment

The Canelos Quichua constitute a significant cultural hinge between the Andes and greater Amazonia. Puyo is the hub of their articulation to national and international systems. Together with their cultural congeners, the Napo Runa radiating out of Tena up the Montaña and down the Napo River system (Reeve 1994; Uzendoski 2004a, 2004b:331, 2005b), they represent deep Amazonian dimensions of thought and feeling conveyed through a cosmovision carried and expressed by what has been known since the sixteenth century as an Andean language. In Quichua dialects of the Oriente, as in other languages of Amazonia, an east-west directionality defines an Amazonian-Andean flow of power. When indigenous people from Amazonia draw maps of their world within their cosmos, they usually place the west on top, east on the bottom, and north and south to the right and left, respectively. The Canelos Quichua fit this pattern perfectly.

The orientation of such a map focuses on the dynamics of the sun rising out of primordial water on the eastern edge of the earth to begin its journey over land, forest, and rivers, moving first northward to cross the apex of the vertical axis at the center—forming the cosmic *axis mundi*—and then back westward, where it goes underwater at the western edge and travels southward and then eastward at night. Day's end signals a dangerous cooling and the emergence of nocturnal forces of chaos and predation controlled by the moon.

The Inca conquest of the Andes destroyed or subverted this east-west primordial directionality in the Tahuantinsuyo Empire of the Andes and imposed a north-south orientation that in many ways cut off Amazonian systems from the centers of emerging Andean political economy (e.g., Richardson 1994). The Spaniards, intrigued as they were by the possibility of El Dorado to the east, and what they took to be the complementary profitable trade in *canela,* capsicum, cotton, and dyes there, maintained the north-south centrality so contradictory to Amazonian and pre-Incaic Andean cosmovision. Actual social relationships, however, among Andeans and Amazonians perhaps intensified during Incaic and later Spanish hegemonic reorientation of space-time (e.g., Salomon 1986; Reeve 1994; N. Whitten 2001).

North-south hegemonic directionality also influenced the growth of professional specializations in the twentieth century so that the academy features Andean studies often devoid of Amazonian systems (e.g., Uzendoski 2005a, 2005c). For a very long time those specializing in greater Amazonia, a region often called "Lowland South America," were caught in the dichotomy between orientations of "cultural ecology," as defined by Julian H. Steward and later Betty Meggers on the one side, and the "structuralism" of Claude Lévi-Strauss on the other. While the former dwelt on the limitations of Amazonian environment (lumping extraordinary diversity into a limiting singularity), the latter assumed collapse of culture (not just population) following conquest so that what remained to be studied were fragments to be imbricated by the analyst savant into universal structures of mind (e.g., Lévi-Strauss 1966; contra this, see Hill 1988; Whitehead 2003).

From the Inca conquest to the Spanish conquest, from subsequent colonial rule to modern academic specialties, not much room, if any, remained for an appreciation of culture in its diversity, the transformative dimensions and potentialities of indigenous lifeways, or the potential forces of change and resistance to be found in peoples of Amazonia, especially those abutting the systems of Andean power and control. Instead of dynamic Amazonian hermeneutics vis-à-vis Andean hegemony, we have been overwhelmed with the hermetics of "tribal" studies. Instead of focusing on people expanding and transforming in the face of systems of domination and hegemony, Amazonianist scholarship zoomed in on the shrinking, disappearing, and "acculturating" processes leading nowhere. The epitome of these unfortunate aspects is found in the typology of Claude Lévi-Strauss of "hot societies" (the West), and "cold societies" (especially those of Amazonia).

Let us take a deep breath, then, and begin anew, at the end of this work, to conceptualize Puyo Runa people, within their framework spearheaded by their assertion, *causáunchimi!* We are Living! A recent, dramatic event underscored by that assertion was the Caminata from Amazonia to Andean Quito, the subject of the previous chapter. But there is much more happening and more stories to tell as precipitous events viewed in retrospect (e.g., Pallares 2002) cascade toward an unknown future at increasing rates.

Cunanrucuguna: Space-Times of "Then-Now"

Topographically there is no place in South America where the Amazonian and Andean systems abut and interlace so closely. The Caminata described in the previous chapter amply illustrates this point. Deeply embedded in the force of some Amazonian people marching westward and then northward toward Quito, the heart and soul of state power and elite hegemony, was the symbolism embodied in the imagery of the anaconda. Such imagery, as manifest in the Tupac Amaru movements in Peru and the Tupac Katari movements in Bolivia (e.g., Stern 1987; for Andean Ecuador, Wibbelsman 2006:205–8), has been evident since the colonial era.

A decade has passed since we completed our analysis of the Caminata from Puyo to Quito. The year 1996, when the Pachakutik social movement formed, is taken by the current president of CONAIE, Luis Macas, to be *the* watershed year of indigenous entry into a system of modernity and millenniarity recently explored elsewhere (N. Whitten 2003a, 2003b; Macas, Belote, and Belote 2003). Some dimensions of the Amazonian cultural wellsprings of Pachakutik must be reiterated because they are the critically important ones often excluded in popular, journalistic, and academic writings. In Western historical time these begin with the 1978 millennial cultural surge in Sarayacu and Puyo, which featured the sequestering of the director of IERAC and Alfonso Calderón Cevallos (the president's first cousin and informal but constant advisor on indigenous affairs, who enters our story in chapter 8), and the issuance of the "Acuerdo de Sarayacu" (the Sarayacu Agreement), which publicly launched the ideology of Amazonian indigenous self-determination (N. Whitten 1986). International events in Sarayacu included visits, at various times, by representatives of the Interamerican Foundation of Washington, D.C., OXFAM-England, the Dominican order, and the Protestant evangelical movement. Over the last quarter century Sarayacu has occupied the international stage as it has systemically resisted persistent encroachment by petroleum companies.

The early-modern (fifteenth- and sixteenth-century) Western schism between Protestants and Catholics came to overt violence in Sarayacu in the 1980s as Catholic and other pressures built up against the Sarayacu evangelicals, most of whom lived along or near the airport or in the eastern sector of Shihuacocha. This conflict culminated in a raid on Shihuacocha and the airport by a group of Puyo Runa joined by others from Sarayacu, some of whom were living full-time in Puyo. This group drove out the indigenous Protestants by force of arms and then dynamited the Protestant homes. The vanquished group moved downriver to Jatun Molino where they flourished after a period of adjustment, established a landing strip with considerable help from the Alas de Socorro World Radio Mission personnel, and later acceded to the establishment of an Ecuadorian military outpost there. Just as conflict raged up and down the Bobonaza River system and into Achuar territory to the south, a remarkable millennial oneness of cultural resurgence took place, eventually including the modern divisions of Christendom and indigenous grassroots political enactment involving Canelos Quichua, Achuar, and Shiwiar.

When the CONAIE-led Levantamiento Indígena of 1990 took place (e.g., de la Torre 2006), its president was Valerio Grefa, a Napo Runa from Arajuno, son of a powerful shaman. Pachakutik itself was brought into being by an Amazonian-Andean indigenous alliance, within which Luis Macas of Saraguro and Grefa were primary figures. Macas had long traveled to the greater Puyo area to meet near Unión Base with formal and informal indigenous leaders in and out of CONFENIAE and to Arajuno, at the juncture of Napo Runa and Canelos Quichua cultural systems (see, e.g., Whitten 1985:217–32). It was during the 1980s that indigenous people from Pacayacu and Sarayacu (including the group that was forced to move to Jatun Molino) began to play a prominent role in the Twelfth of May celebrations of Puyo, performing the dance of the *lanceros* in front of the Catholic church and on several occasions actually "invading" the church during the "staged" Dominario.

On January 21, 2000, eight years after the March for Land and Life, Ecuador became known worldwide in both its global, neoliberal modernity, and in the chiliastic forces simultaneously emerging. At 10:00 A.M. Friday morning, on a signal from the national police, the armed forces guarding the empty Legislative building in Quito pulled back from the doorways and allowed a throng of thousands of indigenous and nonindigenous people to enter. As they waived the national flag and shouted *Ec-ua-dór!*, *Ec-ua-dór!*, *Ec-ua-dór!*, people again parted to allow three emissaries of the new national power figures to enter and take center stage. One of these was Carlos Antonio Vargas Guatatuca, a Canelos Quichua indigenous man from the hamlet of Unión Base, just southeast of Puyo. Another was Colonel Lucio Gutiérrez Borbúa, a Quiteño with roots in Tena, one of the heroes of the Cenepa Valley conflict in Amazonia in 1995, from which Ecuador emerged victorious from its sporadic armed conflict with neighboring Peru. Out of that conflict also emerged the concept of respect for multiculturality, which by the turn of the twenty-first century had become an ideology of *interculturality* championed by indigenous peoples of Sierra, Coast, and Oriente. We return to multiculturality and its transformation into interculturality later in this chapter.

Vargas voiced, loudly and clearly, words that were heard live on national television and ramified worldwide, especially through broadcasts by CNN: *"El pueblo está en poder,"* "The people are empowered." An ephemeral triumvirate formed the Junta of National Salvation; the three joined hands with one another and with other indigenous and nonindigenous people and led the assembled throng in the national anthem. Later they again joined hands and recited the Lord's Prayer.

The coup itself came as no surprise. During the first year of the elected presidency of Jamil Mahuad Witt, supreme confidence was placed in the activities of prominent bankers, in a group of distinguished gringos known as the "Harvard Boys," and especially in the officers and advisors of the International Monetary Fund. Mahuad brought the dignity of a master of arts degree in public administration from Harvard University and his experience as mayor of Quito to bear on the worsening economic situation of the republic. He championed the ideology of a neoliberal political economy, which essentially affirms that "the market" should dictate global economic activities within the sovereign state, as though any market could exist outside of a social and cultural context (e.g., Gudeman 1992, 2001:94–109). Mahuad relied heavily on the ideological trappings of modernity and neoliberal capital enterprise, and he gave those in charge of state and private banks free reign to wheel and deal with millions of dollars of entrusted capital. In the strong and hyperbolic words of Jean and John Comaroff, we might say that Mahuad's image of the state turned to dimensions of "intensified magicalities and fetishes in order to heal fissures and breaches in the fabric of the polity" (Comaroff and Comaroff 2001:36; see also Palmié 2002).

The composition of the coup-makers came as a jarring surprise, however. The coup was not undertaken by members of the political class in alliance with the top brass of the military, as was generally anticipated. Rather, it erupted through forces unleashed by indigenous people, but it was supported and perhaps abated well in advance by the military colonels and captains. Generals of the armed forces were in on agreements to overthrow Mahuad's government, and at first seemed to be in collusion with the colonels, some of whom were engaged in serious conversation with indigenous leaders. But it was not some of the many prominent Ecuadorian members of the "political class" who emerged in the coup; it was an indigenous Puyo Runa leader,

Antonio Vargas, and his military companion, Lucio Gutiérrez, who stole the millennial show (N. Whitten 2003a).

The vice president in the Mahuad regime, Gustavo Noboa Bejarano, was soon named president by Congress after the general who originally backed the coup quickly left it that same night in the face of relentless pressures from spokesman of the United States. One of Noboa's first acts on becoming president was to award a medal to the general who backed out of the coup. Antonio Vargas publicly stated on national television that the general was a traitor to the Ecuadorian people.

In 2002 rebel leaders Gutiérrez and Vargas both ran for president of the republic in a field of eleven initial candidates. Gutiérrez prevailed and was inaugurated president on January 15, 2003 (e.g., Jijón 2003). Two weeks before his inauguration he appointed two indigenous people as his ministers: Luis Macas as Minister of Agriculture and Nina Pacari as Minister of Foreign Affairs. But the president soon moved radically to reject the indigenous and populist movements that propelled him to power, and by early August 2003 he broke all ties with these movements and placed his fate in the hands of the policy structures of the United States, the International Monetary Fund, and the World Bank.

During a crisis in 2004 with a buildup toward a possible indigenous uprising underway, Gutiérrez appointed Antonio Vargas as Minister of Social welfare, thereby dividing the indigenous movement between Sierra as anti-Vargas and coastal and Amazonian indigenous (and other) people as pro-Vargas. The next big crisis came in April 2005 in the "Rebellion of the Forajidos" wherein Quiteños from upper middle classes down to grassroots workers rose up to end the Gutiérrez regime and to drive him into exile (he later returned, was jailed and then released, and is again prominent in Ecuadorian politics). By the time of the rebellion Vargas had turned his position over to his undersecretary and returned to Unión Base, from which vantage point he tried to rally indigenous people to restore the presidential regime, to no avail. The Quiteño forces mobilized against indigenous people and the Gutiérrez regime were too strong. In 2005 the new rift between united Quiteños as *forajidos* (outlaws) and the self-identification of disenfranchisement by indigenous (and other) people of Amazonia on one side of the Andes, and those of coastal provinces on the other side of the Andes, was palpable in multiple domains of dissent and contestation (Araujo Sánchez 2005).

From fall 2003 through the time we write this (May 2007), the nation-state of Ecuador is very widely acknowledged throughout the country and beyond as turning in on itself, going nowhere; it seems to have lost all sense of direction. Journalists now call its pathway the *callejón sin salida* (*El Comercio,* February 23, 2006). Seen from Amazonia, the nation is moving on a trajectory characterized in Canelos Quichua as *mana tuparina ñambi,* a path or road that leads into the unknown where strange and powerful forces reside, and from which no one knows how to return. Forks, mazeways, switch backs, and spirals exist to confound the traveler; there are few if any signposts for guidance, turning back is impossible, and the end is anything but what may be envisioned at the outset of the journey. This pathway constitutes a labyrinth within which the seeker encounters the possibility of *paju,* dangerous powers beyond his or her control. To move into the realm of *paju* is to encounter enshrouded and fearsome imagery of unrecognizable and unknown entities. *Paju* can cause severe illness and even death (N. Whitten 2004).

Let us elaborate. One of the *paju* powers to be encountered is the *cutu amarun,* the "monkey [sounding] anaconda." One takes an unknown fork, comes upon an unknown lagoon, and is completely lost. Moving to another trail on another fork one comes to an area enshrouded by dark clouds; above is the tail and lower body of the great constrictor, but one cannot see this. The head of the *cutu amarun* is in the earth in a dangerous cave occupied by dangerous spirits, *juctu supais.* What brings the person to this place is that the boa constrictor knows how to make the sounds of the red howler monkey, which is food for the indigenous Amazonian people. But the gift of monkey meat from the forest spirit master is an illusion, for above it all is the great constrictor, the great *paju,* that in seeming to offer food actually presents great danger, the awful threat of being crushed and devoured.

This and other stories are used by many indigenous people of Amazonia as tropes of metaphor for the deceptive tactics and devouring potential of the United States of America. Nonetheless, some people voluntarily take the trail that leads them to such conjunctures of political and economic life. As N. Whitten wrote elsewhere, "between the promise of wealth and the reality of poverty lie dynamic symbol systems to enhance critical insights and to sustain movements into and out of liminality and into new dimensions of social relationships" (2003b:29; see also Quiroga 2003). We have sought to explicate such systems throughout the essays in this book.

This takes us again to relationships between indigenous and national politics (and the conjuncture of the two), set in the *mana tuparina ñambi* enshrouded by the two great and interrelated *pajus*: Colombian guerrilla, paramilitary, and terrorist activity and cocaine production and distribution; and the hegemonic policies, strategies, practices, and effects of the United States and its international affiliates.

The ongoing saga of Ecuadorian peoples in the fierce grip of United States policies and practices, combined with the escalating negative affects of Plan Colombia, Plan Patriota, the guerrilla movements, and the right-wing paramilitary movements is oppressive (Taussig 2003, 2004; N. Whitten 2004, 2005). Consequences of these foreign forces ensnare many people in unintentional entanglements. We must, as we have throughout this book, dip below the political, military, and diplomatic surface to come to grips with culturally focused humanity as we have tried to understand it (e.g., Geertz 1983). As understanding emerges, however, we must also retain sight of the furious movements on the global surface of ongoing cultural life.[1]

Interculturality

Beneath the surface of public publications, radio broadcasts, and television presentations lies the indefatigable social movement through sectors of Ecuador toward *interculturalidad* (interculturality) together with its seemingly paradoxical complement of reinforced cultural and ethnic boundaries. Interculturality is very different from an ethos of hybridity or social or cultural pluralism. It is multicultural but it is also *inter*cultural. Interculturality stresses a movement from one cultural system to another, with the explicit purpose of understanding other ways of thought and action, whereas social and cultural pluralism stress the institutional separation forced by the *blanco* (white) elite on peoples. The ideologies of hybridity and pluralism are national, regional, and static; formal consciousness of interculturality is local, regional, diasporic, global, and dynamic.

In chapter 3 we dealt at some length with the concepts *shuj shimita yachai* (other spoken knowledge, or other cultural knowledge) and *ñucanchi yachai* (our cultural knowledge). The relationship between these two realms of knowledge—ours and others, or ours and theirs—is dynamic. *Interculturalidad*, which is pervasive among indigenous and other people of Ecuador, maps perfectly onto the Canelos Quichua base of *ñucanchi yachai—shuj shimita yachai*. As shamans and master potters show us again and again, one cannot understand one's own people's perception without understanding something of the lifeways and thought processes of other peoples.

There is a specific history of the emergence of interculturality in national consciousness in Ecuador. In 1995 during the Ecuadorian war with Peru, multiculturalism gained strength within the military, as well as in the more depressed sectors of the expanding populace (N. Whitten 2003a). President Abdalá Bucaram Ortiz was driven to exile in Panama in 1997 by an indigenous-populist movement that engaged people in all socioeconomic classes and walks of life, and the dramatic ouster of Jamil Mahuad Witt by a combination of indigenous and military rebellion on January 21, 2000, further strengthened interculturality in some sectors, while promoting class and regional divisions in others. The conjoined idioms of military victory, rebellion, and multiculturality carried the principal colonel in this rebellion, Lucio Gutiérrez Borbúa, into a victorious presidential race in 2002 (N. Whitten 2003a).

After the transformational moment in early 2003 that witnessed the president's appointment of two indigenous people to prominent cabinet positions—together with four hundred or so members of the Pachakutik social movement to positions nationwide—the president completely reversed his millennial moves and succumbed to morbid modernity. He allied with global hegemonic forces represented by the International Monetary Fund, the World Bank, high-level representatives of the United States such as Otto Reich and George W. Bush, and his previous arch rivals—great coastal barons and power wielders of Guayaquil, epitomized in the persona of León Febres Cordero, called by many *el dueño del Ecuador* and lauded by the late Ronald Reagan as a "champion of free enterprise" (Corkill and Cubit 1988:77).

On August 6, 2003, Gutiérrez rescinded all four hundred or more of his Pachakutik appointments and reestablished a nation based on a rudderless ship of state foundering on reefs of capitalist modernity and neoliberalism. He took the country into the *mana tuparina ñambi,* which features, especially, a rising and record high price of oil (in a country where this is the number one revenue source) and serious indigenous and populist protests about present, past, and future petroleum exploitation. Government bonds were structured to favor the wealthy of the world and the country became increasingly impoverished in its economic means and wherewithal. The spirit of rebellion, however, intensified.

For Amazonian indigenous people and coastal and Andean colonists, petroleum has reached its fortieth year of severe and dramatic influence on their lives, either direct or indirect. This constitutes a human span of more than two generations of real people of the Upper Amazon–Andean Piedmont. It is part and parcel of the road that seemingly leads nowhere, where great promise of economic wherewithal and wealth for some combines with utter destruction of natural resources, ecological systems, and indigenous environmental management systems that have characterized the Amazonian region since time immemorial. Sawyer (2004) documents some of the Arco-OPIP interactions over issues of oil exploitation in Pastaza Province during much of the 1990s. Petroleum is of high salience today in Ecuador as a major moneymaking company, Occidental Petroleum (OXY), seeks a reimbursement of $150 million in state-withheld taxes because it extracts, rather than manufactures, petroleum. This comes at a time when the state is desperate for revenues to cover its ever-increasing external and internal debts. In 2005 OXY's contract was not renewed, and the subsequent politics and litigations remain the subject for other works.

A dramatic indigenous/oil company standoff in Pastaza Province threatens to break into a "war" between allied indigenous people—Canelos Quichua, especially of Sarayacu, Achuar of the Pastaza drainage, and Shuar from the Macuma River region to Taisha—and the forces of petroleum companies—CGC (the French-Argentine Compañía General de Combustibles), in the north, and Burlington in the south. Each of these was once a subsidiary of Arco, which developed the two oil rigs in Villano and built the secondary pipeline to connect to the Baeza-Quito-Esmeraldas trunk line that runs through one of the world's most fragile ecosystems, one given to severe geophysical disturbances. (The secondary pipeline runs right through the relatively new settlement of San Virgilio at the Cabecera de Curaray, founded by one son of the late Virgilio Santi, from whom the new *llacta* and hamlet take its name.)

In the two petroleum blocks in Canelos, Achuar, and Shiwiar territory wherein subsurface rights have been ceded to the companies, indigenous residents are also stewards of the land, forest, and rivers ceded to them in 1992 and guaranteed to them by the National Constitution of 1998. The only legitimate force that the companies can draw on is that of the Ecuadorian military. The interaction of indigenous forces, petroleum forces, and the military of the Oriente are of critical importance to the entire nation. During the March for Land and Life in 1992 the indigenous people, specifically Canelos Quichua, Achuar, and Shiwiar, gained a national concession of 1,115,574 hectares in their rain-forest–riparian zone of Pastaza Province, about 65 percent of their initial request. This territory, originally granted to OPIP and the evangelical organization, became divided up among different nationalities, including the Waorani, Záparo, Shiwiar, Achuar, and Amazonian Quichua of different organizations. In 2006 the emergent nationality of Andoa seeks its quotient. *But the subsurface rights to exploration and exploitation were retained by the state. In 2006, as in past years, the state retains its rights to wealth that lies beneath the surface, and by the constitutional change of 1998 the indigenous people have their rights to health, welfare, and a satisfactory life in their territory, including healthy and uncontaminated flora and fauna of forest and hydrosphere systems.*

In this situation people struggle with the paradoxes and contradictions before them on their unknown trails in modernity, just as those guardians of *la patria*—the military—increase the numbers of indigenous people in their ranks and debate whether or not indigenous people should be placed in a killing situation vis-à-vis their cultural congeners and family members. Throughout the military it is recognized that the collaboration of indigenous Shuar people in the Cenepa River region of southeast Ecuador was crucial in Ecuador's victory over Peru in 1995, so the idea of killing indigenous people over the rights of foreign oil companies rankles and divides people in all walks of life.

Sarayacu Resistance: Globalization out of Localization

In chapter 1 we noted that "Sarayaquillu represents a condensation and intensive miniaturization of the entire Canelos Quichua cultural region. Many indigenous people share [this] perhaps nostalgic representation" (p. 19). When I first visited Sarayacu in 1970 it was one of two main staging bases for the Western Geophysical Company of America, working as an exploration company for Anglo-Ecuadorian Oil Fields, Ltd. (N. Whitten 1976a:xiii). The other two bases were Villano and Curaray.

In 1938 Royal Dutch Shell took over oil exploration from Leonard Exploration Company, which was granted a concession in the early 1920s. In 1942 it lost a huge concession to Standard Oil of New Jersey (Tschopp 1953; Galarza Zavala 1972) after Peru invaded Ecuador in what became known as the "petroleum war" (Galarza Zavala 1972). From 1943 until a road reached Shell (known as Shell-Mera), all materiel and personnel came and went to and from Shell by air: "This was the first and largest 100 per cent airborne operation of its kind in the history of the oil industry" (Tschopp 1953:2304). The principal air bases outside of Shell in or on the edge of Canelos Quichua territory for Shell Exploration Company were Arajuno and Villano (e.g., Eliot 1975). Shell abandoned its extensive explorations in 1950. When Western Exploration entered in 1969 it also used these two bases. There are now two oil pumping rigs (Lathrop, Slack, and Draper 1999) at Villano.

In 1970 regular flights in and out of Sarayacu from Shell and Villano were by a Twin Otter, complemented by helicopter flights and those of one-engine planes. One Ecuadorian helicopter pilot working with Western traded salt and dry goods to a family in Sarayaquillu for fine ceramics which he sold in Quito and later in Puyo. Some of the Runa came to call him Capitán Mucawa. Today, men and women in their mid-thirties remember this period as the reopening of global capitalism in their locality, and as a time of severe depletion of game animals in their hunting and *purina* territories.

One of the few indigenous Ecuadorian authors, Carlos Viteri Gualinga, is from Sarayacu and was long a resident of Puyo. He now resides in Washington, D.C., where he works in the Indigenous Peoples and Community Development Unit of the Inter-American Development Bank. Before this he was a regular columnist for the Quito Newspaper *Hoy* and advisor to the indigenous leader Nina Pacari when she was a congresswoman. His article on the spirit world of the Sarayacu (and Canelos Quichua people), "Mythical Worlds: Runa," in *Amazon Worlds* (1993) is inspired by the ceramics made by his mother, Rebeca Gualinga (see chapters 4 and 7), and by the deep knowledge and vision of the people of Sarayacu, Puyo, and elsewhere in this region. In the spirit of emerging interculturality he wrote, "in our long journey to the *sumac allpa* [land without evil] we have come face to face with the *chikan*, the foreigner, the unknown, strange, and hostile world that threatens to annihilate our *sumac causai*, our 'harmonious life,' on which the *chikan* also depend. For this reason, at a time and in a space in the future, a life dedicated to correcting the errors now being made will become more and more necessary. We and they, *runa* and *chikan*, must renew our journey toward the same *sumac allpa*" (Viteri 1993:150).

There have been so many dramas enacted within, and ramifying out of, Sarayacu over the past twenty-five years or so that a book could easily be written on this subject alone. For our purposes let us zoom down on very recent events, the consequences and conclusions of which remain to be seen. By 2002, after repeated litigations and confrontations ranging from Sarayacu itself, to other Canelos Quichua settlements on the Bobonaza and Curaray River systems, and to Puyo, Quito, and Washington, D.C., the men and some women from Sarayacu became known as the *guardianes de la selva*, the guardians of the forest. In that year the Compañía General Geofísica (CGG), a French company subcontracted to the Argentine Compañía General de Combustibles (CGC), made a strong move, supported at the time by President Gutiérrez, and with a very reluctant compliance with the military, to act on the side of the Ecuadorian National Constitution (1998) that grants to the state the subsurface rights of territory, while guaranteeing to indigenous people their rights to life, livelihood, and happiness within the very same territory. The CGC had purchased Block 23 (previously Block 10 purchased by Arco, which was thwarted by Sarayacu people in the late 1980s) and intended to repeat and perhaps extend the exploration undertaken in the 1970s by Western. Unfortunately, of course, the only way to get to the subsurface is through the surface.

The move of the company was to bring in more than three hundred pounds (150 kilos, 2,000 sticks) of Pentolite, a dynamite-like explosive, also known as a shock explosive or "flash bang," to be placed in its warehouse (which of course was on the surface of Sarayacu territory). In 2002, and in succeeding years, the people of this Runa territory decided to set aside their annual *ayllu jista* and to focus instead on the logistics of territorial protection. In 2003, instead of hunting camps and *purina* settlements, they established a series of lookout camps composed of men, women, and children on the fringes of their territories (using their system of hunting and fishing regions and *purina* territories). There they waited for the petroleum intruders, who were accompanied by some members of the military. When the latter arrived the Runa moved in, surrounded the petroleum workers and military personnel, and confiscated the Pentolite and military weapons.

The sequestered military personnel were told about indigenous life and human dependence on gardens, forests, and rivers in structured conversations led by Sarayacu women, including Rebeca Gualinga. In this drama there is an uncanny resemblance to the cultural pattern represented by men as predators (hunters, shamans) and women as domesticators (potters, gardeners), though in this case the men were the captors and the women the educators. The latter instructed military personnel in the fundamental humanity and rights of the Runa to forest, river, and soil. Before long, after the period of socialization by women, the arms were returned to the military members, who then left. The oil workers, too, departed.

The Pentolite was left behind. It remains hidden today (2007), overseen in its obscure burial locations by the Sarayacu Runa. It is the fount of stories in major Ecuadorian publications (e.g., "Blanco y Negro 2005," *Hoy,* August 13, 2005: 1–4; www.sarayacu.com). The CGC in 2004 decided to sue the Sarayacu people for theft, while the Sarayacu people struck back with the accusation that the Pentolite was brought to the rain-forest–riparian region that is theirs to cherish and protect without permission. Firsthand accounts by Sarayacu people confirm that the Pentolite is safely buried in a place known to many local people but unknown to outsiders. Burying explosives over a period of time, though, is about as safe as burying a land mine or an anaconda body separated from its head. When one walks over the area the Pentolite may go off—just as when, unknowingly, a person enters a space of great danger by crossing the place where the anaconda body is growing toward its severed head (a process in this region known as *tupaj amarun;* Whitten 1988). Cosmic eruptions may occur, and the world may be brought to the edge of *tucurina,* just as in the Dominario of the *ayllu jista.*

The seriousness of this potentially explosive situation was featured in an editorial "Analysis de Hoy" (*Hoy,* August 15, 2005: 5A) and accompanied by a cartoon by Asdúbal that makes gratuitous racist fun of the situation by primitivizing people of Sarayacu. He depicts them as speaking pidgin or child-talk dialect, as they carry away deadly explosives left behind by those with no concern for human life or limb.

In September 2005, more information came to light about the actions of CGC personnel prior to their departure from Sarayacu territory. The personnel made 467 perforations in the earth in a radius of six kilometers ringing the central population of Sarayacu, and placed charges of Pentolite into these holes (*El Comercio* 7 September 2005). The president of Sarayacu, Hilda Santi, stated that because all people of Sarayacu travel through the forest, there is real danger of someone stepping on an unknown perforation and losing his or her life in an explosion. The imagery of the 1995 war of Ecuador against Peru in the Cenepa valley of the southern rain forest comes to mind, as twenty years later hundreds of antipersonnel mines are still buried, and Shuar people are losing life and limb when they accidentally step on these awful undersoil implants.

Meanwhile, the people of Sarayacu have developed a university in the central part of their territory, the plaza area just north of the river and the airstrip. This is the Universidad de Sarayacu, which now offers a *licenciatura*

Cartoon from *Hoy,* August 15, 2005, portraying indigenous people carrying Pentolite near Sarayacu. Published with permission.

(equivalent to a bachelor of arts degree in the U.S.) in *educación intercultural* (intercultural education) with a specialization in Amazonian peoples (communities). It has received the formal approval of the general and bilingual organizations of CONFENIAE, and now has twenty-six students. Funding comes from organizations elsewhere in Ecuador and in Spain. The Runa founders and teachers also wish to engage systematically in ecotourism that would include lodging, local foods, treks in the forest, river trips, shamanic instruction, instruction in Amazonian pottery, and especially instruction on ethnoecology.

Currently, though, their aggressive stance against the people to the east and west of them has created a system in which ecotourism is at best risky. The people of Jatun Molino to the east now (perhaps assisted by the military) block access to most people from Sarayacu attempting to go downriver. Similar clashes between leaders of Sarayacu and those of Pacayacu and Canelos to the west have resulted in the same blockages. And those from Sarayacu block access up and down the river to their cultural congeners and relatives from east and west. Puyo, though, remains a haven for people from Sarayacu and from Pacayacu and Canelos, as well as Curaray. But to get from Sarayacu to Puyo means chartering one-engine planes, which can cost from US$200 to US$800. Nonetheless, the leaders of Sarayacu maintain an office in Puyo, through which the bulk of communication with NGOs, national, and international agencies take place.

Let us personalize and particularize Sarayacu people a bit, and then move outward in our generalizations. To begin with, Antonio Vargas regards Sarayaquillu as his *quiquin llacta,* the area from which his father's father's family came as Zaparoan speakers from the area near the Rutunu River, to which some people from Sarayacu trek for their *purina llacta.* Marcelo Santi Simbaña's son Marco teaches in Sarayacu, and married a woman there whose mother is a master potter. Events in one place ramify by constant conversations to all other places within this cultural region, and far beyond. Another son, Hugo, is married to a woman from Pacayacu, and he and his wife visit there sporadically. Marcelo himself remains closely tied to people of Canelos, from whence his second wife Faviola came. Each of these people conceptualize *quiquin llactas* and *purina llactas* that range far and wide, cementing through innumerable overlapping networks a regional cultural system with distinct characteristics (for ethnohistorical details see Reeve 1993–94:17–24).

Generalizing the cultural system involves events that people regard as cognate from one territory to another. Just to the north, between the territories of the Canelos Quichua and the Napo Runa, *through their women's association,* the Waorani have rejected all ties and canceled all contracts with Petrobras, the Brazilian State petroleum company. Petrobras secured rights to explore and exploit petroleum, including the building of roads, into the famous Yasuní National Park—one of the most biodiverse and fragile systems in the world, and an ecological reserve to which Waorani people have hunting, fishing, and gardening rights (*El Comercio* 2005: B11). In August 2005, the beleaguered president of Brazil, Luis Inácio Lula da Silva, made a special plea for reopening the reserve and pushing aside the indigenous protest by use of the military (*Hoy,* August 16, 2005: 3A). The issue is unresolved as of this writing.

North and east of Napo Province, in the provinces of Orellana and Sucumbíos, an extended general strike that turned violent stopped oil flow from the northern Oriente for a significant period of time. The strike caused huge losses in state and private revenues and created a stir on the world stage as carried by the British Broadcasting Service and, to a lesser extent, by U.S. network and cable TV. Exacerbating still further a situation of polarizing ideologies that ramify worldwide, in September 2005 Raúl Reyes, a prominent spokesman for the FARC (Fuerzas Armadas Revolucionarias de Colombia; Revolutionary Armed Forces of Colombia) guerrilla force proclaimed that the right of the people of these Ecuadorian provinces to strike was a legitimate movement of people for whom the guerrillas were fighting. This rhetoric, from any position, sets up chains of hegemonic mental associations that come to link indigenous movements and indigenous forms and praxes of resistance to macropolarities such as the one generated by movements of Bolivarianism emanating from the Venezuelan Government, the Colombian FARC, and more recently from a coastal Ecuadorian movement centered in Manabí (e.g., N. Whitten 2003a).

Obviously, the personal, local, regional, supraregional, national, international, and global network systems can and must be considered when we write of Canelos Quichua culture, its Puyo Runa nationalized and urbanized locus, and its Runa territorial ramifications. Each is real, dynamic, transformable, and vitally important to understanding modernity and millenniarity. Let us pursue these issues a bit before returning to some particulars that give special substance to the Canelos Quichua people, their antiquities, and their ethnogeneses.

Modernity and Millenniarity

Although we cover these issues elsewhere (N. Whitten 2003a, 2003b), some reiteration is necessary. Modernity emerged out of medieval European systems to stress the following components as globalizing ideology: profit-seeking; science for economic gain; phenotypic color-coding (racializing) of labor; concepts of humans as vestiges or relics of an antipodal past; the "growth" of wealth; fetishism of commodities; commodification of land, labor, and humans; ethnic cleansing; the hypostasis of racial fixity; and the power of print languages. These imageric features as guiding ideological forces for Western colonial and republican political-economic powers transformed the West and wrecked their savagery on the rest.

Millenniarity in its multiple manifestations confronts these forces as people endeavor to restore human dignity to its inevitable diversity. Capitalism and millenarianism are both intricately linked to Western democracy. The transformation of modern democracy to a system of equitable social relationships and reasonable life chances for all citizens in a civil society has long permeated the struggles now ongoing in Ecuador. The Canelos Quichua, with their modern point of reference in urban Puyo, offer an exemplar of these processes. When people moved out of Puyo in the Caminata in 1992, and when people of Sarayacu confront petroleum exploration and proclaim a revitalized focus on their ecosystem in the 2000s, millenniarity emerges (e.g, Worsley 1957:243).

Modernity and millenniarity are inextricably intertwined. They constitute a mutualistic dynamic that propels Ecuadorian cultural systems from one historical event to another. The conjuncture that they form is impelling and synergistic; it cannot be debundled or its elements dissected. No dichotomy or dialectic can help us understand the transformative dialogues, dramatic events, and charged political and cultural fields and paradigms that punctuate recent and distant history. Only an understanding of the changing significations and resignifications of diversity can lead us to an illumination of real people at local levels, the national results of conjoined localities in motion, and the all-encompassing contradictory and complementary globalizations that constrain and release them (see, e.g., Abercrombie 1998; Guss 2000; Appadurai 2001; Comaroff and Comaroff 1993, 2001; Parameshwar Gaonkar 2001; Warren and Jackson 2002; N. Whitten 2003b, 2004). We have been writing throughout this book to underscore these points of contemporary ethnography.

A Reflexive Interlude on Antiquity and Ethnogenesis

On Thursday, July 28, 2005, Delicia Dagua and Rubén Santi came to visit us in our apartment in the Barrio Obrero across the street from the First of May primary school in urban Puyo. As always we were delighted to see them, having known them since Rubén brought Delicia to Puma Llacta in 1973. It was Delicia, we remember, who explained the full meaning of the word *causáunchimi!* (We are living!) back in 1987 during the discussion in Cushi Tambo of the upcoming exhibition in the Museo del Banco Central. After normal pleasantries and observance of etiquette, our conversation moved to some of the details surrounding the circumstances that led this couple and their entire family to move from Cushi Tambo to a relatively new hamlet at the far end of Nayapi Llacta.

Then Delicia told us of the death of her brother, Tomás Andrés Dagua Tuitui. He was the last of the men and women with full knowledge of the Andoa (pronounced Andua) language and culture. She said he and she would talk back and forth in Andoa phrases, but he had full command of the language and she only had short phrases by which to answer. The couple's local move and the death that took place far away, in Montalvo, ran together in this discourse. Both dealt with tragedy. She began to elaborate on the local-level situation and her *quiquin llacta,* as defined by a *purina chagra,* established in the region of the Ishpingu (Ishpingo) River by her brother and her sister-in-law. She also explained that Ishpingu is the Andoa word for *canela,* the cinnamon so sought after by the initial Spanish conquistadores, from whence comes the name for the region long called "Canelos."

Delicia had suffered greatly over the past year with the loss of her brother and the necessity of a move from her father-in-law's hamlet to another one founded by one of Marcelo Santi's brothers. One of her sisters, from Montalvo, originally from the Río Bufeo region, and now living with her military husband in Shell, had been visiting for some time, and was deeply affected by the events of the internal verbal fighting in Cushi Tampo, and the untimely death by shamanic attack of their brother.

Delicia's sister decided to visit the *wanduj supai* and to do so on Delicia's *chagra,* which is still in the territory of Cushi Tambo. Although one is supposed to take *wanduj* alone, Delicia covertly accompanied her, and watched over her as she moved through times-spaces of the visions to "see" just what was befalling her sister. As the story unfolds this is what Delicia intuited prior to the "return" of her sister from the realm of the Datura and subsequent conversations with her. In this telling the intuitions and the conversations run together to create a flexible text with powerful and explicit imagery of the near future and the recent past.

Her sister came out of the first stage of the drug experience and was assisted by the *supai.* She saw "everything" like a moving picture, *click, click, click,* as the frames came to her. She saw Rubén shooting his brother, and she repeated this future tragedy. She also saw that Delicia was part of this awful future act, something to be avoided, that could be avoided. She flew through the air and looked down on the world, the people, and clearly saw the patterns of their interactions, each of which was standing in relief and providing a staged demonstration of future and past events. Delicia and Rubén, she saw, no longer belonged where they were living; they were too close to an act of death. She wanted to see at the same time the situation in Cushi Tambo and the way by which her (and Delicia's) brother died. She went to the *chagra* of the *supai runa,* and there she "saw" Rubén and Delicia (at a later date) shooting at the brother. It was clearly time to move on in the present to avoid this event in the future.

Then, with the Datura person she went back to the recent past (February 2005) to see how her brother died. The culprit was his cousin, a *sinchi yachaj* whom he trusted. Tomás was fine in the morning and was sleeping near his cousin, though not in the same house. The cousin, who Delicia's sister eventually named, had three black, smooth *supai rumi* (spirit stones), very dangerous and very powerful ones. He put them near where Tomás was sleeping at about 9:00 P.M. and they entered the right side of his body; they killed him. He came into great pain at 1:00 A.M. and he died between 3:00 A.M. and 4:00 A.M. He was buried in a niche in Montalvo, and almost no one came to his wake or funeral. (The implication is that he, too, was a powerful shaman.)

We might pause here to note that there is a deep cosmological and cosmogonic patterning to this trip, as with other journeys with the *wanduj supai.* According to Lawrence Sullivan (1988) in his extensive ethnological presentation of South American religions, wherein Amazonian systems predominate, conceptualizations of death—past, present, and future—are prior to lessons about life. In the section "The Origins of Death" in his chapter "Death and the End of Time," he writes: "Even the end is caught up with the beginning, since death originates at the dawn of time. To study the end, we must begin at the source of all significant imagery. . . . The images of death's origin reveal the significant ways in which death is real and has meaning" (Sullivan 1988:469).

After revealing the insight into the cause of her brother's death, Delicia reentered the story in the first person to tell of the depth of Andoa culture, though now maintained only in Quichua language with words and phrases of Andoa. She began with marriage and kinship. The father of Delicia, Tomás, and two other siblings was a Dagua and his wife, their mother, was a Tuitui. She then said that all Tuituis were Záparo and all Daguas were Andoa. When we gently asked about her two sisters (one now dead) who spoke Shuar, she said that yes, they spoke Shuar, Quichua, and Spanish, but they descended from a Dagua as proper Andoa, and from a Tuitui mother, so they were also proper Záparo.

Next came territory. Her brother and his wife had established a new *chagra* in the territory of the Ishpingu (also written Ishpingo) River, south of the Bobonaza River, on the border of Achuar territory. Her brother wanted her to know that this was also her territory, her *quiquin llacta,* her Andoa roots region. It is near a feeder stream called Jundu, not far from another named Boa Yacu. This is on the Ishpingu Grande, not the Ishpingu Pequeña. The actual site of the *chagra* is Piña Cucha (Angry Lagoon) and her uncle lives there today to maintain occupation of the land. He is the only person there. She plans to go there soon, with her sister-in-law, and Rubén will go with her, though he has never been there. She began to name the seeds in Andoa that were in the region, including *pisiau,* Andoa for peach palm.

Interspersed throughout this conversation, one of the most extensive and intensive that we have ever experienced, was a discussion of a local educator, whom we have known for many years, but whom Delicia had only recently encountered. She asked us what we thought of him, and of a book developed by Andoa descendants through their new organization, ONAPE (Organización de Nacionalidades Andoas de Pastaza del Ecuador; Organization of Andoa Nationalities of Pastaza, Ecuador) to which this educator, with his strong alliances within the Ministry of Education in Quito, attached his name as author. We had just read the book, and found that a significant segment of it was plagiarized from the chapter by Marcelo Naranjo (1977). It was very familiar because it derived from Marcelo's master of arts thesis, deposited at the University of Illinois at Urbana-Champaign in 1974. Delicia pounced on this information to let us know that this local leader with strong ties to powerful people at the pinnacle of the educational bureaucratic pyramid in Quito had taken her brother's photograph and published it in this book with false information, without his consent or knowledge. He could do this because her brother's recent death rendered him unable to protest. But she avowed to work with her relatives through the ONAPE office in Puyo to somehow rectify this wrong.

Our conversation was moving rapidly now, animatedly, ranging through a discussion of a number of recent marriages by young people we all knew fairly well, including those creating new alliances among Puyo Runa, Canelos Runa, Pacayacu Runa, Sarayacu Runa, Napo Runa, Shuar, Achuar, Shiwiar, Waorani, Záparo, Andoa, and Mestizo. We were transported back to the late 1960s and early 1970s when similar phenomena came to light during our initial ethnography—the interculturality of the Puyo Runa of Canelos Quichua native people in a sustained system of resistance to national and international hegemony and a driving ethnogenesis of sustained cultural emergence in the face of modernizing forces (Scott 1985; N. Whitten 1976a). This took us back to Oberem in the 1950s, to Karsten in the early twentieth century, and to Pierre in the nineteenth century, and beyond.

Culture, A-cultured, and Interculturality Revisited

"Acculturation" is an awful word. Its symbolic load can be devastating to people so stigmatized in professional and popular literature and discourse. Originally developed in the 1930s and codified through a Social Science Research Council Summer Seminar by Robert Redfield, Melville Herskovits, and Ralph Linton as the "Memorandum for the Study of Acculturation," published in 1936 in the *American Anthropologist,* and also in the journals *Man, Africa,* and *Oceania,* it became a canon for the "scientific" study of culture change. But it rapidly deteriorated into a synonym for assimilation implying culture loss. In the memorandum this definition is given: "Acculturation comprehends those phenomena which result when groups of individuals having different cultures come into continuous firsthand contact, with subsequent changes in the original cultural patterns of either or both groups" (Beals 1953:626). In Britain "culture contact" was more or less synonymous with the U.S. "acculturation." The term had already been deployed by Melville J. Herskovits as a foundation of African American studies in anthropology, thereby detaching such studies from those of indigenous people, a situation that continues in the twenty-first century (Whitten and Torres 1998).

The reason the word is "awful" is that it is applied by professionals, who should know better, to dismiss the sort of data generated by serious ethnography and history. Ethnographer and philosopher Philippe Descola (1994, 1996) characterizes the Canelos Quichua as acculturated Achuar. His discourse, however, suggests that perhaps he means a-culturated, meaning without "tribal" culture, decultured, and probably denatured.

Michael Uzendoski,[2] in a new serious ethnography titled *The Napo Runa of Amazonian Ecuador* (2005), underscores the negative reaction to this position, which we share, in writing about the perspective of Anne Christine Taylor (spouse of Philippe Descola): "Taylor's otherwise stimulating piece . . . continues this stereotype in arguing that Amazonian Quichua speakers are 'assimilated,' *manso* (weak), and 'generic' natives with 'linear and periodized historical ideologies very different from those of the "traditional" groups of the region' (Taylor 1999:237)." He corrects her position by writing "the people of Napo speak in a different voice. They speak through the voice and poetics of *pachacutic*—destroying, recuperating, and transforming society and history" (Uzendoski 2005b:165). By *pachacutic* here he means "an episteme of transformation" from one space-time system to another" (N. Whitten 2003b:vii).

We concur with Uzendoski's position (see Uzendoski 2004a, 2004b, 2005a). This is not to say that the Napo Runa and Canelos Quichua are the same; they are in many ways very different. It is to say that they are *treated in the same way* in prestigious print sources by learned scholars who are specialists in other cultural systems with which Canelos Quichua and Napo Runa people interact systemically. The treatment harks back to the civilized/savage polarity—promulgated by the earliest Spanish clergy and perpetuated by modern anthropologists—as so brilliantly explicated by Michel-Rolph Trouillot (1991:29) in an article on "the Savage slot": "The dominant metamorphosis, the transformation of savagery into sameness by way of utopia as positive or negative reference, is not the outcome of a textual exercise within the anthropological practice, but part of anthropology's original conditions of existence. Anthropology came to fill the savage slot of a larger thematic field, performing a role played in different ways, by literature and travel accounts" (see also Pratt 1992; Taussig 2004). Later he reaffirmed his theme: "Anthropology must adapt to a world where none of us can take refuge in the illusion that we have found the uncontaminated Savage, the bearer of the pristine culture supposedly untouched by its western alter-ego" (Trouillot 2003:5). He continues this discourse throughout his book *Global Transformations* (2003).

Compare this to Descola's ending thoughts on the Achuar: "the fact remains that even the most scrupulous chronicler [referring to himself], when closely observing an exotic society, always has the insidious feeling of traveling backwards in time. Although they usually deny it, many ethnologists are motivated by an unspoken quest for the very beginnings. Oracular vaticinations and divine decrees no longer rule our destinies, but the illusion of a return to mankind's past crouches, ready to pounce, at some bend in the trail. This illusion is the origin of the metaphysics of nostalgia as well as of the divagations of retrospective evolutionism. But that is perhaps a modest price to pay for the privilege of entering the privacy of certain peoples whose uncertain future still hangs on the ties they have formed with nature's beings" (Descola 1994:331).

To return to "acculturation," it is hard to believe that any highly trained,

creative, competent scholar could regard Canelos Quichua people as acculturated (or a-culturated or "hybrid") Achuar in light of their strong ties
to Zaparoan cultures (as well as to Achuar culture). Certain themes deny a
trajectory from Achuar toward National Ecuadorian–Roman Catholic orientations and demeanors. We note quite specifically, here and elsewhere, their
explicit and continuing ethnogenetic interculturality; their kinship system
with its emphases on intergenerationality and affinity; their system of cultural transmission of knowledge and imagery in a parallel way through men
and women; the deep, feminine Amazonian ceramic tradition of probably
Tupian origin; the *ayllu jista* with its Dominario and dance of the *lanceros;*
and the semantics of knowledge, power, vision, and reflexivity to give just
a few illustrations that refute the imputation of the Canelos Quichua as acculturated (a-culturated) Achuar.

The Puyo Runa of Canelos Quichua culture are Amazonian people who
nonetheless constitute a significant cultural hinge between the Andes and
greater Amazonia. They represent deep Amazonian dimensions of thought
and feeling through a cosmovision carried and expressed by what, since the
sixteenth century, has been known as an Andean language. They are not
collectively moving "toward white-mestizo culture" (e.g., Miller 2004), nor
are they moving from or denying their indigenous identity in any way. They
are what they are: real people in a modern world with millennial outbreaks;
real people seeking an alternative modernity that is satisfactory to them from
both their inner values, their national values, and the global values of which
they are an integral part (Uzendoski 2005b, 2005c).

It is perhaps unfortunate that not only cartoonists and columnists, but
serious scholars of culture and nature, cannot appreciate this simple ethnographic exposition. Lévi-Strauss (1966:234), who separates "hot" (Western)
societies with history from "cold" societies that lack it, writes "the object of
'cold' societies is to make it the case that the order of temporal succession
should have as little influence as possible on their content." This accounts for
Whitehead's sardonic and dramatic opening to his book *History and Historicities in Amazonia* (2003:vii): "Amazonia is something of a last frontier for
the study of history—the epitome of a place where we may yet find 'people
without history.' Amazonia is a place that exists in an eternal present of 'first
contacts.'" These Amazonian peoples are the "cold societies" of Lévi-Strauss.
People such as the "Jívaro," as Taylor and Descola now name them—even
though the appellation is loathed by Aguaruna, Shuar, Achuar, Huambisa,
and Shiwiar when applied to contemporary people—are those whose mythology is said to overwhelm their sense of history.

Cold societies encase people without memory. They are the stuff of the obsolete museum, where human relics are displayed as contemporary ancestors, where data are "pushed" as far as possible toward the exotic (e.g., Whitten and Whitten 1993b; Errington 1998). The Achuar, with whom the Descola-Taylor couple did research and produced excellent ethnography and ethnohistory, illustrate such a "push." Although the Achuar never took heads from human enemies, as far as we know from literature and from their own contemporary exegeses, Descola (1996:273) raises the issue of this custom in his odd and dramatic statement: "I myself know much more about head-hunting than any of the Achuar whom I questioned." Between his deep knowledge of "Jívaro" culture and his and Taylor's assertions about the "acculturation" of the Canelos Quichua, there is no room for the understanding of a regional cultural system such as we have been explicating throughout this work.

They make it sound at times as though to enter modernity Jivaroan people have only to become "Quichua." "Those [Achuar] who feel attracted to change need only travel a few dozen kilometres to find in already familiar Quichua country the by now well-tried apparatus for conversion" (Descola 1996:264). But elsewhere he writes of the "vast distance" between Achuar and "Quichua" culture. In other words, the Achuar are vastly different from "the Quichua" but they may move into modernity by "becoming Quichua," a lifeway with which many, perhaps most, Ecuadorian Achuar are quite familiar, having been intermarrying and intertrading with them for a very long time. If we read Descola and Taylor correctly, such people apparently cannot return from their modernity to live as Achuar. This argumentation does not and cannot make sense; it emanates from an ideology with its locus not in the globalization and transcultural processes found in multiple localities but from the Western imagery of the savage slot explicated so well by Trouillot.

The assertion of acculturated Achuar is as false as the ideological premise of pristine tribal versus semi-civilized life on which it is based. Achuar people not only come and go from residences in Canelos Quichua regions (especially Puyo, Canelos, Sarayacu, and Montalvo), they send children and especially grandchildren to each other to live for a few months to a year or more, and some practice speaking the other language until they perfect both. When crises occur Achuar, Canelos Quichua, and Shiwiar may rise up together, as we saw in the previous chapter about the Caminata, to march shoulder to shoulder into the very maw of morbid modernity to affirm their alternative modernities in a millennial manner.

The historical source of regional polarization stems from the nineteenth-century Dominican administrative division of people into Jívaro and Quichua (see chapter 1). Its recent instantiation by highly competent ethnographers and ethnohistorians is the result of warped Western historicity wherein deviations from the classificatory (and erroneous) "cold" Amazonian societies are offset by the radical (and erroneous) affirmation of "acculturation" for dynamic people who don't fit the "cold" mode.

Explicating Power

Power enters here. In a presentation at the University of Illinois, Marshall Sahlins stated that culture, among other dynamics, may constitute "the organization of empowerment." As such, we have been explicating empowerment throughout this book. Trouillot (1995:xix) wrote of this process: "History is the fruit of power, but power itself is never so transparent that its analysis becomes superfluous. The ultimate mark of power may be its invisibility; the ultimate challenge, the exposition of its roots." After the indigenous rebellion of January 21, 2000, Salvador Quishpe (*El Comercio,* February 20) stated that "Power is an instrument that lets the dreams of the people crystallize." Immediately after the taking of the legislative building Antonio Vargas stated that "the people are empowered." The forces with which this book deals in its focus on the assertion of human cultural life, are suppressed by ideas of "a-culturation" and the entering of civilization or modernity. Understanding is enhanced by the very voices of people in motion, those of the many interculturalities of modern and millennial Ecuador.

Closing Thoughts on Ethnography, Locality, Globality, and Empowerment

Ethnography may be an instrument of empowerment, or it may be an instrument of oppression (for the latter, see, e.g., the review by Geertz 2001). To the degree that it opens a flow of intercultural information it may empower, but to the degree that it hermetically seals off people's lifeways from understanding it constrains.

These essays constitute local-level and regional-level ethnography. By zooming down on the Puyo Runa of Canelos Quichua culture we seek to illuminate an Amazonian regional system that includes Shuar, Achuar, Záparo, Andoa, and Napo Runa, to various degrees, and increasingly Waorani. They are complemented by two other recent works, Uzendoski's ethnography and ethnohistory *The Napo Runa of Amazonian Ecuador* (2005b) and the book of essays published as *Millennial Ecuador* (N. Whitten 2003b). In the latter tome the concept of contrastructural powers, or contrapowers, is applied to modern globalizations and transculturations to underscore the forces latent and occasionally unleashed at local and regional levels within a particular nation-state, in this case Ecuador. Along with contrastructural powers is the notion of alternative modernities, introduced in the preface and chapter 7 and elaborated on in chapter 8 of this book.

By contrastructural powers (called counterpower by Graeber 2004:35–37) we refer to sociosymbolic forces that coalesce against dominant or structural power, such as the nation-state, military, police, or corporations (see also Uzendoski 2005b on the Napo Runa for more illustration and elaboration; the concepts are developed by special reference to the pioneering work of Victor Turner [1974] and Eric R. Wolf [1999]). Alternative modernities constitute a contested domain generated by these same sociosymbolic processes within a nation-state that come to epitomize modernity in such a manner as to make life uncomfortable, unbearable, or simply unthinkable for some of the people within its confines (Parameshwar Gaonkar 2001). Under such circumstances millenniarity may emerge. By millennial we refer to the Quichua concept of *pachacutij*, "the return of space-time (chronotope) of a healthy past to that of a healthy future" (N. Whitten 2003b:x; see also Uzendoski 2005b:165).

One task of the ethnographer is to set forth sociosymbolic processes in unfolding, transculturating, and transforming spaces-times to facilitate understanding across, within, and beyond national borders. Processes of intersubjectivity, expanding hermeneutic horizons, and sustained reflexivity are central to ongoing ethnography. To the extent that projections from Western modernity such as "acculturation," "deculturation," or "assimilation" are painted on the palette of peoples' lifeways, the processes and patterns of life themselves are diminished, ethnography is thinned, and people themselves are omitted from the discourses of continuity and change, hegemony and resistance, reproduction and transformation. This is why we have been harsh in criticizing those who work with adjacent peoples, and who develop, from our perspective, prejudicial and dismissive images of Canelos Quichua cultural dynamics.

Ethnography may offer insights of potential empowerment manifest in innumerable locations around the world, and communicable increasingly by the potential interculturality of horizontal globalization, or "globalization from below" (see Appadurai 2001:16–20). Such a potential requires careful scrutiny that involves not only an inner view of symbol systems, communicative tropes, and the boundaries set up with other systems, but also an understanding of such *systems in action within shifting world frameworks* (see Scott 2005). Understanding of interculturality and its potential for communication globally requires an understanding of contemporary history and ongoing life that eschews the warps of condensed and highly distorted ideologies such as those of millennial capitalism (Comaroff and Comaroff 2001) and millennial fundamentalism (Hopkins, Lorentzen, Mendieta, and Batstone 2001). It is through ethnography and its attendant historicity that such understandings may emerge.

Causáunchimi! We are Living! is an apt proclamation on which to end this work. Luis Vargas and Delicia Dagua so stated to us in 1987 in the small hamlet of Cushi Tambo while discussing a display of imageries and imaginaries of their material culture for a prestigious modern art gallery in the capital city of Quito. As we learned many years ago, and as we write in our preface, "Power emanates from imagery. Imagery is central to all knowledge." Indigenous imagery must be understood in its own cultural matrices, and not from the standpoint of Western ideology. If anthropologists and others can learn to do this, perhaps Canelos Quichua peoples and their cultural transformations and transculturations, together with so many other comparable systems worldwide, can receive the empowering appreciation they deserve. If so, then our concepts of culture can be enriched with diversity, rather than condensed with false hermetic simplicity. With such appreciation the scholarship directed toward ethnography can escape "the Savage slot," and could reemerge as foundational to anthropology.

Notes

1. While this book manuscript was in production Ecuador underwent the processes of another national election. The radical populist candidate Rafael Correa Delgado (who holds a doctoral degree in economics from the University of Illinois at Urbana-Champaign) won the presidency and continued his campaign pledge to destroy the "political class," reject the hegemony of the United States in political and economic terms, and transform national wealth into a program to help the poor and ensure an enduring social justice. As of May 2007, Correa enjoys nearly unprecedented approval by the majority of Ecuadorians. It is not clear at this time where the apparently fragmented indigenous movement stands in the fray of national and global furies.

2. Uzendoski (2005b:165) reviews the literature focused on Amazonian Quichua "acculturation" beginning with Udo Oberem (1971) and carrying through Taylor (1999): "Oberem's account diminishes how the Napo Runa view their history of struggle; Oberem severs the current generation from the past. Far too often people in Ecuador and abroad negate the Napo Runa view of history by asserting that the Napo Runa are 'immigrants' from the highlands or are not proper 'Amazonians.'"

Glossary

Acanga, hawk. *See also* Atatau
Ahijada/o, godchild
Aicha, flesh, meat, body
    Aicha mama, tick
    Sacha aicha, meat from the forest, game
    Yacu aicha, fish
Aisana, covering, embellishment of primary design on polychrome pottery; the finer
    lines and deviations from the primary lines
Ala, fungus, mushroom; mythic brother
Alcalde, mayor; indigenous authority under ecclesiastical colonial rule
Alguacil, indigenous authority under ecclesiastical colonial rule
Allcu, dog
Alli, good
Allpa, land, soil, turf, territory to be protected
    Manga allpa, pottery clay
Allu, mold, fungus
    Allu asua, manioc brew made with fungi
Alzado, unruly animals or people; cannot be applied to "blancos"
Amarun, boa constrictor generally, anaconda specifically
Amasanga, master spirit of the rain forest, male and female, androgynous
Amu, chief
Amulana, burnishing
    Amulana rumi, feminine burnishing stone (pottery), male burnishing stone (dried
        skin)
Andoa, Zaparoan language, for practical purposes same as Shimigae
Antepasados, ancestors

Apamama, grandmother
Aparichina. See pachina
Apayaya, grandfather
Arabela, Zaparoan language
Ashanga, basket
Asua, manioc brew, "chicha"
    Asua churana manga, large polychrome painted pot for storing manioc mash;
      tinaja
    Asua mama, manioc maker and server
Atatau, hawk. *See also* Acanga
Awa, high, Andean, high forest hill
    Awa Llacta, Andes, Andean people
    Awa pacha, sky
    Awa shiri (*Tawa shiri*), distant people of tropical forest hills
Awashca, made
Aya, soul
Ayahuasca (pronounced ayawasca), soul vine (*Banisteriopsis caapi* with plant ad-
    ditives)
Ayllu, kinship system, shared consanguineal and affinal substance

Bancu, seat of power, seat
Barbasco, fish poison
Batea (*bátia*), large wooden bowl for making fermented manioc mash
Biruti, dart
Blanco, white person
Blanco-mestizo, Ecuadorian socioeconomic status groups outside of elite circles
Bulla, noise

Cabecera, headwater region
Cachi, salt
Cachun, daughter-in-law
Cagun, forest spirit with two heads and conjoined tails that eats people
Caja, snare drum
Cajonero (*cajuniru*), drummer
Callana, blackened eating bowl
Callari, beginning
Callarirucuguna, beginning times-places
Callpachina, to cause to run
Calulu, white mushroom (associated with women)
Camai, to prove, proof
Camari, ritual feast
Caminata, long-distance trek or march

Cancha, cleared space around home, or plaza

Capitán, indigenous authority under ecclesiastical colonial rule

Cara, skin, face, countenance

Cari, man

Cariyuj, to possess a man (marriage from woman's perspective)

Caru, distant

Caserío, hamlet

Caucho (*cauchu*), rubber

Caudillo, powerful man who attracts rival factions to him in political arenas; political boss

Causai, life force

Causana, to live

Causáunchimi, we are living!

Chaca (*chacana*), ladder, bridge, axis mundi

 Jilucu chaca, Bauhinia species of vine that fixes nitrogen in the tropical forest

Chagra, swidden garden

 Chagra mama, master spirit of swidden garden. *See also* Nungüi

Challua, fish; family of "bocachica" fish

Chambira, a particular palm (*Astrocaryum chambira, A. munbaca, A. tucuma*)

Charapa, water turtle

Chaupi, half, middle

Chayuj, convener of festival

Chijnina, to envy

 Chijnij, one who envies

Chimbajta, either side

-chimi (suffix), we (chi) with emphasis (mi)

Chiminea, small-bore muzzle-loading shotgun

Chonta (*chunda*), spiny palm, palm dart, palm needle, magical dart

Chontaduro (*chundaruru*), peach palm (*Bactris gasipaes*)

-chu (suffix), asks a yes or no question when attached to verb; may make a statement negative

Chulla, part missing, deformation (*chulla chaqui,* person with feet on backward, or one human foot and another animal foot)

Churana, primary decoration on polychrome pottery

Churi, son

Comadre, coparent, female

Compadre, coparent, male

Comuna, commune

Cucha (*cocha*), lake, lagoon, oxbow backwater of river

Cuichi, rainbow, as an angry and dangerous anaconda

Culqui, money

Cumba, contraction of *compadre*

Cunalla, right now
Cunan, present time, very recent
Cunga, neck
Curaga, leader, cultural broker
Curagazgo, domain of a leader or broker
Curassow, Salvin's Curassow (*Mitu salvini*)
Cusa, husband
Cusca, straight up
Cushi, happy
Cutu, howler monkey

Dominario, last day of kinship festival when people take the world to the brink of "ending everything"

Enganche, system of labor contracting and debt peonage

Fiscal, indigenous authority under ecclesiastical colonial rule
Fuera, out, beyond boundaries (fuera de su lugar, out of place)

Gente (jinti), people, person
Gobierno, government, authority structure
Guerrero, warrior
Gumba. See Cumba
-guna (suffix), plural
Guardian, guard

Ichilla, small
Ila, a giant tree with huge flying buttresses
Indi, sun
Indillama, sloth, place of the sloth
Indio, Spanish for "Indian"
Indiyacushca, area of sun's westward passage just beyond the Andes
Interculturalidad, interculturality
Ishpingo (Ishpingu), "cinnamon," canela (*Ocotea quixos*)
Iwianch, demon

Jacu, let's go
Jacuichi, let's go
Jatari, rise up
Jauya, parents-in-law
Jayambi, iguanid often found on river banks, sometimes known as "Jesus lizard"

Jilucu, Common Potoo bird (*Nyctibius griseus*) or Giant Potoo bird *(Nyctibius grandis),* members of the Nightjar family
Jista, festival
  Cari jista, Quilla Jista
  Jista mama, woman in charge of festival, female host
  Jista wasi, festival house
  Warmi jista, Jilucu Jista
Jucha, sin (for which one must pay)
Juctu, cave
Juing, a frog (*Dendrobatis* species)
Junculu, edible frog (some deny it is edible); daughter or sister of *Nungüi*
Jurijuri, dangerous spirit master of foreign people and master of monkeys; a transformation of Amasanga
Jursa (ursa), force

Lancero, special dancer during kinship festivals in Canelos, Pacayacu, and Sarayacu
Llacta, sector of indigenous territory
Llanchama, bark cloth; tree from which bark cloth is made
Llaquina, sad, nostalgia, love
Llulla, lie, liar
Lluwi, Cock-of-the-Rock bird (*Rupicola rupicola*)
Lubu (lobo), "wolf" but only used as *yacu lubu,* giant river otter; also known as *yacu puma*
Lugar, place (Spanish); time (Amazonian Quichua)
Lulun, egg, fertilizing sperm, very young child
Lumu, manioc, *Manihot esculenta*
Lurira, shield
  Supai lurira, spirit shield

-ma (suffix), totalizing; an emphasis that conveys the subject to be a totality; toward
Macana, fighting club-stick, defensive staff
Machin, Capuchin monkey; foreign person
Mama, mother; feminine presence or force
  Mama churana, primary decoration on polychrome pottery
Mana, to be
Mana, negative when -chu suffix is added to verb
Manalli, bad, evil
Mancharina, to make tremble; to frighten
-manda (suffix), from; of
Manduru, Annatto, a red vegetable dye (*Bixa orellana*)
Manga, pot, pottery clay
  Manga allpa mama, master spirit of pottery clay. *See also* Nungüi

Mani, I am
Masha, son-in-law
Mauca, old; fallow
Mayores, old ones, elders
Mestizaje, ideology of racial miscegenation to "improve the races"
Mestizo, "hybrid," "half-caste"; non-black, non-Indian
Minga, collective work group
Misha, hairball or stone or other hard object found in stomach of game or fish
Montaña, canopied Andean slopes grading into Amazonia or coast
Mucawa (mucaja), decorated ceramic drinking bowl
Mundu (mundo), world
Muqui, reduced human head
Muscui, image, vision, insight, dream
Muscuna, to "see," to dream, to envision
Muscuyuj (muscuj), one who "sees," vision maker

Nacionalidad, nationality; in Ecuador indigenous or Afro-Ecuadorian people, but
   broadening to include previous indigenous people such as "Huancavilca"
Nayapi, swallow tail kite bird (*Elanoides fortificatus*)
-ngui (suffix), you, second-person singular
Nina, fire
Nungüi (Nunguli), master spirit of garden soil and pottery clay, feminine; transformations include *chagra mama, manga allpa mama, Jilucu,* and *sapallu warmi*

Ñambi, trail, path, route
Ñaupa, old, earlier, preceding (time); in front or ahead of (space)
Ñawi (Ñahui), eye, face
Ñuca, I, my
Ñucanchi, we, our

Olla, bowl, jar, pot

Paccha, waterfall, cascade, rushing water, cataract
Pacha, space-time (from about 1990, used as "earth" by some indigenous spokes-
   people)
Pachacutij (Pachacutic), the return of space-time (chronotope) of a healthy past to
   that of a healthy future
Pachakutik, national social-political movement that sometimes serves as a political
   party
Pachama, a totalized space-time
   Jawa (Awa) pachama, sky world

Quillu pachama, times-spaces when the moon illuminated the earth and made crops grow

Ucu pachama, underearth places-times

Pachina (contraction of *aparichina*), special women's plants to make domestic plants grow

Pactana, to arrive, to make a pact

Paju, strong and dangerous power

Páramo, high wet tundra-like grasslands of northern Andes

Parijú, togetherness

Partido, colonial division into ethnic-cultural-geographic sectors

Partimanda, geographic divisions with ethnic-cultural-language implications

Pasuca, killing seance; part of shamanic seance where killing missiles sent to enemy

Paushi, currassow bird (*Pauxi pauxi*)

Pawa, guan bird (e.g., *Penelope jaquacu*)

Pijuanu (*pijuano*), vertical shaman's class flute, often made from tibia of water bird

Pilchi, gourd

Pinduj, river cane (from which derives "Pindo")

Pishcu, bird

Tutapishcu, bat

Puca, red

Pucuna, blowing; blowgun

Pugllana, to play

Puma, wild or feral cat

Taruga puma, mountain lion, cougar

Yana puma, black jaguar

Pungu, portal, entrance; mouth of river

Puñuna, to sleep

Purina, trek

Puru, drinking gourd

Jista puru, festival polychrome drinking vessel

Purungu, drinking vessel made from leaves

Purutu, inedible beans for nitrogen fixation when planting maize

Puyu, fog

Quilla, moon

Quillu, yellow color; lazy person

Quindi, hummingbird

Nina quindi, fire hummingbird

Rayu quindi, lightning hummingbird

Quingu, zigzag

Quiquin, proper

Rama, limb
Rayu, lightning
 Rayu quindi, lightning hummingbird
 Rayu wanduj, Amasanga's Datura
Reducción, colonial forced or induced nucleation of indigenous people
Regatón, river trader
Ricsina, experiential knowledge; to know, to perceive, to comprehend
Rigra, wing
Rina, to go
Ringri, ear
Rucu, old, venerable one
Rullaj, white
Rumi, stone
 Amulana rumi, burnishing stone
 Aya rumi, soul stone
 Charapa rumi, water turtle stone
 Chunda rumi, chonta dart (killing) stone
 Lumu rumi, manoic stone
 Puca rumi, red stone
 Rawai rumi, blood (killing) stone
 Supai rumi, spirit stone
 Tayaj rumi, soul stone
 Yachaj rumi, shamanic stone
 Yana rumi, black stone
Runa, person as unmarked, man as marked, fully human being
 Alli Runa, "good" Christian person
 Sacha Runa, forest person
 Supai Runa, spirit person
 Runa shimi, human speech
Runapura, people living as a group, people among ourselves
Ruya, tree

Sacha, forest
 Sacha allcu, bushdog
 Sacha Runa, forest person, forest spirit Amasanga
 Sacha Warmi, forest (spirit) woman
Sacharuna, forest iguanid
Sacsashca, full, satisfied with meal or drink
Samai, breath; life breath
Sami, class; position in classificatory hierarchy
Samwai, tangible breath; congealed breath; manifest as small snails near recently
 deceased shaman's grave

Sapallu, squash
Saquina, let alone, let be; allow
Saquirina, to stay, remain, endure, last
Sara, maize
Shamuna, to come, to arrive
Shayana, to stand, to "be ready"
Shayarina, reflexive of shayana
Shimi, mouth; word; speech
Shimigae, Zaparoan language; for practical purposes, same as Andoa
-shina (suffix), like, as (simile)
Shinquillu (*shilquillu*), tree resin for coating decorated polychrome pottery
Shitana, to blow evil projectile
Shitashca, hit by evil projectile
Shua, thief
Shuj, one, other, another
Shungu, heart, will
Sicuanga, toucan bird
Simayuca, powder made from various substances to attract friends and neutralize
    enemies; also a love potion
Sinchi, strong
Siqui, rear end (of a person or a garden)
Soldado, soldier
Sumaj, beauty, beautiful
Sungui (*Tsungui*), master spirit of hydrosphere, male and female, androgynous
Supai, spirit
Susto, magical fright

Tambo (*tambu*), temporary shelter
Tamia, rain
Taqui, conductor, musical or rhythmic leader; spirit leader
Taquina, shaman's song, shamanic song
Taruga, deer
Tiana, to be, to exist
Tiari, sit (command)
Tiarina, to sit
Tinaja, large polychrome painted pot for storing manioc mash
Trago, raw cane alcohol; drinking alcohol
Tsantsa, reduced human head
Tsawata, forest tortoise
Tsentsak, spirit dart
Tsintsaca, spirit dart
Tsumi, ability to transform oneself into a jaguar

Tsungui. See Sungui
Tucu, edible palm weevil larva
Tucui, all, every
Tucuna, transformation
Tucurina, ending everything
Tula, digging stick
Tullu, bone
    Aya tullu, soul bone
    Rina tullu, bone sent by shaman as spirit dart (often a catfish bone)
Tupana, to encounter
Tuparina, to return to reencounter
    Tupaj amarun, dangerous situation where boa constrictor's body separated from head grows back toward its head
Tupi (Tupian), language and culture of coastal and central Amazonas that spread expansively in precolonial and colonial times to the base of the Andes and beyond.
Turu, mud
    Turu amarun, dangerous mud anaconda
Tuta, night
Tutapishcu, bat

Uchu, capsicum
    Uchu manga, Amazon pepper pot
Uchuputu, kapok tree
Ucu, down, under
Ucui, within
    Ucui mama, cutter ant
    Ucui yacu, strong *asua* made from drippings
Ullu, penis
Unai, mythic time-space
Ungushca, sick, ill
Upina, to drink; the lip of a drinking vessel or serving vessel
Upiyana, to drink
Urai, downriver
Urcu, hill
Ursa (jursa), force
Ushana, to empower, power; to be capable, to be able
Ushi, daughter
Utipana, to empower, cosmic empowerment
Uunt, great man
Uyarina, to make noise, to be heard

Vara, staff of authority under ecclesiastical colonial rule

Varayuj, holder of staff of authority under ecclesiastical colonial rule

Vinillu, heady alcoholic drink with cyanotropic effects made from drippings of mold or fungal manioc brew

Viuda, widow

    Viuda tutapishcu, bat mother of spirit women givers of crops

Waira, wind

Wamaj, bamboo

Wanduj, "Datura" (*Brugmansia suaveolens*), a hallucinogen

    Allcu wanduj, (variegated leaf species), dog Datura

    Alli upina wanduj, human-drinking Datura

    Rayu wanduj, Amasanga's Datura

    Yacu wanduj, useless Datura

Wangu, bundle

Wañuna, to die

Warmi, woman

Warmiyuj, to possess a woman ("marriage" from a male perspective)

Wasca, vine

Wasi, house, household

Wauqui, brother (male speaker)

Wicsa, stomach; widest part of a pot

Widuj, (*Genipa americana*), black dye

Wira, fat

Yachachina, to teach

Yachai, knowledge, custom, culture

Yachaj, one who knows, shaman; sometimes master potter

    Yachaj sami, shaman's class (level) knowledge

Yachajuí, snare drumming, gathering power

Yachana, to know; deep knowledge, cultural knowledge

Yacu, water, river, liquid

    Yacu lubu, giant river otter

    Yacu mama, anaconda, river spirit master

    Yacu puma, giant river otter

    Yacu supai runa, river spirit people

Yaicui, enter, come in

Yajé (*Yahé*), *ayahuasca* in Tucanoan languages

Yaji, leaf additives to *ayahuasca* to produce visions

Yami, trumpeter bird (*Psophia leucoptera*)

Yana, black, purple, deep blue

    Yana amarun, large, dangerous anaconda

    Yana puma, huge black jaguar

Yanuna, to cook
Yawati, forest tortoise
Yaya, father
Yumbo, healer from the forest; may be pejorative term for forest native
Yumingai, a curse
Yuyana, to think
Yuyarina, reflexive of yuyana, to reflect

Záparo(a), Zaparoan language

Note: Semantics and lexicons vary somewhat from family to family and sometimes from individual to individual. The reader should note that this is especially so between Canelos Quichua and Napo Runa people. Examples include *mucawa-mucaja, shinquillu-shilquillu,* Nungüi-Nunguli. One family uses Tsumi instead of Sungui for the water spirit master. Use of terms as presented here will be understood throughout Canelos Quichua territory.

References

Abercrombie, Thomas A.
    1998   Pathways of Memory and Power: Ethnography and History among an Andean People. Madison: University of Wisconsin Press.

Acosta, Alberto, et al.
    2001   Nada Solo para los indios: El Levantamiento Indígena del 2001. Quito: Abya-Yala.

Almeida, Ileana, et al.
    1992   Indios: Una reflexión sobre el Levantamiento Indígena de 1990. Quito: Abya-Yala.

Almeida Vinueza, José
    1995   Identidades indias en el Ecuador contemporaneo. Quito: Abya-Yala.

Anonymous
    1935   El Oriente Dominicano 8(38):99–102.

Anonymous ("Misionero Dominicano")
    1951   Fundación de San Jacinto del Pindo. El Oriente Dominicano, 111.

Anthropology Today
    1989   News: Auction Houses. 5(5):26.

Appadurai, Arjun (editor)
    2001   Globalization. Durham, N.C.: Duke University Press.

Araujo Sánchez, Diego (editor)
    2005   El abril de los forajidos: Caída y fuga de Lucio Gutiérrez. *Hoy* (Quito).

Armstrong, Robert Plant
    1971   The Affecting Presence: An Essay in Humanistic Anthropology. Urbana: University of Illinois Press.

Babcock, Barbara
    1978   (editor) The Reversible World: Symbolic Inversion in Art and Society. Ithaca, N.Y.: Cornell University Press.
    1980   Reflexivity: Definition and Discriminations. Introduction to Semiotica 30(1/2):1–14.
    1987   Reflexivity. In Encyclopaedia of Religion. Pp. 234–38. New York: Macmillan.

Beals, Ralph
    1953   Acculturation. Anthropology Today. Alfred L. Kroeber, ed. Pp. 621–41. Chicago: University of Chicago Press.

Blomberg, Rolf (editor)
    1952   Ecuador: Andean Mosaic. Stockholm: Ivar Haeggstrom Roktryceri A.B.

Brown, Michael F.
    1994   (editor) Relaciones interétnicas y adaptación cultural entre Shuar, Achuar, Aguaruna, y Canelos Quichua. Quito: Abya-Yala.
    1985a   Individual Experience, Dreams, and the Identification of Magical Stones in an Amazonian Society. In Directions in Cognitive Anthropology. Janet W. D. Dougherty, ed. Pp. 373–87. Urbana: University of Illinois Press.
    1985b   Tsewa's Gift: Magic and Meaning in an Amazonian Society. Washington, D.C.: Smithsonian Institution Press.

Brown, Michael F., and Michael Fernandez
    1991   War of Shadows: The Struggle for Utopia in the Peruvian Amazon. Berkeley: University of California Press.

Bunker, Stephen G.
    2005   The Snake with Golden Braids: Society, Nature, and Technology in Andean Irrigation. Lanham, Md.: Lexington Books.

Bunzl, Matti
    2002   Foreword. In Time and the Other: How Anthropology Makes Its Object. Johannes Fabian. Pp. ix–xxxiv. New York: Columbia University Press.
    2004   Boas, Foucault, and the "Native Anthropologist": Notes toward a Neo-Boasian Anthropology. American Anthropologist 106(3):435–42.

Cabello de Balboa, Miguel
    1945   [1583] Obras, vol. 1. Quito: Editorial Ecuatoriana.

Cabodevilla, Miguel Angel
    1994   Los huaorani en la historia de los pueblos del oriente. Coca: CICAME (Centro de Investigaciones Culturales de la Amazonía Ecuatoriana, Pompeya Río Napo).

Cabodevilla, Miguel Angel, Randy Smith, and Alex Rivas
    2004   Tiempos de guerra: Waorani contra Taromenane. Quito: Abya-Yala.

Calderón Cevallos, Alfonso
    1987   Reflexión en las Cultural Orales. 4th edition. Quito: Abya-Yala.
Carvajal, Gaspar de
    1934   [ca. 1541] The Discovery of the Amazon, According to the Account of
            Friar Gaspar de Carvajal and other Documents. José Toribio Medina,
            comp. H. C. Heaton, ed. Special Publication 17. New York: American
            Geographical Society.
Casement, Roger
    1912   Correspondence Respecting the Subjects and Native Indians Employed
            in the Collection of Rubber in the Putumayo Districts. House of Com-
            mons Sessional Papers 68(14 February 1912–March 1913).
Castner, James Lee
    2002   Shrunken Heads: Tsantsa Trophies and Human Exotica. Gainesville,
            Fla.: Feline Press.
Chango, Alfonso
    1984   Yachaj Sami Yachachina. Quito: Abya-Yala.
Clastres, Hélène
    1995   The Land-Without-Evil: Tupí-Guaraní Prophetism. Jacqueline Grenez
            Brovender, trans. Urbana: University of Illinois Press.
Columbus, Christopher
    1960   The Journal of Christopher Columbus. Cecil Jane, trans. New York:
            Clarkson N. Potter.
Comaroff, Jean, and John L. Comaroff (editors)
    1993   Modernity and Its Malcontents. Chicago: University of Chicago
            Press.
    2001   Millennial Capitalism and the Culture of Neoliberalism. Durham,
            N.C.: Duke University Press.
El Comercio (Quito)
    2004   September 7. http://www. elcomercio.com/noticias.asp?noid-1441414;
            accessed Sept. 7.
    2005   August 11, 2005: B11. Accessed September 16, 2005.
CONAIE (Confederación de Nacionalidades Indígenas del Ecuador)
    1989   Las Nacionalidades Indígenas en el Ecuador: Nuestro Proceso Orga-
            nizativo. 2nd edition. Quito: TINCUI-CONAIE.
    1992   La dignidad de los pueblos: Levantamiento de 21 de enero 2000. Video.
            Quito: CONAIE.
Conklin, Marie W.
    1976   Genetic and Biological Aspects of the Development of Datura. Mono-
            graphs in Developmental Biology, No. 12. Basel and New York: S.
            Karger.
Corkill, David, and David Cubit
    1988   Ecuador: Fragile Democracy. London: Latin American Bureau (Re-
            search and Action).

Corr, Rachel

2000   Cosmology and Personal Experience: Representations of the Sacred
        Landscape in Salasaca, Ecuador. Ph.D. dissertation, Department of
        Anthropology, University of Illinois at Urbana-Champaign.

2004   To Throw the Blessing: Poetics, Prayer, and Performance in the Andes.
        Journal of Latin American Anthropology 9(2):382–408.

Crawford, Neelon, and Norman E. Whitten Jr.

1979   Soul Vine Shaman. L.P. Record with monograph produced and distrib-
        uted by Neelon Crawford. New York: Neelon Crawford and Urbana:
        Sacha Runa Research Foundation. Rereleased as a CD, 2007, by Polar
        Fine Arts.

Dean, Bartholomew

1994   Multiple Regimes of Value: Unequal Exchange and the Circulation of
        Urarina Palm-Fiber Wealth. Museum Anthropology 18(1):3–20.

De la Torre, Carlos

2006   Ethnic Movements and Citizenship in Ecuador. Latin American Re-
        search Review 41(2):247–59.

Deloria, Philip J.

1998   Playing Indian. New Haven, Conn.: Yale University Press.

Descola, Philippe

1981   From Scattered to Nucleated Settlement: A Process of Socioeconomic
        Change among the Achuar. *In* Cultural Transformations and Ethnicity
        in Modern Ecuador. Norman E. Whitten Jr., ed. Pp. 614–46. Urbana:
        University of Illinois Press.

1994   [1986] In the Society of Nature: A Native Ecology in Amazonia. New
        York: Cambridge University Press.

1996   Spears of Twilight: Three Years among the Jivaro Indians of South
        America. New York: The New Press.

Dietrerich, Heinz (compiler)

2000   La cuatra vía al poder: 21 enero desde una perspectiva latinoamericana.
        Quito: Abya-Yala.

Dobkin de Rios, Marlene

1972   Visionary Vine: Psychedelic Healing in the Peruvian Amazon. San
        Francisco: Chandler.

Eliot, Elisabeth

1975   [1956] Through Gates of Splendor. Old Tappan, N.J.: Fleming H. Revell
        Co.

Errington, Shelly

1998   The Death of Authentic Primitive Art and Other Tales of Progress.
        Berkeley: University of California Press.

España Torres, Hugo Efraín

1996   El testigo: El caso Restrepo y otros delitos de estado. Quito: Editorial
        El Conejo and Abya-Yala.

Espinosa, Simón
    1992a   Solidaridad en la Caminata. Marcha Indígena de los pueblos amazónicos Puyo-Quito (Abril-Mayo). Suplemento Especial Kipu 18. Pp. 158–60. Quito: Abya-Yala.

    1992b   "We Shall Overcome." ¡y overcomiarón! Marcha Indígena de los pueblos amazónicos Puyo-Quito (Abril-Mayo). Suplemento Especial Kipu 18. P. 129. Quito: Abya-Yala.

Esterman, Josef
    1998   Filosofía andina: Estudio intercultural de la sabiduría, autóctona andina. Quito: Abya-Yala.

Fabian, Johannes
    2001   Anthropology with an Attitude: Critical Essays. Stanford, Calif.: Stanford University Press.

    2002   [1983] Time and the Other: How Anthropology Makes Its Object. 2nd edition with a new Foreword by Matti Bunzl. New York: Columbia University Press.

Falassi, Alessandro (editor)
    1987   Time Out of Time: Essays on the Festival. Albuquerque: University of New Mexico Press.

Fausto, Carlos
    2000   Of Enemies and Pets: Warfare and Shamanism in Amazonia. American Ethnologist 26(4):933–56.

    2004   A Blend of Blood and Tobacco: Shamans and Jaguars among the Parakana of Eastern Amazonia. In In Darkness and Secrecy: The Anthropology of Assault Sorcery and Witchcraft in Amazonia. Neil L. Whitehead and Robin Wright, eds. Pp. 157–78. Durham, N.C.: Duke University Press.

Ferdon, Edwin N., Jr.
    1950   Studies in Ecuadorian Geography. School of American Research and Museum of New Mexico. Monographs of the School of American Research 15. Santa Fe: School of American Research and University of Southern California.

Ferguson, R. Brian, and Neil L. Whitehead (editors)
    1999   War in the Tribal Zone: Expanding States and Indigenous Warfare. 2nd edition with new preface. Santa Fe: SAR Press and Oxford: James Curray.

Fernandez, James W.
    1973   Analysis of Ritual: Metaphorical Correspondences as the Elementary Forms. Science 182:1366–67.

    1974   The Mission of Metaphor in Expressive Culture. Current Anthropology 15(2):119–45.

Fine, Kathleen S.
    1991   Cotocollao: Ideología, Historia, y Acción en un Barrio de Quito. Quito:
            Abya-Yala.
Fine-Dare, Kathleen S.
    2002   Grave Injustice: The American Indian Repatriation Movment and
            NAGPRA. Lincoln: University of Nebraska Press.
Flad, Rowan, et al.
    2005   Archaeological and Chemical Evidence for Early Salt Production in
            China. New York: National Academy of Sciences of the USA, 102(35,
            August 30):12618–22.
Flornoy, Bertrand
    1953   Jivaro: Among the Headshrinkers of the Amazon. London: Elek.
Galarza Zavala, Jaime
    1972   El festín del petróleo. 2nd edition. Quito: "Cicetronic Cía. Ltda." de
            Papelería Moderna.
Geertz, Clifford
    1973   The Interpretation of Cultures: Selected Essays. New York: Basic
            Books.
    1983   Local Knowledge: Further Essays in Interpretive Anthropology. New
            York: Basic Books.
    2001   Life among the Anthros. *Review of* Darkness in El Dorado: How Sci-
            entists and Journalists Devastated the Amazon. The New York Review
            of Books, February 8.
    2005   Shifting Aims, Moving Targets: On the Anthropology of Religion.
            Journal of the Royal Anthropological Institute 11(1):1–15.
Glave, Luis Miguel
    1999   The "Republic of Indians" in Revolt (c. 1680–1790). *In* The Cambridge
            History of the Native People of the Americas. Frank Salomon and
            Stuart B. Schwartz, eds. Vol. 3: South America, Part 2. Pp. 502–57.
            Cambridge: Cambridge University Press.
Gnerre, Maurízio
    1973   Sources of Spanish Jívaro. Romance Philogoly 27(2):203–4.
Goldman, Irving
    1963   The Cubeo: Indians of the Northwest Amazon. Illinois Studies in An-
            thropology 2. Urbana: University of Illinois Press.
    2004   Cubeo Hehénewa Religious Thought. New York: Columbia University
            Press.
Gow, Peter
    1994   River People: Shamanism and History in Western Amazonia. *In* Sha-
            manism, History and the State. Nicholas Thomas and Caroline Hum-
            phrey, eds. Pp. 90–113. Ann Arbor: University of Michigan Press.

Graburn, Nelson H. H.

 1976 Introduction: The Arts of the Fourth World. *In* Ethnic and Tourist Arts: Cultural Expressions from the Fourth World. Nelson H. H. Graburn, ed. Pp. 1–32. Berkeley: University of California Press.

Graeber, David

 2004 Fragments of an Anarchist Anthropology. Chicago: Prickly Paradigm Press.

Gudeman, Stephen

 1986 Economics as Culture: Models and Metaphors of Livelihood. Boston: Routledge & Kegan Paul.

 1992 Markets, Models and Morality. *In* Contesting Markets. Roy Dilley, ed. Pp. 279–94. Edinburgh: Edinburgh University Press.

 2001 The Anthropology of Economy: Community, Market, and Culture. Oxford: Blackwell.

Guss, David

 1989 To Weave and Sing: Art, Symbol, and Narrative in the South American Rain Forest. Berkeley: University of California Press.

 2000 The Festive State: Ethnicity and Nationalism as Cultural Performance. Berkeley: University of California Press.

Handelsman, Michael

 2005 Leyendo la globalización desde la mitad del mundo: Identidad y resistancias en el Ecuador. Quito: El Conejo.

Harner, Michael J.

 1961 Jívaro Souls. American Anthropologist 64(2):258–72.

 1968 The Sound of Rushing Water. Natural History (77):28–33, 60–61.

 1972 The Jívaro: People of the Sacred Waterfalls. Garden City: Natural History Press.

Harrison, Regina

 1989 Signs, Songs, and Memory in the Andes: Translating Quechua Language and Culture. Austin: University of Texas Press.

Hill, Jonathan D.

 1988 (editor) Rethinking History and Myth: Indigenous South American Perspectives on the Past. Urbana: University of Illinois Press.

 1992 A Musical Aesthetic of Ritual Curing in the Northwest Amazon. *In* Portals of Power: Shamanism in South America. E. Jean Matteson Langdon and Gerhard Baer, eds. Pp. 175–210. Albuquerque: University of New Mexico Press.

 1996 (editor) History, Power, and Identity: Ethnogenesis in the Americas, 1492–1992. Iowa City: University of Iowa Press.

Hopkins, Dwight N., Lois Ann Lorentzen, Eduardo Mendieta, and David Batstone (editors)

 2001 Religions/Globalizations: Theories and Cases. Durham, N.C.: Duke University Press.

Irvine, Dominique
    1987   Resource Management by the Runa Indians of the Ecuadorian Amazon. Ph.D. dissertation, Department of Anthropology, Stanford University.

Izquierdo Ríos, Guillermo
    1960   El indio de lamas. Tarapoto, Peru: Imprenta La Oriental.

Janzen, Daniel H.
    1986   The Future of Tropical Ecology. Annual Review of Ecological Systematics 17:305–24.

Jijón, Carlos
    2003   El colonel y sus laberintos. Vistazo 813(July):34–36.

Jordon, Carl F.
    1982   Amazon Rain Forest. American Scientist 70(July–August):394–400.

Kane, Joe
    1995   Savages. New York: Alfred A. Knopf.

Karsten, Rafael
    1923   Blood Revenge, War, and Victory Feasts among the Jivaro Indians of Eastern Ecuador. Washington, D.C.: Smithsonian Institution Bureau of American Ethnology Bulletin 79.
    1935   The Head-Hunters of Western Amazonas: The Life and Culture of the Jivaro Indians of Eastern Ecuador and Peru. Helsinki: Societas Scientiarum Fennica, Commentationes Humanarum Litterarum, 2(1).
    1998   [1920–21] Entre los Indios de las Selvas del Ecuador: Tres Años de Viajes e Investigaciones. Lars Eriksson, trans. Quito: Abya-Yala.

Kellogg, Susan
    2005   Weaving the Past: A History of Latin America's Indigenous Women from the Prehispanic Period to the Present. New York: Oxford University Press.

Kelly, Patricia, and Carolyn Orr
    1976   Sarayacu Quichua Pottery. SIL Museum of Anthropology Publication 1. Dallas: Summer Institute of Linguistics.

Kimmerling, Judith
    1991   Amazon Crude. New York: Natural Resources Defense Council.

Kipu
    1992a   El Mundo Indígena en la Prensa Ecuatoriana (January–June), 18. Quito: Abya-Yala.
    1992b   Marcha Indígena de los Pueblos Amazónicos Puyo-Quito. Suplemento Especial (April–May), 18. Quito: Abya-Yala.

Kohn, Eduardo
    2002a   Infidels, Virgins, and the Black-Robed Priest: A Backwoods History of Ecuador's Montaña Region. Ethnohistory 49(3):545–82.

2002b   Natural Engagements and Ecological Aesthetics among the Avila Runa of Amazonian Ecuador. Ph.D. dissertation, Department of Anthropology, University of Wisconsin, Madison.

Kunchicuy, Pascual, and Mariano Tsetsekip

2003   Nambeaway: Música de la tradición shiwiar. Quito: Petroecuador and ONSHIPIAE (Organización de Nacionalidad Shiwiar de Pastaza de la Amazonía Ecuatoriana).

Lambek, Michael (editor)

2002   A Reader in the Anthropology of Religion. Oxford: Blackwell.

Lane, Kris

2002   Quito 1599: City and Colony in Transition. Albuquerque: University of New Mexico Press.

Lathrap, Donald

1970   The Upper Amazon. New York: Praeger.

1973   The Antiquity and Importance of Long Distance Trade Relationships in the Moist Tropics of Pre-Columbian South America. World Archeology 5:170–86.

Lathrop, Kenneth, Christopher Slack, and Robin Draper (editors)

1999   The Villano Project: Preserving the Effort with Words and Pictures. Quito: Atlantic Richfield Company.

Latorre, Octavio

1995   La expedición a la canela y el descubrimiento del amazonas. Quito: Artes Graphics.

Layton, Robert

2000   From Clan Symbol to Ethnic Emblem: Indigenous Creativity in a Connected World. In Indigenous Cultures in an Interconnected World. Claire Smith and Graeme K. Ward, eds. Pp. 49–66. Vancouver: University of British Columbia Press.

Leach, Edmund

1976   Culture and Communication: The Logic by which Symbols Are Connected. New York: Cambridge University Press.

1982   Social Anthropology. New York: Oxford University Press.

Ledesma Zamora, Oscar

[N.d.]a   El pasado en el presente de Puyo (Primera Parte 1930). Riobamba: Editorial Pedagógica "Freire."

[N.d.]b   El pasado en el presente de Puyo (Tomo II 1930–1960). Riobamba: Editorial Pedagógica "Freire."

2005   Lo que todos debemos saber de Puyo. Puyo: Gobierno Municipal de Cantón Pastaza.

Léry, Jean de

1990   [1580] History of a Voyage to the Land of Brazil, Otherwise Called America. Janet Whatley, trans. Berkeley: University of California Press.

Lévi-Strauss, Claude
    1954   Social Structure. *In* Anthropology Today. Alfred L. Kroeber, ed. Pp. 524–53. Chicago: University of Chicago Press.
    1966   The Savage Mind. Chicago: University of Chicago Press.

L'Homme
    1993   La remontée de L'Amazone: Anthropologie et histoire des sociétés amazoniennes. L'Homme: Revue française d'Anthropolgie 22:126–28.

Linke, Lilo
    1960   Ecuador: Country of Contrasts. 3rd edition. New York: Oxford University Press.

Lippi, Ronald D.
    1986   La arqueología de los yumbos: Resultados de prospeciones en el Pichincha Occidental. Miscelánea Antropológica Ecuatoriana 6:189–207.

Luna, Luis Eduardo
    1986   Vegetalismo: Shamanism among the Mestizo Population of the Peruvian Amazon. Acta Universitatis Stockhomienis/Stockholm Studies in Comparative Religion 27. Stockholm: Almqvist and Wiksell International.

Luna, Luis Eduardo, and Pablo Amaringo
    1991   Ayahuasca Visions: The Religious Iconography of a Peruvian Shaman. Berkeley: University of California Press.

Macas, Luis
    1991   El Levantamiento Indígena visto por sus protagonistas. Quito: Instituto Científico de Culturas Indígenas ICCI, Amauta Runacunapac Yachai A.R.Y.

Macas, Luis, Linda Belote, and Jim Belote
    2003   Indigenous Destiny in Indigenous Hands. *In* Millennial Ecuador: Critical Essays on Cultural Transformations and Social Dynamics. Norman E. Whitten Jr., ed. Pp. 216–41. Iowa City: University of Iowa Press.

Macdonald, Theodore
    1979   Processes of Change in Amazonian Ecuador: Quijos Quichua Indians become Cattlemen. Ph.D. dissertation, Department of Anthropology, University of Illinois at Urbana-Champaign.

McKillop, Heather
    2005   Finds in Belize Document Late Classic Maya Salt Making and Canoe Transport. New York: National Academy of Science of the USA, 102(15, Apr. 12):5630–34.

Meisch, Lynn
    1994   [1992] "We will not dance on the tomb of Our Grandparents": "500 Years of Resistance" in Ecuador. Latin American Anthropology Review 4:55–57.

Métraux, Alfred
    1927   Migrations historiques des tupi-guaraní. Journal de la Société des Amércanistes 19:1–45.
    1948   The Tupinambá. *In* Handbook of South American Indians, vol. 3: The Tropical Forest Tribes. Julian H. Steward, ed. Washington, D.C.: Smithsonian Institution, Bureau of American Ethnology, Bulletin 143:95–133.

Miller, Marilyn Grace
    2004   Rise and Fall of the Cosmic Race: The Cult of Mestizaje in Latin America. Austin: University of Texas Press.

Monteros, Raimundo M.
    1937   El Oriente Dominicano. (September–October, 54–55):167–68.

Muratorio, Blanca
    1991   The Life and Times of Grandfather Alonso: Culture and History in the Upper Amazon. New Brunswick: Rutgers University Press.

Naranjo, Marcelo F.
    1977   Zonas de refugio y adaptación étnica en el oriente: Siglos XVI–XVII–XVIII. *In* Temas sobre la continuidad y adaptación cultural ecuatoriana. Marcelo F. Naranjo, José Pereira, and Norman E. Whitten Jr., eds. Pp. 107–67. Quito: Ediciones de la Universidad Católica.

Niles, Blair
    1923   Casual Wanderings in Ecuador. New York: Century.

Nuckolls, Janis B.
    1996   Sounds Like Life: Sound-Symbolic Grammar, Performance, and Cognition in Pastaza Quechua. New York: Oxford University Press.

Oberem, Udo
    1971   Los Quijos: Historia de la transculturación de un grupo indígena en el oriente ecuatoriano (1538–1956). 2 Vols. Madrid: Facultad de Filosofía y Letras de la Universidad de Madrid.
    1974   Trade and Trade Goods in the Ecuadorian Montaña. *In* Native South Americans: Ethnology of the Least Known Continent. Patricia J. Lyon, ed. Pp. 347–57. Boston: Little, Brown.

Orr, Carolyn
    1961   Ecuador Quichua Phonology. *In* Studies in Ecuadorian Indian Languages, I. Benjamin Elson, ed. Pp. 60–77. Summer Institute of Linguistics Publication 7. Mexico City: Summer Institute of Linguistics.

Orr, Carolyn, and Betsy Wrisley
    1965   Vocabulario Quichua del Oriente. Série de Vocabularios Indígenas 11. Quito: Instituto Lingüístico de Verano.

Ortiz, Sergio Elías
    1940   Lingüística colombiana. Familia Zaparo o Gae. Revista de la Universidad Católica Bolivariana (8):379–408.

Ortner, Sherry B. (editor)

1999   The Fate of "Culture": Geertz and Beyond. Berkeley: University of California Press.

Osculati, Gaetano

2000   [1854] Exploraciones de las regiones ecuatoriales a través del Napo y de los ríos de las amazonas: Fragmento de un viaje por las dos américas en los años 1846–1848. Quito: Abya-Yala.

Palacio Asensio, José Luis

1989   Los omaguas en el río Napo ecuatoriano. Quito: CICAME (Centro de Investigaciones Culturales de la Amazonía Ecuatoriana, Pompeya Río Napo).

Pallares, Amalia

2002   From Peasant Struggles to Indian Resistance: The Ecuadorian Andes in the Late Twentieth Century. Norman: University of Oklahoma Press.

Palmié, Stephan

2002   Wizards and Scientists: Explorations in Afro-Cuban Modernity and Tradition. Durham, N.C.: Duke University Press.

Parameshwar Gaonkar, Dipip (editor)

2001   Alternative Modernities. Durham, N.C.: Duke University Press.

Paymal, Noemi, and Catalina Sosa (editors)

1993   Amazon Worlds: Peoples and Cultures of Ecuador's Amazon Region. Quito: Sinchi Sacha Foundation.

Peeke, Catherine

1954   Shimigae, Idioma que se Extingüe. Peru Indígena 5(13):171–78.

Phelan, John Leddy

1967   The Kingdom of Quito in the Seventeenth Century: Bureaucratic Politics in the Spanish Empire. Madison: University of Wisconsin Press.

1970   The Millennial Kingdom of the Franciscans in the New World. 2nd revised edition. Berkeley: University of California Press.

Pierre, François

1983   [1889] Viaje de exploración al oriente ecuatoriano 1887–1888. Quito: Abya-Yala.

Porras Garcés, Pedro

1979   The Discovery in Rome of an Anonymous Document on the Quijo Indians of the Upper Napo, Eastern Ecuador. In Peasants, Primitives and Proletariats: The Struggle for Identity in South America. David L. Browman and R. A. Schwartz, eds. Pp. 13–47. New York: The Hague, Mouton.

Postero, Nancy Grey, and Leon Zamosc

2004   The Struggle for Indigenous Rights in Latin America. Brighton: Sussex Academic Press.

Pratt, Mary Louise
  1992   Imperial Eyes: Travel Writing and Transculturation. New York: Rout-
          ledge.
Price, Richard
  1983   First-Time: The Historical Vision of an Afro-American People. Balti-
          more: The Johns Hopkins University Press.
Price, Sally, and Richard Price
  1999   Maroon Arts: Cultural Vitality in the African Diaspora. Boston: Beacon
          Press.
Quiroga, Diego
  2003   The Devil and Development in Esmeraldas: Cosmology as a System of
          Critical Thought. In Millennial Ecuador: Critical Essays on Cultural
          Transformations and Social Dynamics. Norman E. Whitten Jr., ed. Pp.
          154–83. Iowa City: University of Iowa Press.
Quishpe, Salvador
  2000   El Comercio (Quito), February 20.
Radcliffe, Sarah A., and Sallie Westwood
  1996   Re-Making the Nation: Place, Politics, and Identity in Latin America.
          London: Routledge.
Rahimi, Shadi
  2005   Including Indians in Colonial History. New York Times, September 25:
          B15.
Ramón Valarezo, Galo
  1992   Los selváticos nos interpelan. Marcha Indígena de los pueblos
          amazónicos Puyo-Quito: Abya-Yala, Suplemento Especial Kipu 18:118–
          19.
Rangles Lara, Rodrigo
  1995   Venturas y desventuras del poder. Quito: Carvajal, S.A.
Redfield, Robert, Ralph Linton, and Melville J. Herskovits
  1936   Memorandum for the Study of Acculturation. American Anthropolo-
          gist 38(1):149–52.
Reeve, Mary-Elizabeth
  1985   Identity as Process: The Meaning of "Runapura" for Quichua Speakers
          of the Curaray River, Eastern Ecuador. Ph.D. dissertation, Department
          of Anthropology, University of Illinois at Urbana-Champaign. Ann
          Arbor: University Microfilms.
  1988a   Los quichuas del Curaray: El proceso de formación de la identidad.
          Quito: Abya-Yala.
  1988b   Cauchu Uras: Lowland Quichua Histories of the Amazon Rubber
          Boom. In Rethinking History and Myth: Indigenous South Ameri-
          can Perspectives on the Past. Jonathan D. Hill, ed. Pp. 19–34. Urbana:
          University of Illinois Press.

1993–94   Narratives of Catastrophe: The Zaparoan Experience in Amazonian Ecuador. Société Société des américanistes. Bulletin 57–58:17–24.

1994   Regional Interaction in the Western Amazon: The Early Colonial Encounter and the Jesuit Years: 1538–1767. Ethnohistory 41(1):106–38.

Reichel-Dolmatoff, Gerardo

1971   Amazonian Cosmos: The Sexual and Religious Symbolism of the Tukano Indians. Chicago: University of Chicago Press.

1975   The Shaman and the Jaguar: A Study of Narcotic Drugs among the Indians of Colombia. Philadelphia: Temple University Press.

1976   Cosmology as Ecological Analysis: The View from the Rain Forest. Man (Journal of the Royal Anthropological Institute) 11(3):307–18.

1996   The Forest Within: The World-View of the Tukano Amazonian Indians. Tulsa: Themis Books (distributed by Council Oak Books).

Requena y Herrera, Francisco

1991   [1784] Descripción del gobierno de Maynas. In Historia de Maynas: Un paraiso perdido en el Amazonas. María del Carmen Martín Rubio, comp. Madrid: Ediciones Atlas.

Richardson, James B., III

1994   People of the Andes. Montreal: St. Remy Press, and Washington, D.C.: Smithsonian Books.

Rival, Laura

2002   Trekking through History: The Huaorani of Amazonia. New York: Columbia University Press.

Roggiero, Roberto

1991   Una "yumbada" en la Magdalena. Hoy (Quito), May 5:3C.

Roosevelt, Anna C.

1995   Early Pottery in the Amazon: Twenty Years of Scholarly Obscurity. In The Emergence of Pottery: Technology and Innovation in Ancient Societies. William K. Barnett and John W. Mocpa, eds. Pp. 115–32. Washington, D.C.: Smithsonian Institution Press.

Roosevelt, Anna C., et al.

1996   Paleoindian Cave Dwellers in the Amazon: The Peopling of the Americas. Science 272(19 April):373–84.

Rospide, Ricardo Beltrán

1911   Las misiones de maynas. Boletín de la Real Academia de la Historia (Madrid) 59:262–18.

Rowe, John Howeland

1946   Inca Culture at the Time of the Spanish Conquest. In Handbook of South American Indians, vol. 2: The Andean Civilizations. Julian H. Steward, ed. Pp. 183–330. Smithsonian Institution, Bureau of American Ethnology, Bulletin 143. Washington, D.C.: Smithsonian Institution, Bureau of American Ethnology.

Ruiz, Silvana et al.

    N.d.   Pastaza: manifestaciones culturales en la región de el Puyo. Pastaza: Consejo Provincial, 1984–1988.

Sahlins, Marshall

    1976   Culture and Practical Reason. Chicago: University of Chicago Press.

    1981   Historical Metaphors and Mythical Realities. Ann Arbor: University of Michigan Press.

    1994   Goodbye to Tristes Tropes: Ethnography in the Context of the Modern World. *In* Assessing Cultural Anthropology. Robert Borofsky, ed. Pp. 377–95. New York: McGraw-Hill.

    1999   Two or Three Things I Know about Culture. Journal of the Royal Anthropological Institute 5(3):399–421.

    2004   Apologies to Thucydides: Understanding History as Culture and Vice Versa. Chicago: University of Chicago Press.

    2005   Preface. Outside Gods: History in the Pacific. Ethnohistory 52(1):3–6.

Salomon, Frank

    1981   Killing the Yumbo: A Ritual Drama from North Quito. *In* Cultural Transformations and Ethnicity in Modern Ecuador. Norman E. Whitten Jr., ed. Pp. 162–208. Urbana: University of Illinois Press.

    1986   Native Lords of Quito in the Age of the Incas: The Political Economy of North Andean Chiefdoms. New York: Cambridge University Press.

Salomon, Frank, and Stuart B. Schwartz (editors)

    1999a   The Cambridge History of the Native People of the Americas, vol. 3: South America, Part 1. Cambridge: Cambridge University Press.

    1999b   The Cambridge History of the Native People of the Americas, vol. 3: South America, Part 2. Cambridge: Cambridge University Press.

Santos-Granero, Fernando

    1993   Etnohistoria de la alta amazonía: Siglo XV–XVIII. Quito: Abya-Yala.

    1996   Globalización y cambio en la amazonía indígena, vol 1. Quito: FLASCO and Abya-Yala.

Sapir, J. David, and J. Christopher Crocker (editors)

    1977   The Social Use of Metaphor: Essays on the Anthropology of Rhetoric. Philadelphia: University of Pennsylvania Press.

Sawyer, Suzana

    2004   Crude Chronicles: Indigenous Politics, Multinational Oil, and Neoliberalism in Ecuador. Durham, NC: Duke University Press.

Schultes, Richard E.

    1972   An Overview of Hallucinogens in the Western Hemisphere. *In* Flesh of the Gods: The Ritual Use of Hallucinogens. Peter T. Furst, ed. Pp. 3–54. New York: Praeger.

    1978   Richard Spruce and the Potential for European Settlement of the Amazon: An Unpublished Letter. Botanical Journal of the Linnean Society 77:131–39.

Schultes, Richard Evans, and Albert Hofmann

1979   Plants of the Gods: Origins of Hallucinogenic Use. New York: Mc-Graw-Hill.

Schwartz, Stuart B., and Frank Salomon

1999   New Peoples and New Kinds of Adaptation, Readjustment, and Ethnogenesis in South American Indigenous Societies (Colonial Era). *In* The Cambridge History of the Native People of the Americas. Frank Salomon and Stuart B. Schwartz, eds. Vol. 3: South America, Part 2. Pp. 443–502. Cambridge: Cambridge University Press.

Scott, James C.

1985   Weapons of the Weak: Everyday Forms of Peasant Resistance. New Haven, Conn.: Yale University Press.

2005   Afterword to "Moral Economies, State Spaces, and Categorical Violence." American Anthropologist 107(3):395–402.

Scutch, Alexander F.

1970   Life History of the Common Potoo. The Living Bird 9:265–80.

Seymour-Smith, Charlotte

1988   Shiwiar: Identidad étnica y cambio en el Río Corrientes. Quito: Abya-Yala.

Shapiro, Judith

1987   From Tupã to the Land without Evil: Christianization of the Tupi-Guaraní Cosmology. American Ethnologist 14(1):126–39.

Silverblatt, Irene

2004   Modern Inquisitions: Peru and the Colonial Origins of the Civilized World. Durham, N.C.: Duke University Press.

Silverstein, Michael

2005   Languages/Cultures Are Dead! Long Live the Linguistic-Cultural! *In* Unwrapping the Sacred Bundle: Reflections on the Disciplining of Anthropology. Daniel A. Segal and Sylvia J. Yanagisako, eds. Pp. 99–125. Durham, N.C.: Duke University Press.

Simson, Alfred

1886   Travels in the Wilds of Ecuador and the Exploration of the Putumayo River. London: Sampson Low, Marston, Searle, and Rivington.

Smith, Claire, and Graeme K. Ward (editors)

2000   Indigenous Cultures in an Interconnected World. Vancouver: University of British Columbia Press.

Sorenson, Arthur P., Jr.

1967   Multilingualism in the Northwest Amazon. American Anthropologist 69(6):670–84.

Spruce, Richard
 1908 Notes of a Botanist on the Amazon and Andes. Alfred Russell Wallace, ed. London: Macmillan.

Staden, Juan [Hans]
 1944 [1557] Vera historia y descripción de un pais de las salvages desnudas feroces gentes devoradoras de hombre situado en el Nuevo Mundo América. Edmundo Wernicke, ed. and trans. Biblioteca de Fuentes, vol. 1. Buenos Aires: Universidad de Buenos Aires, Museo Etnográfico.

Stanfield, Michael Edward
 1998 Red Rubber Bleeding: Violence, Slavery, and Empire in Northwest Amazonia, 1850–1933. Albuquerque: University of New Mexico Press.

Stern, Steve J.
 1987 Resistance, Rebellion, and Consciousness in the Andean Peasant World: 18th to 20th Centuries. Madison: University of Wisconsin Press.
 1993 [1982] Peru's Indian Peoples and the Challenge of Spanish Conquest: Huamanga to 1640. 2nd edition. Madison: University of Wisconsin Press.

Steward, Julian H., and Alfred Métraux
 1948 Tribes of the Ecuadorian and Peruvian Montaña. In Handbook of South American Indians, vol. 3: The Tropical Forest Tribes. Julian H. Steward, ed. Pp. 535–656. Smithsonian Institution, Bureau of American Ethnology, Bulletin 143. Washington, D.C.: Smithsonian Institution, Bureau of American Ethnology.

Sturtevant, William
 1971 Creek into Seminole: North American Indians. In Historical Perspective. Eleanor Leacock and Nancie Lurie, eds. Pp. 92–128. New York: Random House.

Sullivan, Lawrence
 1988 Icanchu's Drum: An Orientation to Meaning in South American Religions. New York: Macmillan.

Sweet, David Graham
 1969 The Population of the Upper Amazon Valley, 17th and 18th Centuries. M.A. thesis, Department of History, University of Wisconsin, Madison.
 1975 A Rich Realm of Nature Destroyed: The Middle Amazon Valley, 1640–1750. Ph.D. dissertation, Department of History, University of Wisconsin, Madison.

Taussig, Michael
 1987 Shamanism, Colonialism, and the Wild Man: A Study in Terror and Healing. Chicago: University of Chicago Press.
 1997 The Magic of the State. New York: Routledge.

2003 Law in a Lawless Land: Diary of a *Limpieza* in Colombia. New York: The New Press.

2004 My Cocaine Museum. Chicago: University of Chicago Press.

Taylor, Anne Christine

1981 God-Wealth: The Achuar and the Missions. *In* Cultural Transformations and Ethnicity in Modern Ecuador. Norman E. Whitten Jr., ed. Pp. 647–76. Urbana: University of Illinois Press.

1999 The Western Margins of Amazonia from the Early Sixteenth to the Early Nineteenth Century. *In* The Cambridge History of the Native People of the Americas. Frank Salomon and Stuart B. Schwartz, eds. Vol. 3: South America, Part 2. Pp. 188–356. Cambridge: Cambridge University Press.

Trouillot, Michel-Rolph

1991 Anthropology and the Savage Slot: The Poetics and Politics of Otherness. *In* Recapturing Anthropology: Working in the Present. Richard G. Fox, ed. Pp. 17–44. Santa Fe: School of American Research Press.

1995 Silencing the Past: Power and the Production of History. Boston: Beacon Press.

2003 Global Transformations: Anthropology and the Modern World. New York: Palgrave Macmillan.

Trujillo, Jorge Nelson

2001 Memorias del Curaray. Quito: IMPREFEPP.

Tschopp, H. T.

1953 Oil Explorations in the Oriente of Ecuador 1938–1950. Bulletin of the American Association of Petroleum Geologists 37(10):2303–47.

Turner, Victor

1973 Symbols in African Ritual. Science 179(16 March):1100–1105.

1974 Dramas, Fields, and Metaphors: Symbolic Action in Human Societies. Ithaca: Cornell University Press.

1982 (edited) Celebration: Studies in Festivity and Ritual. Washington, D.C.: Smithsonian Institution Press.

1985 On the Edge of the Bush: Anthropology as Experience. Edith L. B. Turner, ed. Tucson: University of Arizona Press.

Uzendoski, Michael A.

1999 Twins Becoming Jaguars: Verse Analysis of a Napo Quichua Myth Narrative. Anthropological Linguistics 41(4):431–61.

2004a Manioc Beer and Meat: Value, Reproduction, and Cosmic Substance among the Napo Runa of The Ecuadorian Amazon. Journal of the Royal Anthropological Institute 10(4):883–902.

2004b The Horizontal Archipelago: The Quijos Upper Napo Regional System. Ethnohistory 51(2):318–57.

2005a   Making Amazonia: Shape-shifters, Giants, and Alternative Moderni-
         ties. Latin American Research Review 40(1):223–36.

2005b   The Napo Runa of Amazonian Ecuador. Urbana: University of Illinois
         Press.

2005c   Writing, Politics, and Culture among Amazonian Quichua Speakers
         of Ecuador. Paper presented at the American Anthropological Asso-
         ciation Meetings, Washington, D.C.

Uzendoski, Michael A., Mark Hertica, and Edith Calapucha

2005   The Phenomenology of Perspectivism: Aesthetics, Sound, and Power
         in Napo Runa Women's Songs of Upper Amazonia. Current Anthro-
         pology 46(4):656–62.

Valladares, Álvaro

1912   Cartas sobre las Misiones Dominicanas del Oriente del Ecuador. Se-
         gunda serie—carta primera. Quito: Imprenta de Santo Domingo.

Vallejo, Raúl

1996a   Seis años después: Pachakutik. El Comercio (Quito), June 4:A5.

1996b   Crónica mestiza del nuevo pachakutik. College Park, Md.: Latin Ameri-
         can Studies Center of the University of Maryland.

VanCott, Donna Lee

1995   Indigenous Peoples and Democracy in Latin America. New York: St.,
         Martin's Press in Association with the Inter-American Dialogue.

Vargas Guatatuca, Carlos Antonio

2000   Nos faltó estrategia. In La cuatra vía al poder: El 21 de enero desde
         una perspectiva latinoamericana. Heinz Dieterich, comp. Pp. 42–48.
         Quito: Abya-Yala.

Viteri, Carlos

1993   Mythical Worlds: Runa. In Amazon Worlds: Peoples and Cultures of
         Ecuador's Amazon Region. Noemi Paymal and Catalina Sosa, eds. Pp.
         148–57. Quito: Oxfam International and Sinchi Sacha Foundation.

Viveiros de Castro, Eduardo

1998   Cosmological Deixis and Amerindian Perspectivism. Journal of the
         Royal Anthropological Institute 4(3):469–88.

2005   Perspectival Anthropology and the Method of Controlled Equivoca-
         tion. Tipití 2(1):3–22.

Warren, Kay, and Jean Jackson (editors)

2002   Indigenous Movements, Self-Representation, and the State in Latin
         America. Austin: University of Texas Press.

Weismantel, Mary

1988   Food, Gender, and Poverty in the Ecuadorian Andes. Philadelphia:
         University of Pennsylvania Press.

2001   Cholas and Pishtacos: Stories of Race and Sex in the Andes. Chicago:
         University of Chicago Press.

Whitehead, Neil L.

2002 Dark Shamans: Kainamà and the Poetics of Violent Death. Durham, N.C.: Duke University Press.

2003 Introduction. *In* Histories and Historicities in Amazonia. Neil L. Whitehead, ed. Pp. vii–xx. Lincoln: University of Nebraska Press.

Whitten, Dorothea S.

1981 Ancient Tradition in a Contemporary Context: Canelos Quichua Ceramics and Symbolism. *In* Cultural Transformations and Ethnicity in Modern Ecuador. Norman E. Whitten Jr., ed. Pp. 749–75. Urbana: University of Illinois Press.

1996 License to Practice? A View from the Rain Forest. Anthropological Quarterly 69(3):115–19.

2003 Actors and Artists from Amazonia and the Andes. *In* Millennial Ecuador: Essays on Cultural Transformations and Social Dynamics. Norman E. Whitten Jr., ed. Pp. 242–74. Iowa City: University of Iowa Press.

Whitten, Dorothea S., and Norman E. Whitten Jr.

1978 Ceramics of the Canelos Quichua. Natural History 87(8):91–99.

1985 Art, Knowledge, and Health. Cambridge: Cultural Survival and Urbana: Sacha Runa Research Foundation.

1988 From Myth to Creation: Art from Amazonian Ecuador. Urbana: University of Illinois Press.

1989 Potters of the Upper Amazon. Ceramics Monthly 37(10), December: 53–56.

1993a (editors) Imagery and Creativity: Ethnoaesthetics and Art Worlds in the Americas. Tucson: University of Arizona Press.

1993b Introduction. *In* Imagery and Creativity: Ethnoaesthetics and Art Worlds in the Americas. Dorothea S. Whitten and Norman E. Whitten Jr., eds. Pp. 3–44. Tucson: University of Arizona Press.

1993c Creativity and Continuity, Communications and Clay. *In* Imagery and Creativity: Ethnoaesthetics and Art Worlds in the Americas. Dorothea S. Whitten and Norman E. Whitten Jr., eds. Pp. 309–56. Tucson: University of Arizona Press.

Whitten, Norman E., Jr.

1976a (with the assistance of Marcelo Naranjo, Marcelo Santi Simbaña, and Dorothea S. Whitten). Sacha Runa: Ethnicity and Adaptation of Ecuadorian Jungle Quichua. Urbana: University of Illinois Press.

1976b Ecuadorian Ethnocide and Indigenous Ethnogenesis: Amazonian Resurgence amidst Andean Colonization. Copenhagen: IWGIA Document No. 23.

1978a Amazonian Ecuador: An Ethnic Interface in Ecological, Social, and Ideological Perspectives. Copenhagen: IWGIA Document No. 34.

1978b   Ecological Imagery and Cultural Adaptability: The Canelos Quichua of Eastern Ecuador. American Anthropologist 80(4):836–59.

1981   (editor) Cultural Transformations and Ethnicity in Modern Ecuador. Urbana: University of Illinois Press.

1985   Sicuanga Runa: The Other Side of Development in Amazonian Ecuador. Urbana: University of Illinois Press.

1988   Historical and Mythic Evocations of Chthonic Power in South America. *In* Rethinking History and Myth: Indigenous South American Perspectives on the Past. Jonathan D. Hill, ed. Pp. 282–306. Urbana: University of Illinois Press.

1996   The Ecuadorian Levantamiento Indígena of 1990 and the Epitomizing Symbol 1992: Reflections on Nationalism, Ethnic-Bloc Formation and Racialist Ideologies. *In* History, Power, and Identity: Ethnogenesis in the Americas, 1492–1992. Jonathan D. Hill, ed. Pp. 193–217. Iowa City: University of Iowa Press.

2001   South America: Sociocultural Aspects. International Encyclopedia of the Social and Behavioral Sciences. Neil J. Smelser and Paul B. Baltes, eds.-in-chief. Ulf Hannerz, vol. ed., Anthropology. Pp. 14607–12. Oxford: Elsevier Science, Pergamon.

2002   *Review of* Trekking Through History: The Huaorani of Amazonia. Tipití 1(2):223–27.

2003a   Symbolic Inversion, the Topology of "El mestizaje" and the Spaces of "Las razas" in Ecuador. Journal of Latin American Anthropology 8(1):14–47.

2003b   (editors) Millennial Ecuador: Critical Essays on Cultural Transformations and Social Dynamics. Iowa City: University of Iowa Press.

2004   Ecuador in the New Millennium: 25 Years of Democracy. Journal of Latin American Anthropology 9(2):439–60.

2005   Indigenous Perspectives on Religion: South America. New Dictionary of the History of Ideas. New York: Charles Scribners Sons (The Gale Group).

Whitten, Norman E., Jr., and Arlene Torres (editors)

1998   Blackness in Latin America and the Caribbean, vols. 1 and 2. Bloomington: Indiana University Press.

Whitten, Norman E., Jr., and Dorothea Scott Whitten

1984   The Structure of Kinship and Marriage among the Canelos Quichua of East-Central Ecuador. *In* Marriage Practices in Lowland South America. Kenneth Kennsinger, ed. Pp. 194–220. Urbana: University of Illinois Press.

1987   Una presencia dinámica indígena en la vida moderna de Puyo, Provincia de Pastaza. *In* Pastaza: Un Municipio al Servicio del Pueblo. Pp. 22–25. Puyo: Revista Municipal.

Whitten, Norman E. Jr., Dorothea Scott Whitten, and Alfonso Chango
  1997   Return of the Yumbo: The Indigenous Caminata from Amazonia to Andean Quito. American Ethnologist 24(2):355–91.
Wibbelsman, Michelle
  2004   Rimarishpa Kaunsanchik: Dialogical Encounters, Festive Ritual Practice, and the Making of the Otavalan Moral and Mythic Community. Ph.D. dissertation, Department of Anthropology, University of Illinois at Urbana-Champaign.
  2005   Otavaleños at the Crossroads: Physical and Metaphysical Coordinates of an Indigenous World. Journal of Latin American Anthropology 10(1):151–85.
  2006   *Encuentros:* Dances of the Inti Rymi in Cotacachi, Ecuador. Latin American Music Review 26(2):195–226.
Williams, Jerry M., and Robert E. Lewis (editors)
  1993   Early Images of the Americas: Transfer and Invention. Tucson: University of Arizona Press.
Williams, Raymond
  1977   Marxism and Literature. New York: Oxford University Press.
Wise, Mary Ruth, and Olive A. Shell
  1971   Grupos idiomáticos del Peru. 2nd edition. Lima: Instituto Lingüístico de Verano y Universidad Nacional Mayor de San Marcos.
Wolf, Eric R.
  1999   Envisioning Power: Ideologies of Dominance and Crisis. Berkeley: University of California Press.
Worsley, Peter
  1957   The Trumpet Shall Sound: A Study of "Cargo" Cults in Melanesia. London: Macgibbon and Kee.
Yepez, Jacinto M.
  1927   Puyo y sus costumbres. El Oriente Dominicano 1(1):6–7.
Zikmund, Miroslav, and Jirí Hanzelka
  1963   Amazon Headhunters. Olga Kuthanová, trans. Prague: Artia.

Index

Abád, César, 181, 184, 185, 186

Acanga (mythic hawk character), 43, 44, 190

Acculturation, 251–55; of Canelos Quichua, 252–53; defined, 251

Achuar people, 2, 10, 11, 14, 19, 54, 185, 186, 240; and Canelos, 10, 17; cultural resurgence, 234; Descola's views on, 251, 252, 254; and March for Land and Life, 206, 207, 218; and Puyo Runa, 11; relation to Canelos Quichua, 252–54; in Sarayacu, 20

Acuerdo de Sarayacu (Sarayacu Agreement), 202, 233

African people, 158

Afro-Ecuadorians, 125; and March for Land and Life, 217, 219, 226; and protest movements, 203

Airplanes: seen in *ayahuasca* trip, 77

Alfaro, Eloy, 32, 33, 158

Alli Runa, 53

Amadora, 186

Amarun, 51. *See also* Big Black Amarun

Amasanga (forest spirit), 45–46, 144, 211; appearing/healing during *wanduj* trip, 46, 72; in ceramic art, 46, 100, 108, 133, 184, 196; and communication with spirit world, 8; essence of in stones, 38; feminine manifestation as lightning, 45; and fog or rain, 56; as a Jurijuri *supai,* 156; and origin myth, 5; as overseer of *sacha,* 45; represented in drumming beat, 121; symbolized in tortoise *bancu,* 35; transformations of, 147, 194

Amasanga *warmi,* 114, 174; appearing during *ayahuasca* trip, 78; in ceramic art, 46

Amazonia: cultural system of, 245–46; in opposition to Andes, 236; prehistory and early historic, 168; after Spanish conquest, 122; ties to Andes, ix, 23, 203, 213, 218, 222, 231, 232, 233, 234

Amazon Rubber Boom, 19, 32; as a time of destruction, 40

Ambato, 213–14

Anaconda, 45, 141; in *ayahuasca* trips, 70, 86; and benches, 35, 50, 210; corporeal representation of Sungui, 35, 49, 110; head separated from body, 243; imagery of in indigenous protest movements, 233; monkey sounding, 237; motifs on pottery, 104, 105; symbolism of, 51; symbolism of during *dominario,* 153; *yacu mama* as, 12. *See also Amarun*

Andes: in opposition to Amazonia, 236; ties to Amazonia, ix, 23, 203, 213, 218, 222, 231, 232, 233, 234

Andi, Rodrigo, 74; *ayahuasca* trip with Taruga, 75–80

Andoa people, ix, 19, 248, 249, 250

Anthropology: failure to understand Amazonian culture system, 253, 254, 255; view of the savage, 252, 254, 257

Arajuno River, 17

Aranda Canelos, Amadora, 181

Arco (petroleum company), 239, 240

Ardilla, 43

Argentine Compañía General de Combustibles, 242, 243, 244
Armstrong, Robert Plant, 198
Asdúbal, 244
Asháninka people, 203
Asua: ceramics for, 99, 100, 112; described, 35, 99; method of drinking/serving during *ayllu jista*, 143–48; preparation of *allu asua*, 129, 139; preparation of *ucui yacu*, 81, 130
Asua mamas, 143, 144, 147, 148
Axis mundi, 141, 191, 231; represented in the *wasi*, 50
Ayahuasca (soul vine), 6, 66, 75; ceramics made for, 92; defined, 69; description of trip with, 69–71, 76–80; and "seeing" reality, 12
Ayahuasca Mama, 144
Ayllu, 50–52, 97; anchoring memory, 31; and cultural performance, 125–26; difficulty in merging, 73–74, 81; gendered origins of, 51–52; knowledge passing through, 33; spanning territories, 53
Ayllu jista, 125–26, 140–55, 194; as a diversionary activity, 163, 194; feast (*camari*) of, 149; and presence of Catholic Church, 157–59, 194, 195; and resistance, 157–59, 166, 194

Babcock, Barbara, 58n2
Balsa wood carvings, 92, 96, 177
Bamboo spirit (Wamaj *supai*), 180
Bancu (stool), 35; in form of turtle, 50, 66; Lluwi's, 6; Marcelo's, 36–37; seat of Sungui, 76, 196; shaman as, 8–9, 71, 78, 79; symbolism of, 35, 116; use of during *ayahuasca* trip, 70, 76. See also Turtle
Banisteriopsis caapi. See Ayahuasca
Bark cloth painting, 136
Bat-widow, 43
Beads, 190, 194
Beauty, 198; in Canelos Quichua culture, 116, 210; and knowledge, 169, 223; proof of, 60; provided by pottery, 128; and song, 223
Bees: represented in drumming sound, 38, 100, 121; spirit-bees as shamanic helpers, 154
Beginning times-places, 98, 116, 185; and festivals, 132
Bell: chapel, 152, 153; costume, 164
Biculturalism, 53
Big Black Amarun (anaconda; song of Clara Santi), 110

Bilingualism, 2, 19, 41, 53, 90, 109
Birds: in Puyo Runa origin myth, 3, 210
Black Woman. *See* Widuj Warmi
Bobonaza River, 14, 15, 17, 19, 23, 53
Bolivarianism, 246
Borja Cevallos, Rodrigo, 97, 203, 218, 225, 227
Breath: of fire, 60, 65; magical, 3, 4, 44, 183, 191; and power, 74–75, 77; and proof of strength, 60, 61, 64
Brown, Michael, 203
Bucaram Ortiz, Abdalá, 238–39
Bush, George W., 187, 239

Cabecera de Bobonaza, 17
Cabodevilla, Miguel Angel, 17, 29n3
Cachi amu (overseer of salt), 92, 187, 190
Calderón, Monseñor, 137–38
Calderón Cevallos, Alfonso, 233
Callarirucuguna, 161–62, 172. *See also* Beginning times-places
Caminata de Pastaza a Quito. *See* March for Land and Life
Canelos, Alegría, 106
Canelos, Andrea, 106
Canelos Quichua, ix–x, 23, 27, 240; and concept of beauty, 116, 223; and concept of power, 61, 62; cosmology of, 100, 110, 113–14, 116, 125, 188–91, 224–25; and cultural emergence, 159–61, 172; and cultural resurgence, 234; culture of, 24, 231–32; and culture loss, 251–52, 253; and globalization, 116; internal conflict among, 11, 31; and March for Land and Life, 206, 207, 218; and pottery trade, 175; relation to Achuar, 252–54; self-identification of, 94, 159
Canelos region, 10, 14, 17; biculturalism in, 53; and cinnamon, 17, 248; and the Curaray Runa, 19; and historicity of Puyo Runa founders, 10; history of, 1, 2, 4, 17–18, 32–33; as juncture of Andes and Amazonia, 17, 18; *runa shimi* dialect, 22
Caninche, 10
Capahuari, 11
Capahuari River, 17, 18
Cari jista, 126, 145, 148
Carlos, 75, 77, 80, 81, 133, 134
Caserío (hamlet), 55
Catalina Chango, Juana, 177, 184; ceramics of, 177
Catfish drinking vessel, 155
Catholic Church: administrative division of people, 122–23, 157–58; control of indigenous people, 52, 149–54, 157–58; conver-

sion dependent on indigenous consent, 20; and destructive powers, 53; and power of the indigenous peoples, 124; state dichotomy, 4–5

Causáunchimi! (We Are Living) exhibit, viii–ix, 36, 92, 179, 181, 183, 184, 185

Cenepa River conflict (Ecuador/Peru), 234–35, 241, 244

Central Villano River, 17

Ceramics, 99, 100, 101, 102, 105, 110–11; Christian symbols in, 156, 195; and cultural knowledge, 65–66, 156, 172, 181, 185; and female visionary power, 98, 169–72, 174–75, 207; and knowledge, 98, 100, 171–72; made for *ayllu jista,* 128, 132–35, 137; made for museum display, 177, 179–80, 183, 184, 185; made for sale, 67–68, 100, 105, 113, 135, 139, 176–77, 183; and male knowledge, 92; methods of making, 65–66, 132–35, 137; as proof of potter's power, 60–61; and shaman's sets, 92–93, 105, 187, 196; subjects of, 179–80; symbolism in, 49, 155, 156; for teaching about culture, 177–78; as teaching tools, 92, 93; technology of, 90, 105–6, 115, 180–81; in Western art markets, 175–78. *See also* Master potter; Pottery

Chaca, 191–92, 199n2

Chagra (swidden garden), 7, 41–46, 129; cultural ecology of, 13; origin myth of, 43–44

Chagra-sacha dynamics, 42–43, 48

Challua, 11, 83, 84, 85, 86, 132; as *chayuj,* 127

Chango, Abraham (Paushi), 32, 109, 111, 224; employment in petroleum industry, 172, 173

Chango, Alfonso, 177–78; and interpretation of Canelos Quichua myth, 187–88, 193; and map of early Puyo, 94, 95, 118n5; and March for Land and Life, 207, 208, 209; paintings of, 184; and planning *Causáunchimi!* exhibit, viii; *Yachaj Sami Yachachina,* 93

Charapa Cocha, 14, 185, 186, 196

Charapa Runa, 186

Chayuj (festival host): actions during *ayllu jista,* 126, 143, 147; chosen by Catholic Church, 126, 150–51

Chichicu (marmoset), 43

Chingosimi River, 13

Chirapas, 10, 165

Christianity: and *ayllu jista,* 148, 149, 149–54; Protestant/Catholic schism and Puyo Runa, 233–34

Chucu Purutu (Bean woman), 43, 45

Clay, potter's, 180–81, 186; Nungüi as master spirit of, 100, 194. *See also under* Myth

Colombia, 237–38, 246

Comaroff, Jean and John, 235

Compañía General Geofísica, 242–43

Comuna San Jacinto del Pindo, viii, 11, 12–13, 14, 17, 33; founding of, 9, 56, 96, 114; map of, xvii; and March for Land and Life, 206, 207, 223

CONAIE (Confederación de las Nacionalidades Indígenas del Ecuador), 15, 234

CONFENIAE (Confederation of Indigenous Peoples of Amazonian Ecuador), 27, 98, 205, 234, 245

Control: by Church, 158; expressed during *dominario,* 152; expressed during March for Land and Life, 215–16

Cooley, Charles Horton, 58n2

Copataza River, 9, 17, 18

Cornet, ceramic, 180; at festivals, 100, 147; and March for Land and Life, 208–10

Corpus Christi, 213, 220, 221

Corral, Victor (Monseñor), 206

Correa Delgado, Rafael, 257n1

Cosmology: of Canelos Quichua, 100, 110, 113–14, 116, 125, 188–91, 224–25

Cotts (British tea company), 9

Coup of January 2000, 234–35

Creativity: and *ayllu jista,* 194; and creation of ceramics, 133–34, 174, 195–98; and use of symbols, 119, 120

Cultural capability, 122

Cultural endurance, 98–100, 106

Cultural knowledge, 38, 39, 65–66, 139, 181, 185; transmission of, 65–68, 188

Cultural ontology, 36, 41

Cultural performance, 119, 120, 125–26, 140, 146, 158, 163, 166

Cultural signifiers: and March for Land and Life, 209

Cultural survival, 22

Cultural transmission, 66–67, 68

Culture: loss of, 251, 252, 254

Cunalla (right here–right now), 40

Cunchu festival, 157

Curaga, 106–7, 123; Nayapi as, 4

Curaray, 18–19

Curaray River, 17, 18, 23

Curaray Runa, 18–19; *ayllu jista* of, 158–59

Cushi Tambo, viii, 14, 33

Dagua, Delicia, 247–50; and planning *Causáunchimi!* exhibit, ix, 248, 257

Dagua, Estela, 102–7, 187; ceramics of, 92, 105, 187, 196; ceramics made for *Causáunchimi!* exhibit, 179–80; as *sinchi muscuj warmi*, 105, 180; trip to U.S., 90–93, 115–16

Dagua Tuitui, Tomás Andrés, 248, 249

Dancing: during *ayllu jista*, 144, 146, 154

Darts, magical, 8, 33; collected during *ayahuasca* trip, 79; described, 34; killing, 71; as proof of shaman's power, 60, 62; and scorpion representation in ceramics, 92; sound of, 35; symbolized by porcupine quills, 145

Datura: Amasanga's, 45; vessel used for, 110–11. See also *Wanduj supai*

Dawn: and spirit world, 6, 11, 12

Death, 249

Deer, 43, 75

Descola, Philippe, 27, 251, 252, 254

Development: in Puyo, 96–97, 107–8

Directionality, 189–90; in Canelos Quichua cosmology, 141, 231–32; and festival houses, 127; and potting, 133, 141; in the *wasi*, 50

Dog, bush, 45, 174

Dominario, 152–55, 195, 234, 243; and *lanceros*, 164

Domination: by Church, 122–24, 137–38, 149–52, 154; indigenous resistance against, 154, 166; by nation-state, 128, 202–3

Dominicans, 17, 160; administrative division of people, 254–55; conversion of Canelos people, 17, 19–20; and Nayapi, 4; and Puyo, 1, 94; and *varayuj* system, 123

Dreams, 68, 69

Drum: construction of, 36–38, 120–21; friction, 143, 148; imagery of, 121; ritual upon completing, 38–39

Drumming: during *ayllu jista*, 143–46, 151, 152, 154; representing Amasanga, 100

Duality, 221, 223; of Alli Runa/Sacha Runa, 53; of attitude toward the Church, 4; in *ayllu jista*, 126, 128, 130; of mythic world, 141; of nation-state/hamlet, 41

Duque, Alejando, 21

Durkheim, Émile, 158

Ecotourism, 245

Ecuador, ix, xv, 114; conflict with Peru, 19, 36, 173, 221, 234, 241; and coup of January 2000, 234; cultural performance in, 125–26; ethnicity in, 22; and globalization, 116; indigenous people and politics, 201, 204; and indigenous protest movements, 14, 246; modern development of, 176–77; multiethnicity in, 108; political indirection, 236–37, 239; and social justice, 14

Education: modern vs. traditional, 88–89, 101, 137–38

Ehlers, Freddy, 228

El Comercio, 98, 115

El Ejido park: and March for Land and Life, 203, 218, 223–24, 225

Elena, 73–74, 75–76, 80, 81

Empowerment, 256–57; and the Canelos Quichua, 59–61; and March for Land and Life, 200, 208, 227–28; and stylized activity, 122

Environment: as cultural, 207; ecological damage to, 240, 242, 246

Ermilinda, 138, 139

Espinosa, Simón, 114, 217

Ethnic-art market, 100, 118n6, 132, 177, 180, 196

Ethnicity, 22

Ethnocide, 159

Ethnogenesis, 52, 53; and antiquity, 247–51; and *ayllu jista*, 157–61; and symbolism, 160

Etiquette, 34–35, 50

Falsetto greetings, 34, 35, 141, 142, 155

FARC (Fuerzas Armadas Revolucionarias de Colombia), 246

Febres Cordero, León, 187, 239

FECIP (Federación de Centros Indígenas de Pastaza), 56, 124

FEDECAP (Federación de Desarrollo Campesino de Pastaza), 206, 216–17

Fernandez, James W., 120

Fernández, Michael, 203

Festivals, 10, 100; ceramics for, 66, 99–100; changing social expressions, 126–27, 131–32; imposed by Church, 157; male/female duality of, 126, 128; preparations for, 81, 127–29; and reversal of the everyday, 126, 128–29, 131–32, 141, 142, 186–87; and territories of others, 127–28, 131

"Five Hundred Years of Resistance" protests, 202

Flowers, 38, 148, 149, 150

Flute, 78, 80, 83; at *ayllu jista*, 144, 147; *pijuano*, 145, 147, 151

Frog, 11, 44, 50

Funeral, 174

Fungi: bracket, 92, 162, 180; and myths of regeneration, 52

Future (*caya*), 98, 208; accessible to the powerful, 40

Galarza, Jaime, 173
García, Alejo, 169
Gardening: and spirit world, 6
Gaye, 19
Geertz, Clifford, 39, 58n2, 125, 158
Gender: role reversals during *ayllu jista*, 128–29, 144; shifting, among mythical figures, 45, 49, 190
Globalization, 116, 118n13, 256; modern beginnings of, 241–42, 247
Grefa, Samuel, 31
Grefa, Valerio, 228, 234; and March for Land and Life, 206, 218, 227
Gualinga, Rebeca, 104, 118n9, 181–83, 185, 186, 193, 242; ceramics of, 46, 114; effigy of Manga Allpa Mama, 182; and resistance to petroleum industry, 243
Gualinga, Santa, 181, 183
Gualinga, Sergio, 90
Guatatuca, Pastora, 102–4, 183
Gutiérrez, Lucio, 104
Gutiérrez Borbúa, Lucio: and coup of January 2000, 234, 236; presidency of, 236, 239, 242

Harvard Boys, 235
Hawk. *See* Acanga
Headdress, 210; of *lanceros*, 164; and March for Land and Life, 206, 208; toucan, 135, 142
Head-hunting, 81, 254
Healing, 71, 80, 87. *See also under* Shaman
Hegemony, 122–24, 201, 202, 208
Herskovits, Melville, 251
Hill, Jonathan D., 160
Historicity, indigenous, 4, 159–61
Horse, 74–75, 80
Houses, festival, 127
Huayusa tree, 43, 162
Hum, shamanic, 78, 121
Human being: being fully human, 16, 18, 27; and power of stones, 38
Hummingbird, 56, 141. *See also* Quindi
Hunting: and *ayllu jista*, 128, 130–32, 141–42; stylized activity associated with, 121–22
Hydrosphere: mythic representatives of, 92, 194

Identity: denied, 22, 27; of indigenous people, 15, 21–22, 27; of people in Runa territories, 19, 160–61; shifting, 20, 30–31
IERAC (Instituto Ecuatoriano de Reforma Agraria y Colonización), 73, 205, 226, 227, 233

Ila tree, 24, 147; assistance with *wanduj* trip, 72, 84; transformation of Amasanga, 47, 147
Illanes Vargas, Eustanquillo, 32–33. *See also* Palati
Imagery: and art worlds, 175–78; in ceramics, 179–84; and creation of ceramics, 133–34; and creativity, 119; during *dominario*, 153; indigenous, 229, 257; during March for Land and Life, 207, 229; private made public, 88–89
Inca Atahualpa, 207
Inca Empire, ix, 16, 231–32
INCRAE (National Institute for the Colonization of the Ecuadorian Amazonian Region), 73
Indi (the sun), 45, 189–90, 213; in ceramic art, 183; and rainbow symbol of anaconda, 56
Indigenous culture: and development in Puyo area, 96–97; silencing of, 1–2
Indigenous people, x, 243; conflict among, 14, 25–26, 40, 104, 245; in Ecuadorian politics, 201, 204; and national politics, 228, 235–36, 237, 239; "outsiders'" view of, 21–22, 27, 223–24; perception of, 115, 223–24; resistance to Church, 152–53, 154; resistance to European dominance, 162; resistance to petroleum industry, 243–44; self-identification of, 23, 159–60, 228; shifting identity of, 15; unifying factors, 25–27, 216, 217, 218
Indigenous protest movements, 201–3, 228, 233, 236; against petroleum industry, 246; feminine presence in, 117, 118n11; journeys to Quito, 114–15, 224; resulting from March for Land and Life, 226–27; and symbolism of the year 1992, 202. *See also* Levantamiento Indígena of 1990. *See also* March for Land and Life
Indillama, 17, 25
Insects, 108, 179
Interamerican Foundation, 22
Interculturality, 235, 238–41, 256, 257; defined, 238; of Puyo Runa, 251
International Monetary Fund, 235, 236, 239
Irvine, Dominique, 28n2
Ishpingu River, 248, 250

Jaguar: appearing during *ayahuasca* trip, 70, 71, 86; breath of, 75; in ceramic art, 114, 184; corporeal representation of Amasanga, 45, 113, 153, 166; mascot of Sungui, 114, 166; shaman as, 9, 166; symbolism of during *dominario,* 153. *See also* Puma

Jaguar woman: women painted as, 108, 111, 113

Jaime. *See* Shiny Shoes

Japa (Deer). *See* Vargas, Venancio

Jatun Machinmi (big monkey person; song of Clara Santi), 111, 175

Jatun Molino, 245

Jayambi (iguanid), 184

Jilucu, 188–91, 193, 194

Jilucu *chaca,* 191–92

Jilucu Jista (Potoo bird festival). See *Cari jista*

Jista mama, 127, 128

Jívaro: defined, 10; as savages, 21, 160

Jivaroan people, x, 18, 19, 206, 253, 254

Juanjiri, 19

Junculu, 43–44; in the form of a frog, 44

Junta of National Salvation, 235

Jurijuri, 48, 71, 77, 211; in ceramic art, 47, 133, 156, 175, 184; guardian of monkeys, 132; and Nayapi myth, 5; origin of, 46; and Puyo Runa origin myth, 5; and shaman's killing power, 76, 77; teeth in a mouth on the back of his head, 46, 156, 184

Kapok tree (Uchuputu), 47, 147

Karsten, Rafael, 33, 102, 107, 169, 251

Kelly, Patricia, 100

Killing debts, 10

Kinship, 9, 11, 31; association with indigenous "places," 18; between groups, 249–50; and identity-placement, 24; and land rights, 172; mythical origin of 50–51. See also *Ayllu*

Kipu, 98

Kite, swallow-tailed, 2, 5

Knowledge, 57, 61–65, 223; and link to environment and cosmos, 98; of "others," 171, 172; and pottery making, 128, 134, 174; relation between ours/others/theirs, 63, 64, 88, 238; of skilled potters, 101, 107, 108, 109, 117, 171–72. *See also* Cultural knowledge

Kohn, Eduardo, 28n2

Kovatch, Ron, 115

Ladder, 191, 192. See also *Chaca*

Lanceros, 10, 234; festival, 163–66; and yumbada, 222

Latacunga, 215–16

Layton, Robert, 116

Leach, Edmund, 160

Leaf bundle, 70, 71

Levantamiento Indígena of 1990, 14, 203, 213, 228, 234; and symbolism of the year 1992, 202

Lévi-Strauss, Claude, 42, 232, 253

Linton, Ralph, 251

Llacta, 23, 49, 97; anchoring memory, 31; defined, 5, 54

Llushín River, 2

Lluwi, 5, 6–8, 9, 11, 12, 13; social and cosmic effects after his death, 59; sons and daughters of, 64–65; teaching Sicuanga, 82

Lucho. *See* Vargas Canelos, Luis

Lula da Silva, Luis Inácio, 246

Lurira (power shield), 66, 67, 76, 121, 122

Macana (club), 164, 166

Macas, Luis, 228, 233, 234, 236; and March for Land and Life, 206, 218

Macdonald, Theodore, 28n2

Machachi, 216

Machin (Capuchin monkey), 43. *See also* Monkey

Machin Runa: effigy abused during *ayllu jista,* 142; as an outsider, 4, 5, 194; priests as, 151; in Puyo Runa origin myth, 3–4, 175

Machoa, Gloria, 106

Mahuad Witt, Jamil, 15, 235, 239

Maize, 45

Male predation, 42, 46, 128

Mamach, 5–6, 9

Manduru (*Bixa orellana*), 6, 43

Manduru Warmi (Red Woman), 188, 190, 210; in Puyo Runa origin myth, 2–4, 135

Manga Allpa Mama (spirit of pottery clay), 105, 178, 181, 182, 183, 184, 191

Manglla, Erlinda, 193

Manioc, 43; and *asua,* 99; and development of pottery, 168; mythical taming of, 5–6; painted red, 44; prepared for *ayllu jista,* 129; sucking blood of babies, 6, 44

Marajó Island, 168, 185

March for Land and Life, 14, 114–15, 200–230; Apacha Vargas and, 108; Clara Santi and, 113; goals of, 203, 204–5, 207, 225; indigenous participants, 200, 206, 207, 212–13, 214, 215, 217, 219; and indigenous rights to land, 203, 205, 240; instructions for marchers, 205; and military and police action, 203, 206, 218, 219; nonindigenous infiltrators in, 215, 216; political results of, 219, 226–27; successes of, 222–23; teaching "others" about indigenous culture, 97–98

María, 81, 82, 83, 84, 87, 89, 127

Marriage, 53. *See also* Partimanda

Marta, 83, 84, 85, 127; actions during *ayllu jista*, 155; preparations for festival, 132–39; songs of, 140–41

Martínez Ampam, Guadalupe Alexandra, 106

Mass, Christian, 149–52

Master potter: and cultural knowledge, 65–66; and shamans, 64, 67, 70

Mead, George Herbert, 58n2

Meat, 141–42

Medical care, modern, 16, 100–101, 214; equipment used by spirits, 77

Meggers, Betty, 232

Meisch, Lynn, 202

Memorandum for the Study of Acculturation, 251

Memory, 31, 43

Mena, Luis, 21

Métraux, Alfred, 169

Military, Ecuadorian: and coup of January 2000, 235; and Curaray Runa, 19; indigenous peoples in, 241; and multiculturalism, 238–39; and petroleum conflicts, 240–41, 243

Millennialism, 22, 246–47, 256, 257; and cultural resurgence, 54, 234

Mindal tree, 162

Modernity: alternative, 256; defined, 246–47; and the hamlet, 55; and indigenous identity, 15, 22

Monkey, 36; in ceramic art, 112; duality of meaning, 112; eaten by Jurijuri, 46; as food, 237; as foreigner, 142, 151; killed during *ayllu jista* hunt, 142; mean monkey person, 92; people as, 3, 4; red howler and *paju*, 237; as stranger, 175

Montalvo, 18, 19

Moon, 70. *See also* Quilla

Mucawa, Capitán, 241

Multiculturalism, 109, 235, 238–39

Multilingualism, 250

Multinationalism, 227–29

Mundu puma (world jaguar), 86

Muratorio, Blanca, 28n2

Museum of the Central Bank of Ecuador. See *Causáunchimi!* (We Are Living) exhibit

Music: and beauty, 60, 223; and communication with spirit world, 100; and festivals, 100. *See also* Flute; Song

Myth: of ending everything (*tucurina*), 161–62; of Nayapi, 2–4; of origin of *ayllu*, 50–51; of origin of *chagra*, 43–44; of origin of pottery clay, 178, 179, 188–91; of origin of Puyo Runa, 1, 2–4; of origin of Sicuanga Runa, 3; of regeneration, 162

Mythic time-space, 39–41, 98, 116, 172, 208; accessed via ceramics, 141, 185; evoked in drumming activities, 121. See also *Unai*

Mythohistories, indigenous, 2

Ñambi (audible path), 34

Napo River, 17, 18

Napo Runa, x, 23, 252

Naranjo, Marcelo, 17, 28n2, 250

Nayapi, 2, 13, 40; as *varayuj*, 123

Nayapi Llacta, 5, 25, 41, 53; cosmology, 68; in early twentieth century, 9–11; origin of, 5; as retainer of traditional cosmology, 53; and use of hallucinogens, 68

Noboa Bejarano, Gustavo, 236

Nuckolls, Janis, 90

Nueva Esperanza, 11–15, 25, 41; representing Puyo Runa in modern world, 53

Nuevo País movement, 228. *See also* Pachakutik-Nuevo País movement

Nungüi, 121, 144, 154; in ceramic art, 100, 183, 184; controlling Amasanga, 8, 48; and domestication of the forest, 43, 44; in form of a coral snake, 44; as Jilucu, 43, 194; as Manioc spirit woman, 45; origin myth of, 6; source of gardening stones, 38; as spirit of pottery clay, 181; as Squash woman, 43

Oberem, Udo, 107, 251

Occidental Petroleum, 240

ONAPE (Organización de Nacionalidades Andoas de Pastaza del Ecuador), 250

OPIP (Organization of Indigenous People of Pastaza Province), 56, 240; and decline in potting skills, 101; and March for Land and Life, 204–5, 207, 226, 227; past officers of, viii

Opposition: and authenticity of indigenous people, 116, 118n12

Orellana, Francisco de, 17, 102, 167, 179

Orr, Carolyn, 100

Ortiz Crespo, Gonzalo, 226

Otter, giant (spirit), 77

Our Knowledge, Our Beauty (video), 183, 187

Owls, 43

Pacari, Nina, 117, 236, 242
Pacayacu Runa, 19
Pachacutij, 252, 256
Pachakutik-Nuevo País movement, 228, 229, 234, 239; bringing indigenous people into modern world, 233
Pachina, 43
Padilla, Inéz, 150
Paint, body: of mythical creatures, 3
Paint, face, 135, 188–89, 210: and *ayahuasca* trips, 69, 83, 84, 85; and March for Land and Life, 206, 208, 210; and seeing as anaconda does, 162, 210; and *wanduj* trips, 69
Painting: of manioc stems, 6, 44
Paju, 237
Palati, 10, 33, 40; as *varayuj*, 123
Papallacta, 22
Paradigm building, 64, 66, 67
Parrots, 142
Partimanda, 52–53
Pastaza Province, xvi, 14, 93–96; and March for Land and Life, 97, 98, 205, 206
Pastaza River, 2, 10, 17, 18, 93
Paushi (bird), 3
Pawa (bird), 3
Paz, Rodrigo, 98, 218
Pazyacu River, 5
Peach-palm tree, 43, 162
Peccary, 36
Penis: in *ayllu* origin myth, 50–51
Pentolite, 243–44
Peru, 9, 19, 234; Peruvian ancestors of Sarayacus, 17; war of 1941, 19, 36, 40, 173, 221, 241
Petrobras, 246
Petroleum industry, 172, 173; employment of indigenous people, 104, 111–13; and indigenous protest movements, 233, 239; indigenous resistance to, 243–44, 246; negative effects of, 239–40; and subsurface rights of territory, 240, 242; and times of destruction, 40
Pierre, François, 151, 251; on early history of Puyo, 2; on history of Canelos region, 17; on *lancero* festival, 163, 165; on Palati, 33; on Ramón Vargas, 58n1
Piripiri, 50
Plaza Lasso, Galo, 179
Polarity: civilized/savage, 1–2, 160, 252; of races, 221
Potoo bird (Jilucu), 191

Pottery: ancient, 184–85, 196; ancient pottery interpreted by modern potters, 170–71, 185–86; and horticulture, 168; in prehistoric and historic South America, 102, 167–68; symbolism on, 171. *See also* Ceramics
Power: of anaconda, 51; and beauty, 61, 62; contrastructural, 256; and culture, 255; denied by "outsiders," 22; expressed in drum sounds, 38–39; indigenous, 208, 229; of indigenous peoples against Catholic Church, 124; of men during *ayllu jista*, 144; in natural environment, 30; against outsiders during *ayllu jista*, 151, 152; Puyo Runa concepts of, 98; of spirits, 47–49; in the *wasi*, 50
Protestants, 234
Puma, 165, 166
Puma Llacta, 9, 13, 16, 33
Puma woman (song of Clara Santi), 113–14
Purina, 14, 23, 24; defined, 54; and productivity of *llacta*, 30, 54; and regional ties, 245
Puyo: coming of machinery to, 12; cultural significance of town, 56–57, 128; development of, 107–8, 172; foreign presence in, 21; founding of, 1, 31, 94; and March for Land and Life, 203, 223, 226; millennial, 247; population growth, 14, 15; symbolism of name, 56
Puyo River, 2, 10, 17
Puyo Runa, 17; historicity of, 4–11; and identity-placement, 24; interculturality of, 250–51; loss of cultural life in urban settings, 53; and millenniarity, 22; myth of founding, 2–4; perception of, 108; ways of knowledge transmission, 18

Quechua language, 16, 19
Quechuaruna, 23
Quichua language, ix, 16, 18, 22, 94; and remnants of Andoan, 249; and self-identification, 159
Quijos, 17, 23
Quilla (Moon Man), 45, 188–91, 194; in ceramic art, 189
Quilla Jista (moon festival), 126, 145, 148
Quindi (hummingbird character), 43, 44, 190
Quiroga, Diego, 216
Quishpe, Salvador, 255
Quito: and coup of January 21, 2000, 15; and Ecuadorian identity, 220–22; and exploita-

tion of indigenous potters, 101; and March for Land and Life, 200; military and police responses to indigenous protests, 202–3, 206, 218, 219; reception of residents to March for Land and Life, 217, 218

Railroad, 173
Rainforest Action Group, 22, 204
Ramón, 137
Reagan, Ronald, 239
Rebellion of the Forajidos, 236
Redfield, Robert, 251
Red Woman. *See* Manduru Warmi
Reeve, Mary-Elizabeth, 28n2, 158–59, 163; on *lancero* dance, 165
Reflection, 61–65, 88
Reflexivity, 61, 63, 58n2, 125, 224; and creativity in Canelos Quichua art, 196–97; in cultural performance, 163; defined, 119; indigenous, 16; in interpreting indigenous knowledge, 188, 193; revealed in song, 109; stylized, 34–39
Reich, Otto, 239
Requena y Herrera, Francisco, 17
Restrepo brothers, 214
Reversal, ritual, 220–23
Reyes, Raúl, 246
Río Chico, 13
Ritual activity, 158
Ritual context, 140
Rival, Laura, 24
River otter, 110
Road: construction, 187; to Puyo, 56, 96, 97, 108
Roggiero, Roberto, 217
Roosevelt, Anna C., 168
Rosa (master potter), 137
Rosario Yacu, 25
Royal Dutch Shell Exploration Company, 9
Rucu, "The Elder," 183, 186
Rucuguna, Alfaro, 32
Runa: term defined, 16
Runa shima (human speech), 22–23
Runga *supai* (water-jaguar spirit), 77, 78

Sacha (forest), 41–46
Sacha Allcu Warmi Mani (I am a bush dog woman; song of Clara Santi), 174
Sacha Runa (forest person), 45, 53. *See* Amasanga
Sacha Warmi, 135
Sahlins, Marshall, 255
Salasaca, 203, 212

Salazar, Luzmila, 207
Salazar Imapanta, Segundo, 222
Salcedo, 214
Salomon, Frank, 221–22
Salt: as cross-cultural insult, 151; mythical origin of, 190; and pottery, 99, 118n8, 187. *See also Cachi Amu*
Santi, Camilo, 9, 224
Santi, Estanislaw, 9
Santi, Faviola, 30, 245
Santi, Hilda, 244
Santi, Rubén, 247–50
Santi, Virgilio, 10, 11, 26, 31, 240; and founding of Comuna San Jacinto del Pindo, 9, 224; and founding of Río Chico, 55; as shaman, 33; as *sinchi yachaj,* 108–9
Santi Simbaña, Bolívar, 216
Santi Simbaña, Camilo, 99
Santi Simbaña, Clara, 32, 98, 108–14, 193; ceramics of, 110–12, 169–75; and myth of Manga Allpa Mama, 184; planning *Causáunchimi!* exhibit, viii–ix; recollections of early Puyo, 94; as *sinchi muscuj warmi,* 109, 174, 224; song composed at March for Land and Life, 223, 224; songs of, 13–14, 109–11, 113, 174–75
Santi Simbaña, Hugo, 245
Santi Simbaña, Marcelo, 19, 229, 245; biographical remembrances, 30, 31–32, 33, 36, 40; and founding of Cushi Tambo, 30, 33, 55; making a drum, 120–21; and manipulation of power of the Church, 123–24; and March for Land and Life, 216, 200, 223, 225; as shaman, 33
Santi Simbaña, Marco, 245
Santi Vargas, Orlando Victor, 34
Sapallu (Squash woman), 43, 45, 184, 190–91
Sara (Maize woman), 43, 45
Sarayacu people, 10, 15, 17, 18, 19, 20; and indigenous resistance, 233–34, 243–44, 241–46
Sarayaquillu, 15, 20; epitome of Canelos Quichua culture, 19
Savage, 22, 150, 175, 215, 220: anthropology's view of, 252, 254, 257; baptism of, 10. *See also* Yumbo
Sawyer, Suzana, 239
Scorpion, 92
Seeing, 20; during *ayahuasca* trips, 70, 71; beyond time, 9; and dream world of images, 36; and formation of images, 39; illness, 109; part of being fully human, 16; in spirit world, 12

Shaman, 108–9; as *bancu,* 71, 78, 79; and beauty, 223; among Canelos Quichua today, 67; and curing, 6–8, 66; inflicting illness, 8; killing power of, 71, 76, 78, 248; and magical darts, 6, 8; and March for Land and Life, 211–12, 213, 223; and master potters, 64, 67, 70; moving between cultures, 61–62, 64; music of, 118n7; paraphernalia of, 66; paraphernalia in ceramic art, 92–93; participation in *ayllu jista,* 145; and power, 207; role during *dominario,* 152; strengthening of *wasi,* 81; use of *ayahuasca* for diagnosing illness, 69; will of (*shungu*), 70

Sharupe, 2, 10, 40

Shell, 1, 16, 187; petroleum operations in, 241–42; and road to Puyo, 56

Shihuacocha, 233

Shiny Shoes, 11–12, 13, 135, 138, 139, 156

Shiwiar people, 19, 24, 93–94, 234, 240; and March for Land and Life, 206, 207, 218

Shuar people, 2, 9, 10, 17, 19, 241

Sicuanga (person), 11, 12, 13, 132; *ayllu jista* hunting trek of, 131; as *chayuj,* 81, 127; *wanduj supai* trip of, 81–88

Sicuanga Runa, 190; appearing during *ayahuasca* trip, 77; in *chagra* origin myth, 44; in Puyo origin myth, 3–4, 5, 39, 175, 210. *See also* Toucan

Sicuanga runa warriors, 10, 165

Sillero, 19–20

Simbaña, Antonia, 9, 109

Sinchi muscuj warmi (strong visionary woman), 101–2, 105, 109, 174, 211

Sinchi yachaj runa (strong one who knows), 6, 34, 211

Singing: during *ayahuasca* trip, 76, 78, 79; during *ayllu jista,* 145, 147. *See also* Song

Sitting-being, 69; during *ayahuasca* trip, 77, 79; and being real, 35

Snail, 60

Snake, coral, 44

Song: and beauty and power, 61, 62, 223; communicated through clouds, 56; and female visionary power, 98, 207; and pottery making, 65, 100, 135, 137; sharing of, 195; symbolism in, 140–41; of women, 109–11, 118n7; use of in storytelling, 2

Soul vine. *See Ayahuasca*

Spirits: cosmology and ecology of, 47–49; during *ayahuasca* trip, 71, 76, 210; during *ayllu jista,* 146, 148, 154; during *wanduj* trip, 86–87; interaction with waking/

human world, 35–36, 38; and March for Land and Life, 211–12, 222; shifting gender of, 100, 190; in territory of "others," 132, 142, 213

Spruce, Richard, 102

Squash woman (Sapallu Warmi), 43, 45, 184, 190–91

Staden, Hans, 102, 167–68, 169, 195

Standing-appearing, 69; and being "seen," 35; during *ayahuasca* trip, 77

Standing/sitting, 66, 71

Steward, Julian H., 232

Stones, 170; *amulana rumi,* 36; *aya rumi,* 38; and being fully human, 38; in ceramic art, 196; and communication with the spirit world, 8; garden, 6, 38; gendered, 38, 170; helping to see meaning of dreams, 24; *lumu rumi,* 170; shaman's, 18, 60, 66; spirits from, 79; spirit stone motifs on pottery, 105; used for killing, 249

Storytelling, 157, 192–93; power of, 13; spiraling nature of, 2, 3, 43, 162

Structure, spatial, 126–27, 127–32

Sturtevant, William, 160

Stylized activity, 140, 166; during *ayllu jista,* 128, 129, 146; and drumming, 121; and empowerment, 122; at funeral, 174; and hunting, 121–22; intertwined with everyday life, 139

Sullivan, Lawrence, x, 163, 195, 249

Sun, 44. *See also* Indi

Sungui (spirit of the hydrosphere), 8, 48–49, 194; in ceramic art, 100, 108, 196; and fog or rain, 56; and hallucinatory trips, 70, 72, 77, 79; symbolized by anaconda, 35, 110, 154; symbolized in turtle *bancu,* 35

Swidden garden. See *Chagra*

Symbolic action, 119–22, 140

Symbolism: and *ayllu* festival, 140; of colors, 141; defined, 120; and March for Land and Life, 203, 208, 213, 220, 222, 229; on pottery, 134–35, 137, 156; representing current events in potter's life, 134–35

Tahuantinsuyo Empire, 231

Tapir, 177

Taquina (shaman's song), 62, 65; power of during *ayllu jista,* 145, 147, 154; revealed in dream, 74; of Sicuanga, 88; sung/played during *ayahuasca* trip, 70, 78

Tariri (Otoñen Escobar), 123

Taromenane, 131

Taruga, 73–81
Taussig, Michael, 220
Taylor, Anne Christine, 27, 251, 254
Teresa Mama, 19
Territory: division of during beginning times-places, 46; reclaiming indigenous territory, 205, 207, 208, 218, 219, 225–26; spatial structure reversed during *ayllu jista*, 128, 131–32. See also *Llacta*
Time of destruction, x, 2, 32, 40, 43, 185, 208
Time of the grandparents, 2, 32, 40, 43, 185
Tingüiza River, 17
Tobacco, 70
Toucan: colors of, 141; eating without killing, 14, 175; feathers, 134, 135; mythical association with sun, 56; myth of Toucan person, 183; Sicuanga as, 3, 210; warrior, 75
Toucan woman (song of Clara Santi), 13–14, 109
Tourism, 21, 97
Tourists, 102, 136; and *ayllu jista* ceramics, 155
Tradition. *See* Cultural endurance
Trail, spirit, 82, 84
Transformation: of beings in beginning times-places, 39, 44–45, 46, 190; of Church into river during *dominario,* 154; and culture, 232; by mythic beings among genders, 45–46; in mythic time-space, 98, 116–17, 194, 208; of self by shamans, 113; of spirits, 45–46, 47–48, 211; between wild and domesticated, 42
Travel, 114, 224–25; virtual and real, 117. *See also* Trekking
Trees: as sources of dyes, 3, 210. *See also* specific tree names
Trekking, 23–24, 230n4; and *ayllu jista,* 130, 131–32, 141; of Clara Santi, 171; by N. Whitten and Marcelo Santi, 16, 18, 20–21, 24; as occasions for learning, 57; to *purina* grounds, 114
Trouillot, Michel-Rolph, 252, 255
Trujillo, Jorge Nelson, 29n3
Trumpet. *See* Cornet
Trumpeter (bird), 210
Tsumi (transformational power), 9
Tsuna (puss person), 3
Tsunki (Achuar spirit of water world), 186
Tucurina (ending everything), 243: and *ayllu jista,* 137; and *dominario,* 154, 161; regeneration after, 162
Tupac Amaru movements, 233

Tupac Katari movements, 233
Tupian people, 168–69, 185
Tupinambá, 167, 168, 195
Turner, Victor, 120, 158
Turtle: form used for stools, 6, 35, 50, 66; motifs on pottery, 105
Twelfth of May celebration, 163, 164, 196, 234

Unai (mythic time-space), 121; humans during, 78
Unión Base, 15, 25
United States: and coup of January 2000, 236; influence in Ecuador, 237–38; U.S. Army in Ecuador, 187
Universidad de Sarayacu, 244–45
Upper Curaray River, 9, 11, 18
Upper Villano River, 17
Urbanity: of Puyo Runa, 55–56
Urcumanda Yao Sicuanga Warmi Mani (song of Marta), 134
Urcu *supai,* 48, 132, 211
Uyarij Runa (noisy person), 77, 78, 79
Uzendoski, Michael, 28n2, 251–52, 255

Valarezo, Ramón, 220
Valladares, Friar Alvaro, 1, 2, 179
Vallejo, Raúl, 228–29
Valverde, don, 136–37
Varayuj, 123, 124, 150, 157–58, 205
Vargas, Acevedo, 9, 15, 25; and founding of Comuna San Jacinto del Pindo, 9
Vargas, Antonio, 255; and coup of January 21, 2000, 15; and March for Land and Life, 205, 206, 218, 227; and Runa unity, 26–27; Sarayaquillu roots of, 245
Vargas, Apacha, 106–8, 183, 229; ceramics of, 46, 49, 92, 108; as ceramics mentor, 102; and March for Land and Life, 218
Vargas, Atanacio, 9–10; and founding of Comuna San Jacinto del Pindo, 9
Vargas, Corina, viii, 30, 31
Vargas, Dario, 107
Vargas, Eliseo, 9, 15, 25, 26, 224; as *sinchi ricsij runa,* 62
Vargas, Eucevia, 10
Vargas, Faviola, 200
Vargas, Isaac, 9, 25
Vargas, Isabel, 31
Vargas, Javier, 4–5, 9, 30, 99; as *sinchi ricsij runa,* 62. *See also* Nayapi
Vargas, Juan, 106
Vargas, Llandro, 9, 10
Vargas, Luis, 102, 104–5, 106

Vargas, Marta, 106
Vargas, Mirian, 103, 106; trip to U.S., 90–93, 115–16
Vargas, Narcisa, 25
Vargas, Pedro, 106
Vargas, Ramón, 30
Vargas, Severo, 106–7
Vargas, Severo (the second), 102
Vargas, Soledad, 99
Vargas, Venancio (Japa), 20, 26, 183, 185
Vargas Aranda, Faviola, viii, 32, 33, 34, 35
Vargas Canelos, Luis (Lucho), viii, 20, 257
Vargas Guatatuca, Carlos Antonio, 104, 234; and coup of January 2000, 234, 235–36
Vargas Santi, Elsa, 111
Velasco Ibarra, José María, ix, 179; and founding of Comuna San Jacinto, 56, 96, 114, 224; healed by Eliseo Vargas, 15, 224
Venezuela, 246
Verduga Vélez, César, 203
Vía Napo, 17
Villano River, 18, 19
Vinillu: effects of, 130; preparation of, 129, 139; use of during ayllu jista, 143, 147
Violin, 8, 171; of shaman, 80
Vision, 61–65, 88, 223
Visions, 68–73; appearing during festival, 144, 146; and creation of ceramics, 133, 174; need for, 69
Viteri Gualinga, Carlos, 118n9, 242
Viuda Tutapishcu, 44

Waira Supai, 211
Wamaj supai, 105
Wanduj supai (hallucinogen), 46; description of trip with, 72–73, 81–88; Nayapi's use of, 5; as a spirit, 86; and visions of Delicia Dagua's sister, 248–49
Wanduj Warmi, 92
Waorani, x, 23, 24; conflict with Záparo, 11; and the Curaray Runa, 19; in Puyo, 97; and resistance to petroleum industry, 246
Warmi jista, 126, 145, 148
Wasi, 50, 81; as microcosm of culture, 40
Whitehead, Neil L., 253

Whitten, Dorothea, 34, 100; From Myth to Creation, 102, 106, 196; territory covered in fieldwork, 28n2
Whitten, Norman, 34, 100, 237; From Myth to Creation, 102, 106, 196; Millennial Ecuador, 255–56; Sacha Runa, 163; territory covered in fieldwork, 28n2; at Yumbo festival, 222
Wichingu, 43
Widuj tree, 188, 189; and bat-widow's daughter, 43; use for paint, 69–70
Widuj Warmi (Black Woman), 188, 190, 210; in ceramic art, 183; in Puyo origin myth, 2–4, 135
Women: and domestication of the forest, 41–42; enactment during ayllu jista, 155–56; and resistance to petroleum industry, 243, 246. See also yachaj warmi
World Bank, 236, 239

Yachaj (one who knows), 61–62, 67; levels of quality, 64–65
Yachaj warmi, 64
Yacu Luba (river otter; song of Clara Santi), 110
Yacu mama: as anaconda, 12; appearing during ayahuasca trip, 70
Yacu puma, 50
Yacu Supai Runa (water spirit), 141. See also Sungui
Yaji Mama, 144
Yami (bird), 3; and trumpet sound, 100
Yasuní National Park, 246
Yu (father of Virgilio Santi), 10
Yumbada, 164, 217, 220–22; and indigenous identity, 220–21; March for Land and Life compared to, 201, 219, 220–21
Yumbo, 22, 201, 212, 219, 224; defined, 221

Záparo, 11, 15, 19
Zaparoan, 15, 17, 19; in Canelos region, 18; and the Curaray Runa, 19; enmity with Shuar and Achuar, 25–26; reclaiming heritage, 93; and regional cultural system, 24; in Waorani territory, 23

NORMAN E. WHITTEN JR. is professor emeritus of anthropology and Latin American studies, curator of the Spurlock Museum, and a Senior University Scholar at the University of Illinois at Urbana-Champaign. He is the author of several books on Ecuador and editor of *Millennial Ecuador: Critical Essays on Cultural Transformations and Social Dynamics.*

DOROTHEA SCOTT WHITTEN is adjunct curator of the Spurlock Museum and research associate of the Center for Latin American and Caribbean Studies, University of Illinois at Urbana-Champaign. She is the senior author of *From Myth to Creation: Art from Amazonian Ecuador,* and senior editor of *Imagery and Creativity: Ethnoaesthetics and Art Worlds in the Americas.*

The University of Illinois Press
is a founding member of the
Association of American University Presses.

Composed in 10.5/13 Adobe Minion Pro
with Meta display
by Jim Proefrock
at the University of Illinois Press
Manufactured by Sheridan Books, Inc.

University of Illinois Press
1325 South Oak Street
Champaign, IL 61820-6903
www.press.uillinois.edu